Medieval Venuses and Cupids

Sexuality, Hermeneutics, and English Poetry

Figurae

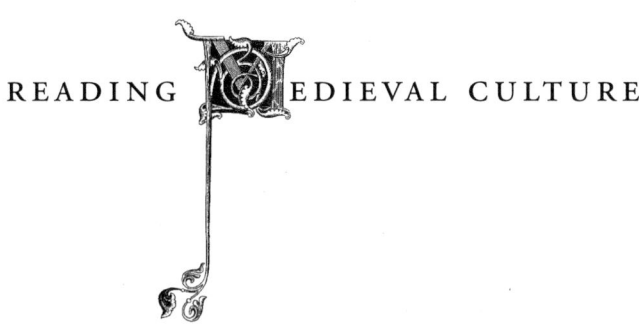

READING MEDIEVAL CULTURE

ADVISORY BOARD

Teodolinda Barolini, Margaret Bent, R. Howard Bloch,
Kevin Brownlee, Marina Scordilis Brownlee,
Brigitte Cazelles, Jacqueline Cerquiglini-Toulet, Georges Didi-Huberman,
Hans Ulrich Gumbrecht, Rachel Jacoff, Sarah Kay, V. A. Kolve,
Seth Lerer, Charles Méla, Jan-Dirk Müller,
Stephen G. Nichols, Lee Patterson, Jeffrey Schnapp, Linda Seidel,
Gabrielle Spiegel, Brian Stock,
Karla Taylor, David Wallace, Rainer Warning, Michel Zink

Medieval Venuses and Cupids
Sexuality, Hermeneutics, and English Poetry

Theresa Tinkle

Stanford University Press, Stanford, California, 1996

Stanford University Press, Stanford, California
©1996 by the Board of Trustees of the Leland Stanford Junior University
Printed in the United States of America

CIP data appear at the end of the book

Stanford University Press publications are distributed exclusively
by Stanford University Press within the United States, Canada,
Mexico, and Central America; they are distributed exclusively
by Cambridge University Press throughout the rest of the world

This book is dedicated
to my friends

Acknowledgments

This is a better book than it started out to be, and I am glad to recognize the generosity of those who helped to improve it. A term of leave permitted me to concentrate on writing the almost-final draft of this book, for which I thank the fiscal powers of the University of Michigan. The Michigan English Department provided a wonderfully stimulating intellectual home during the time I researched and wrote this study, and I am grateful both to my colleagues for their vitality and intellectual engagement and to my students, who always insistently challenge my thinking (if this is not restful, it is nonetheless inestimably helpful). Karla Taylor has been a splendid senior colleague and friend for the past five years, and debating issues and interpretations with her has been great fun; moreover, she cogently critiqued the almost-finished book manuscript and suggested many improvements. Henry Ansgar Kelly, my graduate advisor, also read the book manuscript; his superb eye for detail, his broad learning, and his friendship proved, as always, invaluable. Two anonymous readers wrote very thoughtful reports for the press, giving me much needed and much appreciated perspectives on the argument. I am indeed enriched by being so deeply in debt to so many.

T. L. T.

Contents

A Note to the Reader xiii

Introduction 1

Chapter 1 Beyond Binary Thinking:
The Two, Three, or Ten Loves 9

Chapter 2 Semiotic Nomads 42

Chapter 3 Ambiguous Signs, Contingent Truths 78

Chapter 4 From Latin to Vernacular:
On Poetry and Other Sensual Pleasures 100

Chapter 5 Myths of a Venereal Nature 136

Chapter 6 Unnatural Acts 162

Chapter 7 *Remedia Amoris* 178

Chapter 8 Venus, Cupid, and English Poetry 198

Afterword 211

Notes 217

Bibliography 263

Index 291

A Note to the Reader

Medieval texts offer the modern academic an array of orthographic perplexities. For the sake of consistency throughout my text, I have taken the liberty of silently regularizing all medieval texts: consonantal "v" and "j," vocalic "u" and "i," "th" for ð or þ, "gh" or "y" for ȝ, and "F" for "ff." These are typical modernizations in editions of Chaucer's works, which as a consequence seem spuriously modern when set next to Lydgate or Gower.

Medieval nomenclature makes a similar consistency in the matter of names both difficult and undesirable. I have attempted to use the form of a name most familiar to English readers: English in most cases (William of Conches, Alan of Lille), but the modern Continental vernacular for better known names (Jean de Meun). I follow a similar rule for titles, referring to the title most likely to be familiar to speakers of modern English: Alan of Lille's *Plaint of Nature*, Jean de Meun's *Romance of the Rose*. I translate titles of mythographies (and classical Latin texts) into modern English, and these translated titles appear in the list of works cited along with the original titles.

Translations are my own unless otherwise noted.

Medieval Venuses and Cupids

Sexuality, Hermeneutics, and
English Poetry

Introduction

> When the torch of ancient learning was re-kindled, so cheering were its beams, that our eldest poets, cut off by Christianity from all *accredited* machinery, and deprived of all *acknowledged* guardians and symbols of the great objects of nature, were naturally induced to adopt, as a *poetic* language, those fabulous personages, those forms of the supernatural in nature, which has given them such dear delight in the poems of their great masters. Nay, even at this day what scholar of genial taste will not so far sympathize with them, as to read with pleasure in Petrarch, Chaucer, or Spenser, what he would perhaps condemn as puerile in a modern poet?
>   Samuel Taylor Coleridge, *Biographia Literaria*

Venus and Cupid appear often and prominently in medieval literature, but, as they transform with each new setting, they resemble less a certain antique couple than a motley horde of "fabulous personages." In the course of the Middle Ages, Cupid appears both male and female, blind and sighted, child and adult, playful and sinister, angelic and demonic. He may be a small boy, equipped with bow and arrows, vexing humans who fancy themselves too wise for love. He may be an adult, tyrannizing over the wretched humans subjected to his power—or a mature man introducing a youthful devotee to the mysteries of love. (And both portraits may come to the same thing in the end.) He may be a she. He may be identified with Christ.[1] Venus similarly transforms time and again: in one place a source of life or of death, in others, instructress in the art of love, emblem of changing seasons, genetrix of poetry, guardian of procreation, natural force of physical warmth, corrupter of good warriors, hermaphrodite, and bourgeois paramour. In relation to each other, Venus and Cupid may be mother and small son, queen and king, or wife and husband. Medieval literature obviously discloses not a neatly paired Venus and Cupid, but rather an untidy array of Venuses and Cupids. For metamorphoses of ancient deities promiscuously quicken in the Middle Ages, leading to radical, often perplexing changes in representation. Such frequent alterations seem finally to rob the deities of any stable form, let alone intelligible import.

Even such a cursory overview of the numerous host in medieval literature suggests that multiplicity, change, and ambiguity are all part of the deities' literary function and value. As Venus and Cupid transform to represent varying codes of sexual morality and cultural standards, they vividly embody themes of enduring interest: what sexuality means to individuals, its mutable significances in relation to social orders, its figurative resonances. In the Middle Ages they also typically implicate judgments about the classical past. Yet literary critics have for the most part entirely passed over the potential interest of these marvelously diverse figures. We might initially attribute this collective inattention to the disrepute of myth in nearly all modern critical theories and aesthetic codes. Most of us do not experience Coleridge's genial pleasure in the deities; for many of us, mythic references provoke yawning lapses of attention. What affords no pleasure sparks no interest and is best endured in silence.

Our biases against myth are unfortunate in that they have precluded our exploring the deities' apparently vital roles in medieval poetry. In particular, Geoffrey Chaucer and his contemporaries and successors give these deities a startling prominence, and thoroughly exploit their malleable potential. We might recall Chaucer's familiar representations of assorted Venuses and Cupids in the *House of Fame*, the *Parliament of Fowls*, *Troilus and Criseyde*, the *Knight's Tale*, the *Prologue* to the *Legend of Good Women*, the *Wife of Bath's Prologue*, the *Complaint of Mars*, and the *Complaint of Venus*. Gower features Venus and Cupid in the *Confessio Amantis*. Lydgate gives them salient roles in the *Temple of Glass* (and includes them in numerous lesser known texts). "James I" makes them central to the *Kingis Quair*. Hoccleve's translation of Christine de Pizan's *Epistle of the God of Love* (*Epistre au dieu d'Amours*) obviously depicts Cupid. Clanvowe in *The Cuckoo and the Nightingale* comments on Cupid's minions. If we look further forward in time, we discover Robert Henryson spotlighting the deities in his *Testament of Cresseid*.

In fact, Cupid and Venus closely attend the development of vernacular English poetry in the Chaucerian milieu (the label privileges Chaucer, but then late Middle English poets are frequently Chaucerian in ways they are not, for instance, Gowerian or Lydgatean). Perhaps, as modern critics are sometimes wont to suggest, Chaucer, Gower, Lydgate, and the others suffered an unfortunate failure of both taste and judgment when they so enthusiastically pursued their classicizing revival. These poets certainly did nod at times, some rather frequently. Yet the notable pattern of English references to these deities cannot be fully explained as a collective lapse in poets' judgment. Whatever we think of their aesthetics, their poems raise the question: why are these particular Venuses and Cupids so central to this poetic project? So much space devoted to these deities in so many poems must be purposeful. After all, these are not passing allusions, detachable ornaments, but well-developed portraits woven closely into the poetic fabric.

If we pause to reflect on these many references to the deities, we discover that they map out interesting territories for further exploration. Venus and Cupid are first, of course, representatives of sexuality, depicted in ways that may recommend or discredit specific sexual mores. If we examine them closely, they may open for us new perspectives on medieval sexuality. We may, for instance, be able to detect individual variations on issues such as the priority of reason over passion, the ethics of expressing sexual love, or the class and gender biases of medieval sexualities. Poetic handling of the pair may likewise disclose ideas about what is considered natural in sexual behavior, built into the very order of the cosmos, exempt from human questions or challenges; poems may also help us to discern where and how the supposedly natural may be denaturalized, where and how ideologies and dogmas may be contested. By examining Venus and Cupid, moreover, we may be able better to appreciate the striking alterations in their portraits, such as Cupid's perpetual metamorphoses between child and adult, or Venus's sometimes modest, sometimes immodest, sometimes genteel, and sometimes extravagantly sumptuous attire. Further, if we attend thoughtfully to Venus's usual association with such figures as Fame and Fortune and Minerva, or Cupid's typical alliance with a band of lover-poets, we may be able to perceive how the company they keep influences their characters. Finally, we may come to appreciate why Venus and Cupid appear again and again in these works as patrons of poetry. For Chaucerian poets constantly invoke these deities for poetic inspiration—or blame them for the deceptive seductions of verse. As Venus and Cupid make their way through English verse, then, they often betoken tenuous links between sexual love and the sensuous appeal of poetry; they speak to a medieval (and modern) intrigue with the sensuousness of verse. In short, these deities are worth studying if only because they may point to Chaucerian negotiations of the classical past, to integrations of sexuality and poetics, to posited relations among divine and natural and social orders. They may help us to comprehend how ancient myth may be used to encode medieval social mores, aesthetic values, and ideologies.

If we would recover the English myths, however, we must accept that poetic traditions are not autonomous, not hermetically sealed off from other discourses. For Venus and Cupid are written and rewritten in many of the competing discourses that construct medieval sexualities and poetics, and each discourse grafts new meanings and implications onto them. The ancient world knew a number of Venuses and Cupids, which partly accounts for the confusion and multiplicity of medieval representations. As the multiplicitous deities are then taken up by various medieval discourses, they accrue still more meanings. For example, astrology treats Venus as a planet, medicine and natural philosophy as a figure of sexual physiology, sermons as a moral exemplum, historians as an ancient prostitute, and so on. Cupid too is inscribed within several discourses, and a writer's perspective frequently determines the god's moral and other significances. As the deities enter into poetry, they perforce trail behind them long clouds of meaning. In order to appreciate their possible and likely implications, we must refer not to poetry alone, but to the numerous discourses that formulate and rationalize those implications.

Conveniently, medieval mythography (that is, writing about myth) allows us to examine the deities from just this multi-discursive perspective. This most obvious advantage of the discourse has been lost to modern scholarship, for literary critics have almost universally been content to treat mythography as a source of moral allegories that may be inflicted on poetic texts. Mythography has been reduced to nothing more than a set of moralistic commonplaces, though it actually consists of far more than moral allegories. In fact, moralization garners little or no attention in many mythographic texts. Mythographers both repeat and invent interpretations of the deities from a wide variety of disciplinary perspectives, drawing on many hermeneutics and often gathering their interpretations into encyclopedias. Mythographies include not only moralizing interpretations of Venus and Cupid (as of other deities and figures of classical legend), but also medical, philosophical, theological, etymological, astrological, historical, and iconographic explanations. From their participation in many discourses, scientific and philosophical as well as literary, the deities acquire an essential multivalence and come to bear contradictory meanings. Medieval mythography can therefore help us to apprehend Venuses and Cupids rather than an artificially unified Venus and Cupid; mythography can lead us to expect a play of polysemous meaning rather than strict representational coherence. That multivalence constitutes the distinguishing feature of mythography is in fact well recognized in existing scholarship: Jean Seznec, Rosemond Tuve, and Judson Boyce Allen long ago laid out the basic intellectual traditions, and more recent work supports and extends their conclusions.[2] Contrary to much current opinion, we will find that what mythographies proffer is not the historically "correct" meanings of Venus and Cupid, but the ever-changing, interdisciplinary perspectives and ideologies bound into medieval discursive constructions of sensual love and sexuality.

We should realize at the start that medieval treatments of Venus and Cupid—whether mythographic or poetic—do not promise straightforward expositions of uncomplicated and transparent meaning. Mythographers and poets alike use the deities to naturalize and legitimate (or denaturalize and challenge) particular sexual and poetic values. For instance, in referring to the planetary Venus, mythographers and poets often advance social ideologies in the guise of innocent facts of nature. At the same time, moralization usually generates clear boundaries between good and evil, between licit and illicit desires; these categories also cloak particular and mutable ideological programs with the appearance of unchanging Truth. In their turn, philosophers read their own designs into the receptive figures of the ancient deities. Each of these discourses yields particular, sometimes conflicting, sometimes complementary ideas of sexuality and love. In order to understand the potential significances of Venus and Cupid, and their import in English poetry, we must therefore inspect the medieval discourses that devise for them a whole plethora of meanings—not in order to force those meanings upon poems but in order to comprehend the discursive strategies that together create multivalence, and in order to think cogently about the possible relations between those strategies and poetic representations.

As Venus and Cupid accrue multiple meanings and appearances in diverse discourses, their import becomes perplexingly contradictory and ambiguous, gradually challenging any notion that signs necessarily manifest semiotic unity. Perhaps recognizing an analogy between medieval mythography and the more fashionable post-structuralism might help us to value anew the medieval traditions. Post-structuralist theories can at the least help us to appreciate the signifying play, the unstable multiplicity always apparent in medieval mythic traditions. Discovering post-structuralist multiplicity is not the ultimate goal of this study, however, and the medieval traditions are finally not best illuminated by clichés about linguistic instability. The more challenging objective lies in perceiving how discourses on sexuality and myth and poetics relate (or fail to relate) to each other. For example, encyclopedic mythographies juxtapose many interpretations, one after the other, and thereby raise questions about just how all these disparate meanings—all these diverse inscriptions of both sexuality and the classical past—make sense together. How does an understanding of Venus as a planet reinforce or conflict with ideas of her as a moral exemplum or as a poetic patroness? Mythography encourages us to investigate how various disciplinary perspectives complement or oppose each other in medieval constructions of sexuality and love; it summons us to heed dialogues and non-dialogues among many discourses. Examining poetry and mythography together likewise allows us to ponder how they do or do not relate to one another. And, finally, poets too may develop multiple, disparate representations of Venus and Cupid, inviting us to discern concord in the discord (or discord in the seeming concord).

As we examine more than one discourse about sexuality, we will discover both complicities and discrepancies among, for example, ecclesiastical, scientific, and belletristic treatments of sensual desires.[3] No one discourse on sexuality predominates in all situations throughout the Middle Ages. Although medieval discourses about sexuality may have been "markedly unitary,"[4] they were obviously anything but monolithic.[5] Ecclesiastical writing is dramatically influential, but only in a limited context; other discourses, such as medical writings, depart from ecclesiastical guidelines on some points. A canon lawyer, an astrologer, a natural philosopher, and a poet may advance very different perspectives, may support diverse social and ideological imperatives. Thus as we approach Venus and Cupid in mythography and poetry, and as we consult heterogeneous discourses, we should be alert to how they compete with one another in the construction of medieval sexualities. We should

Introduction   7

expect not a fixed hierarchical relation among ecclesiastics and scientists and mythographers and poets, but rather an ongoing and ever-changing series of dialogues.

This is therefore a book about dialogues and, as significantly, about non-dialogues among medieval discourses: among the academic disciplines that together construct sexuality, among the intellectual traditions that formulate strategies for understanding the ancient mythic figures, between Latin and vernacular literary conventions and ways of reading, and within English poetry. Most centrally, I seek to investigate the relations between English poetics and Latin intellectual traditions—between poetry and conventional mythographic hermeneutics drawn from a variety of disciplinary perspectives.

This effort must initially consist of clarifying the discourses that make up mythography, an effort necessitated by the widespread but erroneous impression that it unfolds unified, coherent, perhaps even simplistic moralizations of the deities. Chapter 1 below therefore reviews the prevailing critical uses of mythography in order to delineate their problematic aspects, and concludes by outlining a new interpretive model. Chapter 2 surveys mythographic treatments of Venus and Cupid from late antiquity to the fifteenth century in order to describe the intellectual force of this discourse in the Middle Ages and in order to intimate its potential appeal to poets.

Once we have a fuller comprehension of how medieval mythography works, of how it produces and theorizes multivalence, we can turn to relations between poetry and mythographic hermeneutics. Chapters 3 through 7 take up this topic, concentrating particularly on how both mythographers and poets (especially Chaucer, Lydgate, and Gower) manipulate the deities' images and their "natural" (astrological, physiological) meanings. As we will find, poets may simply import mythographic methods, recounting the stock hermeneutics and commonplaces. Poets may also refer to mythographic models in order to question their authority, or in order to license poetic ambiguity and multivalence. It is, after all, not the function of poetry merely to embrace whatever ideas happen to be current in a culture, but at least sometimes to show us the familiar in a strange new light, to alienate us from the quotidian. When late medieval English poets refer to mythography, they may or may not bow to an authoritative system of interpretation, and they may as well revise as adopt the principles of that discourse. We will discover that poets, like mythographers, can and often do use standard hermeneutics and traditional material for their own purposes.

Chapter 8 focuses on connections between the deities and poetry, on the Chaucerian development of a poetic ideal that shuns Cupid's deceits in favor of Venus's patronage. As we will see, this venerean poetics suggests an integration of sensuality and intellect. Further, Chaucer's and others' venerean poetics direct attention to nationalistic as well as classicizing imperatives: whereas Cupid stands as the grand patron of medieval French verse, Venus is the mother of both ancient Roman and medieval English poetry. In short, we will discover finally that the venerean myth of English verse implies a (somewhat equivocal) turn from French models and toward a poetics implicated in a "natural" order that extends beyond the merely social, class-bound order of Cupid's Gallic cult.

As we begin to pursue the mutable poetic and sexual semiotics that medieval writers inscribe in Venuses and Cupids, and as we try to comprehend the multifarious values the deities may represent, we might ask what is at stake for medieval writers in treating of Venus and Cupid. What and whose purposes do the deities serve? What ideologies do writers invoke to legitimate and rationalize their sexual and literary values, and just how do they drape those ideologies over the deities' accommodating figures? By pursuing such questions, we may at the least recover a genial sympathy for the dessicated literary conventions of another age. Though the mythic figures long ago entered the shadowy underworld, they may still lead us through strange labyrinths to unexpected vistas.

Chapter I

Beyond Binary Thinking

The Two, Three, or Ten Loves

> She is all there.
> She was melted carefully down for you
> and cast up from your childhood,
> cast up from your one hundred favorite aggies.
>   . . .
> She is so naked and singular.
> She is the sum of yourself and your dream.
> Climb her like a monument, step after step.
> She is solid.
>
> As for me, I am a watercolor.
> I wash off.
>   Anne Sexton,
>   "For My Lover, Returning to His Wife"

> As the antients agree, brother Toby, said my father, that there are two different and distinct kinds of love, according to the different parts which are affected by it—the Brain or Liver—I think when a man is in love, it behoves him a little to consider which of the two he is fallen into.
>   Laurence Sterne, *Tristram Shandy*

Because Venus and Cupid so often change form and role in the Middle Ages, they challenge literary critics trying to decipher the nuances and implications of any particular representation. In response to this challenge, readings of Venus and Cupid have for the most part settled into two schools: the deities have for decades been almost universally explicated as symbols of "courtly love" or of "two loves" ("good" and "evil," either one of which may also be "courtly"). There are other valuable interpretive paths laid down, but few American or British scholars travel them.[1] Indeed, ideas about "courtly love" and "two loves" have come so routinely to guide interpretation that literary criticism often seems mechanical or routine when touching on Venus and Cupid. The problem lies less in the interpretive models—for even the best of models eventually turn into mechanical systems that preclude rather than provoke thought—than in their perhaps inevitable simplification over the years. I therefore propose in this chapter first to review the dominant interpretive models in order to recover their lost subtleties and to reassess their advantages and disadvantages. I will then concentrate on the theoretical and other consequences of "two loves" as an interpretive model, before projecting a model more in keeping with both current understandings of medieval sexuality and recent theoretical developments in literary studies.

"Courtly Love"

Over the years numerous literary critics have serenely declared—sometimes as if doing so straightaway clarified all obscurities—that Venus and Cupid symbolize courtly love.[2] This fashion, still current, skirts the fact that "courtly love" can itself mean almost anything. The term has at various times in its history identified behavior that is infantile, sophisticated, narcissistic, chivalrous, playful, genuine, fictional, carnal, spiritual, Ovidian, Arabist, Catharist, "Fontevraultian,"[3] blasphemous, natural, unnatural, adulterous, and chaste. That "courtly love" opens a semiotic abyss has been well documented and frequently remarked upon.[4] When literary critics do not offer a stipulative definition (a routine oversight) to clarify which meaning is intended, they tend to recall Humpty Dumpty with his capricious linguistic habits: "When *I* use a word . . . it means just what I choose it to mean—neither more nor less."[5] Humpty Dumpty by and by tells Alice what he means. Given that critics usually avoid the complete emulation that would supply such a gloss, their designating Venus and Cupid symbols of courtly love adds little to our understanding of the deities or of medieval sexual love. Indeed, we end with an enlargement of the confusion brought about in the first place by the perplexingly varied Venuses and Cupids of medieval literature.

At present, "courtly love" serves as a critical shorthand to designate an amorphous set of social attitudes, literary conventions, and behaviors; as long as it remains a shorthand sign of an undefined and undefinable code, the term and the interpretive model will open few if any new insights on sexual love in medieval culture. That the Venuses and Cupids in Guillaume de Lorris's *Romance of the Rose*, Juan Ruiz's *Book of Good Love* (*Libro de Buen Amor*), and Chaucer's *Parliament of Fowls* may all be designated symbols of courtly love finally tells us nothing about the representations themselves, or about why they differ so radically from one another. In other words, applying the universalizing label "courtly love" erases the marked conceptual and representational differences among these figures. An apparent homogeneity replaces particular differences, perhaps the most remarkable of which are the diversities in attitudes toward sexual love among national literatures. Treatments of love by French, English, and German writers evidence marked disparities.[6] Viewing Venus and Cupid as ambassadors of courtly love, therefore, at worst obfuscates literary meaning and elides cultural differences, and at best yields critical clichés. In order better to understand the love deities, we need something other than a repetition of what we think we already know.

Two Loves: The Modern Origins

Much recent literary criticism on Venus and Cupid steers around the well-posted courtly-love quagmire, only to slip into the rut of two loves. This interpretive model derives from the hypothesis that in the Middle Ages love was widely understood in terms of a dichotomy—good/evil, spiritual/carnal. According to this model, Venus or Cupid in any literary appearance incarnates a good or an evil love. (Actually, duality may characterize any ancient deity, just as it may be absent from treatments of the love deities.)[7] Thus far the idea of two loves, if unsubtle and unexciting, sets up no insuperable obstacles. Certainly, we can all generate examples of antithetical loves. Augustine of Hippo wrote of love being directed in two ways, toward God or toward the world.[8] Walter Shandy distinguishes two loves according to the body part affected, brain or liver. Anne Sexton divides women into permanent monumental wives and ephemeral watercolor lovers, and so on. Bipolar opposition is demonstrably commonplace, in ideas about love as in all other human phenomena.[9]

The modern scholarship that concentrates on sketching out how medieval Venuses and Cupids embody two loves confirms that dichotomy is a widespread conceptual norm, in recent years as in the far distant past. Erwin Panofsky, D. W. Robertson, Jr., George D. Economou, and Robert Hollander give us the seminal analyses. Although modern critical notice of two loves (usually as a rhetorical *topos*) predates this scholarship, these scholars give form and substance to the idea, as well as research support for later literary criticism. Most of their attention centers on Venus; Cupid attracts little sustained inquiry and is typically mentioned only in passing, often as interchangeable with Venus. Thus models of two loves tend to suppress gender difference in favor of polarized feminine stereotypes—Eve and Mary.

Basing his analysis on poetry, mythography, and visual arts, Panofsky explicates celestial and natural Neoplatonic Venuses; the exception among the founders of two-love paradigms, he also distinguishes two Cupids, one (a mythographic figure) signifying an illicit love and the other (a poetic figure) a divine love. Panofsky organizes images into these general prototypes and then examines how artists appropriate and modify them. One sixteenth-century Neoplatonist pictures a battle between love and reason; since Venus appears only in her lesser, "earthly" guise, the division between a putative two Venuses seems absolute. Titian, on the other hand, depicts two very like Venuses, stressing the similarity between eternal and transitory pleasures.[10] Panofsky discovers considerable variation even within his targeted circle of Italian Neoplatonists, who may choose to highlight the discrepancy or the similitude between the two loves (and who may, when two figures seem inadequately nuanced, add a third).

Robertson does not, as far as I can discern, refer to Panofsky's argument in devising another two Venuses, these representing an always identical Augustinian love (*caritas*) and lust, passion, or desire (*cupiditas*). Robertson takes Cupid and Venus to be interchangeable.[11] For Robertson, what matters in any literary representation is less how an artist employs or adapts the tradition than the single truth hidden by the fictive veil: the unchanging, hierarchical relation of flesh and spirit, and thus of the two loves, carnal and spiritual. Robertson bases his conclusions on several textual traditions, but mythographies seem particularly prominent.[12] Although he discusses two Venuses in mythographic and other traditions, he tends to discern just one in poetry—a Venus signifying idolatrous concupiscence, everywhere and always condemned in medieval literature.[13] This model has been much criticized, but the extensive original research apparently validating it has had a powerful influence on later studies.[14] Indeed, Robertson synthesizes an enormous range of literary traditions, including Latin and vernacular commentaries and poetry, as well as pictorial traditions; and even those who disagree with his general interpretive model tend to take for granted his research on the two Venuses, which now constitutes the unchallenged (in some cases, likely unrecognized) basis of nearly all critical commentary. In this vein, critics have failed to perceive how his theoretical model biases his selection of evidence and shapes his conclusions. As we will find, his research may yield far different conclusions than those he draws from it.

The influence of Robertson's research is apparent in the subsequent work of Economou and Hollander, both of whom accept as authoritative the idea of two Venuses, with one illustrating concupiscence. Economou and Hollander, however, modify Robertson's model by inserting a licit (third) goddess of "earthly" but virtuous love between Robertson's extremes. Economou in fact defines two earthly Venuses: "the one, legitimate, sacramental, natural, and in harmony with cosmic law; the other, illegitimate, perverted, selfish, and sinful."[15] Economou follows Robertson in contending that mythography provides a definitive medieval model for the two Venuses (though Economou shows an unsure command of the texts, which renders his assertion less than persuasive).[16] Economou's point is that these dualistic literary images of Venus encode positive and negative judgments about "courtly love." This constitutes nothing if not a significant departure from Robertson's Augustinian model.

Hollander concentrates on tracing Boccaccio's portrayal of two Venuses in his *opere minori in volgare*: a "celestial" Venus of marriage, and an "earthly" Venus of lasciviousness. According to Hollander, Boccaccio creates two distinct Venuses by means of iconography and by stating his intention (in a gloss on the *Teseida*).[17] The persuasiveness of Hollander's argument rests on our willingness to agree that Boccaccio's gloss on the *Teseida* accurately and fully explains his many representations of Venus, and on our ability to read his texts ironically. That is, if Boccaccio seems to praise carnal love, he must be referring us to a rigid system of religious values that reveal this praise to be an error. I have reservations about this reading of Boccaccio's Venuses, for I do not perceive two distinctly opposed Venuses in the gloss, let alone in the *Teseida* as a whole (or in all of Boccaccio's works considered together); I will shortly deal with the gloss in some detail. Also, I fail to detect the irony (as I do with many of Robertson's analyses). My failure does not, of course, invalidate this line of interpretation. It does point up the fact that such discoveries of irony depend on readers' assuming that medieval texts refer us to unchanging moral constants.[18] This is, I think, precisely what we cannot assume about a period as long and full of change as the Middle Ages. Instead of debating the irony—likely an irresolvable and futile point of contention—I would have us reconsider our assumptions about medieval moral codes and sexual mores.

This body of scholarship and criticism supports the conclusion that various types of antithetical love persist throughout the Middle Ages and well into the Renaissance.[19] This scholarship also argues adamantly against any idea that a single dichotomy of two loves prevailed. Each study advances two or three Venuses or Cupids—but not the same two (or three). The two loves are variously referred to Neoplatonism, to Augustine's *caritas* and *cupiditas*, to codes of courtly love, and to Boccaccio's attempt to separate lasciviousness from marriage. We should further mark that some of these scholars' conclusions specify unique historical contexts and do not lend themselves to period generalization: Panofsky's Italian Renaissance Neoplatonic Venuses are no more universal types than are the two Venuses Boccaccio attempts to distinguish in his gloss on the *Teseida*. All the modern scholars obviously share the organizing principle of antithesis, but their emphatic disagreements about precisely what this antithesis consists of fully establish that a single, unified medieval tradition of two loves never existed.

In pursuing binary loves, scholars necessarily minimize what does not cohere with the model. Panofsky stresses the model of two Venuses and outlines Pico della Mirandola's three Venuses in a note.[20] Although such a subordination of alternatives is necessary to logical exposition, a prepossession for dichotomy can also inevitably bias the collection and interpretation of textual evidence. Robertson's exposition at times shows this tendency. For example, he refers to John Scotus Eriugena linking the concupiscent Venus with original sin. As given, the citation appears to justify a scheme of two loves:

The expressions "concupiscence of the flesh" and "mother of all fornication" suggest the Augustinian conception of the malady of original sin, and, indeed, John the Scot had explicitly identified the shameful Venus with that malady. Like her celestial sister, she was frequently associated with music in medieval iconography. Thus there are, in effect, two very different kinds of "melodye"—one the music of the spirit and the flesh in harmony with created nature, and the other the music of the flesh as it seeks inferior satisfactions as a result of its own concupiscence.[21]

Robertson slides easily from John on original sin to conclusions about two melodies and the dichotomy of flesh and spirit, all of which ostensibly reinforces his model of two loves. If we turn to the cited passage from John's text, however, we actually find much that argues against Robertson's idea of two loves, of a simple opposition between flesh and spirit. John begins this passage by interpreting Venus as a natural force, the seed of all living things. This idea of origins leads him to contemplate the source of virtue, and to note that original sin produces a mixture of vice and virtue in human lives, passed on by the pleasures of Venus. This interpretation develops swiftly from natural to spiritual meaning, and the connection between Venus and original sin is the same as that discovered by Augustine—pleasure in sexual intercourse passes essential sin to the progeny. Yet this does not exhaust Venus's possibilities. Directly before this passage, John identifies her as Vulcan's wife, their marriage teaching us that sexual desire depends on physiological heat (Vulcan's forge).[22] Later, John describes two Venuses, pleasure and chastity—since the latter is again Vulcan's spouse, we are presumably now to ignore Vulcan's metaphorical fires, which would dispute the alleged chastity.[23] And still later, John offers that Dione, or sense, brings forth Venus because "all desire is born of the delight in carnal senses."[24]

Although the evidence of this commentary points to ambiguity and to multiple, unreconciled traditions, Robertson uses it only to affirm dichotomy.[25] His erudite model has deservedly had a tremendous influence, even over critics who may disagree with his larger argument. We could multiply examples of his influence, but one should suffice for the moment. Richard Hamilton Green endorses Robertson's hypothesis about two Venuses—even though Green demonstrates that John's Venuses establish "the flexibility of the mediaeval writer's handling of his mythological material," and even though Green shows a keen interpretive sensitivity to literary multivalence.[26] The interpretive model forces an awkward leap from a discussion of multivalence to a conclusion about two Venuses. Like almost any interpretive model, this one determines what we perceive and what we repress in our readings.

Much effort has now been invested in modern scholarship supporting the principle of dichotomy in medieval love, and this effort has been valuable. We gain from it lucid and comprehensible ways to organize disparate ideas surrounding the problematic topic of medieval love. We also gain insight into the cognitive categories attractive to both medieval and modern writers faced with the complexities of sexual love. And, indeed, bipolar opposition proves even seductively appealing. It surfaces in works as diverse as D. W. Robertson's *Preface to Chaucer* and Michel Foucault's *History of Sexuality*. Either scholar could have written that sexuality exists in a binary system, "licit and illicit, permitted and forbidden."[27] Although such modern academic dualities function to organize our knowledge and to illuminate medieval traditions, we should recognize their limitations. They do not, after all, delineate absolute medieval truths but only modern constructions of the past. We should not be so content with these constructions that we stop seeking more fully to understand the past.

Two Venuses: The Medieval Origins

As Robertson's and Green's treatments of John Scotus Eriugena indicate, we preserve dichotomy—or imagine a universal dichotomy—only by overlooking variations in medieval and modern treatments of Venus and Cupid. In short, a bipolar opposition of two loves depends on the suppression of differences among many loves. This is to say that a bipolar opposition is a fabrication: it organizes information for some functional purpose. We might assume that we know this purpose to be conformity with rigid medieval moral codes that strictly distinguish good from evil in the matter of sexual love. If we examine particular medieval dichotomies more closely, however, we find something quite different and more interesting.

There are several striking medieval instances of Venuses and Cupids interpreted as two opposed loves, and these frequently appear in modern criticism as the *loci medii aevi* of "good" and "bad" figures (significantly, use of these loci obscures the modern origins of the idea). The two most cited texts, both from the twelfth century, are Bernard Silvestris's *Commentary on the "Aeneid"* and Alberic's mythography (the so-called Third Vatican Mythography). A brief consideration of these works shows that just as modern scholars define various sets of two loves, so do medieval writers. According to Bernard,

We read, therefore, that there are two Venuses, namely one lawful, and the other the goddess of wantonness. The lawful Venus is the harmony of the world, that is, the even proportion of worldly things, which others call Astrea, natural justice. She is in the elements, in the stars, in the seasons, in living beings. But the shameless Venus and the goddess of wantonness we declare to be concupiscence of the flesh, which is the mother of all fornication [illicit sexual activity].[28]

For Bernard, these two Platonic Venuses distinguish two kinds of union. The Venus of wantonness symbolizes inconstant sexual union, and the licit Venus, the cosmic love that binds all elements in universal harmony. With all their antitheses—mutable and immutable, illicit and licit—both Venuses signify physical union. Sexual intercourse and the cosmic unification of elements and stars are thus represented as variations on the same principle. If we compare this passage with other writings of Bernard, we discover a consistent appeal to the "idea of cosmic fertility" embodied in the licit Venus.[29] Bernard's doubling of Venus therefore serves to display the congruence of seemingly dissimilar things, the sisterhood of cosmic and earthly unions.[30]

Platonism is not a static philosophy, and Venus is not the sole mythic figure even twelfth-century Chartrian Platonists use to embody two loves. Bernard's model does not suffice for all his contemporaries. William of Conches, for instance, employs Hymenaeus.[31] Platonic interpretations of Venus also change over time, so Bernard's model does not necessarily answer for later writers. In Marsilio Ficino's system, the two loves are heavenly and common Venuses, both laudable because with each love we seek beauty and thus God. Neither of Ficino's Venuses represents illicit sexuality, which he sees as a form of bestial insanity rather than any kind of love. Whereas Bernard emphasizes the similarity of two loves, then, Ficino stresses the division between them. On the other hand, Pico della Mirandola locates bestial insanity under the auspices of a common Venus, adding a "second celestial Venus" (that is, a third Venus) to symbolize a love both earthly and admirable.[32] Thus in its turn Ficino's model does not suffice for all his contemporaries. As the two Venuses multiply and transform into triplets, changing philosophical contexts determine the precise meanings of and values attached to "celestial" and "earthly." The point of doubling the sign is obviously to designate an opposition, a division between earth and heaven; but bipolarity can serve also to unify the two opposed elements, to express the resemblance of earth to heaven.

Alberic, citing Remigius of Auxerre, draws on more mundane and moralistic principles to distinguish two loves. Alberic does not specify his source text, but it is most likely Remigius's commentary on Martianus Capella's *Marriage of Mercury and Philology*. Throughout this text, Martianus presents Venus or sensual pleasure as a necessary balance to the austere pursuit of the seven liberal arts. Remigius's commentary replaces this approval of sensual pleasure with a rigidly binary morality:

> There are two Venuses, one chaste and modest who presides over honorable loves, who is also married to Vulcan; the other a goddess of lusts, devoted to pleasures, whose son is Hermaphrodite. Likewise there are also two loves; one good and chaste, by whom virtues and wisdom are loved; the other unchaste and evil, whom we call "loves," in the plural, for the sake of distinguishing the good love.[33]

These two loves allow Remigius to distinguish between the presence and absence of sexual pleasure, which corresponds to an antithesis of virtue and vice. By means of this binary, he rewrites Martianus's interrelation of pleasure and study, drawing heavy lines between delight (vice) and diligence (virtue). In short, Remigius turns the ambiguities of venerean delights into a binary system, interpreting Venus in a way that replaces Martianus's authorization of pleasure with a rigidly Augustinian denial of pleasure.[34] We can understand Remigius and Martianus, or Remigius and Bernard, as recapitulating the same idea of two Venuses only by overlooking their central ideological differences. For Bernard, sexuality parallels the structure of the cosmos, and must therefore have an approved role to play within that order. For Remigius in the commentary on Martianus, sexual morality depends on marriage (and on heeding the *auctores*), which at best excuses sexual activity. Interestingly, the idea of two Venuses does not surface in the Second Vatican Mythography, which has been attributed to Remigius.[35] That text describes just one Venus, one Cupid.[36] Perhaps Remigius fits the explanation to the occasion, as John Scotus Eriugena does. In any event, as Remigius's model of two Venuses appears in Alberic's mythography, it becomes just one way of understanding Venus and Cupid: Alberic does not present this as a single, authoritative explication of the deities, but simply as one of many possible ways to think about them.[37] We might take one further example of how Remigius's concept was received. One anonymous commentator on Ovid's *Fasti* repeats it—but then quite rightly points out that Ovid names only one Venus.[38] If we survey Bernard, Ficino, Martianus, Remigius, Alberic, and others, we discover not a single idea of two loves but a series of formulations and reformulations.

To ignore the differences among these writers is perforce also to bypass just how ideology forms and authorizes judgments about sexuality. In other words, focusing on the common strategy of dichotomy causes us to miss how medieval minds conceptualize sexualities out of sex. From such diverse sources, we can collect two loves only by absolutely privileging bipolar opposition over a multiplicity of differences. In doing so, we allow the law of two loves to efface the particularities of literature, history, philosophy, and theology. Good and evil become universal categories, always and everywhere the same throughout the Middle Ages.

Surely two loves oppose one another across the centuries, even monotonously so, but we do not find the same two at every point, whether we compare Panofsky and Robertson or Bernard and Alberic. In the epigraphs to this chapter, Walter Shandy and Anne Sexton similarly draw on the organizing principle of dichotomy. Yet while that principle is commonplace, a single, universal set of two loves does not develop from it. Bernard symbolizes a cosmic fertility, Remigius stigmatizes pleasure, Walter Shandy pragmatically diagnoses organic disturbances, Sexton imagines two degrees of aesthetic permanence. To read all these passages as setting forth the same two loves would devalue their markedly distinct conceptual, ideological, metaphoric, and historical implications.

Simplifying Love

Whether we examine medieval or modern writings on Venus and Cupid, we discover not a universal duality but particular and discrete dualities. Literary critics with the most disparate theoretical bents nonetheless often reduce all these subtly devised pairs of deities to the simpler (and surely more accommodating) set of a "good" and a "bad" Venus or Cupid. The marked and explicit differences among the original modern scholarly models (and among medieval models) have thus been eliminated in favor of what they occasionally share, the principle of dichotomy. What began in modern scholarship as an organizational device has come to seem a static feature of medieval culture, and the "two Venuses" or "two loves" have gained over the years all the historicist authority of an unquestioned medieval discourse. Witness Donald R. Howard (certainly no Robertsonian critic) referring perfunctorily to "the 'two Venuses,' good and sinful love" in Chaucer's *Parliament of Fowls*.[39] More recently, R. F. Yeager takes the idea of two loves as his model for interpreting the Venus of Gower's *Confessio Amantis*.[40] In this critical tradition, the arguments of Panofsky, Robertson, Economou, and Hollander have been simplified, displaced onto the past, and accorded the status of fact. In short, a series of distinct modern constructions have been reduced to a vague idea of "two loves" (or, still more generally, to a sense of a "moralized" Venus). However naturalized, this model is obviously contingent, dependent on certain modern ideologies. This becomes apparent if we review earlier criticism. For instance, C. S. Lewis in *Allegory of Love* detects in medieval literature an integration rather than an opposition of secular and holy loves. Indeed, Lewis's idea of integrated love provoked the idea of two opposed loves as an alternative "historicist" model.

The model of two Venuses is usually attributed to mythographers, who are supposed to have interpreted the deities as good and evil (*in bonum* and *in malum*). Notably, all the seminal studies of Venus and Cupid (except Hollander's book) rely on mythography, arguing that it straightforwardly advances an idea of two loves. Further work on Venus and Cupid by Meg Twycross, John Mulryan, Doris Ruhe, Earl G. Schreiber, and Theodore L. Steinberg also concentrates on mythography and may further the tacit suggestion that this discourse definitively articulates the deities' medieval import, that it elucidates the hermeneutics of sexual love in the Middle Ages.[41] For example, Lee Patterson states that Chaucer's *Knight's Tale*, "consistent with the major traditions of medieval mythographic writing," presents Venus in terms of "moral allegory."[42] In fact, Patterson in *Chaucer and the Subject of History* several times adopts Robertson's methodology to explicate Chaucer's references to myth, introducing into yet another "historicist" model the problematic use of mythography as an uncomplicated (and positivist) source of literary meaning.[43] Moralizing continually appears the *sine qua non* of mythography, and, where critics elaborate (Patterson does not), duality its fundamental mode.

As the existing scholarship on mythography proves, however, and as we will see in the next chapters, the interpretive rule in mythography is not duality but multiplicity, and moralization is neither mandatory nor everywhere dominant.[44] Mythographic literature seldom proposes a single, coherent model of two loves that would necessarily exclude other explanatory models. While mythographers advance many dichotomies, they often also surround those with a wide assortment of other ways to interpret the ancient deities, much as we have seen John Scotus Eriugena do. Furthermore, John Scotus Eriugena, Bernard Silvestris, Remigius of Auxerre, Alberic, and company demonstrate the absence of a single dualizing norm, of a single set of moral values. If we pursue the idea of two loves into still more medieval texts, we discover that dichotomies of love have no monopoly on the interpretive market in the Middle Ages. Triune or single loves also prosper. Boccaccio (in his mythography) names at least three Venuses and a number of Cupids (Boccaccio's genealogies similarly produce three Jupiters and six Mercurys). Another influential mythographer, Fulgentius, finds only one love depicted by Venus and Cupid. We might notice that dualities can themselves also multiply: for instance, Richard of Fournival distinguishes good from evil love, then divides good love into spiritual and temporal loves, and finally separates temporal love into natural and inborn loves.[45] And for all Augustine's implicit authority over the "two loves," he scathingly reports extensive pagan confusions and challenges all such models for the deities:[46]

> Is it not insupportable that while they ascribe to fire so much honour and, one may say, purity, they are not ashamed sometimes to identify Vesta with Venus, thus making nonsense of the virginity which is honoured in her attendants? For if Vesta is Venus how could the virgins do her due service by abstaining from the works of Venus? Or are there two Venuses, one a virgin, the other a wife? Or, rather three! One for virgins, who is the same as Vesta; one for married women; one for harlots? This last was the goddess to whom the Phoenicians used to give a present, earned by the prostitution of their daughters, before they gave them in marriage. Which of these is the lady wife of Vulcan? Certainly not the virgin, since she has a husband. Not the harlot; perish the thought! We must not seem to insult the son of Juno, and Minerva's fellow-worker. Then we infer that Vulcan's wife was concerned with married women. I hope they will not imitate her behaviour with Mars![47]

Augustine is responding to Roman syncretism, which does indeed present us with a confused assortment of goddesses all bearing the same name. Exploiting those confusions, Augustine rejects any doubling of the deities, for doubling would grant the deities a spurious legitimation and coherence. That is, if we attribute all the questionable aspects of the myths to a unified evil Venus, we gain an entirely good double; but she remains a pagan deity, and the more dangerous because wholly attractive.

Augustine has cogent reasons for symbolizing two loves not with two Venuses but with two cities. In short, the widespread idea that two loves constitutes a universal medieval scheme lacks universal medieval support. Not only do the particular two vary, but a good many notable authorities (though certainly not all medieval writers) reject binary models altogether. The most extensive discussions of mythography to date—Jean Seznec's *Survival of the Pagan Gods*, Rosemond Tuve's *Allegorical Imagery*, and Judson Boyce Allen's *Friar as Critic*—fully establish a mythographic tendency toward multiplicity. Medieval and modern scholarship alike, therefore, should direct us toward an interpretive model that allows us to perceive not only bipolar oppositions but also potential multiplicities.

Though medieval and modern scholars argue that there are indeed more (or fewer) than two loves, literary critics continue to discover two greatly simplified loves in moralized Venuses and Cupids. Indeed, a great number of these discoveries have occurred since Panofsky, Robertson, Economou, and Hollander first led their paired loves to the sacrifice. In this simplification of two loves, criticism displays an oddly tangential relation to that scholarship, which aimed at complicating and refining our ideas about medieval love. Given the current widespread misapprehensions about the medieval conventions, we should pause to untangle the interpretive and theoretical knots in this critical tradition before attempting to weave the threads into a new design.

Alan of Lille, Chaucer, and the Critics

We may discriminate the most typical critical issues resulting from a simplified model of two loves in responses to Alan of Lille's *Plaint of Nature* and Chaucer's *Knight's Tale*. The two Venuses in Alan's work are usually discovered in his first lines and are sometimes presumed to correspond exactly to Bernard Silvestris's celestial and earthly Venuses.[48] (In much the same way, Alan's Venus is often supposed to be identical with Guillaume de Lorris's and Jean de Meun's.)[49] This reading creates rather more difficulties than it does solutions to the problems inherent in Alan's thorny text. The *Plaint of Nature* opens with the speaker mourning the human condition:

I turn from laughter to tears, from joy to grief, from merriment to lament, from jests to wailing, when I see that the essential decrees of Nature are denied a hearing, while large numbers are shipwrecked and lost because of a Venus turned monster, when Venus wars with Venus and changes "hes" into "shes" and with her witchcraft unmans man. (Trans. Sheridan, 67)[50]

Here as elsewhere in the text, Alan describes one Venus becoming a monstrous perversion of herself. By contrast, the Platonists' (say, Bernard's) two Venuses serve conceptually to separate divine love from just such earthly, sensual perversions. The point of the doubling—a point so obvious as to pass unnoticed—is that it produces two distinct figures, however ambiguously interrelated those two may be. Divine love does not transmogrify into a monster. Were Alan to incorporate both celestial and earthly into this one figure that so radically degenerates,[51] he would call divine love into question. A Venus signifying a "lawless" sexuality (and particularly sodomy) is itself a tradition, but this has little enough to do with Platonic or other doublings.[52] Referring Alan's Venus to models of two loves merely introduces unnecessary philosophical dilemmas into our inquiry.

The meaning of Venus in the opening metrum can easily agree with her dominant role in the work, a role Alan clearly explains. As Nature outlines the sexual precepts humans are supposed to follow, Venus literally signifies sexual intercourse (*venus*), and Cupid names desire (*cupido*).[53] Whether Venus engages in marital coitus with Hymenaeus or in adultery with Antigenius, she remains literally a figure for intercourse, with all of its potential variations. Both intercourse and desire are in themselves neutral, capable of participating in or violating natural order. As Nature details Venus's ordained labor, Venus controls how hammers and anvils—male and female reproductive organs—meet or fail to meet:

I [Nature] selected Venus to be in charge of the work of propagation of earth's living things so that she might in producing things mould various materials and submit them for examination.... To insure that the reliability of the instruments should preclude confused and defective workmanship, I assigned her two approved hammers with which to nullify the snares of the Fates and also make a variety of things ready for existence. I also set aside outstanding workshops with anvils in which to do this work, giving instructions that she should apply these same hammers to these same anvils and faithfully devote herself to the production of things and not allow the hammers to stray away from their anvils in any form of deviation. (Trans. Sheridan, 155–56)[54]

Alan prosaically visualizes coitus as a hammer meeting an anvil. More generally, Venus represents the bringing "together in contraposition differing parts of the different sexes so as to effect the propagation of things" (trans. Sheridan, 156; pr. 5.35–37). This representation is as functional as Bernard's, but has distinctly different implications. Alan's metaphor depicts not erotic pleasure but the exercise of a rational, creative skill. Just as the hammer imposes form on the matter held upon the anvil, so also in one model of generation men provide the "key of life" or form and women the "matter for shaping."[55] That reasonable activity here seems exclusive of sensual delight; the desire to shape matter appears the entire motive for sexual intercourse. In other words, Alan pictures in Venus's forging activity a complete subordination of sexual pleasure to the rational end of procreation. (A bizarre visual tradition develops from this idea: Nature stands at a forge, literally hammering out a baby.)[56]

Cassian, one of the founders of the ascetic system, may help to illuminate Alan's metaphor. Cassian describes the penultimate stage in achieving chastity as the ability to "[contemplate] the act [of coitus] in a mood of calmness and purity, as a simple function, a necessary adjunct to the prolongation of the human race, and [depart] no more affected by the recollection of it than if it had been thinking about brickmaking or some other trade."[57] Alan's metaphor precisely pictures this fundamental ascetic ideal of rational sexual control.[58] The metaphor also implicitly supports an orthodox Catholic sexual code: at this time, faced with the Catharist rejection of marriage, Catholic theologians and canonists are defending marriage via the value of procreation, and suspecting any sexual pleasure, including delights that lead to the approved end of coitus.[59] By describing Venus at the (unpleasurable) forge, Alan employs myth against heterodoxy.

With this understanding of Venus's dominant import in the text, we can return to the opening metrum. What of this "Venus fighting against Venus" ("Venus in Venerem pugnans")? I would propose that here Alan is indulging in an arcane grammatical wit that anticipates the myth of the generative forge. His wit depends on the correspondence between language and sexuality that Nature explores at somewhat tedious length and in tendentious detail. Most simply, in Alan's view of natural sexuality, a man takes the active role and position in sexual intercourse, a woman the passive. These roles translate into elaborate grammatical (and other) metaphors: the male should act in intercourse as does the agent of action, the subject of the verb, in a sentence; and the female should serve as recipient of the action, as the grammatical predicate.[60] Alan opens his allegory with a graphic perversion of this natural sexual grammar. Let us return to the crucial lines:

> Cum Venus in Venerem pugnans illos facit illas
> Cumque sui magica devirat arte viros

when Venus wars with Venus and changes "hes" into "shes" and with her witchcraft unmans man

Here Alan makes the feminine *Venus* both agent (the male role) and recipient (the female role) of the action of *pugnans* ("fighting"); as both agent and recipient of action, *Venus-Venerem* participates in a pseudo-reflexive masturbatory grammar. Next, Venus turns the masculine *illos* ("hes") into the feminine *illas* ("shes"). The change of gender ending has sexual implications: "In grammatical terms *signaculum* refers to the masculine ending of a noun, but in real life the *signaculum* ['distinguishing trait'] of a man would be his genitalia."[61] Alan's lines give man a feminine *signaculum*, a thorough grammatical unmanning of the already predicate (passive, feminine) pronoun. Finally, *Venus* as agent (again the male role) of *devirat* ("unmans") graphically dominates the predicate *viros* ("men"), with men relegated once again to the passive and feminine position. As Venus assumes an active male grammatical and sexual role, she becomes hermaphroditic and men become womanish things, grotesque bodies made up of disparate parts that transgress their ontological and social boundaries. Alan's opening lines manifest not two Venuses but alterations in sex roles producing grammatical and ontological changes. In this, he unfolds a central theme of the allegory: transgressions against "natural" order pervert sexuality and grammar. The grammatical consequences of sexual perversion are inscribed in the opening metrum.

Though not precisely applicable to the opening lines, an idea of two Venuses can illuminate Alan's allegory. We have seen that Alan treats Venus literally, as the act of sexual intercourse; he also treats her naturally, as a planet, one of the gems in Nature's diadem. If we must have two Venuses, these are Alan's two, the product of his encyclopedism. Another tradition for Venus enters the work as well, for Alan's Nature is but "a thinly disguised classical Venus."[62] Alan's Nature, like Bernard Silvestris's celestial Venus, has a long ancient as well as medieval poetic lineage: for Ovid and Lucretius as well as for Bernard, Venus can represent the source of life and natural impulses, the love that unites humans and cosmos.[63] Alan alters this tradition by explicitly dismissing Venus from her cosmic role, thereby calling attention to his own symbolic system. He consistently symbolizes in Nature alone the generative vitality of the universe and the bonds of love traditionally ascribed to Venus.[64] The scant disguise of Venus as Nature serves a fundamental allegorical purpose, for by it Alan detaches divine love from the pagan pantheon, and cosmic love from sexuality. The division between Nature and Venus suggestively distances the approval of procreation from sexual acts. Nature appears as a remote figure condoning procreation, dictating its natural forms, but also disdaining any sensual pleasure apart from what inheres in poetic language (and apart from what she and other feminine figures enjoy together). Nature takes the role of a medieval monastic, one who, having taken a vow of chastity, devises an orthodox sexual code for others, and then presents it obscurely so as not to disclose possibilities for perversion to the laity and the uneducated. Alan completes his Christian rewriting of myth by making Nature rather than Saturn the progenitor of Venus (Nature's chastity is apparently not absolute; pr. 9.94–95). Removed from her higher offices, Venus symbolizes a physical sexuality separated from cosmic love. Alan's Nature and Venus emphasize a division between love and sexuality; by contrast, Bernard's two Venuses accentuate the eroticism and the continuity of celestial and earthly loves, of sexuality and love.

In sum, Alan sets up contrasting pairs rather than doubling any figure: we encounter in his text not two loves but assorted sets of opposed loves—Nature and Venus, Hymenaeus and Antigenius, Cupid and Jocus. The pairings serve to heighten moral (and other) differences between the figures. Just as Nature and Venus separate the approval of procreation from actual sex acts, so Hymenaeus and Antigenius, Cupid and Jocus, function to distinguish marital sex from adultery, procreation from contraception, marriage from concubinage, toil from ease, refinement from boorishness, and urbanity from provincialism. The orthodox norms of marital and procreative sexuality come coded in terms of fairly specific social and class values. At the same time, that specific social value system appears as part of a universal nature. By mistakenly discovering two Venuses in the opening metrum of the *Plaint*, we miss how Alan veils his discussion of sexuality with these allegorical figures, how he locates them within his own carefully invented mythic system, and how he turns that myth to an ideological purpose.

We encounter very different critical issues in modern responses to Chaucer's *Knight's Tale*. Chaucer recounts that the lovelorn knight Palamon prays to the goddess Venus for possession of Emelye. According to the paradigm of two loves, this Venus typically manifests Palamon's earthly, lustful passion (though she may also be taken to represent his holy affection—the critical model polarizes responses). With one Venus located in the oratory, critics can discover the second, "good," Venus in Theseus's speech about a fair chain of love.[65] That Chaucer offers no textual evidence for this second Venus goes unremarked. Critics who find two Venuses in the *Knight's Tale* support their reading not with Chaucer's text but with that of his source, Boccaccio's *Teseida* (much as Bernard's two Venuses sponsor discoveries of two in Alan's prosimetrum).[66] One of Boccaccio's glosses on this work argues that Venus represents the "concupiscible appetite," which he initially explains as follows:[67]

> Venus has two aspects: the first is that of honest and permissible desire, like that of having a wife and children, or similar ones. Of this, we shall not treat here. The second is lascivious desire in general, for which Venus is generally called goddess of love. (*Teseida*, 463, gloss to 7.50; trans. Boitani, *Chaucer and Boccaccio*, 201)

The two aspects of the concupiscent appetite obviously overlap: the specific desire for a wife forms a subset of desire "in general." In the lengthy gloss that follows, Boccaccio belies himself by explicating desire in both the promised general sense and in the ostensibly eschewed particular sense. One sense is of course not entirely extricable from the other. He begins his discussion with sexual desire as a universal natural phenomenon, and explains common principles of sexual-reproductive physiology. The temperateness of Venus's home on Mt. Citheron, for instance, tells of the physical conditions required for coitus—a person must be neither cold nor overheated. Although this sexual physiology pertains to all, Boccaccio continues, those we call "lovers" are excited by further particulars (such as love, elegance, and courtesy). Throughout the gloss, he alternates physiological and moral commentary. Thus he notes that Venus's temple is made of copper or brass, the planetary metal, "because it is by virtue of her [astral] influence that all natural couplings [aim] at procreation";[68] brass, having the appearance of gold, also indicates both the initial delights of these couplings and their later bitterness. None of this actually distinguishes two Venuses, though it does outline general and more specific aspects of the concupiscent appetite (the appetite Palemone indulges seven times on his wedding night). How adequately this gloss explains the immediate action is arguable.[69] It certainly does little, if anything, to account for the poet's invocation to Venus in Book 1, so the gloss has at best a limited, local relevance.

Boccaccio unquestionably tries to present two aspects of Venus as the concupiscent appetite in his gloss on the *Teseida*, but Chaucer does not in the *Knight's Tale* (he may never have seen the gloss, or, having seen it, he may have dismissed it, or may plausibly have read it as describing one appetite).[70] Chaucer omits the temple of Venus in which Boccaccio's couple marry; in place of that ceremony, Chaucer has Theseus praise the fair chain of love. Theseus never names the goddess, any more than Boethius does in the passage from which Chaucer borrows (*Boece* 2, metrum 8). Two Venuses arise from the *Knight's Tale* only if we substitute "Venus" for "love" in Theseus's speech. I would offer that the semantic difference between "Venus" and "love" is substantial here: Theseus's fair chain of love signifies what Venus cannot—once again, a love separated from the pagan pantheon.[71] Like Boethius, Chaucer employs an ambiguous sign that is neither entirely Christian nor completely pagan. Astrologizing the deities furthers this ambiguity. By means of the planetary deities, Chaucer recreates the emotional power of the pagan divinities in another of his sources, Statius's *Thebaid*. Where Statius portrays cruelly menacing Roman deities, Chaucer offers conflicting astral forces.[72] This substitution creates natural forces that a medieval audience would find believable. At the same time, like the chain of love image, the planets thwart easy distinctions between Christian and pagan systems of thought. In this way, Chaucer brings the threat of Statius's deities alive, evoking a pagan world even while permitting his audience to discern the planetary aspects of those deities—and thus their relation to a Christian sense of cosmic order. Pursuing Boccaccio's gloss into Chaucer's poem simply rips away the spiderweb of poetic influences out of which Chaucer designs this continuity of paganism and Christianity.

In some existing criticism, the central ambiguities of this Venus are erased in order to make the text conform to critical presuppositions. Preconceptions about a known hierarchy of two loves lead to our overlooking Chaucer's equivocation between Christian and pagan, and to our filling in what Chaucer leaves out: determinate sexual values. Stubborn attention to the interpretive model of two loves also leads to our slighting such aspects of Chaucer's poem as his alterations in Boccaccio's narrative and his debts to Boethius and Statius. We can read Chaucer's poem without attention to his sources, but if we would interpret the *Knight's Tale* on the basis of Boccaccio's gloss, then we need to compare the texts. When we do this (rather than taking Boccaccio as Chaucer's glossator instead of his own), we inevitably recognize each poet's independence from his sources, just as we do with Alan of Lille and Bernard Silvestris.[73]

Though Venus obviously could represent cosmic love, Chaucer's tale limits her to a planetary sphere, subordinate to the patriarchal First Mover.[74] The chain of love image and Venus's astral limitation preclude the possibility of her developing into an independent feminine power. Venus is to the First Mover as the conquered Amazon Hippolyta is to Theseus, and as the sought-after Emelye is to her suitors and guardian. Theseus's image carries to the cosmos the repeated primacy of the masculine and subjection of the feminine at each conceptual level in the tale—international, national, and domestic. I am not arguing that gender is the only hierarchy here, but that gender relations align with political and cosmic power structures. Just as the planets are subject to the First Mover, so are the Thebans and Amazonians to Theseus's Athens, and so too are women subject to men, the feminine (body) to the masculine (reason).[75] Within the larger context of the *Canterbury Tales*, this neat conceptual order assumes a distinctly ephemeral, fictive quality. For where Chaucer delineates such a hierarchal order, he adumbrates also what challenges it, what calls it into question.[76] He pictures not a single absolute order but, rather, provisional myths of hierarchical orders. That is, Chaucer does not develop the eternal verities of Robertson's static "medieval world with its quiet hierarchies," but something much closer to Mikhail Bakhtin's sense of "the official and serious tone of medieval ecclesiastical and feudal culture," always dynamically challenged by "carnival."[77]

Setting aside the chain of love in the *Knight's Tale*, we are left with a single Venus, signifying, according to existing criticism of the poem, either concupiscence (the "mythographic Venus") or an improving astral force.[78] (How critics read Venus has influenced their views of Palamon as a sadly lustful youth or as a noble, even mystical, lover.)[79] Obviously, two loves multiply profligately wherever we turn. I would have us focus for the moment just on the Venus of concupiscence, who seems to appear with greatest frequency in critical commentary after Robertson.[80] While some scholars modify many of Robertson's positions and supplement his evidence, his basic argument retains currency: Venus signifies cupidity (apparently the only interesting term in the two-love model) in accordance with a fixed medieval value judgment. The idea persists because it seems to articulate a final historical truth about medieval attitudes toward sexuality, a truth evident in poetry as in mythography, visual arts, theology, canon law. Poems thus speak for us a (conveniently) unified truth about medieval sexuality, a truth pervading every discourse throughout the period.

This "historical" understanding of Venus assumes that mythographies, poems, theological tracts, and so on all speak the same truth, that being a truth of simple and lucid divisions between licit and illicit sexuality; assumes that those truths are fixed, unchanging within the period; and assumes that this rigid value system applies to all texts, all cultural milieus. None of these assumptions proves satisfactory in the light of recent scholarship in the history of sexuality, which abundantly demonstrates that sexual values varied widely throughout the Middle Ages.[81] To posit that Venus or Cupid signify unchanging values attached to "concupiscence" replaces these historical shifts with a false universal. Few truths about sexuality accurately characterize the entire period, in fact, even if we regard only orthodox ecclesiastical writing. Although an Augustinian distrust of sexual pleasure dominated theology throughout the period, even the rigor of that position modified over the course of centuries. We find, for instance, a rehabilitation of sexual pleasure in the thirteenth century. We do not need a hearing aid to make out dissenting voices and multiple opinions among theologians and canon lawyers, for the Catholic Church was no more unitary on sexual doctrines than on any other topic. Nor were secular or sacred communities everywhere alike in their orthodoxy, or even particularly well informed. Popular and learned attitudes toward sexual pleasure, socially acceptable sexual behavior, contraception, clerical marriage, concubinage, prostitution, homosexuality, and rape altered according to time and place. The differences between canon law and social custom are striking. The differences among social classes in the same time and place can be as notable.

Against this field of diversity within and between popular and ecclesiastical milieus, a universalized notion of concupiscence inadequately defines sexual desire in any medieval text. Even medieval texts that refer to Venus as "cupidity" or "concupiscence" or "lust" may signify with the same label various behaviors or attitudes. A continuous use of one label need not indicate a continuous endorsement of one idea, and an apparent continuity often hides genuine ruptures in many medieval commentaries and allegorical traditions.[82] "Cupidity" may identify a desire for adulterous or homosexual liaisons, or a desire for marital but contraceptive sexual pleasures, or a desire for pleasure during procreative intercourse with a spouse. Adding to the heterogeneity of the period is the fact that a single author may advance more than one model of sexual morality. In Chaucer's *Canterbury Tales*, for example, one woman commits adultery with impunity, another has sexual intercourse with her husband only to conceive a child, and a third renounces sexuality even within marriage. One definition of concupiscence does not suffice for all. If we understand Venus and Cupid merely as "concupiscence," their specific import and valences elude our grasp. As Ernst Robert Curtius succinctly remarks about four twelfth-century texts, attitudes toward Eros can and do range widely even within a limited temporal frame: "the ascetic ideal curses him, profligacy debases him, mysticism spiritualizes him, and gnosticism consecrates him."[83]

The point here (I will return to the *Knight's Tale* in a later chapter) is that Chaucer does not represent two Venuses in this tale, and that we cannot simply refer the one he does depict to a static, fixed, and known code of sexual morality. If we would comprehend Venus in this tale, we need another interpretive model. Chaucer and Alan of Lille and Bernard Silvestris and Martianus Capella and Remigius of Auxerre (and so on) obviously do not all agree about the role of sexuality in life, the threats sexuality poses to social order, or the nature of acceptable sensual pleasure. What these authors share is the blatant co-optation of Venus and Cupid for their own purposes. Each author advances specific ideologies of sexuality, ideologies revealed by the details of representation. In order to recover these ideologies, we cannot adhere to a single model of two loves.

Beyond Binaries; Or, Getting Off the Horns of a Dilemma

Preconceptions about two loves can foster literary criticism that finds no need to examine material texts and sets up a supposed medieval intellectual tradition—binary opposition—as the authentic text.[84] With knowledge of "the tradition," critics can make literature yield conclusive meanings; they find in "tradition" and "source" certain answers to the questions posed by literary texts. Hans Robert Jauss examined this impulse in literary studies following the war, and his acute analysis directs our attention to what such a critical practice risks: in seeking "the focal point of knowledge in the origin or in the atemporal continuity of tradition," literary scholars doggedly ignore "the presence and uniqueness of a literary phenomenon."[85] The vagaries of texts, and the aesthetic particularities of poetry, are displaced by a critical control that assures us of limited, known meanings. Although such control may comfort us, particularly in the wake of the post-structuralist ebb of signs, personal comfort seems an inappropriate critical goal. Those who have most extensively studied the commentaries that carry these traditions in fact argue against precisely this practice.[86] Any division between problematic "literary" and pellucid "source" texts is, quite simply, untenable. "The tradition" itself requires interpretation, and is itself the product of scholarship that creates apparent coherence by picking and choosing among pieces of evidence. Rather than determining the meaning of a text, reference to a source or tradition merely defers that resolution.

This does not mean that we should eschew attempts to define traditions or to locate poems in relation to those traditions. It does mean that we should distinguish between a general pattern and a universal one, between a tradition and any individual manipulation of it. Literary traditions are the product of historical human activity, and they are subject to change, to redefinition, to individual modification. And a tradition, however widespread, does not in the end constitute a tyrannical aesthetic imperative. Our interpretive models, I would propose, need to respect both the integrity of traditions and the particularities of literary texts; our models need also to allow for the possibility of a dialectic between individual text and relevant traditions.

Since conjectured traditions of binary loves raise rather obvious difficulties in critical practice, the remarkable tenacity of this scheme merits analysis. Why, in the end, does bipolar opposition appeal to so many who write of love, now as well as in the remote past? Why does it emerge as a normative pattern and other possibilities continually recede? Why these particular antitheses of good and evil, represented by two women (not a man and a woman, not two men)? What, and whose purposes, do such lucid dichotomies serve? One quick answer to all these questions would be that this tendency proves structuralists right, that people really do organize reality according to binary opposition. I would defer on this point to Carol P. MacCormack: "We do not wish to deny that binary contrasts are vital to human thought; it is the allegedly universal meanings given to some category nouns which concern us."[87] That many writers treat of sexual love in binary pairs is undeniable; what particular binaries achieve is less obvious and worth consideration. By comprehending the values embedded in the oppositions now so firmly attached to Venus and Cupid, we may hope to denaturalize, and thus begin to move beyond, binary thinking.

For a start, we might realize that bipolar oppositions meet human and scholarly needs for order, method, and comprehensibility. Out of multitudinous individual experiences of sexuality, a bipolarity creates a hierarchical relationship between just two loves. On the one side we set clearly distinguished goods (the spirit, sexual renunciation, reason, procreation) and on the other equally understandable evils (the body, pleasure). This hierarchized opposition clarifies morality, producing a clear normative division between superior moral and inferior immoral sexualities. It identifies what we are to praise, what repudiate, creates apparently lucid and self-evident normative values from the raw material of contradictory and ambiguous cultural systems.

We encounter a similar effect with binary thinking about gender. If we focused on Venus and Cupid as a pair, for example, we could readily discover a stereotypical gender opposition: Venus and femininity would align with the body and with nature—would be defined according to biological and sexual characteristics; masculinity and Cupid would be associated with culture, with transcending nature through symbolic activity and reason. In a structuralist context, this opposition between Venus and Cupid could be taken to reveal corresponding differences between female and male, flesh and spirit, emotion and intellect, sensuality and reason, lust and self-control, nature and culture.[88] Indeed, Venus and Cupid can be read as manifesting this gendered opposition in much medieval literature. Such a pattern has long been recognized and owes nothing to structuralist, gender, or feminist theories: C. S. Lewis, for instance, remarked that in the *Romance of the Rose* "Venus is the sexual appetite—the mere natural fact, in contrast to the god of Love who is the refined sentiment."[89] Placing gender into binary oppositions of this type functions to remove ambiguity, to locate unmistakable and hierarchized differences between masculine and feminine.

If we forsake straightforward binary formulas, we are left without distinct guides to medieval ideas of good and evil, or to medieval sex and gender systems, and we find ourselves in a swarm of ambiguities. We might note that this logic applies to many dichotomies, whether the subject is language or medieval love or gender or periodicity.[90] Much as a model of "two loves" may help us discriminate between good and evil, allowing confident judgment about the presumed effects of a text on its medieval audience, so may a concept of medieval/modern promote security about what constitutes past and present values and mores. We pay a price for the clarity and confidence gained by means of such binary thinking, for binary sex and gender systems are no more—and no less—than cultural myths. The danger of naturalizing these binaries is that we ossify ideology: we turn the products of our own cognitive activity into seemingly immutable constants.[91] In order to reduce many representations of Venus and Cupid to such lucid antitheses as feminine/masculine or good/evil, we have to overlook what would confuse our categorical thinking, and to eliminate textual and historical specificities. We gain a marvelously clear outline by cutting off what does not happen to fit into the mold; coherent dichotomies depend on our not seeing what would complicate and refute simple differences.

Entrapment in binary thinking almost always leads to the same kind of oversimplification: a logical false dilemma that excludes possible alternatives. At best, binary thinking imposes a spurious coherence and clarity on the host of Venuses and Cupids we encounter in medieval literature. But surely such unproblematic binaries have grown implausible, as post-structuralism has subjected them to a remorseless analysis that exhibits their constructed quality, allegiance to hierarchies, and analytical limitations.[92] As this analysis has taught us, exclusive attention to two opposed elements compels a repression of any third (fourth, tenth) term. For instance, the binary homosexuality/heterosexuality excludes bisexuality and autoeroticism and celibacy; similarly, a male/female opposition ignores hermaphrodites. The focus on binary opposition also makes each element seem unified (all homosexuals or heterosexuals seem the same, as do all men, all women). In sum, binaries effectively deny multiplicity and diversity. Accepting such conceptual models severely limits the medieval traditions we are willing and able to perceive. If we comfortably expect two Venuses, we do not notice the inconvenient third Venus. The implications of binary thinking extend beyond Venus, of course, and lead us to overlook many medieval conventions. For instance, attention to gender opposition and to licit/illicit sexualities has all but buried a vigorous medieval tradition of comparing two quite different loves—homosexual and heterosexual, Ganymede and Helen.[93] Yet this tradition would doubtless reward further study.

Whatever values we attach to modern binaries, they manifestly simplify subjects and produce a reductive understanding of the past. The idea of the two loves imposes a misleadingly neat order on discrepant textual details, satisfying a desire for clarity by hierarchizing and oversimplifying the terms of the discussion. Conceptual simplification is sometimes useful, even necessary, in that it can permit us to recognize larger patterns. A case in point: attending to stereotypical gender differences can help us locate power relations and inequities operative in a culture. Analysis of such stereotypes is sometimes valuable, even vital, to the purposes of feminist politics. (It is worth noting that stereotypical gender opposition, like any other binary, is not fixed to a single political agenda but may be appropriated for radically other propositions.)[94] If we never leave the sweeping and panoramic views offered by such analyses, however, we advance but little. We need not only universal models but also awareness of details that contradict or challenge those models.

The persuasiveness of universalizing dualities rests on their seeming comprehensiveness, their power to organize our experience of medieval culture and literature. As dichotomies are repeated in medieval texts and in modern criticism, they produce the recurrent illusion of coherent, simple distinctions between good and evil, licit and illicit, male and female (and so on). The oppositional differences by slow degrees develop the appearance not of a contingent cultural arrangement but of a factual system inherent in the unchanging universe. This naturalization of binaries and the eventual disappearance of their contemporary human origins helps explain part of their modern scholarly appeal: binary constructions of sex and gender systems have attained the status of historicist veracity. The bipolar opposition of two loves, like a simple gender antithesis, functions to create a past that is both known and different, though different in ways that we seem fully to understand. This effect is heightened by the supposed mythographic basis of two-love or moralized-love schemes, for the naturalization of a medieval origin has encouraged some scholars eager to historicize critical practice to adopt the idea of moralized or dualistic loves. As modern binary constructions of the past have been naturalized, they have come to support what may look like a value-free, historicizing, and ideologically neutral critical practice. By reference to binary paradigms and the moralization of myth, we make judgments about past sexual morality or gender roles seem historically verified, untouched by modern cultural influences or personal subjectivity.

The problem with this is self-evident: once again, the advantage is illusory. Mythography (or any other medieval discourse) does not universally advance an idea of two loves or of moralization, and reference to mythography does not necessarily permit a historicist understanding of literature. We need something more thoughtful and complicated than an idea of two mythographic, moralized loves if we wish to historicize our readings of Venus and Cupid. But we should not in any event imagine that historicism is the final answer to the problem of deciphering literary meanings. Texts can resist historical contexts and can stand in deeply ambiguous relation to history, which, after all, is also an interpretive category.[95] Appeals to history do not necessarily validate literary criticism; some such appeals are merely reductive.

Perhaps the most popular modern notion about the Middle Ages is that the period evidences a clear and simple antithesis between licit and illicit sexuality, between the sacred and the profane.[96] Yet when we concentrate on the details, we find that the universal moral code promoted by a static binary opposition of good and evil loves goes against the conclusions of recent studies on the history of sexuality, and this is probably the most serious limitation of the model of two loves, as of ideas about the so-called moralized Venus.[97] Two Venuses, or Venus moralized as concupiscence, may have effectively defined medieval sexuality at one time, but that time has certainly long passed. In view of new developments in conceptions of sexuality, we need models that acknowledge the multiplicity and change that we know to characterize medieval (and other) constructions of sexuality.

While a binary model of medieval love pretends to historicist authority, it facilitates the illusion of scholarly objectivity, of a lucid and immediate comprehension of past attitudes. Since morality and gender roles look objective within this limited context, an objective critical stance seems possible even for the topic of sexual love, which I would guess evokes anything but impersonal, detached responses in most of us. Dichotomies therefore fashion for modern literary critics the mask of interpretive objectivity. If we dispense with binary models, we will be left to speak as individuals who are anything but serenely omniscient about and disinterested regarding human sexual behavior. We will be left to speak as embodied scholars. This is in fact inescapable; we have no other position from which to speak. If a fully objective, universally "human" critical stance is possible, we have yet to invent it.[98] Certainly, the subjectivity inherent in the discipline of literary study can spawn excesses, but we can attempt to correct problems without overcorrecting, without pretending literary criticism is or should be an objective science. This is a flaw in the discipline only if we assume that the sciences provide the only possible model of knowledge (and only if we take the sciences to be perfectly objective—a very dubious proposition). The power of criticism as a discipline, however, may well lie in our always diverse subjectivities, which lead us to heterogeneous readings that in the long run prove mutually illuminating. From our pluralism as critics and scholars has arisen a fuller knowledge, a more complete comprehension of our subject, of our methodologies, and of our theoretical presuppositions: our subjective diversity and consequent disagreements enrich our analyses.

Thus far, then, we find that bipolar opposition entices us to pursue mirages of hierarchical order in sex and gender systems, illusions of historicism and objectivity. The particular binary of two loves has at least one more telling effect. It always speaks finally of a unity: the two loves exist in union, each defined by and dependent on the other. If Venus or Cupid appears confusingly disunified in a text, then, the model of two loves can remedy the difficulty. For example, when Alan of Lille presents Venus not only as a figure for intercourse but also as an anthropomorphized force of sexual desire and as a planet, critics can refer to two loves to discover a unified import in keeping with dominant modern academic aesthetics. The prevailing critical model and critical practice therefore testify to unchallenged assumptions about organic unity in representation: Venus or Cupid must point to one coherent, unified meaning in any one text. Where they obviously do not, the binary opposition serves to resolve textual contradictions, producing organically unified portraits in place of disparate, puzzlingly incompatible references.

If we abandon the model of two loves, the texts may fragment, leaving us with sundry pieces obscurely related to one another. I will argue in the following chapters that medieval texts do sometimes juxtapose unreconciled elements and leave them unreconciled. This may even be the most characteristic effect of medieval treatments of myth; it certainly emerges as a very pronounced feature of the texts we turn to in the next chapter, the mythographies that willy-nilly pile up explanation after explanation of the ancient gods, discerning in Venus and Cupid manifold and conflicting significances. Indeed, the preeminent characteristic of the mythographies considered in the following chapters is the marked plenitude and variability of meanings they advance for the ancient deities. Authors can jump with sometimes astonishing rapidity from one interpretive category to the next and back again. Of course, not all mythographers interpret myths at any length, and not all multiply interpretations. Mythography may incline toward handbooks of mythic narrative or toward hermeneutic compendia, though multiple interpretations appear the more common tendency. To follow the logic of these texts, we need to understand their strategies for reading, their acceptance of contradictions among those strategies, and their license to manipulate hermeneutics for particular occasions. We need also to recognize mythographers' role in creating and arguing for polysemous signs. For instance, Pierre Bersuire promises to develop various levels of meaning—literal, allegorical, natural, spiritual; similarly, Christine de Pizan repeatedly stresses the possibility of multiple readings, which she must overlook for the sake of a unified design.

Mythography is not alone in the medieval acceptance—even celebration—of multivalence. The letter to Cangrande that purports to be by Dante offers one familiar systematization of a widespread idea about reading a single text through several conceptual paradigms. Much medieval sign theory similarly accepts polysemous signs.[99] As we wander in the byways of poetry, we repeatedly encounter the same basic position. A gloss on Lydgate's *Reason and Sensuality*, for instance, indicates that "among the poets, Jupiter is interpreted in many ways."[100] Bipolar opposition, like moralization, constitutes one, but only one, of the "many ways" of mythography.

The explanatory diversity advocated by mythographers and many other medieval writers holds signs in tension between indeterminacy and univocality, arguing that we understand the meaning of these signs (the deities) as neither completely arbitrary and indeterminate nor entirely fixed and univocal. The example of mythography suggests that the creation of meaning actually falls between those absolutes. The mythographic signs are not indeterminate, for each meaning is momentarily stable; they are not univocal, for each meaning may always give way to others. We find that mythography mediates between absolutes. It promulgates temporary univocalities, immediately displaced by other and equally transient univocalities. In other words, the commonplace binary opposition of absolute indeterminacy and absolute determinacy, a major conceptual basis of deconstruction, does not adequately describe what we find in these texts.[101] We might think rather in terms of local and limited determinacies (better: near-determinacies). Although the deities are multivalent and as a consequence always potentially ambiguous, we may yet seek to discern what meanings are temporarily advanced, what meanings are held in equivocal suspense. We may also discover cultural meaning in the very conflicts among hermeneutics, as well as in the issues left unresolved or insistently resolved. If something in literature escapes such defining acts, that only points to the limits of criticism—and to the pleasures of the text.

Instead of using mythography as a sourcebook for poetic meaning, therefore, we might seek to appreciate how the hermeneutic impulse toward multiple meanings for the ancient deities (or for multiple figures of each deity—this difference *is* often indeterminate) might enter into literature. I would propose that medieval encyclopedism, together with medieval (and ancient) confusions about just how many Venuses and Cupids there are, makes possible, even likely, diverse representations of Venus and Cupid in a single literary work. Just as Alan of Lille in the *Plaint of Nature* treats Venus as a poetic figure for sexual intercourse, a planet, and a symbol of sexual desire, so in the *Anticlaudianus* he depicts Venus at one point as a figurative force of sexuality attacking the good and perfect man, at another point as a planet. The planet is in each case distinct from a poetic figure for sexual desire, and both are distinct from a euphemism for sexual intercourse. Alan's handling of Venus evidences something quite distinct from an absolute organic unity. Of course, encyclopedism does not mandate such disjunctions. Jean de Meun's *Romance of the Rose*, though nothing if not thoroughly encyclopedic, presents unified portrayals of Venus and Cupid. The example of encyclopedism and of classical texts alike should nonetheless alert us to the likelihood of our encountering in the literature either a deity with multiple imports, or multiple and unreconciled appearances of a deity in assorted guises. Resolving the differences into bipolar oppositions—however much clarity, unity, or security we may gain by doing so—misrepresents medieval (and classical) mythology. We will have instead to accept Venus and Cupid as they come to us in these texts: as inherently multivalent and disunified signs, semiotic nomads. In order to approach them, we have to be willing to query our assumptions about organic unity, univocality, and representational consistency.

This does not mean that discovering fragmentation or discrepancy ends the critical endeavor. Such is the beginning, not the end, of my argument. The end lies in exploring what the fragments intimate within their own systems of thought, and in discerning how those systems, those fragments, relate to each other. I would draw an analogy here to Bakhtin's theory of dialogic discourse in the novel. A discourse becomes dialogized when it is brought into relation with other discourses, which relativizes each of them, exposes how each must compete with the others to promote its own definitions.[102] This idea of de-privileged, rival discourses can help us to make sense of how various systems of thought generate meanings for Venus and Cupid, and how those systems and their definitions may come into competitive relations in both mythography and poetry.

This is therefore not a study that advances an argument about oppositional sex and gender differences, but one that seeks to challenge the hold such dualisms exert over our imagination, and to dislodge binary opposition from the center of our attention in the study of medieval sexuality and hermeneutics.[103] This is, moreover, a study that seeks to delineate some of the ways various medieval disciplinary perspectives compete for precedence in the definition of sexual love. In sum, I would propose that we extricate sex and gender systems from naturalized binary models, and attempt to move beyond binary thinking by seeking to comprehend what binaries accomplish in particular instances, what terms they repress, and what terms they privilege. When we encounter two loves, as we will, we might ask ourselves, "Why these two? What agenda do they advance?" Further, I would argue that we would do well to respect the essentially polysemous and fragmentary character of the deities. If the deities appear disparate in a single work, we might attempt to understand whether the discourses that inscribe them are also disparate. As we do this, we might investigate how discourses interact with one another, how they disclose tensions and complicities. That is, we might attempt to be alert both to dialectics between texts and traditions, and to dialogues among discourses within a single text. Finally, given the tremendous change and diversity implicit in medieval constructions of sex and gender systems, and given the multivalent potential of the deities, we might simply respect the omnipresent possibility of multiplicity and ambiguity. Instead of resolving all ambiguities into more manageable bipolarities, and instead of reducing all moral codes to one, we might in analyzing literature ask what is rendered ambiguous and, perhaps, to what effect; we might adopt a critical method that seeks to explore rather than eliminate ambiguity. Put briefly, then, I suggest that we query binary oppositions, that we attend to the possibility of multivalence and polysemy (thus of ambiguity), which may complicate our ideas about the necessity of strict representational unity and coherence, and, finally, that we listen for dialogues among the competing discourses that treat of Venus and Cupid.

As we will find, the deities of love most typically stand somewhere between the poles of holy renunciation and unholy deviance, embodying a sexuality of everyday life, neither exalted nor debased. Venus and Cupid seldom illustrate cultural ideals about holiness, about sexuality cast off or turned into sacred metaphor; they accordingly reveal little about monastic ethics of renunciation, one extreme of licit sexuality.[104] Yet if they do not typically express that extreme, they also rarely become symbols of repudiated "deviant" sexualities: they are not usually lepers, heretics, or homosexuals.[105] Venus and Cupid can therefore allow us to glimpse the subtle tones and hues in medieval attitudes toward sexuality: the acceptance of sexual pleasure, but not of "excess" or "deviance"; the encouragement of rational moderation rather than an insistence on renunciation. They can help us to get beyond a division between licit and illicit that persistently oversimplifies medieval sexualities for the sake of creating a past that is both comprehensible and different from the present.

Chapter 2

Semiotic Nomads

> Keep your head
> up. They are calling to you—slut, mother,
> virgin, whore, daughter, adultress, lover,
> mistress, bitch, wife, cunt, harlot,
> betrothed, Jezebel, Messalina, Diana,
> Bathsheba, Rebecca, Lucretia, Mary,
> Magdelena, Ruth, you—Niobe,
> woman of the tombs.
> Tess Gallagher,
> "Instructions to the Double"

Since much of the potential diversity and interest of mythography have been repressed for the sake of two-love schemes, the traditions have come to seem conceptually impoverished. Most modern commentators in fact appear to assume that these texts advance unimaginative moralistic agendas. With this impression of the traditions, literary critics have no good reason to examine them. Still, the prevailing lack of interest in mythography derives less from its conceptual poverty than from the limited questions we have asked of it, the limited attention we have granted it. As long as mythographies remain unproblematic sources for "primary" or "literary" texts, they will predictably disclose little of literary (or other) interest themselves. The prevailing indifference toward the verbal texture of mythography, and the widespread positivist uses of mythographic writing, testify not to the texts' inherent lack of interest but to their exile from the canon—from the country of texts that merit critical attention, that need interpretation. In spite of their gaining frequent notice in criticism, therefore, the texts are seldom analyzed critically, though they have rewarded such efforts.[1]

We might begin to think anew about mythography by coming to terms with its most obvious feature: it presents interpretations of the deities and legends of classical literature. These interpretations, like our own, are never innocent of bias. We might consequently expect that mythographies, in taking up Venus and Cupid, reveal not only ways of understanding the pagan past but also ways of encoding the politics of interpretation and of sexuality. If we approach the texts with this expectation, we will more likely read them as worthy of our critical attention. As we do this, we will be able to detect how meanings are invented and rationalized, and we will be in a position to appreciate how this discourse supports, questions, or complicates gender issues, social power relations, and ideas about sexuality.

Since mythographic texts are relatively unknown, this chapter serves as an introduction to some of the major texts and their hermeneutics.[2] Beyond that descriptive and functional purpose, it will demonstrate some crucial lines of historical change within the traditions, outline the shifting contexts of interpreting ancient myth, and set forth the diversity and attractions of mythographic hermeneutics. I would emphasize the importance of heeding change and diversity. Although we are able to trace historical tendencies in medieval writing about sexuality, clearly no medieval era witnesses a homogeneous interpretation of sexuality; consequently, no era discloses a homogeneous interpretation of Venus and Cupid. In the twelfth century, for example, canon law revives a rigorous Augustinianism (thus rejecting sexual pleasure),[3] but at the same time Platonism may legitimate sensual pleasure. Attitudes at each of these extremes emerge in mythographic literature of the time. In the thirteenth century, some theologians rehabilitate the value of sexual pleasure;[4] yet mythography in this time may formulate extensive moralizing condemnations of precisely what those theologians permit. Instead of torturing all medieval discourses until they confess the same truth, we might best seek to appreciate what mythography (or, for that matter, poetry) actually reveals—the possibility of variations on the dicta found in such official texts as penitentials and canon law. There is no universal value, mythographic or ecclesiastical, to which we can refer for a fixed understanding of all medieval Venuses and Cupids. Instead, we must heed the multiplicity of medieval voices that articulate their meanings.

An Overview of Mythography

Mythographic comments on Venus and Cupid form one of very few discourses on sexuality that span the entire Middle Ages. Because of their historical breadth alone, mythographies can help us comprehend how ideas about sexuality and gender develop and alter, and how these ideas are variously encoded in the deities of love. As explanations of ancient myth unfold over these centuries that witness massive shifts in the theological and social formation of sexual codes, broad historical changes inevitably affect interpretations of Venus and Cupid. Hence mythography can intriguingly complicate our understanding of medieval sexual mores and values. It can show a range of norms by which sexual behaviors and attitudes are judged in various contexts, discourses, and times, and by various writers, all of whom have their own purposes for inscribing various ideological and sexual codes in Venus and Cupid.

Since a single study of mythography that attempted exhaustively to chronicle its diversity for the entire period would fill many volumes and lifetimes with wearisome repetition, I limit the nucleus of my discussion in this book to a few vastly influential texts, and to a few more eccentric ones. My purpose in referring to these texts is not to catalogue each incidence of every interpretation (I am not attempting to write an encyclopedia), but to suggest the methods of mythography and its interest. For the purposes of this descriptive chapter, the following texts will let us sample the methodologies and scope of mythographic traditions for Venus and Cupid, and the changes within them, from the fifth to the fifteenth century, without putting us in the position of mechanically collecting repetitive details: Fulgentius, *Mythologies* (*Mitologiae*); Isidore of Seville, *Etymologies* (*Etymologiae sive origines*); Alberic, The Third Vatican Mythography, *On the Gentile Gods and Their Allegories* (*De diis gentium et illorum allegoriis*); John Ridewall, *Fulgentius Metaphored* (*Fulgentius metaforalis*); Pierre Bersuire, *On the Gods' Appearances and Figures* (*De formis figurisque deorum*); Giovanni Boccaccio, *Genealogy of the Gentile Gods* (*Genealogia deorum gentilium*); Christine de Pizan, *The Epistle of Othea* (*L'Epistre Othéa*).

One could certainly add many other texts (and I will refer to others in passing here and in later chapters), yet each addition leads to an increase in discursive repetition (and a possibly superfluous exercise in scholarly patience).[5] The listed texts suffice fairly to represent mythographic concerns and strategies. We should begin by recognizing that these mythographies differ markedly from each other in methodology, organization, and purpose. Mythography does not constitute a formal genre or display a stable literary form; mythography may augment a commentary on an ancient or medieval text, or develop into an independent discussion of myth. In addition, the purposes and rationales of mythography alter radically from the beginning to the end of the period, and mythographic hermeneutics undergo significant changes. Mythography continually renews itself from the classical period into the Renaissance, and its long life doubtless owes much to its conceptual and discursive flexibility: its ability to adapt with changes in education, philosophy, social codes, milieus, and concepts of authority.

We might take two texts as exemplary of how much mythography alters in the course of the Middle Ages. In the late fifth or early sixth century Fulgentius writes a book of mythologies in order to correct the lies promulgated by ancient fables; he defines himself by his overt opposition to antique myth, which he allegorizes in order to read acceptable meanings into the narratives. In the fourteenth century, John Ridewall reads Fulgentius's own text allegorically. The commentary must itself eventually be rewritten.[6] Between Fulgentius and Ridewall, education and philosophy have changed, as have the relations between Christianity and paganism, commentary and primary text; hermeneutics alter with the times. Throughout the Middle Ages, mythographic writing follows eddying intellectual and social currents, and, especially regarding Venus and Cupid, participates in the flux of changing sexual norms.

Since conceptualizations of both mythography and sexuality clearly alter in the course of the Middle Ages, it becomes easy to mark out discontinuities and breaks in the traditions for Venus and Cupid. The more difficult task lies in attempting to detect continuities; for this we would need, ideally, a more complete historical and textual record of mythography than we have.[7] Some of the most important mythographies presently exist in a state of dishabille, frustrating any study of their contents and making precise conclusions about their relations to other texts next to impossible. We do not yet have complete, reliable critical editions of all the major texts, including the Vatican mythographies and John Ridewall's *Fulgentius Metaphored*. Some mythographies went through several revisions, to which we do not necessarily have access, any more than their medieval audiences did. Boccaccio's *Genealogy of the Gentile Gods* circulated widely in its 1370–71 form, without his final revisions.[8] Pierre Bersuire completed two major redactions of his mythography, *On the Gods' Appearances and Figures*. We may take the last version in either case as definitive of the author's intention, but earlier as well as later versions obviously influenced medieval writers and would form part of any comprehensive picture of mythographic sources and influences.[9] After reviewing the extensive difficulties of tracing Bersuire's influence on other writers, in fact, William D. Reynolds sensibly concludes that "If Bersuire studies are to continue to progress, what is needed is easier access to what he actually wrote."[10] We could say the same of almost any mythographer. The absence of reliable critical editions can also generate sham continuities: for example, editing practices create dependence on presumed sources as well as obscuring reliance on common lost sources for the important Vatican mythographies.[11] Not surprisingly, source studies of mythographies concentrate on tracing the sources and influence of a single text, which does little to advance our understanding of how traditions might continue throughout the period.[12] In the absence of critical editions, manuscript studies, and source studies, we clearly lack access to much of the information we would need in order to discriminate continuous mythographic traditions, in order to discern with any confidence the relations among texts. We can detect borrowings between some texts and among discrete groups of texts; a few classical tags recur, as do iconographic details and several interpretive commonplaces. Since scholarship cannot wait on ideal conditions, we may sketch out general traditions, yet we should remain conscious that the present state of the scholarship makes many conclusions about texts and traditions necessarily tentative.

Beyond these pragmatic difficulties in determining what constitutes mythographic traditions, particular lines of interpretation vary greatly from text to text, making conclusions about continuities problematic. Let us take one popular mythographic moment—the story of Mars, Venus, and Vulcan—as an example. Both Fulgentius and Alberic offer (as one of several explications) that Mars signifies a good warrior infected by Venus or lust and gripped by the fetters of desire, Vulcan's net. Not only entrapped, Mars is "corrupted," even physically "polluted."[13] The language corresponds to that of penitential manuals, which would suggest we understand pollution and corruption as indicating a "state of ritualistic impurity" resulting from seminal emission.[14] Since even the epitome of martial valor is not safe from Venus's sexual prowess, all men seem intensely vulnerable, subject to women and uncleanness because subject to desire. Yet not all mythographers interpret the tale according to exactly the same ethical or social code. In contrast to this focus on ritual impurity, Lactantius Placidus concerns himself with the loss of reason implicit in sensual pleasure: "For what is the pleasure of Venus except pure madness?" Therefore Venus is joined to Mars and Vulcan, *furor* and fire.[15] Here sensual pleasure threatens rational self-control. Taking a still different perspective, the anonymous twelfth-century Digby mythographer views the adultery as indicating Venus's ("shameful") contempt for her husband.[16] Such fabliaulike sympathy for Venus and ridicule of the cuckolded Vulcan are common. All these explanations demonstrate the independence of commentators, whose particular interpretations respond to different contexts, different imperatives. What, then, constitutes "the" mythographic tradition?

If we move forward in time a bit, we find Jean Molinet, in a commentary on the episode in the *Romance of the Rose*, asserting that Vulcan signifies Christ.[17] The potential for variation becomes even more obvious if we compare a few still later accounts. Christine de Pizan drolly notes that Mars's fate reminds the good knight not to be forgetful of time—to watch so that he is not surprised by a returning husband.[18] ("If it were done, when 'tis done, then 'twere well / It were done quickly.")[19] This surely constitutes one of Christine's least profound moral lessons.[20] As she continues, the lesson becomes universal and less comically pragmatic: the good Christian should guard against such spiritual enemies as covetousness, lechery, and gluttony. Christine also comments that the fable may be read according to astrology. Though she does not explain further, this analysis would disclose the adulterous copulation to be a figure for a planetary conjunction of Mars and Venus. In his turn, Thomas Walsingham tells the story of adultery twice, making a different point each time. From one perspective, "the man of strength is destroyed in Venus," or sexual desire; but from another point of view Vulcan's "baseness" and "ugliness" are laughable.[21] None of the participants gains this commentator's sympathy. And finally, if a short digression from strictly mythographic texts be allowed, we might note that Guibert of Nogent explains that Venus, "the heat of lust," eventually "boils over into cruelty" with Mars.[22] In his turn, Genius in Gower's *Confessio Amantis* reads the tale as teaching married men not to reveal their shame (5.698–713). And Lydgate in *Complaint of a Lover's Life* presents the story as one in a series of exempla demonstrating that true lovers like Mars "fynde mercy comfort noon" while false lovers like Vulcan have "many nightis glade."[23] Explications of the myth clearly run the gamut from fabliau winks to romance to harsh denigration.

Drawing on three accounts of the myth, one modern scholar asserts that "in mythographical commentary the story of Mars and Venus is consistently taken to signify the bondage of the 'chains' of illicit and irrational desire"; these "specific implications in the context of medieval thought" in turn explain the episode in the *Romance of the Rose*.[24] We do not need mythography to arrive at this understanding of the tale in the *Romance*, but the reference to the specificity and consistency of mythographic explication gives the reading an apparently historical validity. This exemplifies the most common critical use of mythography. The obvious problem with this practice is the necessity of a coherent and unbroken mythographic tradition of a particular import, which we have not got. If we sought long enough, we could unearth nearly any explanation we desired in order to authorize an interpretation of a literary text, yet such a selective choice of evidence would not constitute a historical understanding of the myth. A more defensibly historicist use of mythography would recognize the historical particularities of and alterations in sexual norms—the difference, say, between an early medieval concern for ritual purity and a late medieval worry that young men not be embarrassed (perhaps endangered) by being discovered *flagrante delicto*.

Mythographies certainly provide historical evidence of reading. They manifest not a single, repeated interpretation of any mythic moment, however, but a set of more or less commonplace strategies about reading, strategies always subject to change and modification. We can trace in the examples given above the shared hermeneutic traditions of moralizing allegory, astrological interpretation, and social commentary. The mythographic tradition lies in the hermeneutics, not in their particular applications. Each writer treating of Mars and Venus shares assumptions about the flexibility of the myth, about its adaptability to various purposes; each produces a different explanation of the episode. Thus although mythographies do not evidence a "correct" or "historical" understanding of myth, they disclose what is perhaps more interesting—the negotiable uses of hermeneutics.

The mythographers' more common ways of understanding ancient myths are drawn from various models; the most typical are based on historical, etymological, scientific (natural or astrological), allegorical, moral, dualizing, and philosophical categories of thought. For instance, Venus may be historically a prostitute; naturally, a planet; allegorically, feminine vanity; morally, libido or licit and illicit loves; philosophically, celestial or earthly love. Mythographers typically develop more than one of these models, and Venus may signify all of these meanings within a single text. The choice of interpretive models is frequently telling, for the models invoke different kinds of authority and develop diverse ideological purposes. In the medieval historical analysis, for instance, the goddess's origin is located in the pagan past, and the politics of Christian-pagan relations inform the analysis. These politics of course alter between the classical period and the late Middle Ages. Astrological interpretation, which identifies the goddess with planetary influences misunderstood by pagans, can similarly expose pagan errors. But whereas historicizing the deity bestows on her a kind of illegitimacy, astrology grants her scientific legitimacy. In addition to the politics built into the interpretive models, moreover, mythographers often advance particular ideological agendas. Their acts of interpretation, in short, are never neutral.

Mythography from Antiquity to the Later Middle Ages

One of the most obvious impulses behind medieval mythography is the need to offer Christian explanations of ancient pagan literature and religion. The earliest medieval mythography develops in the context of religious polemics, and attempts to answer the claims of paganism. As the ages pass, the threat of ancient Roman religion disappears, replaced by the successive challenges of Teutonic, Viking, Moslem, Judaic, and heterodox religions. From the time of the Crusades forward, ancient Roman myths offer the safe and escapist appeal of inoculated myth; they express a dead paganism, a counterfeit threat (unlike Jewish and Moslem religious texts). The very topic of Roman myth declares in the later Middle Ages the triumph of Christianity: the Roman Empire gave way to the Holy Roman Empire, and its gods to the Christian God. In the Middle Ages, the myths begin as stories associated with religious practices and end simply as fictions. Negotiations of classicism alter according to this and other patterns of change; the methods of mythography similarly shift in response to new contexts.²⁵ The remainder of this chapter maps out some of these patterns, beginning with the late antique world and ending with the early fifteenth century.

The Classical Legacy

The routine modern perception of one Venus and one Cupid—that is, of coherent, unified deities—is largely the product of scholarship that synthesizes and consolidates the ancient figures. Many ancient places claimed a Venus or a Cupid type, but they did not all claim the same deities. Cicero delineates four Venuses and three Cupids; in his turn Boccaccio similarly describes three Venuses and a small host of Cupids and Amors.²⁶ Roman syncretism begins a process of consolidating the local deities by identifying a number of Venuses with one imperial Venus. Yet though the many local deities gradually resolved into an almost coherent pantheon, medieval mythographers inherit from the classical period a confusing multiplication of deities, and genealogical and other perplexities remain unresolved.²⁷ Mythographers may preserve the multiplicity—as Cicero and Boccaccio do—or they may consolidate all the Venuses and Cupids into a more manageable pair. Whichever choice they make, their legacy consists of confusingly disparate figures: a bald Venus, a bearded Venus, a matronly Venus, a prostitute Venus, a planetary Venus, a vegetable Venus, and so on (all of whom we will meet in due course). When all these Venuses are incorporated into one figure, that one evidences inherent and inescapable disunities.

Ancient philosophers compound the conceptual difficulties of this multiplicity by formulating numerous and contradictory ways of understanding the deities. According to these arguments, the gods are poetic fictions—for historical personages, or for astral or other natural forces, etymological verities, or for philosophical, ethical, or psychological truths.²⁸ Some of these interpretations come from critics of religion, who may argue, for instance, that the gods were invented by priests for their own mercenary or other purposes; such ancient critiques of pagan religion can provide medieval writers with conveniently disparaging, informed analyses of paganism. Other interpretations arise to preserve religion from the degradations of poetic (particularly Homeric) narratives. The ancients' interpretive strategies persist through the Middle Ages, continually recast to fit writers' diverse ideological agendas and purposes. In other words, the interpretive shell often endures, but the kernel of truth goes through a series of transformations. The apparent continuity of a hermeneutic may misleadingly suggest a unified conceptual tradition, whereas in fact conceptual ruptures have occurred.[29] After all, the point of the analysis cannot be at all the same for an Augustan Roman, a patristic or Carolingian writer, and a late medieval Englishman. Early Christian apologists and mythographers often enough represent themselves as opposing ancient philosophical readings of myth—even, or perhaps especially, when borrowing from them. In the early Middle Ages, the pagan world remains vivid, and borrowings from it are imbued with tension. As the threat of paganism gradually shifts from ancient Romans to medieval Vikings and Moslems, ancient Greco-Roman myth grows more innocuous. At this point, as we will see, the old myths begin to participate in new mythic systems.

The Early Middle Ages: Augustine, Fulgentius, and Isidore

Although Augustine of Hippo does not write a mythography, his *City of God* (*De civitate Dei*) includes an extended argument against paganism that draws on ancient mythographic ways of understanding the deities. As an argument against paganism, Augustine's treatise exemplifies an ideologically motivated deployment of mythography, and it promises to show the interested ways in which ancient hermeneutics are transmitted to the later Middle Ages. Augustine may thus prepare us to be sensitive to the potential utility and value of mythographic modes of thought.

Augustine makes central to his argument against paganism in *City of God* several pagan theories about the origins of the deities. He chiefly relies on a historical understanding of the pantheon. According to Euhemerus (ca. 300 B.C.E.), the founder of this hermeneutic, the gods and goddesses were originally men and women, who because of some remarkable qualities or actions were revered and eventually divinized by their contemporaries. In a world that obviously did deify humans—witness Hercules, Romulus, and Octavian Augustus—it makes sense that all the deities in the pantheon would originally have been human. According to this logic, the human Venus had made herself memorable by founding prostitution or by exercising a remarkable amorousness. People gradually forgot the historical person and worshipped her image. By reversing this process and extricating the human from the deity, euhemerism discovers an original secular history covered over by religion.[30] Medieval writers in turn appropriate historical interpretations in order to affirm that the Christian God reigned unrecognized even while Greeks and Romans were blindly elevating humans to divine status, extending biblical truth back through time and to non-Hebraic cultures. In medieval hands, then, the hermeneutic induces the past to confess the supremacy of Christian myth.

Throughout the *City of God* Augustine repeatedly asserts that the deities were originally mortals—the pagan sense of the divine was merely superstitious error. His historicization, in other words, reduces the daunting mythic foundation of Rome to purely secular and human origins, to actions deprived of divine agency. As Peter Brown aptly puts it, Augustine shrinks the empire "to the level of any other state, in order to beat out the gods from its history."[31] However ordinary their lineage, though, the deities from Augustine's perspective had the power of demons: demons beguiled people into worshipping deified humans, and demons inhabited their idols.[32] That is, Augustine both explains away the deities (as divinized humans) and explains them as demons.[33] His interpretive strategy thereby deprives the empire of its mythical divine origins—and denies erudite, elite Roman citizens any cause for ancestral pride.[34] Historicizing admirably suits the evangelical purposes of *City of God*.

Augustine also calls on etymology to interpret the ancient deities. Etymology may seem unpromising to those of us who think automatically of brief entries in modern dictionaries, but it had considerable intellectual force in the Middle Ages. Some ancient and medieval theorists posited that knowing a word's origins constituted understanding the objective reality it signified; medieval epistemologies are sometimes rooted in etymology.[35] Augustine comically exploits the theoretical implications of classical etymologies when he derives *Venus* from a scenario in which a pagan man needs an excessively long procession of deities (Jugatinus, Domiducus, Domitius, Manturna, Virginensis, Subigus, Prema, Pertunda, Venus, and Priapus) to marry and bed a woman:

> If the husband finds the job altogether too much for him and needs divine assistance, would not one god, or one goddess be enough? Do you mean to tell me that Venus alone would not be adequate? She is, they say, so called (among other reasons) because "not without violence" (*vi non sine*) can a woman be robbed of her virginity![36]

Surely, Augustine continues, imagining the presence of all the requisite deities—those voyeuristic attendants—would squelch sexual desire. The very number of scrupulously counted deities suggests that each lacks any real power. The final mock etymology functions to provide Venus herself, erstwhile powerful goddess of love, with a degraded origin. She signifies not the charms of love or the compulsion of sexual desire, but the masculine use of force: force replaces seduction, and that on a wedding night. Etymology, like history, thoroughly discredits the aura of beneficent divinity often surrounding the pagan goddess.

With these historical and etymological interpretations, Augustine employs ancient philosophy against paganism, appropriating the familiar hermeneutics for his own purposes. Together, these interpretations establish the absence of the divine in Roman religion; they serve as handmaidens to Augustine's polemical revision of Roman history. At the same time, the analyses of myth appear literal and demystifying treatments: the pagan divinities were "really" just humans and demons, and their names reveal nothing so much as the absurdity of worshipping these ignoble creatures of fable. Significantly, Augustine establishes the fallacy of paganism on the basis of Roman philosophy. He chooses hermeneutics that would appeal to the educated Roman pagans of his time, inviting them to take up that part of their intellectual heritage that accords with Christian revelation.

Whereas in *City of God* Augustine smoothly deploys ancient historical and etymological hermeneutics for his own purposes, in his earlier *On Christian Doctrine* (*De doctrina Christiana*) he repudiates another ancient hermeneutic: allegorization. The passage in *On Christian Doctrine* may help further to account for the choice of hermeneutic strategies in *City of God*. According to the ancient method of allegorization,

> If . . . any of them wished to interpret the idols as signs, they referred them to the worship and veneration of creatures. Of what use is it to me, for example, if Neptune is not taken as a god but as a sign of all the sea, or, indeed, of all other waters that rise from fountains? . . . This husk shakes sounding pebbles inside its sweet shell, but it is not food for men but for swine. . . . Even if you transfer your affections from these signs to what they signify, you still, nevertheless, do not lack a servile and carnal burden and veil.[37]

By opposing figurative readings of the pagan deities, Augustine declares his difference from the pagan philosophers who viewed the myths (the sacred religious texts of pagans, Jews, and Christians) as shells covering kernels of truth. From Augustine's perspective, allegorization should not be found in just any text, and most particularly must not be employed to discover any redeeming value in myths about the pagan gods. Rejecting allegorizations of pagan texts, he reserves that ancient philosophical method for Scripture (this restriction of method retains currency throughout the Middle Ages).[38] That is, he turns the ancient allegorical tool to a new field, and discovers buried treasure in Scripture alone. Jupiter's debaucheries are merely debaucheries, but depravities in Scripture teach us spiritual truths. The unequal value of religious texts determines how we are to read them; the choice of hermeneutics both declares and creates the superiority of Scripture. Augustine's argument here and in *City of God* challenges the value of the pagan myths, even as the framing of that challenge indicates his debt to pagan learning. His choice of historical and etymological hermeneutics for his goal of selective debunking is suggestive. While rejecting allegorization, Augustine could have developed natural interpretations of the deities: Venus signifies passion, Saturn is time. But those readings would validate the myths, would give them a kind of scientific authority. Augustine seeks a more complete rejection of pagan myth, a more thorough repudiation of its prestige. He achieves those ends by means of well-chosen demystifying historical and etymological analyses, deploying pagan learning against pagan fictions.

Augustine reveals the potential utility of mythographic modes of thought. His adroit manipulation of ancient hermeneutics establishes the power of mythographic models, and he showed the way to many later writers. There are, of course, limits to his influence. Most notably, we will straightaway find that whereas Augustine scorns allegorization, other medieval mythographers allegorize any and every text, ancient and medieval alike. We might imagine that it is but a small step from the hermeneutics Augustine does authorize to those he does not (chiefly natural and allegorical). We should nonetheless recognize that allegorization directly counters Augustine's method in *City of God*: mythographic writing does not follow a single authoritative model of interpretation. Instead, writers choose and adapt interpretive models to suit occasions.

One of the most influential of medieval mythographers, Fabius Planciades Fulgentius wrote his *Mythologies* (*Mitologiae*) in the late fifth or early sixth century.³⁹ Like Augustine, Fulgentius intends to rewrite pagan tales, though his purpose is not to argue for the superiority of Christianity—he takes that for granted—but to demonstrate the allegorical truths, the edifying morals, hidden within pagan narratives. As he asserts, "I look for the true effects of things, whereby, once the fictional invention of lying Greeks has been disposed of, I may infer what allegorical significance one should understand" (Prologue to Book 1).⁴⁰ The problem is not persuading pagans to convert but discerning a morally useful import in their fiction, particularly in their erotic poetry. The solution lies in allegory—which is to say, in a commentary that replaces mythic narratives with didactic exposition.

Although Fulgentius denounces the lies and follies of poets, he does not denigrate fiction or poetry as such. He claims to be a poet and in fact designs his mythography as a fiction, with Calliope explicating the myths. In the course of those explications, we discover that Calliope is the last of the Muses to be involved in the process of learning: she represents the attractive form in which knowledge should be communicated (1.15). Fulgentius thus presents mythography as incorporating both textual pleasure and edification. He promises the appeal of fiction as well as the moral discourse of a schoolmaster. And he carries out this promise, for the eroticism repudiated in poetry enters into the mythography. Calliope "with a playful touch of her palm branch, stirred the sweet itch of poetry," Fulgentius reports, after which she is to be found "stroking my neck more tenderly than was becoming" (Prologue to Book 1).⁴¹ The text finally establishes no strict difference between erotic poetry and mythography, but rather their close interdependence.

Fulgentius employs iconographic, historical, etymological, natural, and allegorical hermeneutics to return us to the "truths" from which poetry sometimes strays. The multiple hermeneutics do not, however, seek a single, coherent truth for any mythic figure. Fulgentius refers to some figures several times, with a new explanation attending each new appearance; the particular meaning of any figure depends on and is limited to the immediate interpretive context. For example, he explains the story of Venus's birth from Saturn's severed sexual organs as a natural allegory about how crops are cut down and cast into the belly, represented by the sea, where they produce lust, or Venus (1.2, 2.1). In this passage, Saturn actually signifies both glutting (from *saturando*) and divine intelligence—a notable combination. Similarly, Juno at one point represents the element air (1.3), at another the active life (2.1). Venus turns up again in reference to the judgment of Paris, where she symbolizes devotion to pleasure, completing the triad of the contemplative, active, and voluptuous paths of life (2.1). Venus next signifies the lust that corrupts valor in the tale of her adultery with Mars (2.7), and simply lust in the tale of Cupid and Psyche, where Cupid embodies desire and Psyche the spirit (3.6). Venus is not alone in representing lust (see, for example, Semele at 2.12 and Anteia at 3.1). The multiplication of lustful figures is not surprising, since Fulgentius decries the eroticism of myth. At the same time, lust appears a natural phenomenon, the seemingly inevitable result of eating and drinking (1.2, 2.12): food and wine produce physical warmth and thus desire. Sexual desire is also the predetermined and seemingly constant state of youth (see Hero and Leander at 3.4). Fulgentius's moral allegories therefore coexist with a naturalization of inescapable sensual desire. Sexual morality ultimately emerges as an inevitable product of old age, not of moral choice: "for either sex desire [*libido*] dies with the extinguishing of the ardor of youth. . . . All the little fire of ardent youth grows cold in the decline of numbing dullness" (3.4).[42] In the meantime, sexual desire remains inevitable (and so, it seems, does sexual activity).

As a sample of Fulgentius's method, we might compare his etymology for Venus with Augustine's: "She is called Aphrodite, for in Greek *afros* is the word for foam, either because lust [or sexual desire] rises momentarily like foam and turns to nothing, or because the ejaculation of seed is foamy" (2.1).[43] Allegorical imperatives override linguistic logic, which would separate the Latin *Venus* from the Greek *Aphrodite*; this is nevertheless a popular etymology. Part of its appeal doubtless comes from how very thoroughly it rewrites the myth of Venus's birth. Where the poets give us a woman born from her father's severed sexual organs and the ocean waves, the mythographer offers us a woman allegorically representing sexual desire or passion (*libido*), and ocean foam signifying seminal fluid. With this explanation, scientific reality replaces fiction, for, according to Pythagorean theory, seminal fluid is foamy because it contains hot air. No less authority than Aristotle pointed out how aptly Aphrodite was named.[44] By adapting this etymology, Fulgentius substitutes for a lying fable a moral allegory about always ephemeral physical desire. He revises the myth so that it locates the origins of the goddess in the physical production of semen. The name signifies, in the best fashion of classical (Stoic) etymologies, its human origins in physical reality. In Fulgentius's treatment, moreover, the scientific turn of the etymology decisively reduces that reality to the lowest common denominator. Etymology totally effaces the divine or supernatural aspect of sexual desire.

For Fulgentius as for Augustine, the choice of hermeneutics is revealing. Throughout Fulgentius's text, natural interpretations conflict with moral allegories: although we are to reject the life of pleasure, sexual desire controls youths (as well as their elders who unwisely eat and drink). The hermeneutics do not, except accidentally, reinforce each other or work together toward a coherent single meaning for any figure. Venus represents a corrupting sexual desire, a voluptuous life, an ephemeral sexual physiology. The hermeneutics provide convenient ways of reading the myths, not coherent or stable ways of understanding the mythic figures. We might therefore seek to appreciate just what the conflicting hermeneutics destabilize or render equivocal. With Fulgentius (and he is hardly alone in this), the mythographic project exposes a recurrent and unresolved tension between moralism and naturalism.[45] He represents sexuality in such a way as to preclude individual moral action even while requiring it. Further, his mythography manifests a central struggle between the wish to disclose the allegorical truth of licentious, poetic fictions and the impulse to write allegorical and erotic fiction. His text unfolds not a lucid truth of sexuality or mythography but points of stress in the construction of each.

With *Etymologies* (*Etymologiae sive origines*) by Isidore of Seville (ca. 560–636), mythography becomes part of a larger, encyclopedic project.[46] Commenting directly on the pagan deities, Isidore asserts that they are to be understood historically: people esteemed their brave men and the founders of their cities, made images of them, and from contemplating them came little by little, with the help of demonic persuasion, to worship them as gods. Thus Crete has Jupiter, Athens Minerva, and Paphos Venus (8.11.1–5). In comparison with Augustine, Isidore's summation suggests a detached antiquarian interest without any urgent occasion for polemic.

Although Isidore declares in favor of a single hermeneutic, he actually draws on several, including etymological and natural interpretations.

His etymology for Venus agrees with Fulgentius's: the name Aphrodite, from *aphros*, refers to the foam and blood of coitus (8.11.76–77). Isidore infers from this etymology that bodily humors and heat are necessary for sexual intercourse—again, a physiological rather than a moral lesson. Elsewhere, Isidore adds a complementary natural explanation of the goddess: she signifies the sexual desire (*libido*) that results from eating and drinking (1.37.9). Thus while proclaiming the priority of historical analysis, Isidore also develops etymological and natural interpretations of Venus; as we will find in the next chapter, he reserves moralizing for Cupid. Isidore's assertion of a single hermeneutic provides a semblance of coherence and an indication of priority, but when the one strategy clearly fails to accommodate every interpretive occasion it is readily supplemented with others.

With Isidore, as with Fulgentius, the reference to multiple hermeneutics testifies to the encyclopedism of much mythographic writing. This in turn significantly limits the possibility of single, stable understandings of the mythic figures: etymological, historical, natural, and allegorical explanations do not readily produce a coherent, unified signification for any deity. Furthermore, the multiplication of hermeneutics almost inevitably leads to conceptual disparities. Historical and etymological analyses in these texts vividly demonstrate this tendency: although each locates an originary meaning, those origins differ. When writers add natural and moral explications of myths, the confusing multiplicity merely intensifies. Even in its medieval infancy, then, this discourse does not offer us a single, authoritatively historical, transcendent meaning for Venus and Cupid. What it offers is glimpses into the categories of thought found persuasive in particular times and for particular purposes, and into the unresolved tensions among those categories.

These early interpretations of Venus focus on perceived historical, etymological, allegorical, and natural (physiological) realities: interpretive categories that remain valid options throughout the period. Appeals to history, nature, and etymology refer us to originary physical realities; they ostensibly stabilize meaning. The combination of these hermeneutics simultaneously destabilizes origins by multiplying them. Similarly, allegorical readings establish transcendent truths that disappear in the face of other, equally persuasive truths. Mythographic hermeneutics testify to a perpetually thwarted desire for originary stability. What these texts reveal is therefore a momentary fixing of meaning (through any one interpretation) and a cumulative unfixing of that meaning (in the combination of interpretations). They map out a terrain between univocality (Venus represents libido) and indeterminacy (Venus signifies anything and everything). Clearly, what is at stake in mythography is not the establishment of unified meanings for myths but the strategies of interpretation themselves—their ideological flexibility, their conceptual clarity and adaptability, their classicizing prestige. Most of all, mythographic hermeneutics prove to be interpretive models anyone can employ, for a wide variety of purposes (we have a fine modern analogy in the adaptable paradigms of critical theories).

We find in these early texts that Cupid garners little attention. Indeed, Cupid is curiously fugitive in medieval mythography and therefore in this study, sporadically emerging and then flitting away as swiftly as if he were fleeing the scene of some soon-to-be-discovered mischief. This has to do in part with the classicism of mythography—Cupid is not an important Roman deity—and in part with hermeneutic choices. For example, as a child of Venus, Cupid does not invite historical interpretation; children are usually deified because their parents' love creates idols, not because of their own notable actions. Since Cupid was not a significant Roman deity, and since he is not associated with a planet, he has no strong early associations with natural forces. He does not come ready furnished with ancient natural interpretations, as Venus does. He also invites no etymological interest: the Latin *cupido* ("desire") or *amor* ("love") generally seem self-explanatory.[47] (Unfortunately but perhaps predictably, the mythographers do not, as far as I can discover, develop an etymology for Cupid from the Greek *eros*, with its homosexual connotations.) As writers translate these names into vernaculars, some variation emerges. Grammatical gender creates personified female Loves, which leads to Cupid being pictured as a woman in Provençal poetry (as *Amors*) and in German iconography (as *Liebe* or *Minne*).[48] Yet Cupid's meaning remains essentially that of "desire" or "love"—the equivocation is telling. With him, we would do well to employ Bakhtin's proposition that "meaning is rooted in the social, but the social conceived in a particular way."[49] Cupid refers us to distinctly social constructions of love and desire. Accordingly, we might note that Cupid's resistance to historical, etymological, and natural interpretations would not preclude moralizing or allegorical readings. Moralizations of Cupid nonetheless tend to develop late. It is surely not historical accident that places Venus rather than Cupid, feminine rather than masculine sexuality, in the spotlight of moral analysis. Silences about Cupid may be expressive.

The High Middle Ages: Alberic and Encyclopedism

Like much else, mythography revives in the twelfth century, and the preeminent witness to the new standardization of learning is Alberic's *On the Gentile Gods and Their Allegories* (*De diis gentium et illorum allegoriis*), also known as the Third Vatican Mythography.[50] Alberic is above all an enthusiastic encyclopedist, and he manages to collect a good number of earlier accounts, some of them notably disparate. The result is a text that, although somewhat chimerical, most fully displays mythographic hermeneutics.[51] Alberic certainly provides a convenient reference work, for he includes iconographic, historical, etymological, allegorical, moral, philosophical, natural, and astrological interpretations. Although most of these are already familiar to us, the interest in astrology is fairly new: it was fueled by the recovery of ancient scientific treatises at the time of the Crusades, and it comes into prominence in mythography between the twelfth and fourteenth centuries.[52] In this period, astrology tends to dominate natural interpretation.

What most impresses one about Alberic is simply his accumulation of meanings and the ease with which he repeatedly empties and refills signs. That is, he empties the sign of mythic meaning—of historical contingency, intentionality, cultural import—not of literal meaning.[53] His interpretations do not come to the reader in tidy categories, ordered, separated, prioritized, or labeled. They come tangled, and Alberic offers few indications of preference for one or another authority or interpretation. For example, Alberic begins his discussion of Venus with three ancient authorities for her name (228). Since she represents pleasure (*voluptas*), the Epicureans interpret her as a "good thing" (*bona res*), the Stoics as a "vain thing" (*vana res*). In a third case, Cicero derives *Venus* from *venire* (to come): "let her come to all" ("Venus, quod ad omnia veniat"). With this mythology, Cicero's character Balbus designates a universal natural and generative desire and an affirmative life force, a goddess worshipped by devout Romans. Cicero in the same sentence associates *venus* also with *venustas* ("charming"); this positive sense of the goddess does not emerge in mythographers' etymologies, as far as I can tell.[54] Alberic does not adjudicate among the Epicureans, Stoics, and Academics, but simply invites all of them into his text.

The structure of Alberic's text emphasizes that his purpose is just this gathering of interpretations. For each major deity, he outlines a series of mythic tales more or less involving that deity; for each tale, he includes a set of interpretations. In other words, he develops a sequence of diverse interpretations of discrete mythic narratives. From the opening etymologies for Venus, Alberic passes rapidly through iconography, an allegorical reading of the three Graces, a historical interpretation of Hymenaeus, an astrological analysis of a scene in the *Aeneid*, a recounting and allegorization of Venus's adultery with Mars and its consequences for the daughters of the sun (who caught the lovers), a natural interpretation of Mars, a report on Romulus and Remus, a lengthy denunciation of augury, a return to Venus with a natural interpretation of the story of Adonis, a note on Cupid, an account of Hero and Leander, and an allegorical reading of the judgment of Paris. Much of this obviously touches but slightly on Venus or Cupid, who in their turn emerge in the similarly eccentric progresses of Alberic's other deities.

The very organization of this text, let alone the encyclopedic collection of authorities and interpretations, precludes the emergence of coherent meanings for the myths or mythic figures. Alberic does not seek to reconcile or unify his disparate material, but simply to collect it. His encyclopedic text forcefully emphasizes sequentiality in the creation of meanings and the utter disparity among different meanings; his encyclopedism engenders chaotic polysemy, not fixed, monolithic, or univocal meanings. (We should recognize that an analogous multiplicity characterizes other twelfth-century and later discourses.)[55] We can, if we wish, point to any one spot in the text and conclude: Alberic interprets Venus as the voluptuous life (241). But we could also point to other spots and conclude that she signifies sexual desire (228–29), the beauty of earth (155, 238), two loves (239), a planet that protected Aeneas from astral influences injurious to eroticism (230), and so on. Identifying a coherent meaning for any mythic figure on the basis of this text would be grossly reductive.

Alberic reinforces and deepens our conclusions about early mythography, while his encyclopedia also signals something new in the discourse. For with this complete guide to authorities, this compendium of hermeneutics, Alberic attempts to incorporate all authority, all learning, into a single reference work. The selection of hermeneutics witnesses to a totalizing concept of the subject. This work conceives mythography as a discourse in itself, not a mere tool in an argument as it was for Augustine, not dependent on such literary devices as Fulgentius's framing fiction, and not part of a larger encyclopedic project such as Isidore's *Etymologies*. For Alberic, mythography can stand on its own merits.

We should not make the mistake of imagining that these works by Fulgentius, Isidore, and Alberic define the discourse or exhaust its possibilities in the early medieval period. Although commonplace, allegories, moralization, historical analysis, and etymologies are not mandatory. Nor is the focus on interpretation absolutely essential. For example, the First (ca. eighth or ninth century) and Second (ca. ninth or tenth century) Vatican Mythographies are less hermeneutic compendia than handbooks to the mythic narratives.[56] (Although quite different from Alberic's text, these nevertheless anticipate his respect for mythography *per se*.) Similarly, the anonymous Digby *Book on the Nature of the Gods* (*Liber de natura deorum*, after 1159 and probably shortly after 1180)[57] delights in realistic narrative rather than in encyclopedic interpretations, in examining social relations rather than in expounding moral or philosophical ideals. Although this text is certainly not in the traditions epitomized by Alberic, it too had an influence.[58] And, like the First and Second Vatican Mythographies, the Digby text demonstrates that telling tales can take precedence over interpreting them. The discourse of mythography fosters endless variations—not only in particular interpretations but also in the overall purpose of particular texts.

The Later Middle Ages: Rewriting the Discourse

Fourteenth-century mythographers display a flourishing authorial individuality, even in comparison with the diversities of earlier writers. It is hardly coincidental that a comparable idea of authorial individuality emerges in thirteenth- and early fourteenth-century exegesis;[59] various commentary traditions all depend on very similar intellectual models and academic training. The writers I have selected from this period are John Ridewall, Pierre Bersuire, Giovanni Boccaccio, and Christine de Pizan.

When we move from earlier mythographies to these writers' texts, we gain the immediate impression of striking revisions in the discourse. Most obviously, these writers tend not to be encyclopedic in the way Alberic is. Even though they still aim to produce reference texts, they offer markedly individualistic readings of myth that work against a standardization of learning: in other words, individual readings take priority over established, authoritative interpretations. What constitutes a reference work alters slightly, allowing invention overtly to supplement or replace the collection and repetition of authorities. Even more notably, these writers tend to unify their texts by imposing thematic and conceptual cohesion on their disparate materials, and by articulating and to some extent following coherent methodologies. Priorities among interpretive methods become both more clear and more consistent. Finally, they may offer organizing and framing fictions that emphasize the literariness of their texts; perhaps they take a hint from Fulgentius. We will find that these late medieval mythographers at times suggest a fusion of literary and scholarly purposes, an intention less to comment on ancient literature than to recreate the myths as their own fictions. While this is not surprising for the two poets, it also and less predictably applies to the religious. Later, Renaissance (and modern) scholars will reject the late medieval belletristic trend in mythography as unscholarly, proving that the discourse remains subject to the changing purposes and status of classicism. But for now let us pursue the methods and designs of the fourteenth-century mythographers without an immoderate prejudice against belles lettres.

John Ridewall with *Fulgentius Metaphored* (*Fulgentius metaforalis*, ca. early 1330s) seeks to impose on the ancient deities unified ethical meanings.[60] He begins the discussion of each deity with mnemonic descriptive verses, then elaborates the meaning of each feature. His exegesis produces highly unified, transcendent meanings for each figure. For example, every visual feature in the image of Saturn corresponds to an aspect of prudence: his old age testifies to the fact that prudence does not belong to youth, and he is shown castrated because prudence cuts off carnal desires. Ridewall similarly recasts each deity as a coherent ethical abstraction. Jupiter signifies kindness or goodwill; Juno, memory; Neptune, understanding or intelligence; Pluto, foresight; and so on until we arrive at Venus and the voluptuous life (we will examine Ridewall's image of her in the next chapter). As Judson Boyce Allen concisely describes Ridewall's method, his "allegorization is the assertion of a parallelism between organized systems, rather than the elucidation of some referentially symbolic meaning."[61] The meanings of the mythic figures do not derive empirically from readings of the mythic narratives (which Ridewall mentions only when convenient) but from an arbitrary parallel between the systems of myth and ethics. The deities become static, imagistic embodiments of ethical principles. (Needless to say, Fulgentius's text disappears behind the metaphorizing.)

By the simple expedients of focusing on a single hermeneutic (iconography) and of fitting every visual detail to one meaning, Ridewall discovers in each deity's image a unified abstract concept. Diverse potential meanings and ambiguities are suppressed for the sake of the overriding conceptual scheme—conventional systems of ethics. Saturn as prudence is followed by the parts of prudence: Juno as memory, Neptune as intelligence, and Pluto as foresight. Later, Minerva, Juno, and Venus represent the contemplative, active, and voluptuous lives. As the double appearance of Juno here indicates, unified signification for each figure is not absolute but temporary—meanings change to meet occasions. If we look up the birth of Venus in the account of Saturn, we learn that she represents two kinds of desire; in the judgment of Paris, she apparently signifies only one. For Ridewall, the goal is less a particular transcendent meaning than the exemplification of conventional ethics.

Ridewall's invention of unified meanings for the deities nonetheless departs from the more familiar encyclopedism that fosters a multiplication of authorities and hermeneutics. Indeed, he supplants the typical priority of authoritative hermeneutics with individualistic allegorization. This does not mean he discards the old hermeneutics—in its longest version, his text begins with an Augustinian history of the origin of idols—but that he gives clear precedence to coherently allegorized ethical systems. Within the conventional systems, he salts his text with constant citations of well-known authorities: Fulgentius, Seneca, Juvenal, Isidore, Aristotle, Apuleius, Cicero, and Boethius, to name a few.[62] Underwritten by these authorities and by conventional systems of ethics, Ridewall's highly individualistic interpretations appear to have a significantly classicizing authorization. The original allegories look conventional and ancient. Such an authorization of new ideas by attributing them to the ancients is a common strategy in mythography as in other discourses. As Adelard of Bath candidly acknowledged, "when I have a new idea, if I wish to publish it I attribute it to someone else."[63]

By thus interweaving myth and ethical philosophy, Ridewall creates an ethical system that seems timeless, unchanging, the same for Christian and pagan alike. His analyses in fact greatly minimize the distinctions between Christian and pagan, between medieval and ancient authority, that so centrally motivate early mythography. In this the text hints at its own purposes. It clearly does not serve a need for simple accounts of the myths, or for ways of reading ancient literature. It is properly neither handbook nor commentary. Instead, Ridewall formulates a thorough redemption of the past through his synthesis of ancient authorities and Christian truth: in displaying the riches of Egypt, his mythography at once promulgates, exemplifies, and advertises a classicizing model. What is at stake in this text is this classicizing model, rather than conventional mythographic hermeneutics or conventional ways of understanding particular myths. In short, Ridewall's mythography serves the purposes of a "classicizing friar."[64] It popularizes the ancient mythic figures and shows their amenability to ethical analysis.

Pierre Bersuire's *On the Gods' Appearances and Figures* (*De formis figurisque deorum*, in several versions ca. 1340–60)[65] presents a similarly individualistic allegorization, and an analogous if quite different conflation of Christian and pagan. This text, an account of the deities' images and meanings, prefaces Bersuire's commentary on Ovid's *Metamorphoses*; the mythography serves to theorize the commentary. In his Prologue to the whole, Bersuire explains his methodology. He argues that all ancient poets designed fictive veils to cover specifically Christian truths: the Christian meanings he uncovers in myths, he asserts, were original, even intended by ancient authors.[66] He thus identifies the methods of Scripture with those of pagan literature. Like Ridewall, Bersuire does not define his purpose as opposing paganism but as appropriating its insights. In order to reveal the truths hidden in pagan fables, he promises to develop literal, natural, historical, moral, spiritual, and allegorical readings. He does not actually develop each hermeneutic for each deity, and he includes analyses not anticipated by the Prologue (etymology, for instance). In practice, moreover, the promised and conventional mythographic hermeneutics are continually displaced by Scripture, which serves as the final authority to confirm (or create) the truths discovered.[67]

Since the deities' forms and figures constitute Bersuire's base text in this preface to his commentary on Ovid, the account of Venus begins with the image of Venus, Vulcan, and Cupid (*Appearances and Figures*, 22–25). Bersuire develops multiple readings of that image. He first and "literally" refers the image to astrology, explicating the visual details by their natural import. He then rereads the image allegorically, finding that Venus signifies a life of pleasure. This leads to a biblical analogy in which Venus is imagined born in the sea because *luxuria* (which denotes extravagance, licentiousness, luxury) is begotten from waves of delights, "just as" Scripture tells of prostitutes: "Pass thy land as a river, O daughter of the sea."[68] Here as elsewhere Bersuire articulates an unproblematic, biblical value for mythic fables—though the connections to Scripture often seem to require a leap of faith.[69] Bersuire rereads the image again to demonstrate that Venus represents a pleasure-loving woman. Venus thus signifies in turn a planet, a life of pleasure, pleasure itself, and a pleasure-loving woman (besides alluding to a subtext about prostitution and gold-digging women). Bersuire ends the account with similarly multiple readings of Cupid and the three Graces (Vulcan gets short shrift).

The emphasis on multiple readings serves a fairly specific purpose: Bersuire seeks to turn the raw material of mythic figures and myths into convenient, ready-made exempla for sermons.[70] He does not concentrate on writing an encyclopedia of preexisting interpretations (although he gathers together an impressive collection), but on furnishing simple moral analyses for any and all occasions. For example, the three Graces embody the three faults of riotous living (avarice, carnality, and infidelity), the three sins of the prosperous (luxury, avarice, and pride), the three theological virtues (faith, hope, and charity), and, finally, kindness and service (*Appearances and Figures*, 24–25). The Graces, like Venus and Cupid, are handily prepared for the likely requirements of a wide range of classicizing sermons.

Bersuire's interpretations are at the service of predetermined and commonplace moral truisms, and a prescriptive moralization dominates the work. In spite of this moralizing focus, and in spite of the clear difference between interpretation *in bonum* and *in malum*, moral dichotomies are less the object than is the proliferation of readings. Bersuire produces not a single good and a single evil import, but as many of each as he can find or invent. They tend, as these examples indicate, to advance a conservative moral code of charity, self-control, and social responsibility. Under the cover of interpreting ancient myth, Bersuire devises a homily against the contemporary sins of the upper classes (especially luxury, avarice, pride, injustice, lack of charity) as well as the lower (especially violence, deposition of rulers, carnality) and against clerical as well as lay faults. Many of the readings recommend the duty of defending just government, secular as well as ecclesiastical: a message cut to the more conservative fashions of the times. This social commentary weaves a thread of coherence into the text, in spite of the sometimes wildly disparate multiple readings of particular mythic details. The multiple and disparate interpretations therefore do not finally preclude a significant measure of thematic and conceptual unity.

We might digress a moment to note the vagaries of influence in mythographic traditions. Thomas Walsingham in *On the Mysteries of the Gods* (*De archana deorum*, ca. 1400–25) draws some material from Bersuire, but omits all biblical quotations and moralizations, the most notable feature of Bersuire's final redaction. This need not indicate a purposeful revision of Bersuire's method, for Walsingham may have had access to Bersuire's text in a form that did not include such material.[71] The most complete form of a mythography was not necessarily its only influential form. Walsingham also seems unaware of the classicizing friars' interpretive approaches, indicating once again the historical discontinuity of mythographic traditions even within a fairly limited time and place. Walsingham produces an inchoate and encyclopedic compendium that strongly resembles Alberic's much earlier text. Hermeneutics and overall designs clearly do change. Although a survey of the sort undertaken here necessarily imposes a certain order and coherence on the discourse, mythography demonstrates no tidy evolutionary progress toward ever greater complexity, individuation, or sophistication. The tendency of individualism in late medieval mythography is just that: a tendency, not an absolute rule.

Boccaccio's *Genealogy of the Gentile Gods* (*Genealogia deorum gentilium*, ca. 1350–74)[72] evidences a more obvious formal design than is typical of mythography, though this does not in the end lead to greater clarity in the deities' imports. He organizes his text on the basis of the deities' genealogies, plainly stressing their human, secular, historical origins. In keeping with that emphasis, his explication downplays moralizations and focuses on historical and natural hermeneutics, and he typically depends on explanations given by classical or early medieval authorities. The organization of the whole, and the choice of hermeneutics, decisively grant precedence to ancient authorities. As part of his classicizing approach Boccaccio preserves the ancient multiplicity of Venuses and Cupids.[73] By distinguishing these separate figures, Boccaccio attempts to sort out the most obvious disparities in their meanings. Thus he discriminates three Venuses—most simply, the planet (Venus *magna*, 1: 142–48), an allegorical exemplum (Venus *secunda*, 1: 148–52), and an immoral historical woman (Venus, daughter of Jupiter, 2: 543–44)—instead of applying the three distinct hermeneutics to one figure. This design promises a lucidity it does not always deliver: Cupids and Amors multiply into utter confusion.

Ideally, the discrimination of genealogically distinct figures would function to resolve disparities and to eliminate ambiguities, but an examination of Boccaccio's Venuses shows the ideal to be unfeasible and unfulfilled.[74] Of the three Venuses, two gain the same historical origin. Venus *secunda*, one daughter of Caelus, has a Cyprian history: Cyprus was rightly the place of this Venus's birth since it was famous for lasciviousness and venereal hospitality (1: 150–51). Cyprus also claims Boccaccio's third Venus, a daughter of Jupiter, who was worshipped by Cyprian prostitutes (2: 543–44). Though distinguished by their parentage, these two Venuses become one in historical origin. If we refer to linguistic origins, we similarly discover that "Venus" names all the figures, though the first two have separate etymologies. We also find overlaps between Venus *magna* and Venus *secunda*: the planet and the moralized figure both come to signify comparable natural forces and moral imports. If we turn to the genealogy itself, we find the same collapse of the design. Venus *secunda* is the mother of (one) Cupid, but Cupid also appears as the son of Venus *magna* (1: 146–47). Here the difference between the two Venuses collapses because the mythic narratives do not fall neatly into place under the categories of astrology and moralization.

While neither the structure of the text nor the individual interpretations actually achieve the aim of discriminating separate and unified figures, the genealogical design and the choice of hermeneutics and authorities reveal a classicizing imperative. Hence the design encodes Boccaccio's ideological intention: his goal to recover the ancient deities as they existed in the pagan era, not to graft onto them explicitly Christian meanings. The three Venuses and multiple Cupids achieve this end, for they do indeed simulate the disorderly classical pantheon. Indeed, the confusions produced by Boccaccio's genealogies offer a copy beautifully true to those in Roman religion (an unintended and dubious boon, to be sure). That the design collapses at points, that Boccaccio sometimes slides into Christian moralization, is probably inevitable, given his resources and the confusion implicit in mythic traditions. Still, this does not destroy the significantly classicizing effect or the notable measure of scholarly order and comprehensibility he imposes on the myths.

While Boccaccio's explications stress the invocation of ancient authorities and the spectacle of a detached, painstaking classicism, the proems to the books of the *Genealogy* keep us very much aware of the present and of Boccaccio creating his text.[75] In his proems, Boccaccio elaborates a fiction of himself as writer: just as Prometheus stole fire from heaven, so Boccaccio steals the spark of wisdom, of poetry, from God.[76] This continual thread of fiction explains in part what Boccaccio means by claiming that his mythography is "wholly poetical."[77] Yet fiction is not the whole of the "poetical." According to his definition, poetry is "whatever is composed as under a veil."[78] Any text that hides meanings under a fictive veil qualifies as poetry. As the proems veil Boccaccio's truths in poetical fictions, so the explications of myth unveil the truths of ancient writers. This conjoining of poetry and scholarship speaks, therefore, of simultaneous desires to veil and to unveil meaning. These contradictory purposes can undermine the mythographic task, but they can also reinforce it. For instance, the genealogical structure of the work on one level emphasizes the deities' secular, human origins; on another level, it recalls the genealogies of scriptural history.[79] The structural implications appear particularly noteworthy in that Boccaccio is probably the first writer to employ such genealogical trees for a secular text, which would surely draw attention to the device.[80] Hence the genealogy demonstrates the human origins of the gods even while revealing a loaded correspondence between pagan and Christian histories. At the same time, the submerged Christian perspective (like the occasional Christian reading) counters Boccaccio's ostensible avoidance of explicitly Christian interpretations. The text ultimately manifests a delicate balance between the classicizing project and a Christian perspective, and between scholarship and poetry.

While Boccaccio attempts to present the myths divested of their medieval encrustations, and while his *Genealogy* argues for a central concern with scholarly classicism and the authority of the ancients, he also appropriates myth as a literary device with his fiction of the mythographer as Promethean poet. The text poises the mythographic embalming of a dead and past mythology against its poetic revivification. This double treatment of myth exemplifies a fairly widespread phenomenon in the later Middle Ages. With the rise of a new classicism, writers gain a sense of the conceptual and emotional power of myth: they become aware of its poetic potential. The myths, long empty of any religious feeling, become part of the store of tales begging to be rewritten, whether for poems or for sermons.[81] Boccaccio, Bersuire, and Ridewall, in their very different ways, all share this new awareness of the creative possibilities of myth. All demonstrate the ease with which myth may be adapted to diverse ideological and conceptual systems. And, finally, all testify to the shifting fortunes of classicism, its tenuous, continually negotiated relation to Christianity.

The last text in this survey, Christine de Pizan's *Epistle of Othea* (*L'Epistre Othéa*; 1399–1400), contributes a highly innovative design to the history of mythography.[82] Christine develops her text as a letter sent by the goddess Othea to the young knight Hector, teaching him the codes of earthly and heavenly chivalry. Othea recounts one hundred brief poetic texts, "story moments" (to borrow Rosemond Tuve's apt description) involving mythic figures; alongside each verse passage, she offers a gloss and an allegory, the former explicating the lesson for the earthly *chevalier*, and the latter universalizing the lesson and turning it to the purposes of heavenly chivalry. This method unifies the text, for each story moment advances a coherent social and religious code.

Since the social code promulgated by Othea values most of all the defining characteristic of chivalry—valor—her didacticism in the glosses is overwhelmingly class- and gender-exclusive.[83] For instance, a central danger to earthly chivalry is aristocratic masculine idleness: the idleness of the noble hunt (pictured in Diana, 63; Adonis, 65; and Actaeon, 69), and of noble amusements like music (Orpheus's failing, 67). Although the *chevalier* should be engaged in deeds of prowess, he should not be merely rapacious. He is rather to avoid becoming embroiled in disputes (had Peleus done so, the judgment of Paris would have been precluded and the Trojan war averted, 60). Through her treatment of the Trojan war, Christine constantly affirms a kingdom's need for political stability, urging the *chevalier* to foster that by speaking diplomatically and by avoiding disputes. This formulation of the chivalric code is plainly aimed at nobles and knights in Christine's faction-ridden and tumultuous France (one manuscript also addresses the English side of the long war between the two countries).[84] The parallel between medieval France and ancient Troy has a double edge: it both implicitly valorizes France by identifying French knights with the mythic Trojan origins of chivalry, and warns the French that they too may fall because of a derelict chivalry. The vehicle of myth facilitates Christine's mild social criticism by distancing it from contemporary society. The code of religious chivalry developed in the allegories is equally lucid: Othea advocates engagement in continual spiritual warfare and, ultimately, renunciation of the world. For instance, Achilles' disastrous love for Polyxena teaches us first that the earthly *chevalier* should not pursue foreign loves, and second that the heavenly *chevalier* should flee everything foreign, which is to say, the world (93).

Christine's code of sexual morality and commentary on Venus and Cupid follow from this general schema. Along with developing an ideal of temperate, married love, Christine identifies Cupid with a moderate love that improves the young noble: the knight who serves Cupid pleases Mars (47), though excessive passion leads a young man to risk his life for a futile cause (the lesson of Leander, 42). In this, Christine both reinforces noble ideals about the eroticism of chivalric combat and points to the wisdom of avoiding unnecessary dangers.[85] On the spiritual level, Cupid represents the penitence that battles against sin and pleases Jesus Christ, the God of battle. The disjunction between gloss and allegory here calls attention to an ever-present potential division between earthly and heavenly chivalry, between the actions of worldly knights and those of world-renouncing saints. Christine resorts to conventional historical and astrological interpretations for the gloss on Venus, both a planet that influences love and idleness, and a particularly promiscuous queen of Cyprus (7). The good knight should avoid her, for Venus—besotted or excessive love—and chivalric arms are mutually exclusive (as shown by Pygmalion, 22; Achilles, 40; and Paris, 73). Allegorically,

Venus signifies vanity, a besetting failure of the *chevalier* and finally equated with original sin (7). Cupid and Venus suggest a particular and historically vigorous discrepancy: the privileged exemption of aristocratic masculine codes (Cupid, chivalric love) from searching criticism, and the vulnerability of feminine sexuality (Venus) to precisely that.[86]

Christine turns mythography to the clear purpose of social and political commentary, and her commentary is ideologically conservative.[87] She unequivocally endorses the code of chivalry, noble social mores (in moderation), and, above all, the preservation of royal and aristocratic power, on which she hangs the future stability of France. She critiques abuses but leaves the structures of power unquestioned. She also supports the preeminent values of the (early) Church: the priority of the contemplative life and the necessity of renouncing the world. These social and religious programs present a conflict between approving and rejecting the world-as-it-is, a conflict continually surfacing in the juxtaposed glosses and allegories. The very structure of the text, the equivalence of gloss and allegory, declares the equivalence of Christine's social and religious agendas, but also their conceptual isolation. This hints at unresolved tensions at the center of the mythographic design. The good knight must both pursue and eschew love. The excessive passion disavowed in the figure of Pygmalion (59) returns to be praised in that of Alcyone (79).

The discourse seems to invite the exposure of such irresolutions in the formation of social codes, here amatory mores in the code of chivalry as against those recommended by a world- and flesh-renouncing religiosity. The juxtaposition of several meanings and the relation of many myths once again reveal tensions among categories of thought. Such conflicts apparently went unnoticed or were simply permitted free play. For the discourse continually foregrounds the construction of social meanings, the points of balance as well as the conflicts among naturalism and moralism, classicism and Christianity, chivalry and religion.

We find with Christine that mythography is turned to precise ends, albeit ends that at times struggle against each other. Most notable is her parallel between ancient myth and medieval France, between ancient and medieval chivalry, by which she turns myth to the purposes of a precise and even nationalistic social commentary. The strategy of using myth to develop such commentary is not original with Christine. Bersuire similarly employs myth as a vehicle for social analysis, and Giovanni del Virgilio (an earlier fourteenth-century mythographer) likewise focuses on social mores.[88] Christine nevertheless stands out for the precision, coherence, consistency, and thoroughness of her social commentary—as well as for the thematic coherence of her mythography. She also deserves attention for so closely integrating mythography and fiction. She treats the ancient world of myth as a text to be reshaped into a new fiction with immediate contemporary import. In this she goes beyond the vast majority of her contemporaries and predecessors, though others also (and perhaps more controversially) invent new myths and flirt with the interdependence of fiction and scholarship.[89] In the up-so-down fortunes of mythography, Christine's *Epistle of Othea* offers us yet another variation on the possible concepts and purposes of the discourse. Significant also is the fact that Christine translates mythography into the vernacular, implicitly questioning the status of Latin in the transmission of classicism. One of her models for this translation project is the *Ovide moralisé*; the other is doubtless Dante's *Divine Comedy*. By translating clerkly mythography into the mother tongue, and by bestowing it on an authoritative woman speaker, the mythical Othea, Christine redefines the discourse.[90]

Reading as Rewriting

A quick review of the texts may help to clarify our understanding of mythographic methods. Augustine turns ancient learning against ancient religion, appropriating conventional hermeneutics for his own polemical objectives. Fulgentius, Isidore, and Alberic similarly adopt hermeneutics that meet their purposes—whether exposing pagan "lies" or rewriting pagan history or simply gathering together the shreds of others' learning. Each of these writers collects diverse hermeneutics that propound disparate but equally authoritative originary meanings for the myths and mythic figures. In the later Middle Ages, Ridewall advances one transcendent, ethical meaning for each mythic deity; multiple meanings are incidental products of the fact that the deities unavoidably enter into each others' myths and participate in more than one transcendent meaning. Bersuire encourages moral meanings to proliferate while referring them ultimately to the authority of Scripture, to the Transcendent Signified, and while developing through the diverse readings a unified social commentary. Boccaccio aims to disentangle the confusingly multiplicitous gods and goddesses and to reproduce an ancient understanding of the pantheon; by discriminating separate and coherent figures in ancient myths, he tries to arrive at a unified meaning for each figure. That is, he designs univocality for each deity, and multivalence signals failures of the design. Christine presents an intentional dualism, earthly and heavenly chivalry. Accepting polysemy allows her to view the myths from a variety of worldly and otherworldly perspectives. Ideas about the point of mythography clearly vary as significantly as do methodologies. What these texts share is simply participation in the traditions of creating (and collectively destabilizing) meaning. They disclose not a single authoritative historically correct meaning for Venus and Cupid but rather the notable absence of such a meaning.

Each of these mythographers allows us to perceive the useful flexibility of their hermeneutics. In historicizing the deities, for example, writers may assert the superiority of Christian revelation, may claim a difference between a pagan worship of demons and a Christian reverence for the one true God. The same historicizing logic can as easily serve to integrate Christian and pagan insights, making the two appear continuous and complementary. The prestige associated with historicizing explanations of the ancient deities corresponds closely to the always-shifting status of classicism. Venus's fortune rises and falls with those shifts: if historicism can degrade her as a prostitute of Cyprus, it can also crown her queen of Cyprus. Etymology similarly demonstrates the malleability of mythographic conceptual categories. By means of etymologies, writers can (temporarily) fix Venus to a demystifying, a degraded, or a "natural" origin. As this hermeneutic shades into a heuristic, the same etymology can as easily invite natural philosophy as moralization—can teach us about reproductive physiology as well as about the polluting ephemerality of sexual desire. Either way of developing the etymology appears equally credible, and the choice of direction depends on the writer's immediate purposes and perspective. As with euhemerism, the conceptual model does not constrain or limit specific applications. The same may be said of moralization, natural and philosophical explanation, or ethical analysis, all of which are eminently accommodating to an almost endless variety of individual purposes.

Mythography reveals not only the flexibility of hermeneutics but also the conflicts that can arise among medieval categories of thought. Thus by placing a euhemeristic explanation of Venus next to an etymological account, writers foreground the essential illogic of her multiple origins.

The one origin challenges the other, calling into question the very idea of originary stability. More provocatively, interpretations of Venus continually expose tensions between moralism and naturalism. If naturalism teaches that sexual desire is inescapable, part of the reproductive cycle of life, moralism may nonetheless condemn it: apparently, we are at once to participate in and to reject the life to which we are in any event inextricably bound. Mythography also discloses tensions between the ideals associated with the upper social classes and religious ideologies—as with Christine's difficulty in reconciling the dictates of chivalry with a paradigm of world renunciation. Where the accepted behavior of the upper classes and moral dogma differ, we encounter unresolved discord: not an automatic privileging of one or the other but their uneasy coexistence.

Mythography often suggests in fact a double (or triple, quadruple) perspective—an awareness simultaneously of the claims of class and religion, nature and conventional morality, historical and linguistic origins. If mythographers seem even eager to put discordant explanations next to one another, however, they tend rarely to account for the relations among the multiple perspectives they employ. There the explanations rest in their separate locations on the page, refusing to be synthesized into coherent views of Venus and Cupid. We see the deities as a fly would, through multiple lenses. Yet for all the confusions and discrepancies, each of these texts quite plainly establishes an articulate and generally lucid dialogue between paganism and Christianity, for mythography is perhaps above all a discourse devoted to negotiating these religious worldviews. As the meanings of Venus and Cupid grow ever murkier, attitudes toward the pagan past clarify. Mythographers thus carry on a perpetual dialogue with ancient days, testifying to an enduring fascination with that lost but still vital world.

An examination of mythographic methodologies argues that we should not assume that poets, in depicting the deities, would refer us to mythographers' moral (or other) lessons. Mythography offers few constant morals for poets to repeat (and, after all, even mythographers need not merely repeat others' interpretations). Since mythography promulgates multiple meanings rather than an absolute fixity of meaning, it can offer no unproblematic guide to poetic meaning. Mythographers do not themselves advance pellucid explanations. The example of mythography recommends that we discard the expectation of finding continuous "historical" meanings for medieval myths. The tradition of mythography is nothing more nor less than the development and theorizing of literary and imagistic multivalence. Surely, poets are more than likely to respond to this theorizing, to the attitudes toward multiplicity, and to the hermeneutics that most obviously characterize mythography. We might expect, in fact, that poets would also develop multiple figures of the deities, would also understand the deities in terms of the broad conceptual categories of history, etymology, philosophy, nature, and so on. And, finally, just as mythographers may appropriate, refigure, and reauthor myths, so too may poets. We should anticipate that poets may adopt precisely what mythographers do—the conceptual paradigms—and not necessarily the specific applications of their predecessors.

According to their various purposes, these mythographers plainly employ various allegorical techniques. Mythographers often refer to their method as reading through the fictive "veil."[91] The continuity of expression covers over the manifest breaks in hermeneutic practice. While many writers refer to the veil of fiction, they differ markedly in how they value that veil and what it achieves for them. They may mean us to disregard the harmful, deceptive literary surface for the sake of the truths they find it to cover. They may mean us to value precisely that surface, with its ambiguities, interpretive challenges, and aesthetic rewards. They may straightforwardly invent allegories, or they may claim that the allegories reside in the original text. They may ignore the veil, the fiction. And they may accompany their demystifications with new fictions. Writers similarly differ in what they find behind the veil of poetry: philosophical, dualistic, scriptural, ethical, natural, historical, allegorical, moral, spiritual, etymological, or chivalric truths. If Augustine altogether rejects allegorizations of pagan myth, reserving allegory for readings of Scripture, Bersuire quite explicitly takes the Bible as the ultimate Signified, and exegesis as the ultimate model for interpreting just those pagan myths. We might take the Chartrians, Bernard Silvestris among them, as mapping out a middle way between these extremes. Chartrians detect in fiction the philosophical order of the cosmos, discovering primarily philosophical and only secondarily Christian truths; they do not concentrate on generating specifically Christian moralizations and do not adopt the methods of biblical exegesis.[92]

Countless other variations are possible, for mythographic theories of literary criticism are nothing if not heterogeneous. This being the case, we should be careful not to universalize a binary opposition of veil and hidden truth, shell and kernel.[93] Mythographies tend to pile on as well as remove veils; certainly, they do not manifest a static binary between worthless fictive veil and valuable hidden truth. Mythographers continually perplex distinctions between fiction and commentary, interspersing their moralizing bits with erotic tales, threading poetic fables through their learned expositions, glossing their own verses, always and everywhere confounding any difference between interpretation and invention, between reading and rewriting a text.

Many mythographers view interpretation not as an empirical act but as a generative one. And their ways of reading can easily become heuristics. The heritage of mythography is perhaps best imagined as just this emphasis on inventive acts of reading, on a way of reading that is finally indistinguishable from a way of rewriting ancient (and, for that matter, medieval) literature. If mythography offers us no sure and certain guide to the interpretation of poetry, then, it does illuminate medieval systems of interpretation: the strategic uses of hermeneutics, the potential for disparities in ways of understanding (or counting) the deities, the possibility of conflicts and tensions among interpretations, the likelihood of simultaneous multiple perspectives. Whether we look at mythography or at poetry, therefore, the critical problem ultimately remains how to heed the details and contexts of representation, how to listen carefully to the textual voices.

Chapter 3

Ambiguous Signs, Contingent Truths

> A good legible label is usually worth, for information, a ton of significant attitude and expression in a historical picture. In Rome, people with fine sympathetic natures stand up and weep in front of the celebrated "Beatrice Cenci the Day before her Execution." It shows what a label can do. If they did not know the picture, they would inspect it unmoved, and say, "Young girl with hay fever; young girl with her head in a bag."
>
> Mark Twain, *Life on the Mississippi*

Iconology is traditionally thought of as a language of symbolic forms: a *logos* of the *icon*. Like any language, it depends on signifying conventions. A cruciform halo identifies a person of the Trinity; a man, an ox, an eagle, and a lion represent the four evangelists. For the symbolic images to function as a language—to communicate meanings—the audience must know and artists adhere to the conventions. Respecting the need for conventionality, artists do not suddenly or inexplicably replace the cruciform halo with a floral garland, or place that halo over a pope, or portray the Apostle John as a carp. This is not to say that change never occurs in a convention, but that conventionality necessarily takes precedence over innovation. Although the conventions are as arbitrary in this as in any other language, and sometimes as obscure, they nonetheless constitute an agreed-upon public language that we can decode.[1] If we imagine, however, that we can equate visual signs directly with specific, unambiguous meanings, then we arrive at something very like a New Criticism of the visual arts, in which a properly informed reader claims to discover the (only) correct meaning embedded in the work. Arriving at such a conclusion, we would oversimplify iconology, which like other languages can generate ambiguities and multivalence. Although we can distinguish many conventionally symbolic images from the Middle Ages, moreover, not all medieval art hides some profound significance or buried meaning.[2] Sometimes an ox is just a farm animal. As we approach images of Venus and Cupid, we need to recognize that they may or may not suggest conventional iconological meanings, and that in any event those meanings need not be utterly fixed and certain.

Mythographic iconography (that is, writing about iconology) reveals how the visual and verbal conventions arise, and how sometimes complex meanings can be attached to visual signs. In mythography, though, the forms and attributes of Venus and Cupid both concretize meanings and serve as a basis for interpretation; in other words, mythographers assert that the images bear at once one meaning and many meanings. This hermeneutical practice destabilizes the import of the visual signs. As visual details accrue disparate meanings in explication, they lose the capacity to signify limited, clear meanings independent of the commentary.[3] When iconology grows uncertain, artistic innovation becomes both more likely and more necessary. In the fourteenth century, Cupid's nude body can signify guilt, shame, or innocence. Unable to rely on the concrete detail of nudity to indicate guilt, mythographers and artists strike Cupid blind, manifesting his dangerous moral obliviousness and thereby (temporarily) resolving his ambiguities. The mythographers' hermeneutics finally impose ambiguities and multivalence on conventional visual signs, which come to represent specific values only through explication. Interpretation displaces and replaces iconology.

Even while complicating how and what the images can signify, mythographers standardize and disseminate those images. What they pass on to artists, then, is a set of fairly conventional images that bear problematic, ambiguous, uncertain, and diverse meanings. As a consequence, mythography once again offers no positivist last resort to critics seeking the sense of poets' images. It offers instead a range of explicit statements about sexual love, which may serve us as useful guides to medieval constructions of sexuality, and to the points of tension within that construction. For mythographers lay bare the class and gender ideologies they find pictured in Venus and Cupid, demonstrating just how cultural norms may be naturalized in representational details. As significantly, mythographers preserve recognizably classicizing images of the deities, and this constitutes one of the dominant representational traditions of the Middle Ages. Eventually, the mythographers' portraits of Venus and Cupid gain the aura of scholarly classicism. As we will discover in the next chapter, a later medieval English poet can adopt the mythographers' images for precisely this implication.

Early Medieval Visions

The basis for medieval classicizing images of Venus and Cupid lies in Roman temple statues and artifacts, and in written descriptions of the deities. This initially deprives Cupid of any significant status. Although the Greek Eros was the first of the gods and supremely powerful, Romans view Cupid as a mere child of Venus, ancillary to and dependent on her.[4] Eros may be aged or youthful; Cupid is always a boy, winged, carrying a torch or bow. When further demoted, he becomes the little unnamed "loves" (*amores*) accompanying Venus. Venus's appearance varies more considerably, partly because what we call "Venus" is a syncretic version of many goddesses, each having her own cult image.[5] Art historians have nonetheless sorted out the more common visual types, several of which are vital to our study of the Middle Ages: Venus *anadyomene* (of the sea), Venus *pudica* (modest), and Venus *genetrix* (of procreation or fertility).[6] These types contain the seeds of several medieval visual traditions. As the classical *anadyomene*, Venus emerges from her birth in the sea, often with her arms raised to arrange her hair. She may or may not be nude, and she may carry, ride, rest against, or emerge from a conch or scallop shell.[7] This figure will become the medieval mythographic type. Venus *pudica*, a nude, stands with hands shielding middle and breasts (the posture Botticelli adapted for his *Birth of Venus*). Venus *genetrix* appears robed or veiled, with the look of a respectable Roman matron; this is the Julians' ancestor, the dignified founder of an empire. Accompanying Venus we may find doves or swans,[8] dolphins, the three Graces, Vulcan, Cupid or *amores*, Priapus, Hermes, Adonis (and so on). Her usual attributes are a mirror, a comb, jewelry, a shell, roses, and myrtle. Less common but neatly complementary versions of the goddess include a bearded Venus and a bald Venus.[9]

In late antique and early medieval culture, these Venuses are sculpted in statues and statuettes, engraved on lovers' gifts or wedding presents, pictured in mosaics, and carved in gemstones. As these representations influence developing iconographic traditions, Venus becomes a model for images of women—Eve and prostitutes as well as saints and the Virgin Mary.[10] Throughout the Middle Ages, people would know surviving local conventions for Venus and Cupid, and travelers would encounter a wider variety of traditions.[11] A number of Roman mosaics of Venus survived in Britain, for example, and preserve the basic outlines sketched above, though the character of the art varies.[12]

In the late fifth century in North Africa, Fulgentius would have confronted mosaics of Venus *anadyomene*, a popular motif for baths and fountains.[13] Setting out to correct poetic lies about Venus, he visualized that image of sensuous beauty and turned on it his hermeneutical spotlight:

> They depict her naked, either because she sends out her devotees naked or because the sin of lust is never cloaked or because it only suits the naked. They also considered roses as under her patronage, for roses both grow red and have thorns, as lust blushes at the outrage to modesty and pricks with the sting of sin; and as the rose gives pleasure, but is swept away by the swift movement of the seasons, so lust is pleasant for a moment, but then disappears forever. Also under her patronage they place doves, for the reason that birds of this species are fiercely lecherous in their love-making. . . . They also depict her swimming in the sea, because all lust suffers shipwreck of its affairs. . . . She is also depicted carrying a seashell, because an organism of this kind . . . is always linked in open coupling through its entire body.[14]

Here Venus takes on her medieval *anadyomene* attributes—nudity, roses, doves, and shell.[15] Venus's classic *anadyomene* posture, her hands raised to her hair, alters in the medieval type. This mythographer also eliminates such details as veils, jewelry, and mirror, all of which would heighten her association with sensual pleasures; all these attributes persist in other traditions.[16] According to Fulgentius, each detail signifies the "life devoted to pleasure" (*voluptaria vita*) chosen by Paris. This transcendent meaning unifies the account while permitting, if not fostering, multivalence for individual details. Venus's nudity at once pictures her devotees, the impossibility of concealing lust, and the appropriateness of bareness to sexual acts; her roses similarly indicate the pain and blush of sin, and ephemeral sexual pleasures. As we view the doves and conches, we are asked to imagine sexual union. Fulgentius separates the three Graces from Venus's transcendent meaning: they are naked because grace is unadorned. In all of this, he ignores the Cupids typically attending Venus *anadyomene*; elsewhere he notices Cupid as the archer god but neither provides nor analyzes iconology for him.[17] Cupid retains his Roman insignificance.

Fulgentius's interpretation powerfully refigures the popular image of Venus, reinscribing the triumphant ancient deity with an early Christian sexual code of renunciation and shame.[18] A life of pleasure is a life of pollution and impurity. Devoting themselves to pleasure, humans become "effeminate by lust or bloodied by murder or burnt up by theft or soured by envy"—in a word, "corrupted."[19] Fulgentius's emphasis on defilement agrees with that of many other early Christian writers, who similarly contend that sexuality is intrinsically sinful and productive of impurity. From the patristic to the Carolingian period this seems a particularly insistent theme.[20] Fulgentius grafts this ideology onto Venus. The goddess who in the visual arts from North Africa to Britain had for centuries risen from the sea as if reborn, purified,[21] becomes a sign of corrupting sexual desire. The appropriation of Venus *anadyomene* for a Christian sexual code could hardly be more complete.

Whereas Fulgentius concentrates on the impurity attending sexual intercourse, Isidore a century later emphasizes its procreative end. This end legitimates his Venus *anadyomene*, who now exemplifies the orthodox function of coitus: procreation.[22] Her birth from the sea reveals to Isidore the basics of reproductive physiology: the moisture, blood, and heat needed for generative coitus. He therefore induces from the fable of her birth the lesson that nothing would be created unless that physical *humor* had descended from heaven.[23] For Isidore, physiology and dogma complement each other, and both authorize a procreative Venus.

In contrast, Cupid, a "demon of fornication," or of any illicit sexual activity (*daemon fornicationis*), attracts Isidore's severe reprobation: "Cupid is depicted winged because nothing is found lighter than lovers, nothing more changeable. He is depicted as a youth because love is foolish and irrational. He is represented holding an arrow and a torch. An arrow, because love wounds the heart; a torch, because it inflames."[24] Isidore's absolute terms and his brevity (about a quarter of the space devoted to Venus) emphatically dismiss the god. He has, in fact, classical precedent for such a treatment of Cupid, for the Romans created this moralized image.[25] According to this analysis, Cupid's inflaming arrow and torch produce only irrationality, foolishness, and changeability.[26] Cupid has no part in the approved end of coitus. Isidore's focus on a violation of reason implicit in fornication derives from his adherence to the ethics originally developed by the Stoics and adapted by the Church in the patristic period. According to the Stoics, sexual desire, like all else in life, should be governed by reason. One should have some rational rule for copulation: reason approves an attempt at procreation, but rejects the pursuit of mere pleasure.[27]

While Venus signifies a rational coitus seemingly without pleasure, then, Cupid or fornication violates the rule of reason. This division between a generative Venus and an irrational, pleasure-seeking Cupid exemplifies the orthodox divorce between procreation and pleasure. Even in the context of authorizing procreative coitus, Isidore condemns sexual pleasure. His contemptuous treatment of Cupid, fornication, and pleasure likely responds to popular resistance to the official sexual code. In Isidore's time, as in most times, Church and laity did not always agree about sexual mores; and the rule of sex only for procreation (now sometimes called the Alexandrian rule) was not readily accepted by all lay people and clerics.[28]

With Isidore as with Fulgentius, iconography obviously serves ideology. The mythographers' Venus *anadyomene* is gaining not a single, conventional import, but a sequence of contextually determined implications. Already the images require explication to signify anything more precise than "sexuality" or "sexual pleasure," for Venus can as readily encode a corrupting sensual pleasure as an approved generative vitality. In considering variations in the traditions, moreover, we should heed silences: not every mythographer describes visual images. The First Vatican Mythographer discusses the fable of Venus's birth from the sea as a story rather than as a picture, with Venus briefly interpreted as "goddess of sexual desire" (*dea libidinis*), not quite the point of either Fulgentius or Isidore.[29]

The Second Vatican Mythographer repeats the idea of Venus as goddess of desire but lends that meaning different nuances.[30] Venus *anadyomene* once again appears as Venus *naufraga* (shipwrecked), floating in the sea "because all desire suffers shipwreck of its affairs."[31] The shipwrecked Venus repeatedly, even proverbially, links sexuality and economic disaster. This mythographer follows Fulgentius for a few other details: Venus's red roses indicate the shame of sexual desire, the sting of sin; her conch and doves again reduce to coitus. Conventional as these details are becoming, however, the hermeneutical focus varies: this Venus *anadyomene* embodies sexual shame more than sexual pollution or the reproductive teleology of sex.[32]

Departing from earlier models, moreover, this mythographer includes Saturn's castration in the picture of Venus's birth, giving the image a new set of implications.³³ She is represented (*fingitur*, suggesting both image and fable) born from male mutilation "because all masculine strength is weakened by venereal practice." Indeed, intercourse cannot be accomplished without male loss.³⁴ Such mythographic uses of sexual physiology demonstrate, if nothing else, how medicine can reinforce cultural values. Here the surety of masculine loss argues against frequent sexual exercise. The fabulous image also implies a principal masculine role in generation: a man's experience of debility accompanies his manifest contribution to new life. Medieval reproductive physiology similarly caters to the cultural need to establish paternity.³⁵ As Venus is born directly from her father, without the mediation of a mother's body, the image erases the obvious role women play in creating new life. Thus myth and physiology shore up the shaky cultural order of paternity.³⁶ In short, this Venus *anadyomene* pictures not only sexual shame but also paternity; we view in her both a suspicion of sexuality and a value for procreation, the two-sided attitude informing much of the official Catholic sexual code.

Cupid further complicates Venus's meaning: the "god of love" is her son "because the venereal act cannot take place without *amor*."³⁷ *Amor* encompasses both love and ardent sexual desire, an ambiguity exploited in much poetry. As a definition of Cupid, this passage either implies that people engage in sexual intercourse in order to express love or proffers a truism about male sexual physiology. Contemporary Catholic theologians rarely recognize, let alone approve, the possibility of a confusion between love and desire; they typically find sexual pleasure dangerous and sexual acts corrupting, as Fulgentius and Isidore do.³⁸ Both Isidore and the Second Vatican Mythographer embody in Cupid (very different) ideologies at odds with that official code. That the early official Catholic code excludes both seeking pleasure and expressing love testifies to its narrowness. While inspiring discordant interpretations, Cupid's portrait remains the same—he materializes as a nude, winged boy, equipped with a quiver and torch. The continuity of the image does not preclude radical discontinuities of meaning.

Reading Cupid's quiver, this writer finds that "love wounds the mind"—a condition of helplessness that in this context may evoke sympathy.³⁹ Cupid's nudity pictures the shame (*turpitudo*) of love, his torch its heat and fervor. His wings speak of love's quickness and mutability.

And his youthfulness tells that just as the eloquence of boys fails through inexperience, so that of lovers fails through excessive pleasure.[40] Inarticulateness similarly evidences lovesickness, the complaint of noble men.[41] Given these characteristics, Cupid epitomizes an ardent, inexperienced, and mutable love that may imply an aristocratic milieu. His visual image, like Venus's, can carry markedly diverse nuances, prompting stoical disdain for the irrational pursuit of pleasure, as well as sympathy for youthful, eager, and tongue-tied love. The images are all but empty semiotic vessels, to be filled with whatever meanings the mythographer wishes; without the commentary, we cannot discern the precise values associated with Cupid. That is, the image by itself signifies a confluence of sexuality, love, and desire, but not specific judgments on that confluence.

A comparison of this mythographer's Venus and his Cupid is instructive. Whereas Venus is a shameful and potentially ruinous sexual desire, Cupid is an inexperienced love. She commits adultery (*adulterium*) and manifests the pain of sin (*peccati aculeus*). He suffers from ignorance (*imperitia*) and reveals the shame of love (*turpitudo amoris*). Venus elicits a rigorous suspicion of sexuality, and Cupid evokes the bond between love and sexuality. This distinction implies a gender bias: Venus, woman, the feminine flesh receive the blame for sexuality; Cupid, man, and masculine emotion are spared this blame. Such gendered partiality does not preclude similarities, for each combines sin and shame, physicality and emotionality. Gender inequities also do not prevent their family relationship from signifying something rather surprising: the complementarity of sexual desire and love. Whatever they indicate separately, together this Venus and Cupid authorize a sexuality that potentially expresses love. Set against the typical attitudes of early medieval theologians, this seems a boldly humane position. It appears that the Second Vatican Mythographer is as much concerned with secular or pragmatic sexual codes as with monastic or idealizing ones—and more concerned with describing than with judging sexuality. If Remigius of Auxerre wrote this mythography, then he was capable of significantly different perspectives on love: his commentary on Martianus Capella's *Marriage of Mercury and Philology* insists on an unambiguous opposition of licit and illicit loves, whereas this text presents less straightforward and shifting correspondences between sexual shame and sin, male and female sins, love and sensual desire.[42]

Encyclopedism in the High Middle Ages

Alberic (the next of the so-called Vatican mythographers) collects a wide variety of earlier analyses, which makes his account less than coherent. When Alberic relates the fable of Saturn's castration, for example, he repeats all three of the conclusions we have examined thus far (*Gods and Allegories*, 155). Still, such hermeneutical variation does not inhibit the development of stable visual conventions for Venus and Cupid (*Gods and Allegories*, 228–29, 239). Alberic's Venus *anadyomene* significantly duplicates that of Fulgentius, both in visual details and in explication of nudity, roses, doves, sea, and conch. For the goddess's declared transcendent meaning, however, Alberic follows the earlier Vatican mythographers (who name her the goddess of sexual desire) rather than Fulgentius (who repudiates in her a life devoted to pleasure). The meaning explicitly proposed does not matter in one respect: whatever Venus is said to represent, she manifests little enough of pleasure in any of these texts. Indeed, denying the pleasure of venerean sexuality forms one of the more obvious and consistent early mythographic designs. Once again, then, Venus drifts on the sea as shipwrecked *libido*, emblem of the financial ruin brought about by passion, a warning rather than an enticement to young heirs.

Yet Alberic does not develop a tonally consistent, unified account of Venus as *libido* (or as anything else). For example, he departs from Venus's posited transcendent meaning in order to account for the Graces, who are painted nude because they are without deceit. Their linked arms show the bonds of friendship. The Graces can obviously complicate moralized iconography: no matter how fervently a mythographer asserts that Venus signifies the shame or pollution of sexuality, the Graces associate her with pleasing and virtuous charms, with attractions to love. The incongruity in the image can, as here, fragment the interpretation. Since mythographers typically defer to their authorities, the Graces nonetheless remain part of the image, sometimes leading the severest of moralizers into apparent ambivalence.

Alberic passes easily from moral to natural interpretation, which further divides his concept of the goddess. Myrtle is associated with Venus because it grows near the sea, from which she was born; or because coitus induces a salty sweat; or because it is "appropriate for the necessities of women" (myrtle was used as a remedy for gastrointestinal problems, which perhaps included morning sickness);⁴³ or because myrtle does not produce seeds. Alberic's syntax—his habit of stringing clauses together with "or" (*vel*)—indicates a lack of priority among hermeneutic alternatives. All of these physical processes appear simply analogous natural phenomena. In this context, the sweat of coitus seems a physical fact no more shameful or guilty than a medical treatment or plant physiology. Alberic does not reconcile this twelfth-century naturalism with the preceding austere moralization borrowed from Fulgentius. Once again, naturalism and moralism seem at odds.

After describing the Venus *anadyomene* established by Fulgentius, Alberic recapitulates another visual tradition, introducing further disparities into his account. Alberic discovers that the Cypriots worshipped a bearded virgin Venus (*barbata virgo*), so, true to his authorities, he describes her as well. Alberic finds this mutation not at all remarkable—being incorporeal, a deity can assume any form (*Gods and Allegories*, 231). Although this logic ingeniously explains a sidekick of the syncretic Roman deity, it simultaneously raises questions about iconology. Can there be a conventional image for a deity that can assume any form? Alberic does not labor with such questions, does not attempt to synthesize his material; he merely collects details, hermeneutics, tidbits of ancient lore. Images serve him as a basis and excuse for interpretation. They provoke rather than limit the possibilities for meaning.

Moving on to Cupid, Alberic discovers something similar to the Second Vatican Mythographer's unity of love and sexual desire. According to Alberic, Venus brings Cupid forth because "it is certain the love [*amor*] arises from the desire for pleasure."⁴⁴ Representing the desire for pleasure as the first step in the development of love or passion, Alberic's allegory implies the possibility of recuperating sensual pleasure (an implication that arrestingly contrasts with his iconographic explanation of Venus, but then Alberic is not troubled by inconsistency). The potential union of emotionality and sensuality differs from the dominant theology of the time, but the twelfth century is a time of pronounced cultural diversity.⁴⁵ In the development of canon law, Gratian and the early decretists similarly argue that two people attracted by physical desire would come to love each other after marriage.⁴⁶ Thus decretists as well as mythographers imagine that sexual desire can lead to authorized emotional bonds. Other twelfth-century discourses would agree. Chrétien de Troyes and Marie de France, for example, often depict lovers experiencing an immediate physical attraction and then proving enduringly faithful to that love in spite of all trials and temptations. In these poetic discourses, sensual desire (sometimes, anyway) becomes love. For poets and mythographers alike, Cupid, son of Venus, can symbolize this progression.

Alberic's attitude toward Cupid necessarily alters the focus of iconographic exposition. Alberic explicitly finds him guilty of nothing worse than callowness. He is pictured as a boy because "desire for baseness is foolish, and because conversation is unfinished in lovers, as in boys."[47] Although Cupid's wings are once again emblems of the lightness and mutability of lovers, that weakness simply characterizes youth. His faults, such as they are, appear inevitable—experienced, and thus condoned, by almost all. Alberic's portrait of Cupid romanticizes youth as a time of irrepressible, irresistible passion. This is nothing if not a common medieval attitude. Cupid's dart strikes, as Gower later puts it, with the "irresistible concupiscence of youth."[48] Some quite respectable medieval authorities in fact assumed that the nature of youth made sexual continence impossible. Since the young were thought to be helplessly swept about by the tides of desire, clerics as well as poets often excused their sexual sins (and that even in the assumed absence of reproductive capacity).[49] The social ideology tends, not surprisingly, to exonerate men more than women, making Cupid an apt exemplar. While excusing Cupid, however, Alberic binds him to an orthodox sexual code: Cupid's arrows and nudity speak of his shame and consciousness of crime. Condoning sexual sin evidently need not argue against its sinfulness. Alberic's combination of excusing and blaming Cupid suggests a compromise between ecclesiastical and secular sexual codes, for ecclesiastical concessions to youthful passion are matched with a secular acceptance and internalization of the general theological precepts. In this, Alberic exemplifies a fairly common double attitude toward youthful sexuality.[50]

Thus far, Alberic seems to present a cohesive iconography for Cupid, but only thus far. Immediately after establishing a coherent meaning, Alberic contradicts it by recapitulating Remigius of Auxerre on the two loves: "Likewise there are two Loves: one good and virtuous, through whom wisdom and virtues are loved; the other without virtue and evil, through whom we are inclined to vices" (*Gods and Allegories*, 239).[51] At his best, Alberic's Cupid does not actually rise to such virtue, nor, at his worst, sink to such vice. (Remigius's "chaste and modest" Venus likewise has no place elsewhere in Alberic's account.) Quite obviously, delineating unified meanings for the deities constitutes no part of Alberic's purpose. The meanings generated by iconography do not in any way constrain other hermeneutics. This consequence of Alberic's encyclopedism whispers provocatively about an acceptance of diverse points of view, and an indiscriminate enthusiasm for learning—all of which place Alberic securely in the twelfth-century renaissance. His work allows us to view sexuality and desire from many perspectives, and it reminds us that medieval Venuses and Cupids are created from many perceptions, and from a gathering of discourses. Walsingham's much later *On the Mysteries of the Gods* (21, 32) offers two descriptions of Venus, inviting similar conclusions. That Walsingham largely repeats Alberic's account implies its enduring authority.

Late Medieval Revisions

As mythographers impose on the visual images diverse implications dependent on their particular contexts, they turn the images themselves into virtually empty signs. The iconology vaguely suggests pleasure, a life of pleasure, sexual desire, love, but we need mythographers' explanations in order to ascertain what values they attach to these figures. We have seen with Cupid that the visual signs of nudity and bow cannot tell us whether we are to condemn him or sympathize (or both). At this point writers must alter or add to the conventions if the image is to signify in more limited and unambiguous ways. Fourteenth-century mythographers, Bersuire and Boccaccio among them, accordingly invent for Cupid a new attribute—he becomes blind or wears a blindfold, designating the mental and moral blindness of love. As an iconological feature, his blindness links Cupid with the ominous figures of Fortune, Death, and Night.[52] Like many iconological details, this one undergoes later transformations. An enlightened Cupid, for instance, may remove his own blindfold.[53] Iconology is never more than temporarily stable. Nor is it, as Bersuire and Boccaccio will demonstrate, absolutely lucid or unequivocal even with such an innovation.

Bersuire describes Cupid as blind and winged, just fleeing to his mother's lap after angering the gods (*Appearances and Figures*, 22–25). Although blindness may seem to clarify Cupid's import, Bersuire passes this image through several interpretations and imposes on it new equivocations. In the "literal" interpretation, Cupid is the offspring of the planetary Venus and pictures "concupiscence of the flesh" (*carnis concupiscencia*). Next, Cupid is "fleshly love, son of pleasure" (*carnalis amor, filius voluptatis*). In this interpretation, his wings connote the swift flight and suddenness of such a love. His blindness tells that love does not discriminate between poor and rich, ugly and lovely, religious and lay, but aims its arrows at all alike. Cupid's blindness also represents people inflamed by "evil love" (*malus amor*), and those who love the unattainable, as Narcissus loved his reflection, or as a commoner will perchance love a noble. Blindness pictures a universal physical desire that preempts class and other differences, and threatens social order. The image speaks less of a concern for religious orthodoxy than of an anxiety about social disorder.

Bersuire elsewhere interprets Cupid again and arrives at a new sequence of meanings.[54] Cupid is now "the god of love" according to the Gospel of John: "God is love" (*caritas*). Cupid's arrows become "divine commands," either inflaming "good love" or extinguishing "evil love." Or, finally, if Cupid is "immoderate" (*luxuriosus*), he nevertheless carries the "arrows of divine eloquence." For Bersuire, Cupid can as easily represent the Christian God as concupiscence of the flesh. The point of Bersuire's explication is always to generate meanings, never to arrive at an absolutely determinate or unified meaning. In pursuing this goal of polysemy, Bersuire displays an enviable interpretive agility. Striking Cupid blind does nothing to limit his multivalence, though it momentarily pins him wriggling on the wall. The point to pause over here is perhaps what Bersuire's equivocation centers on: his suspension of the image between carnal and spiritual meanings. In this, Bersuire emphasizes Cupid's semiotic range.

As we might expect, Bersuire also pictures Venus *anadyomene*, describing her as a nude and "most beautiful" woman, adorned with roses, holding a conch, and attended by Cupid, doves, the three Graces, and her base, ugly husband, Vulcan.[55] This image invites Bersuire once again to a series of explanations. The image of the woman first pictures a planet with a "feminine complexion"; the sea and Vulcan indicate a planetary effect on moisture and warmth, which generate concupiscence (Cupid). Next, the image signifies the "life of pleasure" (*vita voluptuosa*), inconstant as a woman. She is depicted nude because voluptuaries do not conceal their indecencies, in the sea because they always float in pleasures.[56] In this interpretation, the doves become wanton people, and the three Graces stand for the faults of licentiousness or luxuriousness (*luxuria*)—avarice, carnality, and infidelity.[57] Lastly, Bersuire reads the image "literally" (and still more misogynistically) as a nude woman, licentious, inconstant, immodest, and accompanied by doves that represent licentious men. The three Graces now indicate this woman's three faults: avarice (the woman is a gold-digger), concupiscence of the flesh, and inconstancy (when she has emptied a man's coffers, she sends him away). The same image serves to represent Venus as a planet, as a life of pleasure, as licentiousness, and as a woman. The Graces accompany her through these changes, but then they take a final turn away from her in order to appear as the three theological virtues—faith, hope, and charity.

In Bersuire's ludic sobriety almost any interpretation is possible: Diana also becomes *luxuria*, a bawd inciting youth to serve lust. Any sign—Diana as well as Venus—can be filled with rank sexuality or with a divine presence. Bersuire's Venus and Cupid epitomize the hermeneutic flexibility of the conventional images. Bersuire does not set out to shape a single authoritative meaning for the images, and does not even pretend (as Alberic does) to fix on such a meaning. As he states in his Prologue, he wishes us to view the deities through literal, natural, spiritual, and allegorical lenses. His goal is to present a diversity of rapidly changing perspectives, not a single unified meaning. He succeeds admirably.

Textual corruptions eventually produce comic permutations of Bersuire's iconology, demonstrating another kind of medieval variation.[58] Bersuire reports that Venus holds the conch shell in her right hand ("Venus . . . in manu sua dextera *concham marinam* continens").[59] In one manuscript the shell becomes a sea goose (*aucam marinam*). One illustrator draws Venus grasping this avian novelty by its neck, while another, with superb ingenuity, transforms a common goose into a sea goose by drawing in a fish tail and scales. The goose in this way bears an intelligible relation to Venus *anadyomene*. Elsewhere the shell becomes a slate (*canam laminam*). This is inscribed with a love poem in one illustration: the new visual detail produces a new interpretation, making Venus a patroness of poetry. Out of textual corruptions illustrators craft new perceptions of the goddess, perceptions that have little to do with mythographic hermeneutics.

An important fourteenth-century handbook for artists, the *Notebook on the Images of the Gods* (*De deorum imaginibus libellus*), standardizes the mythographers' Venus *anadyomene* and youthful Cupid.[60] Although the *Notebook*'s adoption of this image demonstrates the forceful influence mythographers had on iconology, it presents the deities' images without interpretations, disseminating an iconology detached from its mythographic function. The image is very close to Bersuire's. Venus is a "very beautiful girl," nude, floating in the sea, holding a conch in her right hand, wearing on her head a garland of white and red roses. Doves circle her. Beside her appears the "base and ugly" Vulcan. Three nude little youths, the Graces, stand face to face. And Cupid, blind, winged, bearing his bow and arrows, has just struck Apollo and is escaping to the safety of his mother's lap.[61] With this description, the mythographers' visual type—still recognizably an *anadyomene* in her attributes, however distinct from the classical model—becomes a standardized artistic convention.

This image has passed from mythographer to mythographer as a nearly empty vessel: suggesting in turn a life of pleasure, procreation and fornication, *libido*, youthful pleasure, love, concupiscence, and charity. The *Notebook* passes the image on as an ambiguous sign, separated from commentary, adaptable to any hermeneutic or narrative purpose. Mythographers create the ambiguities and equivocations as well as the image; and because mythographers do not, either singly or as a group, impose on the image a single, strictly delimited set of values, the image alone directs us to none.[62] It signifies sexual love, pleasure, and desire, but without a context we lose any sense of the specific values attached to these conditions of mind and flesh. As a consequence, the image passed on by the *Notebook* may illustrate any text with equal appropriateness, for its content is largely determined by its context. This description of the goddess and her escorts is quite minutely realized, for instance, in the frontispiece to one manuscript of Chaucer's *Complaint of Mars*.[63] It carries to Chaucer's poem little meaning but takes its meaning from that poem. The adaptability of the image becomes one of its more noteworthy merits.

Boccaccio receives images in need of renovation if they are to convey his (or anyone else's) attitudes and values. In fact, Cupid's always ambiguous image becomes for Boccaccio nearly useless. His genealogical multiplication of figures would be terminally confusing if all the Cupids and Amors ended up looking the same, and Cupid's iconology offers too few features to distinguish all of them from each other. Boccaccio consequently dispenses with iconography for most of his Cupids and Amors, and devises a memorable image for just one Cupid.[64]

This figure seems conventional enough at first sight: a nude, winged boy bearing a quiver, bow and arrows, and torch (2: 451–54). Boccaccio's lengthy analysis seeks the nuances of these details, delivering in part a familiar naturalization of youthful (masculine) sexual desire. Cupid's youth indicates boys' susceptibility to passion, for boys are driven by passion rather than reined in by reason; his wings picture the instability of this ardor. Significantly, this Cupid represents not love (*amor*) or desire (*cupido*), but passion (*passio*), a god of tremendous power. That *passio* was a medical synonym for disease indicates the morbid severity of the disorder embodied in Cupid.[65] This transcendent meaning signals Boccaccio's departure from the tendency of some earlier mythographers—Cupid's power makes him dangerous rather than excusable. Boccaccio more definitively breaks with earlier mythographic conventions by ascribing to this Cupid three arresting features—a blindfold, a girdle of hearts, and the taloned feet of a griffin.[66] These details dramatically refigure the mythographers' conventional emblem of youthful passion, giving it a distinctly threatening import. Boccaccio explains that the blindfold tells of lovers led wholly by their passion and oblivious to all else, while the griffin's feet picture the intractable and tormenting hold of passion. Cupid becomes a frightening, even demonic figure.

None of Boccaccio's Venuses picture such tormented desire. Interestingly, though, the griffin's feet have an old basis in depictions of Venus. As a death goddess, Venus is taloned; transferring the talons to her companion separates her from her power of death.[67] With Venus, Boccaccio's genealogical multiplications once again complicate iconography. The mythographers' *anadyomene* can hardly be rewritten for each of Boccaccio's three Venuses, nor does he try. He does not include iconographic commentary on the third of his Venuses, the daughter of Jupiter, the ancient deity associated with prostitution (2: 543–44). As the wife of Vulcan and lover of Mars, she could be pictured with one or both of them; however, this could beget confusion since Venus *magna* is also married to Vulcan. The third Venus has a pleasure garden, which medieval artists would picture as a conventional garden of love; once again, though, this would merely create problems, for that would confuse this Venus with Venus *secunda*. Foregoing iconography for the third Venus, Boccaccio concentrates on differentiating Venus *magna* from Venus *secunda*. For the first, the planetary Venus, he both borrows from and alters the familiar mythographic image. He assigns to her the three Graces, doves, myrtle, roses, a chariot pulled by swans, and a cestus (a band supporting the breasts—the famous girdle, 1: 142–48). The Graces signify the charm (*gratia*) attendant on love; the doves, as ever, stand for impassioned coitus. Myrtle and roses belong to Venus because their fragrances incite humans to love. Her chariot indicates her planetary motion. Swans pull it because their whiteness points to "womanly elegance," and because their death song resembles the songs that draw lovers, as well as the songs in which lovers "practically dying from excessive desire, reveal their passions in song."[68] Boccaccio associates Venus's cestus with marriage. Iconography establishes the astral Venus as a force of sexuality, to be understood within a fairly limited cultural milieu—she presides over songs and elegance as well as over any and every sexual act.[69] (She in fact very much resembles the Venus of Boccaccio's gloss on *Teseida* 7; some details are the same.) This Venus incites people to authorized charms and pleasures of sexual love. Retaining some of her conventional mythographic features (the roses, doves, myrtle, and Graces), Boccaccio detaches them from moralization.[70] Of course, Boccaccio is not alone in thus rehabilitating a "natural" sexual pleasure. The thirteenth century witnesses an official relaxation of earlier Catholic rigor, and this tendency continues in the fourteenth century.[71] Theologians thus anticipate Boccaccio: Thomas Aquinas and others defended marital sexual pleasure as good. Canonists argued similarly. Boccaccio's naturalization of venereal pleasure here differs only in deemphasizing the conjugal prerequisite.

Boccaccio's second Venus appears as Venus *anadyomene* in the tradition established by Fulgentius. Her attributes and features—roses, shell, nudity, ocean—once again signify the "life of pleasure" (*voluptuosa vita*, 1: 148–52). Boccaccio repeats much of Fulgentius's explication: Venus's nudity manifests the impossibility of hiding luxury; the ocean indicates the bitterness and shipwreck of a lover's life; the roses denote the blush, sting, and ephemerality of desire (with the first Venus they entice us to pleasures); and the conch shell stands once again for the creature's coitus. If Boccaccio celebrates sexual pleasure with the first Venus, he seems to deny it with the second. In spite of this explicit agenda, though, he proceeds to a natural interpretation that significantly modifies the Fulgentian Venus. As Boccaccio continues, the castration of Saturn symbolizes the "seeds of all things" flowing down from heaven, and Venus's birth from the sea indicates the generative roles of salty sperm, nourishing moisture, and food. Venus *secunda* now embodies the faculty of procreation, much as she does for Isidore. This naturalism complicates the initial moralism, for Venus *secunda* finally unites desire and generation.

Boccaccio's hermeneutics confuse his differentiation of two Venuses. Both Venuses symbolize forces of nature: Venus *secunda* refers us to the humors involved in one sexual physiology, and Venus *magna*, the planet, signifies another theory of sexual physiology. In fact, given the close interconnections between medieval astrology and medicine, the planet cannot be absolutely separated from humor physiology.[72] Whereas Venus *magna* presides over pleasure (she is *voluptuosa*), Venus *secunda* depicts a life of pleasure (*voluptuosa vita*). Hence Boccaccio's interpretations recombine the Venuses he takes such pains to separate iconographically and genealogically. His iconography creates an illusory difference, one of seeming rather than being. The attempt to distinguish two Venuses is nonetheless telling, for the design itself suggests ambivalence about sexuality—a simultaneous legitimation and prohibition of sexual pleasure. Boccaccio witnesses less to two distinct Venuses than to a very common double perspective on sexuality.

Ridewall also describes Venus twice, but this doubling is merely incidental. Ridewall's method is to set a deity's iconology into mnemonic verse and then explicate the meaning of each attribute.[73] The phrase "deprived of his shameful [member]" (*pudendis orbatus*) describing Saturn leads to a discussion of Venus's birth in the sea. Later, Ridewall analyzes the judgment of Paris, and here he versifies his rendition of Venus *anadyomene*. Both accounts suggest an authorization of sexual pleasure similar to one of Boccaccio's attitudes.

For the first image, Ridewall explains that Saturn is shown castrated because prudence, which he signifies, cuts off the desire for venereal pleasures. Ridewall continues: "poets say that the goddess Venus is doubled," one a goddess of "orderly and chaste delights," and the other a goddess of "wanton and fleshly pleasure."[74] Ridewall claims that he reduplicates the two Venuses of Remigius's commentary on Martianus Capella's *The Marriage of Mercury and Philology*, as Alberic claims when he discusses two Venuses. Ridewall and Alberic and Remigius certainly do not all describe exactly the same pair. Most notably, Remigius mentions no "delights" in connection with chastity, as Ridewall does. The authority of Remigius sanctions but does not constrain the idea for later writers.[75] Ridewall draws a contrast between the good and sanctified delights in which prudence rejoices, and the disorderly and dangerous pleasures of the flesh (the "feminine blandishments of the body")[76] that cannot coexist with virtue. He leaves unclear just which sensual delights he would sanction, but prudence emphatically does enjoy some pleasures. The distinction between these two Venuses or kinds of sensual pleasure appears dependent not on moral choice, but on age. Saturn or prudence is pictured as an old man because old age produces immunity to venereal pleasures and thereby facilitates prudence. Ridewall's point is the inevitability of venereal desire in youth; prudence arises from the natural aging process—from a loss of physical heat and the consequent physiological extinction of sexual desire.

Ridewall's full account of Venus has not yet been edited, but the descriptive verses have been. She appears

nude, displayed on the sea, set amid greenery, her skin whitened, adorned with flowers, wafting unguents, accompanied by Graces, and placed on a conch.[77]

As does every mythographer, Ridewall uses iconography to advance a sexual ideology; and Ridewall's ideology is far from the Fulgentian rigor with which we began this chapter. Just as Fulgentius refigures the Roman image of the *anadyomene*, Ridewall rewrites Fulgentius's image. Whereas Fulgentius describes a life of pleasure as a life of ritual pollution, Ridewall imagines a life of pleasure as pleasurable. He accordingly details fair nudity, flowers, greenery (presumably myrtle), and sweet fragrances, all of which refer us to sensual pleasure. In sum, Ridewall recuperates the pleasure condemned by Fulgentius. We might note that, in his turn, Ridewall is also rewritten. John de Foxton in the early fifteenth century turns Ridewall's deities into emblems of the virtues; now a bearded, male Venus symbolizes audacity. This delightfully nonstandard account also attributes to Venus a crown, naked sword, lantern, and jug.[78] No mythographer is obliged to depict Venus and Cupid according to just one prototype; however dominant, the Fulgentian *anadyomene* is not universal. Besides, even that model may be drafted to bear a distinctly non-Fulgentian message, and it may be replaced with entirely other imagery.

Competing Discourses, Contradictory Perspectives

We can trace some faint patterns in the shifting sands of mythography. When mythographers explicate the image of Venus *anadyomene*, we hear the insistent note of religious scruples about sexuality. Venus may encode a notion of physical and spiritual pollution attendant on sexuality, a suspicion of pleasure, a reproductive teleology of sex, or, finally, an authorization of pleasure. Through all these variations, she directs our attention to ecclesiastical ideologies imposed on sex acts. This image of feminine sexuality elicits from the mythographers a set of generally conservative and theologically grounded judgments about the sexualized body, though that conservatism does not necessarily equate with a repudiation of sexual pleasure, as modern clichés about medieval sexuality might lead us to expect. In the late Middle Ages even conservatives may condone sexual pleasure. On the other hand, Cupid embodies a fundamental equivocation between desire (*cupido*) and love (*amor*). With him, moreover, the center of attention often shifts away from the body or sex acts and toward the mind, toward the emotions attending desire. This focus on interiority does not typically lead to penitential rigor. The mythographers' Cupid most often represents a particular social construction of sexuality—youthful masculine license. Certainly not all mythographers approve of this construction, but all seem to recognize it.

The fact that Venus represents sexuality and Cupid an equivocation between desire and love is probably not historical accident. In a tradition constructed almost exclusively by male writers, Venus is often defined primarily as the Other, the source of the sexual desire or generative vitality projected onto her. Sexuality is perhaps more comfortably judged as an aspect of the Other, more readily condoned as a part of oneself. This formula does not account for all treatments of Venus and Cupid, but it may help to explicate the pervasive double standard in the iconographic analyses surveyed here. These treatments of Venus and Cupid demonstrate that writers seldom exhibit a single, consistent view of sexuality; rather, they express opinions conditioned by the contexts of sexual desire—by such factors as gender and age and social standing. Even within the seemingly limited opportunities provided by iconographic exposition, we encounter multiple and shifting points of view on sexual love and desire. We confront the relativity of human attitudes toward sexuality.

The standard mythographic images of Venus and Cupid grow increasingly ambiguous—not in spite of but because of mythographers' explications. If iconography temporarily imposes a single, fixed meaning on this image, the forward march of hermeneutics ignores it. Both in individual texts and in the tradition as a whole, Venus and Cupid come to embody polysemy rather than any univocal, conventional morality. Iconology in the hands of mythographers becomes less a conventional visual language than a language of empty signs with contextually determined values. The mythographers' discussions argue against any modern notion that iconography divulges the deities' "proper" or historical medieval meanings.

For all the semiotic variations, though, the visual conventions remain relatively constant in their rough outlines. When these mythographers describe the deities at all, they almost always describe Venus *anadyomene* and the youthful, winged Cupid. The steadiness of the conventions suggests the mythographers' deference to authority. Perhaps, though, the stable images also owe their long lives to their essential ambiguity—their need to be interpreted. Venus *anadyomene* can picture rebirth as easily as sexual pollution, sexual pleasure as readily as moral anguish. The young Cupid can likewise manifest serious transgressions against an official Catholic sexual code or predictable, excusable youthful peccadilloes. The very absence of a clear and simple meaning encoded in the images becomes one of their key mythographic advantages: because the details cannot in themselves indicate absolutely determinate meanings, the mythographers' expositions are justified, even necessary. The limitations of the images paradoxically constitute their value.

Mythographic visions and revisions of Venus and Cupid disclose significant variations, for writers have their own ideological imperatives, their own biases, which may or may not agree with those found in other contemporary discourses. By providing us with access to a number of such individual attitudes, mythographies allow us to distinguish a good assortment of medieval sexualities. Some writers, especially in the early Middle Ages, concentrate on the ritual impurity attending sexuality; other writers, especially later ones, emphasize the pleasures of sex. Some bind sexual desire to procreation, others to marriage, some to love, and still others to youth. The essential ambiguity of the mythographic forms taken by Venus and Cupid permits the inscription of any number of sexualities.

Iconographic accounts of Venus and Cupid sometimes display conflicts, equivocations, and ambivalences in medieval constructions of sexuality. Most often in the iconographic accounts surveyed here, mythography reveals implicit contradictions between moralism and naturalism, between condemning and condoning sexual desire. When mythographers examine Venus in terms of natural philosophy, they unveil physiological aspects of sexuality—the heat and moisture needed for generative coitus, the peculiar fervency of youthful desire. Venus often emerges from these accounts as an approved figure of procreative sexuality. When the same writers turn to moralizing, philosophical equanimity disappears, and the discourse invites repudiation of this embodiment of feminine sexuality. Juxtaposing these two discourses in one text relativizes both, exposes their rivalry in advancing definitions. Neither achieves a securely privileged status. Likewise, other categories of thought (such as etymology, euhemerism, astrology, Platonic or Stoic philosophy) generate meanings to impose on the images of Venus and Cupid, and, within mythography, those systems and their definitions also come into competitive relation. Mythography grants no single discourse the exclusive power to define Venus and Cupid. As a consequence, mythographic iconography does not impose coherent meanings on the deities, but reveals how competing discourses may be brought to bear on their ancient images.

Mythography suggests, then, that particular discourses correspond to particular points of view, and that point of view significantly affects a writer's conclusions. By drawing many discourses together, mythographers not only multiply potential insights but also betray the biases and limitations in each point of view. This enhances our sense of discourses entering into competitive relations, one discourse picking up where another leaves off, one filling in what another leaves blank. Ultimately, however, the almost complete lack of dialogue between and among the several discourses indicates the conceptual segregation of disciplinary perspectives within mythography. Each point of view, each discourse, appears merely different, and they come together not in choral harmony but as many distinct voices speaking their own limited and contingent truths. In this, mythography discloses not a unified, hierarchical worldview but the difficulties of reconciling heterogeneous perspectives on life.

Chapter 4

From Latin to Vernacular

On Poetry and Other Sensual Pleasures

> Age cannot wither her, nor custom stale
> Her infinite variety. Other women cloy
> The appetites they feed, but she makes hungry
> Where most she satisfies.
> — Shakespeare, *Antony and Cleopatra*

The last two chapters may insinuate that mythography is limited to a set of specialized texts, yet mythography—in the general sense of writing about myth—enters into and borrows from a wide range of discourses. Though some texts concentrate exclusively on interpreting myths, earning the label "mythography," other texts also rely on selected mythographic hermeneutics. We find the standard hermeneutics incorporated into such diverse works as commentaries on ancient and medieval texts, patristic polemics, sermons, and poems. Mythographic methods of reading constitute part of an education in ancient literature, and a medieval writer need not study a particular mythography to be familiar with the basic methods of analysis. The hermeneutics and images we have been tracing were widely diffused and doubtless had considerable influence, albeit sometimes indirectly, on conceptions of the deities. At the same time, knowledge of the conventions need not lead to a servile conformity. Venus *anadyomene* may always float free of natural-astrological, moralizing, euhemeristic, etymological, dualizing, and philosophical hermeneutics; and any of those hermeneutics may be applied to other images. In short, mythographic concepts may be variously received.

Just as mythographers may write poetry, so too may poets appropriate mythographic hermeneutics or images. Like mythographers, poets have choices about which hermeneutics to employ, if any, and which patterns of imagery to adopt. For example, Chaucer depicts Venus and Cupid according to standard mythographic images in the first book of the *House of Fame* and in the *Knight's Tale*, but he does not gloss that imagery. Chaucer's treatments of the deities in the *Parliament of Fowls*, *Troilus and Criseyde*, the *Prologue* to the *Legend of Good Women*, and elsewhere exemplify still further variations in image and import. While Chaucer exiles mythographic commentary from these poems, other poets employ the conventional hermeneutics, either working them into the verse or relegating them to scholarly glosses. We encounter these strategies in the works of Gower and Lydgate (in *Confessio Amantis* and *Troybook*, for instance). When poets versify mythographic hermeneutics, consolidating narrative and commentary traditions, they silently repudiate any straightforward opposition between (lying, vernacular) poetry and (true, authoritative, Latin) commentary. (We can sometimes detect a similar message in mythography, as when Christine de Pizan presents in the vernacular both verse "story moments" and glosses.) Gower and Lydgate elsewhere present the deities without the academic keys that purportedly unlock their definitive meanings (as in *Confessio Amantis* and *Temple of Glass*). If Chaucer, Lydgate, Gower, and others omit explicit mythographic commentary, however, their scribes may always add it. For the medieval poet did not exert absolute control over the text, and scribes could and did gloss texts in order to indicate conventionally authoritative ways of reading the ancient myths. Mythographers, poets, and scribes may all adapt (or not) conventions befitting their immediate purposes. In fact, as this and subsequent chapters will argue, later Middle English poetry resembles mythography in one vital respect: all of the texts demonstrate the flexibility of the intellectual traditions, their openness to diverse appropriations and revisions.

When poets and scribes elaborate mythographic hermeneutics for Venus and Cupid, they imply a perceived need to interpret the deities for the audience, suggesting a desire to control meaning. Indeed, later medieval literature manifests repeated authorial and scribal attempts to gloss, explicate, or otherwise fix the meanings of Venus and Cupid, hinting that their ambiguities were well recognized and occasionally considered something of a problem. These references to mythographic modes of thought appeal to what seem authoritative systems of reading. Such appeals characterize one kind of response to translations and appropriations of Latin traditions in the later Middle Ages. For we must remember that this is the dawn of vernacular Bible translation, a project that raised both many anxieties about and much delight in the loss of stable official interpretations of texts. Much as poets may depart from mythographic analyses of the pagan deities, so too may Wycliffite translations of the Bible (and Lollard readings of Scripture) diverge from official exegesis. Ralph Hanna III comments insightfully on the potential tensions implicit in such projects:

> Perhaps most distressing for the conservative, Englished Latin had been cut free from the Latin tradition and its learned practice of reading. It had become "open." Englished texts were now consultable and interpretable, perhaps in ways unforeseen, seditious and dangerous. They had lost the support provided by that system of control and indoctrination by which Latin had always been approached—the grammatical education which made "fit" and trained readers. Such Englished texts . . . were now part of a more general discourse where they might be abused.[1]

Similarly, mythographic iconology and hermeneutics implicate authoritative scholarly systems of reading, by means of which poets and scribes may attempt to stabilize portrayals of Venus and Cupid, may try to direct readers' interpretations. Poets who remove Venus and Cupid from these conventional systems expose them to possible misunderstandings, for "untrained" readers may well depart from established ways of explicating ancient myth (as, of course, may "trained" readers). The already polysemous figures of the deities may gain as many interpretations as there are "fit" and "unfit" readers. The translation of mythographic hermeneutics and iconology into English poetry likely seemed to some writers a loaded project, for translating mythography could either guide readers' interpretations or provide opportunities for them to refuse the guidance of conventional authorities. As we will find in this and subsequent chapters, English poetry reveals numerous experiments in controlling (or not) how the deities are read, announcing sometimes uneasy, sometimes playful reactions to the opening up of interpretation. English translations of mythography may thus help further to illuminate the complex interactions between vernacular eloquence and conventional Latin authority systems.[2]

Of course, the mythographers' images of nude Venuses and Cupids—with their roses, shells, doves, bows, and arrows—constitute only one tradition; and none of their hermeneutics becomes universal. All is not encompassed by strictly mythographic texts, however all-encompassing they sometimes seem. Mythological figures are treated in many discourses and literary genres, not all of which classicize the deities or multiply hermeneutics. Venus and Cupid therefore approach later Middle English poets by many paths: mythographies and texts directly or indirectly indebted to mythographic modes of thought; sermons by preachers taking advantage of the materials prepared by the "classicizing friars"; French and Italian poetic models, with their own very different classicizing programs; and ancient poetry, which cultivates a variety of Venuses and Cupids typically ignored by mythographers. The deities inhabit multiple discourses not only within mythography but also within literature more generally conceived. Writers of commentaries, sermons, court poetry, romances, collections of exempla, florilegia, chronicles, and autobiographies all shape the deities to their own purposes. If a preacher mentions Venus in the course of censuring the judgment of Paris, a poet may beseech her to help him generate rhymes. One writer praises Cupid as the patron of a moral and gentle love, and another scorns him for encouraging amatory deceits. Any one of these or a dozen other definitions is specific to a context, and none necessarily retains its persuasiveness or appeal apart from that context.

Venus and Cupid stand always in the nexus of rival discourses, and each writer creates that nexus anew. When choosing to portray Venus or Cupid, later Middle English poets must mediate the competing discourses that inscribe their meanings—poetic as well as mythographic discourses, and courtly as well as academic traditions. In order to examine how Chaucer and Chaucerians treat the deities, then, we must not consider mythographers the final authorities. However useful mythographers are in delineating academic traditions, most of them apparently turn deaf ears to dialogues carried on by poets from Lucretius to Edmund Spenser. Since we would find it hard to rationalize emulating this insensibility, let us consider two important traditions that usually enter only tangentially into mythography: the cosmological and the courtly. As we will discover, later Middle English poets borrow heavily not only from mythography but also from these traditions. Equipped with the several threads spun out of mythographic and other discourses, we may the more easily follow the labyrinthine turns Venus and Cupid take as they enter into Chaucer's *House of Fame* and *Knight's Tale*, Lydgate's *Troybook* and *Reason and Sensuality*, and the Lydgatean *Assembly of Gods*. Together these poems offer splendidly various examples of how poets may fashion anew the diverse and contradictory discourses that converge on Venus and Cupid.

Art and Sensuality

Throughout his works, Ovid gives Venus and Cupid preeminent roles to play in inspiring (or otherwise affecting) his poetry, and in sponsoring a code of love. His conceptions of the deities significantly influenced the later development of both cosmological and courtly Venuses and Cupids. Part of this influence is likely direct: his poetry was widely available in the later Middle Ages, and the *Art of Loving* (*Ars amatoria*) in particular was basic to an education in classical literature.[3] Other ancient writers also locate their poetry under the auspices of the love deities, but, since pragmatism forbids an extensive survey of ancient literature here, Ovid's works may provide us with a logical and convenient focus for examining Venus and Cupid in guises rarely attested by mythography. If mythographers pay little attention to the deities in their roles as amatory and literary patrons, poets throughout the Middle Ages adopt and revise Ovid's figures.

In the early poems of *Loves* (*Amores*), Ovid self-mockingly defines himself as a poet conquered by the vagrant arrows of Cupid, the mighty ruler of love and love poetry. Ovid depicts the god as patron of several key amatory conventions: the poet's pose as a lover, the madness common to both writing and loving, the tyrannical mastery of love (*Loves*, 1.1, 1.2). All of these poses are utterly common in Roman literature before Ovid takes them up, but he displays their essentially comical implausibility. He pictures the lover-poet ingloriously and immediately surrendering to the all-conquering deity, who leads him (along with a host of personifications) in a parodic military triumph through the city streets. The stock figure of the poet as a lover painfully yet lyrically subject to his own desire becomes, in Ovid's hands, impossible to take seriously (not incidentally, so does the idea of the military triumph). Ovid employs the lover persona to emphasize its artificiality, its empty conventionality; he defamiliarizes the pose of lover-poet, and with it the poet's distressing subjection to love. As Sara Mack concludes about Ovid's use of elegiac commonplaces, he is "asking us to see the conventions as conventions."[4]

Ovid carries his play with amatory conventions further in the *Art of Loving*. Here Venus gives the poet the pseudo-epic charge of schooling Cupid to a civilized code—an art—of love (*Art*, 1.1–34). Cupid embodies a wild, overmastering passion, a love that must be controlled by rational arts and disciplines, which the poet promises to deliver. This untamed youthful love contrasts vividly with the Cupid of *Loves*, a military leader imitating his cousin Augustus. Perhaps in part because the uncivilized boy Cupid would be an inappropriate poetic patron, Venus takes over that role for the *Art of Loving*. Ovid invokes her aid at the beginning of his enterprise (*Art* 1.30), closely coupling her sensual pleasures and his art:

> nos Venerem tutam concessaque furta canemus
> inque meo nullum carmine crimen erit.
>   (*Art*, 1.33–34)
> I sing a safe Venus and pleasures indulged,
> And in my song will be no crime.

With the paronomasia of *carmine crimen* undermining the avowal that there will be no crime in the song (or no poetic fault? the language is provocatively ambiguous), Ovid both promises and mocks moral probity. As this goddess of safe sex presides over a poetics that equivocates about its own truthfulness, she represents a wittily contested relationship between art and morality. Whereas Cupid proves a somewhat tyrannical taskmaster over poetry in *Loves*, Venus promises more pleasant and less arduous endeavors.

In *Fasti*, a partial account of the Roman religious calendar, Ovid again prays Venus to lend beauty to his verse. This invocation is partly derived from the hymn to Venus *genetrix*, *alma* Venus (Venus the mother, the lifegiver) that opens Lucretius's *On the Nature of Things* (*De rerum natura*).[5] At least parts of this poem would have been known, directly and indirectly, in the Middle Ages: fragments of the text survive, it was quoted in such well-known texts as Isidore of Seville's *Etymologies*, and it most likely entered into florilegia.[6] Lucretius's poem merits quotation for its considerable beauties as well as for the sake of comparison with Ovid's and others' developments of this Venus:

> quae quoniam rerum naturam sola gubernas
> nec sine te quicquam dias in luminis oras
> exoritur neque fit laetum neque amabile quicquam,
> te sociam studeo scribendis versibus esse
> quos ego de rerum natura pangere conor
>   (*On the Nature of Things*, 1: 1.21–25)

And since thou alone dost guide the nature of things, and nothing without thine aid comes forth into the bright coasts of light, nor waxes glad nor lovely, I long that thou shouldest be my helper in writing these verses, which I essay to fashion on the nature of things (trans. Bailey)

This cosmological Venus assists in the creation of poetry as in other life-giving activities, and poetry is one expression of the sensuous, generative order of things. While that order cannot finally be represented by Venus in this poem, any more than Lucretius's philosophical poetry can remain long in her domain, the opening hymn exquisitely depicts Venus in terms familiar from conventional Roman religion: as a force of love and polymorphous generative capacity, as a cosmological *genetrix*. Ovid does not, even in *Fasti*, emulate the Epicurean seriousness of Lucretius, but he alludes to this conception of Venus by naming her *alma mater* (4.1) and by celebrating her power over both sexual and poetic generation:

> illa quidem totum dignissima temperat orbem;
> illa tenet nullo regna minora deo,
> iuraque dat caelo, terrae, natalibus undis,
> perque suos initus continet omne genus.
> (*Fasti*, 4.91–94)

She indeed sways, and well deserves to sway, the world entire; she owns a kingdom second to that of no god; she gives laws to heaven and earth and to her native sea, and by her inspiration she keeps every species in being. (trans. Frazer and Goold)

Ovid then praises the cosmological power of this goddess who ensures the continuance of species and finally civilizes humans. Ovid incidentally describes Venus's children, "twin loves," who help to portray her as fecund *alma mater* ("Alma . . . geminorum mater Amorum," 4.1). This cosmological Venus leaves nothing for Cupid to do, and his sovereign role in *Loves* fades into distant memory. Even as a cosmological force, Ovid's Venus manifests her civilizing power chiefly through arts of love. Venus *genetrix* transforms into Venus *artifex*:

> primus amans carmen vigilatum nocte negata
> dicitur ad clausas concinuisse fores,
> eloquiumque fuit duram exorare puellam,
> proque sua causa quisque disertus erat.
> mille per hanc artes motae; studioque placendi,
> quae latuere prius, multa reperta ferunt.
> (*Fasti*, 4.109–14)

A lover was the first, they say, to serenade by night the mistress who denied him entrance, while he sang at her barred door, and to win the heart of a coy maid was eloquence indeed; every man then pleaded his own cause. This goddess has been the mother of a thousand arts; the wish to please has given birth to many inventions that were unknown before.

The Venus *genetrix* who elsewhere appears in Roman literature as a source of the love that binds all things together (witness Lucretius's hymn), or as a goddess of empire (as in Virgil's epic treatment of her) gains with Ovid a significantly revised tie to culture. As the *genetrix* she usually refers us to the sober claims of Roman religion and empire, to the order of nature and its relation to human society, to a poetry of sensuous joy. Yet even while referring us to the *genetrix*, Ovid also undercuts precisely those traditional claims. Her power over the natural order of things becomes a precedence over amorous contrivances, and civilization culminates in the production of amatory poetry and arts of love. In *Fasti* and the *Art of Loving*, Venus presides not only over Ovid's poetry, but also over the deceptive verbal arts that open hard doors closed against men.[7] She represents well Ovid's equivocations about his own art.

Ovid's works serve as a fair introduction to what will become prestigious medieval amatory conventions: the pose of the suffering lover-poet, the service to an all-mastering Love, the madness of passion, the notion of a rational code to civilize love. Ovid also devises an important dual patronage system for poetry, associating his works alternately with a sportively tyrannical Cupid and with a somewhat frivolously cosmological Venus. These conventions (which are of course not at all unique to Ovid) undergo a number of transformations in their passage through the Middle Ages. Just as Ovid reshapes ancient Roman conventions to suit his purposes, so do later poets revise his and others' arts of love and poetry.

Many writers, both ancient and medieval, treat the cosmological Venus with rather more respect than Ovid does, associating her with the divine power of love, its ordering force, its heavenly character. At her zenith, this Venus can symbolize the love that rules the sun and all the stars.[8] She presides over poetry as a force capable of uniting and ordering all things, including body and soul, sensuality and intellect. The basic outlines of the cosmological Venus remain discernible throughout the Middle Ages. We might take two examples as expressive of her conjoined influence over love and poetry: the *Eve of St. Venus* (*Pervigilium Veneris*, third or fourth century C.E.) and Boccaccio's description of Venus *magna* in the *Genealogy*. The "Eve of St. Venus" details her conventional influence over vernal loves, shaping the classical tradition to a fresh and explicit sensuousness:

> facta Cypridis de cruore deque Amoris osculo,
> deque gemmis deque flammis deque solis purpuris,
> cras ruborem qui latebat veste tectus ignea
> uvido marita nodo non pudebit solvere.
> cras amet qui nunquam amavit quique amavit cras amet.
>
> (st. 7)

Compounded of Venus's blood and of Love's kiss and of jewels and of flames and of flushes of the sun, tomorrow the bride unashamed will unfold from the wet cluster the crimson that lurked hid in its taper sheath.

Tomorrow shall be love for the loveless, and for the lover tomorrow shall be love. (trans. MacKail)

The poem ends with a contrast between Venus and the poet excluded from this spring of life and love, and thus from poetry:

> illa cantat, nos tacemus: quando ver venit meum?
> quando fiam uti chelidon ut tacere desinam?
>
> (st. 22)

She sings, we are mute: when is my spring coming? When shall I be as the swallow, that I may cease to be voiceless?

Arts of love and of poetry—a sensuousness of flesh and of mind—are unified in Venus. Whereas she sings of love and desire satisfied, the poet sings voicelessly in the absence of sexual fulfillment. Exclusion from the lovers' *reverdie* leads the poet to aestheticize sensuality in verse: absence and exclusion transform desire into poetry. Symbolizing the "natural" forces of desire, Venus presides over sexual couplings as well as over the lyrical evocation of sensuous pleasure. Needless to say, she does not receive a mythographic commentary within the poem.

Boccaccio's depiction of Venus *magna*, the astrologized deity in the *Genealogy*, demonstrates a crucial later medieval revision of this Venus: the astrologizing of the cosmological deity. Boccaccio lists her planetary influences over sensual pleasures, including "all sorts of illicit sexual activity and wantonnesses, and a multitude of couplings."[9] This planet also sponsors writing and poetry, something of a surprise since astrologers normally identify not Venus but Mercury with arts of writing.[10] Yet in the later Middle Ages the astral influence best represents the ancient broadly conceived cosmological power over both sensual love and art, and Boccaccio seeks to place this Venus in precisely that tradition. Early in the account, for instance, he cites Ovid's description in *Fasti*, naming her the life-giving mother of twin loves ("alma . . . geminorum mater amorum," *Genealogy*, 1: 142). By linking Venus to poetry as well as to procreation and diverse sexual acts, Boccaccio grants the planet a generative and sensual power that fosters mental as well as physical creation. Later in the explication, he cites Cicero's etymology, as befitting the cosmological goddess (*Venus* from *venire* because she may come to all; *Genealogy*, 1: 148). The entire account neatly resurrects the classical goddess of generative vitality: Venus *genetrix* in her most extensive, cosmological role. This Venus fully evidences a union of physical sensuality and verbal art—in other words, she fully represents the sensuousness of poetry, its appeal to both mind and body. If we follow the hints, the passage suggests that Boccaccio, Italy's "second Ovid,"[11] is deftly appropriating (and refashioning) the mantle of Italy's first Ovid by declaring himself another poet of Venus. If so, his poetic invocations to Venus receive their final gloss here, in his mythographic art.

Both ancient and medieval writers embody in the cosmological Venus a union of sensuous pleasures and verbal art. Writers may indeed equivocate about this Venus, as Ovid does, but they clearly do not address her with the faintly ecclesiastical tones evident in much mythographic commentary on the *anadyomene*. Indeed, as a symbol of the love that sustains universal order, she represents an ideal both Christian and pagan. Hymns to Venus may therefore serve as models for hymns to the Virgin, also conceived as universal *alma mater*. The association with both sensual love and poetry does not define the whole of the cosmological figure, but it suffices to indicate the far-reaching effects potentially implicit in her power over sensuality. As the son of this Venus, Cupid retains his classical character: a small child attending his powerful mother, attesting to her fertility and linking her to youthful pleasures. He gains no particular attention in this guise. Meanwhile, however, courtly conventions elevate him into a mighty adult god, ruling over gentle lovers and their codes of refined love. This god descends from figures like the autocratic Cupid who dictates the form and content of Ovid's *Loves*, but his appearance and character mark his medieval rise to courtly preeminence. With Cupid's assumption of an adult male courtly status, Venus may remain powerful but often loses her association with poetry. At medieval courts, lover-poets generally serve Cupid, ambiguously naming him the God of Love. Thus courtly conventions as well as mythographies locate in Cupid a union of love and sexual desire, and an equivocation between Christianity and paganism.

The courtly Cupid perhaps most famously appears as Amor in the *Romance of the Rose*, with Venus his helpful consultant in the uses of flaming arrows. Guillaume de Lorris and Jean de Meun picture these deities less in conformity with ancient models than in deference to contemporary expectations about the proper appearance of sexual love: they look genteel.[12] Guillaume's portraits of the pair epitomize their typical appearances in courtly literature, which displays them as sponsors of noble love, expensively dressed according to the fashions of the time. As Guillaume describes her, Venus holds a blazing torch and is lavishly adorned with the lace, gold, and other accoutrements of an elegant lady. Cupid appears in his usual romance guise as the unmistakably adult God of Love, dressed in elaborate natural materials: his garments appear to be made out of blossoms woven into intricate representations of flora and fauna. In manuscript illuminations and in later literature, these floral garments are usually replaced by more conventional fabrics, loosening Cupid's bond with nature.[13] He retains the wings attributed to ancient *amores* and the mythographic Cupid, but here they align him with angels—at least in the narrator's eyes. Numerous companions attend him and ease his labor by bearing his cumbersome double set of bows and arrows. With these descriptions of Venus and Cupid, Guillaume crafts what is to become a very popular imagery, both in France and in a later medieval England enamored of French romance.[14]

The vision of Cupid as a lord surrounded by underlings notably departs from mythographic and classical representations of a childlike or boylike figure engaged in careless sport, though Ovid's *Loves* provides ample justification for imagining a princely Cupid. Still, we need not refer to the *auctores* to realize that this image neatly captures ideas of Cupid as the irresistible power of love and the license of youthful passion. Whether as caesar or as a feudal lord, Cupid stands at the center of power, an entirely appropriate emblem of love's compelling force. At the same time, Guillaume's medievalized Amor once again suspends us between love and sexual desire.[15]

Guillaume de Lorris and Jean de Meun enlarge Amor's Ovidian power by having him rule the codified language in which the *gentil* lover expresses himself. Thus Amor, dethroning Venus in his maturity, rules over the poetic cultivation of sensual desire. In Jean's hands, a refined Amor explicitly endorses the ambiguities and hypocrisies (false seemings) inherent in a codified language of love. By locating the dubious effort to civilize love and the avowedly false language of love under Cupid's patronage, Jean makes explicit what Ovid only implies in *Loves* and *Art of Loving*. Both Guillaume and Jean present Venus as a vaguely cosmological force, a force beyond Cupid's sphere of command, but she exercises a severely limited power. Cupid maintains a strict rule over lover-poets, and Nature takes over as generative force. Venus appears as little more than a sexual appetite (especially a feminine one). She nonetheless discloses a witty literalism. Jean de Meun has Venus shoot the masculine, phallic "arrow" that enters the feminine tower's "narrow aperture," located between two "pillars." Manuscript illuminations bring out Venus's hermaphroditism in this sequence. One illustrator pictures Venus shooting the arrow at a woman with her genitalia aflame.[16] In the end, then, Venus literally signifies intercourse, the union of male and female in one flesh. She also gains an innovative mythographic commentary in Jean's contribution to the allegory: the Old Woman uses the fable of Mars's and Venus's adultery to propose that women and men are born free and should remain sexually available to all. The interested proponent of mythography here undercuts its scholarly authority, giving just the sort of nonstandard explication that an "untrained" reader is supposed to produce.

In much French courtly literature, the love deities wear the representational garments Guillaume de Lorris and Jean de Meun fashioned for them. During the later Middle Ages, the meanings of these images are often remade, and we might recall the concurrent remaking of meaning in mythography. For example, Christine de Pizan, who famously resisted the influence of Jean de Meun's *Romance of the Rose*, takes over the poem's celebrated visual tradition in order to invest it with new meanings. Her illustrations of Venus and Cupid in the *Epistle of Othea* (*L'Epistre Othéa*) and elsewhere look very like those attached to Jean's poem, but they suggest somewhat different implications.[17] Her iconology preserves the deities' social status as she subjects to critical commentary the values they represent. We also encounter the adult courtly Cupid in numerous works of Chaucer's French contemporaries, such as Guillaume de Machaut and Jean de le Mote, who in their own ways enlarge on the convention of suffering lover-poet serving a sovereign and imperious Love.[18] Venus often becomes a mere adjunct to her son in this tradition—she signifies a feminine sexual power acknowledged but marginalized in illusory feudal orders.

Venus and Cupid metamorphose time and time again as various Latin and vernacular discourses appropriate them. Each discourse shapes and clothes and invests them with meanings. Images of the deities are no more fixed than are their implications, within or apart from mythography. The scholarly, classicizing imperative evident in much mythography mandates that they retain their ancient nude forms, and that Cupid appear as a child. Courtly writing envisions Cupid as adult lord and adorns both deities with the expensive and rare materials that mark a socially exclusive love. Either the cosmological Venus or the courtly Cupid may incite lovers to write poetry. The courtly and cosmological traditions are not necessarily separable from one another, but we should recognize the very different implications and nuances of a cosmological Venus nurturing poetry (as when Lucretius and Ovid invoke her aid for their poetic flights) and a courtly magnification of Cupid as poetic patron (after his triumph in Ovid's *Loves*). The one refers to a feminized power of love, the other to a masculine cultural rite. We should also note differences of representational conventions: the cosmological Venus appears as *alma mater*, universal life-giving mother; the courtly pair exemplifies the fashions of love among the gentle classes. These traditions may of course be variously synthesized and reconceptualized. Thus Boccaccio invokes both Venus and Cupid at the opening of the *Teseida*, bringing together the cosmological Venus and the courtly Cupid (in order, Boccaccio continues, to reveal their shortcomings). With the *Genealogy*, he drafts much the same Venus into a validation of sensuous pleasure and poetry. If we are to interpret images of the deities, we need to attend closely to the details of particular representations, appreciating how those details point to the competing discourses that write and rewrite the deities' meanings, and acknowledging how details may speak to poetic revisions in traditions.

Absent Hermeneutics: *The House of Fame* and *The Knight's Tale*

When Chaucer decides to include Venus and Cupid in the *House of Fame* and the *Knight's Tale*, he draws on mythographic, cosmological, and courtly conventions. By bringing these conventions together, he manages to achieve one of the vital effects of poetry: he defamiliarizes all of them. While courtly images of the deities materialize beside every rosebush in French literature, Chaucer adopts the mythographers' classicizing images. These new images of sexual love denaturalize both courtly and mythographic conventions, thereby permitting new kinds of social and aesthetic commentary. In his poems, moreover, the ancient and mythographic images of the deities retain their inherent ambiguities, and he exploits these ambiguities to distinctly unmythographic ends.

Multiplying Traditions in the House of Fame

In Book 1 of the *House of Fame*, Chaucer envisions a temple of glass filled with ancient artistic images—"olde werk" done in a "queynte maner" (126–27). This temple testifies to superfluous wealth expended on images made of gold, "rych tabernacles," paintings, and pinnacles adorned with precious stones. The dreamer concludes that this is the temple of Venus, for her portrait appears among the magnificent architectural embellishments. At this point, when Chaucer's original audience doubtless expects the god and goddess as depicted in the *Romance of the Rose*, Chaucer describes Venus *anadyomene* and blind Cupid:[19]

>   in portreyture
> I sawgh anoon-ryght hir figure
> Naked fletynge in a see,
> And also on hir hed, pardee,
> Hir rose garlond whit and red,
> And hir comb to kembe hyr hed,
> Hir dowves, and daun Cupido
> Hir blynde sone, and Vulcano,
> That in his face was ful broun.
>   (131–39)

Chaucer's mythographic image emphasizes sensuality itself, not the finery of a cultural elite. The few indications of class status serve only to perplex class exclusivity. While the detail of Venus's comb adds the implication of feminine vanity and aristocratic leisure,[20] she is paired with Vulcan, whose brown complexion indicates his unattractiveness and probably his boorishness. Cupid's blindness hints at a passion lacking in discrimination, oblivious to all things other than desire: a sensuality that takes no account of social or other hierarchies. These fleeting implications generalize the idea of sensuality, extending it to all ranks. Indeed, the deities' nudity represents sensual desire as a common human condition not restricted to the upper classes. By offering these particular images, and by separating them from authoritative hermeneutics, Chaucer enhances the ambiguities and universality of sensual desire. In other words, whereas the portraits of Venus and Cupid in the *Romance of the Rose* and in much of French literature restrict love to the wealthy and leisured classes, Chaucer pictures sexual love and desire as a more broadly human phenomenon.

The setting deepens these implications. The mythographers picture the deities in empty space or at the seaside, but Chaucer places them in an ancient temple, imagined in terms of medieval architecture.[21] The ancient religious setting refers us to a pagan deification of sensual desire and pleasure, to the pagan error of idolizing Venus and Cupid.[22] Yet the temple description also focuses on an ostentatious medieval display of wealth, implicating Chaucer's contemporaries. Even while Chaucer classicizes the deities' images and setting, then, his details do not restrict idolatry or sensuality to pagans. The setting and iconology remain enigmatically poised between the ancient and the medieval, between the upper and lower classes, and between the scholarly and the courtly. Medieval Christians as well as pagans may idolize sensual desire, and lower as well as upper classes are comprehended. The imagery confounds easy oppositions based on religion, era, class, or gender. (David Wallace points out a similar effect in *Troilus and Criseyde*, where Chaucer's inscription of the deities explores the "uncertain space" between Christianity and paganism.)[23] Though all are implicated in Chaucer's mythographic imagery, however, none is judged. By itself, the iconology advances no specific values.

Chaucer's poetic indirectness and universalizing set him very far apart from the mythographers. His imagery is not about moralization but about poetic representation. It is nevertheless important that Venus *anadyomene* and blind Cupid are distinctly mythographic images, identified with the learned Latin tradition that produced them.[24] The iconology points to a pagan past as understood through a particular scholarly tradition. By selecting these images, Chaucer classicizes the deities, but he also calls attention to his departure from the larger tradition: his erasure of mythographic hermeneutics.[25] He essentially frees meaning from the control of the authority systems involved in Latin commentary and glosses on poetry. In other words, Chaucer alludes to the commentary tradition in order to disavow it.[26] His imagery exists for the sake not of hermeneutics but of poetry, with all its uncertainties and ambiguities. He implies, as many French writers do, a poetics detached from moral allegories and from theories about the fictive veil (the *integumentum*).[27] Hence Chaucer's first temple of Venus declares the precedence of English over Latin (for with several notable exceptions mythography is a Latin discourse), of poetry over commentary, and of poetic puzzles over interpretive clarity.[28] If we come to this temple with Dante's more confidently idealizing elevation of the vernacular fresh in mind, Chaucer's move may seem nervous and self-mocking.[29] Chaucer nonetheless affirms English as a replacement for both Latin and French, albeit a risky and sometimes inadequate one.

From translating medieval Latin mythography, Chaucer moves on to treat Latin poetry—Virgil's *Aeneid* and Ovid's *Heroides*—in a similar fashion. The temple of Venus becomes a complete statement about displacing Latin traditions, and a model of how they may be replaced by English poetry.[30] Virgil narrates Troy's fall by detailing a mural on the wall of Juno's temple in Carthage. Chaucer places the *Aeneid*, enveloping an epistle of Dido from *Heroides*, on the wall of Venus's temple. The change of venue signals a shift in narrative focus: Chaucer concentrates on the love affair of Dido and Aeneas, subordinating Virgil's celebration of the Roman empire to its most memorable private consequences. If we recollect Dante's very different rewriting of Virgilian epic in the *Divine Comedy*, Chaucer's anything-but-idealizing reception of the Latin classics becomes all the more apparent. He domesticates the epic.

Chaucer's retelling of the *Aeneid* concentrates on bringing out Venus's maternal solicitude, on magnifying her role as *genetrix*, mother of Aeneas. She appears at every dramatic turn of Chaucer's mini-epic. First, she views the conflagration of Troy and, descending from heaven, bids Aeneas to flee. A storm threatens him with shipwreck, so she goes "wepynge with ful woful chere" to Jupiter (214) and prays mercy for her son. When the stranded Aeneas and Achates meet her out hunting, she comforts the complaining Aeneas and sends him on to Carthage. (Virgil's goddess denies him this comfort, and Aeneas eloquently blames her for denying their relationship.)[31] Finally, Chaucer's Venus brings Aeneas into Dido's "grace" (240). (Virgil's Venus must petition Cupid to disguise himself and inspire Dido's passion.) At every point in Chaucer's compact narrative, we encounter Venus directly interceding for Aeneas. As Chaucer tells it, Aeneas achieves his task of founding the Roman empire only by means of her (and others') conspicuous intervention.[32] The last half of the *Aeneid*—the battle to possess Italy—becomes trivial, easily recounted in a few lines, "For Jupiter took of hym cure / At the prayer of Venus" (464–65). A precise summation: Aeneas achieves his empire through his mother's influence rather than, as Virgil would have it, by epic fortitude against superhuman adversaries.

Through all of this, Chaucer identifies the Venus *anadyomene* of the temple portrait with the Venus *genetrix* of Virgil's epic, fusing the two Roman traditions. Chaucer's conception of Venus in fact comically subverts Virgil's epic and the glories of the Roman empire. The Roman Julians claimed to descend from Aeneas; his mother, Venus, was also their *genetrix*, the divine force behind their claim to power. As such, she usually appears not nude but robed, in the garb of a dignified Roman wife and mother. Virgil provides an illustrious epic mythology of the Julians' divine origins. In Chaucer's retelling, the goddess of sensual pleasure, Venus *anadyomene*, displaces the august power behind the Roman empire (a most Ovidian revision of Virgil).[33] Far from being an epic conqueror, Chaucer's Aeneas pursues a life of pleasure. He seems very like the medieval Paris, in fact, and we might recall that in mythography Venus *anadyomene* often pictures the life of pleasure chosen by Paris.[34] (Of course, following his conflicting traditions, Chaucer both defends and accuses Aeneas; the vacillation calls the defense into question.)[35] It is difficult to imagine a strategy better calculated to undermine Virgil's pious hero than to align him, even obliquely, with Venus *anadyomene*, Paris, and the apple of discord.

The narrative within the temple further enlarges the import of the opening iconology. While Venus remains an image suggestive of pseudo-idolatrous sensuality, Chaucer adapts her to a provocative political commentary. Within the mini-epic, Venus *anadyomene* is associated with both the fall of Troy (through the judgment of Paris) and the eternally flawed foundation of pagan Rome (as Aeneas's mother). A devotion to Venus *anadyomene*—to sensuality—links the two cities. One senses this causal chain stretching forward from ancient Rome to the Holy Roman Empire, and thence to Chaucer's London, New Troy, with its potential for a similar loss of knighthood in sensuality. Chaucer presents sensual desire as the shadow dogging military exploits, and as the trait always potentially undermining chivalric achievements. Although this lesson most forcefully concerns men of the gentle classes—military leaders—Chaucer's treatment does not exclude anyone. The mythographic images serve to generalize the implications of sensuality, to make sexual love and its consequences notable as a human experience rather than exclusively a noble and chivalric diversion.

Chaucer encloses within Virgil's epic an epistle of Dido from Ovid's *Heroides*, and this constitutes a further commentary on both Latin letters and on sensual desire. From Virgil to Ovid to Chaucer, Dido exists as little more than a marker in a masculine poetic traffic in Woman.[36] Just as Ovid rewrites Virgil's Dido, Chaucer revises Ovid's Dido. Whereas Ovid seeks to express Dido's perspective (with dubious success), Chaucer turns her into a medieval moral exemplum, at key points distancing us from our fragile Ovidian identification with her. When Dido grants Aeneas her love, for instance, Chaucer launches into a homily against both masculine deceit and feminine gullibility. Charging Aeneas with betrayal, Chaucer indicts Dido for the fault of indiscriminate love: "Loo, how a woman doth amys / To love hym that unknowen ys!" (269–70) Chaucer also lingers over Dido's "nyce lest," because of which she "loved al to sone a gest" (287–88). Countering Dido's Ovidian lament with overt moral commentary, Chaucer plays sympathy off against judgment.[37]

This moralizing constitutes one of very few points in the *House of Fame* at which Chaucer overtly fixes and limits meaning. That this love affair must be discursively controlled is telling. Chaucer openly accuses Aeneas of treachery, besides implying his sensuality through his relationship with Venus *anadyomene*. Similarly, Chaucer directly moralizes Dido's actions, and she illustrates the passionate lack of discrimination, the potentially anarchic sexuality, symbolized by blind Cupid. The overt moralization repeatedly directs our eyes to the social consequences of noble love in late medieval times, calling attention to a social context that makes women vulnerable to masculine deceit. The problem devolves from upper-class gender roles: feminine passivity and masculine aggression, feminine pity for masculine suffering, and finally feminine trust complemented by masculine deceit. Although Chaucer finds it unnecessary to comment on pagan religion or sexual love in the abstract (thus on Venus and Cupid), he does purposefully explicate the dangerously ambiguous social contexts of love.[38] His overt moralization circumscribes a problem area in the construction of a class-specific sexuality, while the symbolic echoes broaden the perspective, making the problems of specifically genteel sensuality seem applicable to all ranks, in all ages. Between the deities' images and the love narrative, we encounter an equivocation between universal human nature and class-specific behaviors.

When commenting on Dido, Chaucer's tone varies between detached sympathy and proverbial dismissal ("Al hir compleynt ne al hir moone, / Certeyn, avayleth hir not a stre"; 362–63). The proverbial lowerings demolish both Virgil's tragedy and Ovid's pathos.[39] Chaucer's moralization consequently translates mythography not only into English but into the communal register of proverbs. The collective native wisdom of England, condensed into proverbs, serves as wryly sufficient commentary on pagan literature. The English, it seems, need no special learning, no academic traditions, no mythographers, to comprehend the import of ancient literature. A reliance on native wit and common sense will ensure an appropriate interpretation.

If the *House of Fame* is a text about textuality, a poem about poetics, a discourse about discourses, it is at first about Latin mythographic and poetic traditions.[40] And here Chaucer evokes those elite, prestigious traditions only to displace them with England's native conventions (or at least with his own poem). He likely learned to think of vernacular poetry as a vehicle for such nationalism from Latin and Italian poets, but he does not simply follow other writers.[41] His uses of literary traditions demonstrate that he definitively reauthors the texts he translates. As Karla Taylor proposes about his relation to Dante, he shows not only "dependence on" but also "independence from" his sources.[42] As he handles the mythographic images of the deities, they call attention to a poetics that detaches classical mythology from commentary traditions—and they reveal a poetics that relies on sensuous rather than didactic effects. Chaucer probably learned both this approach to myth and this ideal of poetry from contemporary French writers.[43] The first book of the *House of Fame* thus demonstrates how Chaucer negotiates both scholarly and poetic traditions, both Latin and vernacular conventions.

Chaucer's first Venus *anadyomene* and blind Cupid embody a sensuality that brings together upper and lower classes, Christian and pagan, men and women; in their temple setting, they signify both the class exclusivity of sensual love and its universality. His imagery revises courtly conventions that insist on the class specificity of sexual love, undermining the widespread cultural myth that the gentle classes are naturally superior in love. Further, the implications embedded in the deities' portraits introduce and pronounce an implicit commentary on the epic action. As the *anadyomene* of sensual pleasure and the *genetrix* of empire become the same figure, we discover a link between military deeds and commonplace sensuality—between the chivalric empire-builder and the churl. By combining disparate traditions, Chaucer makes them new: he reveals affinities between contemporary social mores and the mythographic image of sexual love, between paganism and Christianity, between human nature and exclusionary class norms, and between the *anadyomene* and the *genetrix* (we might reasonably suspect Ovid's influence in this last stratagem). Chaucer represents sensual desire as profoundly ambiguous—an import brilliantly introduced with the mythographic images. He also portrays sensual desire as intrinsic to a universal human nature: the mythographic images serve a humanist ethos.

As Book 1 of the *House of Fame* closes on Latin epic and mythographic traditions, Book 2 opens with an invocation drawing on myths of Venus as patron of the arts. Within Book 2 Venus and Cupid preside over the making of love poetry, in the French fashion. Chaucer progresses from mythographic iconology to cosmological and courtly models for the deities. Since he writes not an encyclopedia but a poem, a work distinguished by aesthetic patterning, these various representational conventions enter into something very like a dialogic relation. In the proem to Book 2, Chaucer follows Dante and Boccaccio in seeking Venus's help for his work:[44]

> Now faire blisfull, O Cipris,
> So be my favour at this tyme!
> And ye, me to endite and ryme
> Helpeth, that on Parnaso duelle,
> Be Elicon, the clere welle.
>
> (518–22)

Venus now assumes her typically cosmological role as the deity who nurtures poetry.[45] We may still picture her as the *anadyomene* since that image readily accepts almost any meaning. Her association with the Muses refers to conventional parallels among them, the planets, and the liberal arts; rhetoric and the Muse Terpsichore are in Venus's sphere.[46] Taken as a whole, the invocation refers us to venereal pleasures as well as to the intellectual and sensuous aspects (especially rhyme) of poetic composition. In Book 1 and in this invocation, Chaucer suggestively connects the *anadyomene* and the cosmological patroness of poetry. The presence of this unmistakably sensual deity in the invocation creates for some readers a problematic equivocation between the sensuous appeal of verse and its moral import. This tension inheres in the cosmological convention, and Chaucer only magnifies it when he begins with the classicizing image of naked desire. By incorporating both *anadyomene* and cosmological traditions, in fact, Chaucer insists on the sensuous aspects of his poetry.

The language of this invocation—particularly the reference to "enditing"—initiates an important pattern of self-definition in Chaucer's poetry, one often associated with Venus and Cupid. Further on in Book 2, the eagle notes that the narrator "ever mo of love enditest" (634). The eagle also calls him a poet of Venus and Cupid, one who "make[s] bookys, songes, dytees" (622) in the service of love. Thus Chaucer first identifies Venus with the "enditing" of this poem, then names both Venus and Cupid in relation to the "making" and "enditing" of his love poetry. Chaucer frequently uses the terms "making" and "enditing" to define his poetry, and this usage has been astutely analyzed by Glending Olson and Anne Middleton. As Olson argues, "making" refers to a French theory that emphasizes poetry's pleasures more than the moral intent or learning that goes into it. "Making" names a secular poetics of courtliness, and raises expectations quite distinct from the "exalted moral and religious functions claimed by much medieval literature and literary theory" (for instance, in the theories of the exegetes, Petrarch, or Dante).[47] The "makers" are the poets of Cupid's courtly band. On the other hand, Anne Middleton proposes that Chaucer's use of "enditing" locates the poet in a broader arena than that occupied by the "makers," with responsibilities beyond the celebration of narrow courtly values. The "enditer," she submits, takes a "middle way" between the courtly entertainments of the "makers" and the high ideals of "poets" such as Virgil and Dante. Whereas the "maker" addresses a small, elite audience in fairly circumscribed ways on the subjects of love and chivalry, the "enditer" seeks a wider audience and a more varied range of treatments, if not subjects.[48]

The *House of Fame* does not support a strict division between "making" and "enditing," but rather suggests their complementary aspects. The proem to Book 2 yokes Venus to the Muses and the "enditing" of this poem. The ideal of poetry momentarily harks back (through Italian poetry) to the classical model of a sensuous Venus who inspires poetic and other generative acts.[49] This ideal of poetry is not entirely separable from the French model of "making," with its emphasis on musicality (that is, on sensuous effects such as rhyme).[50] Venus embodies the virtue common to both classicizing and French models: the sensuous side of poetry. Thus far, "making" and "enditing" overlap. Then, within Book 2, Chaucer describes "making" poems as service to Cupid, referring us to the traditions of contemporary love poetry modeled on a French heritage that owes much to Guillaume de Lorris's and Jean de Meun's *Romance of the Rose*, but also to Guillaume de Machaut and his followers and imitators.[51] As we have found, in this courtly tradition Cupid usually reigns supreme over his troupe of lover-poets, and so he does in Book 2. Although he retains his attribute of blindness, just as Venus remains "faire" (617–18), Cupid now assumes the lordly status elaborated by courtly verse. Poets and lovers are his servants. By alternating in this book between Venus and Cupid, "enditing" and "making," Chaucer implies a vital interaction among classicizing, scholarly, amatory, and sensuous ideals for poetry. The deities' repeated appearances suggest interconnections among seemingly disparate traditions. They refer us to an ideal of poetry as both sensuous and learned, and to an ideal of love that is not only class exclusive.

Elaborating on his poet-persona's relation to this Cupid, Chaucer asks the audience to view the makers' conventions from the perspective of one who emphatically does not write from his own experience of love, but who only hears of love on the winds of fame. That is, he rewrites the persona of the lover who versifies out of the madness of passion, and under the despotic rule of desire (Ovid and French poets similarly revise and comment on the conventions).[52] No longer even pretending to be a lover, Chaucer's narrator is significantly distanced from the type, emphatically insistent on its conventionality: he out-Ovids Ovid. The pose of nonparticipant in the cult of love, deriving poetry from reading texts rather than from experience, comments on the fictive self-fashioning seemingly omnipresent in conventional amatory verse. Amatory poetry is often implicitly based on the absence of sexual joy, on unfulfilled desire, and Chaucer's creation of the nonlover persona makes this convention visible.[53] Chaucer's text renders not only apparent but inescapable the fiction of the lover persona. By turning the convention of lover-poet into comedy, Chaucer casts doubt also on the idea of a tyrannical god of love dictating the poem's matter or style. He denies this courtly tradition a privileged role in defining his poetics.

Chaucer challenges the priority of "making," but he does not here exclude it from his poetic self-definition. "Making" and "enditing" identify not mutually exclusive or strictly hierarchized values in this poem, but rather complementary aims: poetry associated with both Venus and Cupid, with feminine sensual influences as well as with highly conventionalized masculine arts. Chaucer thus draws for Book 2 on both cosmological and courtly traditions for Venus and Cupid in order to emphasize what they share—an appreciation of pleasure, the sensuous virtue of poetry. This common ground among classical, Italian, and French models becomes a tacit early definition of Chaucer's poetics, represented by a collaboration between Venus and Cupid, "enditing" and "making." Although this does not elucidate the whole of Chaucer's poetics, it calls attention to some important early emphases.[54] (The invocations to Morpheus for Book 1 and to Apollo for Book 3 indicate, however, that any definition within this poem is only temporary, meant to be supplanted by others: just as Venus supplants Morpheus, so Apollo takes her place.)

As the narrator tours the house of Fame in Book 3, he spies a depiction of Ovid, "Venus clerk" (1487), topping a copper pillar. Copper befits Venus's poet, for it pertains to the planetary deity. Chaucer credits Ovid with spreading the "grete god of Loves name" and "fame" (1489–90). At this point, we discover the fictive origins of the courtly and puissant God of Love, the cosmological Venus, and the mythographic pair: Ovid's poetry. The diverse conventions at last find a common origin in the house of Fame. In short, Venus and Cupid enter the poem as mythographic figures of sensual desire and love, gain associations with the "enditing" and "making" of classical and French poetry, and end as the sponsors and subjects of Ovidian amatory arts. Chaucer's poem reverses their pilgrimage through literature, through the circuits of fame.

Literary traditions for Venus and Cupid, like all tidings, multiply in the house of Fame. As Chaucer's eagle declares:

> Everych ayr another stereth
> More and more, and speche up bereth,
> Or voys, or noyse, or word, or soun,

> Ay through multiplicacioun,
> Til hyt be atte Hous of Fame—
> Take yt in ernest or in game.
>
> (817–22)

The tidings of Fame continuously reproduce and multiply, begetting not only Latin poetry and mythography but also vernacular poetics. Pursuing the variants of fame, Chaucer explores and recombines several literary traditions for the deities. His diverse representations of Venus and Cupid finally suggest a quasi-encyclopedic survey of literary traditions, with each portrayal of the deities drawing on slightly different literary conventions.[55] This kind of diversity is not entirely due to encyclopedism, for the lyric poetry of Chaucer's French contemporaries reveals a similar "discontinuity."[56] Lyric and encyclopedic influences harmonize in this poem that fully testifies to the diversity of literary "aventures."

As tidings multiply in the house of Fame, we discover the rich variety of, and the potential for dialogues among, literary traditions.[57] Chaucer grants no tradition more than ephemeral precedence in this sublunar realm, as he introduces various traditions—mythographic, cosmological, and courtly—into an evanescent series of contingent and mutually illuminating definitions of sexuality and poetry, a series that precludes any single definition or fixed meaning. By bringing these traditions into a complex system of aesthetic relations, he discloses surprisingly wide-ranging implications about a sensuality at once common to all and unique to the upper classes, a sensuality that may be a diversion from military achievements or the basis of poetic arts. Through their interactions, each convention comes to mean something slightly different, slightly more interesting than it meant on its own. Each appearance of the love deities thus comments on and complicates associations between sensuality and poetry, between sexual desire and amatory literature, between the classical past and contemporary society. As Chaucer recombines conventions, he also re-creates them. Whereas a mythographer typically draws on multiple explanatory discourses and leaves them unreconciled, disparate, Chaucer takes in diverse representational conventions but ultimately suggests their unified origin in the house of Fame. For behind each word stands a speaker; the poem sketches out a myth of originary presence underpinning the vagaries and uncertainties of convention.[58]

Sexuality and Social Class in the Knight's Tale

When Chaucer locates the mythographers' iconology in another context, the *Knight's Tale*, he once again reshapes its import. Each new poetic context vividly alters the implications of the imagery. Here once again the deities appear in a pagan setting, one that still more forcefully combines scholarly and courtly conventions. For the final combat of Palamon and Arcite, the battle to determine which will possess Emelye, Theseus designs an amphitheater and adorns it with temples to Venus, Mars, and Diana, all intended for his religious rites. This amphitheater epitomizes Theseus's construction of social and cosmic order, his imposition of an idealizing, chivalric order on the wild incivility of Palamon and Arcite's fight to win Emelye.[59] Situated around the amphitheater, the deities' temples bring within the compass of Theseus's idealizing order the primary forces of disorder in the narrative—sexual desire, military aggression, and chastity (a surprising third, until we consider the much-repressed threat of the Amazon women). The amphitheater functions, then, as Theseus does, to organize, to ritualize, to idealize the violent competition on which the tale hangs.[60] In it we meet chivalric ideals and chivalric ferocity, the ideology of the medieval cavalry as well as the physical realities of combat.[61]

Within the amphitheater, the forces designated by the three deities seem at once separate and inextricable: they resolve into discrete temples yet participate in the single chivalric order. Their unity in chivalric ideology is vital and repeatedly displayed in the narrative, where it appears as the fusion of masculine sexual desire and military aggression, and the link between that desirous offensive and the feminine rejection of men (or *daunger*). Both Arcite and Palamon exemplify this union of masculine sexuality and aggression. On his escape from prison, Palamon intends to conquer Athens and gain Emelye by force (1482–86); later, he prays in the temple of Venus. Released from prison, Arcite endures lovesickness (1355–79);[62] he prays in the temple of Mars. To make the pattern complete, Theseus "conquered al the regne of Femenye" (866) and married the queen. For each knight, love equates with military conquest. The narrative presents masculine assault and feminine resistance as complementary gender roles. The resistance justifies, even eroticizes, the aggression.[63] This narrative unity of desire, aggression, and resistance characterizes chivalry throughout the poem. The narrative thus naturalizes the alliance of desire and aggression, aggression and resistance in the chivalric code. Within the narrative, Mars, Venus, and Diana are inseparable, though their unity is invisible.

Viewed as a whole, the amphitheater with its temples represents this ideological paradigm. It also displays the contingency of the social construct, for it turns out that the forces of aggression and resistance are separable. In the individual temples if not in the narrative, we view sexual desire as a force distinguishable from armed aggression. Recognizing the isolation of sensual desire from military force, we query their interrelationship within the circle of the amphitheater and in the narrative. We denaturalize the unity of the chivalric code. We also puzzle over the priorities these temples so clearly fail to establish. The amphitheater sets us a conundrum: What does this ideology privilege—sensuality, military and erotic aggression, or chastity? Decades of modern critical debate prove the entertainment value of the question.[64] It remains, however, irresolvable, like the question at the end of the poem's first part. With the amphitheater and its temples the aesthetic point is the paradox, the separate but inseparable disposition of masculine desire and aggression and feminine resistance. Whereas chivalry naturalizes the formation, Chaucer depicts it as a constructed and therefore contingent social order.

Within this setting we find the mythographers' Venus *anadyomene* and blind Cupid, their meaning now dependent on their relation to chivalric ideology.[65] Chaucer's description appropriately begins with the somatic signs of eros among the nobility, before progressing to an elaboration of other courtly conventions:[66]

> First in the temple of Venus maystow se
> Wroght on the wal, ful pitous to biholde,
> The broken slepes, and the sikes colde,
> The sacred teeris, and the waymentynge,
> The firy strokes of the desirynge
> That loves servantz in this lyf enduren.
>
> (1918–23)

Such sleeplessness, sighs, and tears favor a diagnosis of lovesickness, the complaint particularly of noble men.[67] Inscribed on the body, this susceptibility to passion appears natural; it proves the innate superiority of noble blood and breeding, for lesser creatures experience neither this intensity of emotion nor its somatic consequences. These symptoms of love are, in fact, so common among the nobility that they effectively constitute a claim to aristocratic status. By fashioning themselves according to such conventions of love, late medieval men establish both gender and class identity.[68] Chaucer characterizes Palamon and Arcite as noble men by attributing to each these symptoms of love.[69] Their failure to master the refined language of love talk, the preeminent literary mark of an aristocratic man, insinuates the limits of their gentility.[70] Their aggression remains militaristic, not diverted into seductive language. Accordingly, when given a year to prepare for their final combat, they return to Thebes instead of staying to woo Emelye (as Boccaccio's knights do in the *Teseida*). Their ephemeral symptoms of love nonetheless tenuously establish Palamon and Arcite as members of an elite masculine community.

On the wall of Venus's oratory, the description of lovesickness gives way to personifications and behaviors that further characterize youthful, noble love:

> Plesaunce and Hope, Desir, Foolhardynesse,
> Beautee and Youthe, Bauderie, Richesse,
> Charmes and Force, Lesynges, Flaterye,
> Despense, Bisynesse, and Jalousye,
> That wered of yelewe gooldes a gerland,
> And a cokkow sittynge on hir hand;
> Festes, instrumentz, caroles, daunces,
> Lust and array, and alle the circumstaunces
> Of love. (1925–33)

Much of this recalls Guillaume de Lorris's and Jean de Meun's *Romance of the Rose*: love's prerequisites are youth, beauty, wealth, joy, charms, dancing, and music. Just as lovesickness demonstrates noble self-fashioning, so does conspicuous consumption for the sake of love—spending much, dressing well. Significantly, only those with wealth and leisure (the upper classes or aspiring bourgeoisie) can adopt this code. Love, like pleasure, appears a class privilege. The conventions of noble love thereby delineate class differences, excluding commoners and reinforcing a naturalized social hierarchy.[71] Yet Chaucer interweaves this exclusionary ideology with social realities: flattery, jealousy, force, and deceit. This list recapitulates the narrative unity of sexual desire and force. It also hints at a recurrent point of tension in Chaucer's (and many of his contemporaries') constructions of sexuality: social conditions that foster masculine perfidy (deceit, flattery) and feminine victimization.[72] As Chaucer sets the ideals of nobility against these social realities, love comes to seem a class distinction of dubious worth.

The temple mural locates all of this in the garden of pleasure, with Idleness at the gate. The personifications of Plesaunce, Hope, and company, the garden with its porter, all vividly recall the *Romance of the Rose* and anticipate its Venus and Cupid. This anticipation grows into certainty when Chaucer notes that Venus dwells on "the mount of Citheroun" (1936), where, in Jean de Meun's *Romance of the Rose*, she attempts to seduce Adonis before participating in the lover's denouement. But Chaucer cheats the reader's expectation and replaces the French deities with the mythographers' Venus *anadyomene* and blind Cupid. In the explicit context of noble love, the switch is arresting:

> The statue of Venus, glorious for to se,
> Was naked, fletynge in the large see,
> And fro the navele doun al covered was
> With wawes grene, and brighte as any glas.
> A citole in hir right hand hadde she,[73]
> And on hir heed, ful semely for to se,
> A rose gerland, fressh and wel smellynge;
> Above hir heed hir dowves flikerynge.
> Biforn hire stood hir sone Cupido;
> Upon his shuldres wynges hadde he two,
> And blynd he was, as it is often seene;
> A bowe he bar and arwes brighte and kene.
> (1955–66)

The emphasis on light and color, on the music and fresh flowers, recalls courtly aesthetics. Yet Chaucer once again represents not a spectacle of noble wealth but a naked sensuality. In this temple, as in the *House of Fame*, he strips away the medieval fictional embellishments over the classical deities. Removing the garments denoting class privileges, elegance, and expense, he pictures what they cover over. Beneath the elaborate rituals and exalted aspirations of noble love, beneath the claims to class exclusivity, we find, quite simply, sensuality, the human trait that, like death, levels king and peasant.

Chaucer's iconology thus opens the heart of chivalric love, and there he stops. The very choice of iconology makes moral judgment uncertain, enigmatic: this imagery signifies sensuality but not judgments about sensuality, certainly not a verdict against a class-specific carnality. A contemporary courtly audience need not notice Chaucer's implicit social critique, for several reasons. It is quite possible that the Knight and his youthful heroes point to a recognizably old-fashioned chivalry, for the definition of gentility in Chaucer's time is shifting away from its military basis.[74] This emphasis would perhaps distance the critique from the immediate audience. The classicizing context also potentially distances the subject of sensuality, referring it to the pagan past. To critique noble love through mythic iconology in a classicizing romance is, in any event, to critique it with surpassing tact and deftness.[75] Though the context insists on class exclusivity, moreover, the mythographic images of Venus and Cupid universalize sensual love, creating an equivocation between the context of noble love and the generalized images of sensuality. The temple and images of the deities, taken together, confuse a class-exclusive code and a human condition. The iconology (like the tale) confuses past and present, pagan and Christian, ancient and chivalric. The tale suspends us between the lot of "pilgrymes, passynge to and fro" (2848) and that of knights who "haddest gold ynough" (2836). And in the end, for all their universality, the images of Venus and Cupid belong to a high poetic style, a mythic register. As John Boswell claims about an analogous context, putting sex into the register of myth elevates it: it lends to the representation of sex the "connotations of mythological sanctions, cultural superiority, and personal refinement."[76] The poetic register of myth heightens the ambiguous implications of the mythographic iconology.

In the *Knight's Tale*, Chaucer once again juxtaposes mythographic iconology and courtly conventions of sexual love, welding together commentary and romance traditions. He once again refuses to privilege a single established construction of the deities. This implication is reinforced by the tale's obvious denaturalization of the courtly Cupid. As Theseus asserts,

> The god of love, a benedicite!
> How myghty and how greet a lord is he!
> Ayeyns his myght ther gayneth none obstacles.
> He may be cleped a god for his myracles,
> For he kan maken, at his owene gyse,
> Of everich herte as that hym list divyse.
> . . .
> Who may been a fool but if he love?
> Bihoold, for Goddes sake that sit above,

> Se how they blede! Be they noght wel arrayed?
> Thus hath hir lord, the god of love, ypayed
> Hir wages and hir fees for hir servyse!
> (1785–90, 1799–1803)

Every youth must serve this god, he continues, but the mighty god in time loosens his grip. The courtly god of love is relegated to a temporary tyranny—and then subordinated to Venus. In this tale, sexual love chiefly pertains to Mars and Venus, not to the French god of love.

As the *Knight's Tale* fits the classicizing iconology into a well-developed description lifted straight out of medieval romance, the close proximity of these two perspectives creates a powerfully unresolved tension. The whole description suspends us between the pagan past and contemporary Christian customs, as well as between human nature and class-specific ideologies of sexual love. Chaucer thus leads us in this temple (as in the tale) to adopt shifting and unstable perspectives on sexual love, which we view as at once pagan and Christian, universal and exclusionary. Adopting these multiple perspectives, we discover alternatives to the Knight's aestheticized sensuality; the values of the noble lovers become questionable, contingent. The juxtaposition of mythographic and romance conventions challenges the assumptions of both.

Ephemeral Hermeneutics: Lydgatean Poetry and Commentary

Among English poets, Lydgate's works exemplify what we might think of as more typical deployments of the authoritative, scholarly regulatory systems begotten by mythographers. Rarely trusting images of Venus and Cupid to the reader's imagination, Lydgate includes mythographic commentary on their portraits in *Troybook* and *Reason and Sensuality*. One manuscript of *Reason and Sensuality* has in addition extensive Latin annotations on the action; the seemingly ample authorial direction must have appeared inadequate.[77] *The Assembly of Gods, or the Accord of Reason and Sensuality in the Fear of Death*, once attributed to Lydgate,[78] similarly depends on mythographic modes of thought. The poem is most likely not Lydgate's, but it neatly exemplifies a variation on his strategies for dealing with myth. Each of these poems illustrates a reliance on mythography that reverses Chaucer's erasure of hermeneutic commentary. Even so, these poems are not all cut from one bolt, and they also offer us both disparate views of poetry and diverse evocations of interpretive authority. Given his restless experimentation with new interpretations and strategies of interpretation, in fact, Lydgate foregrounds problems of interpretation and authority, a central issue in much late medieval English poetry. He and the author of the *Assembly of Gods* may help to reveal points of stress where Latin hermeneutics meet vernacular poetry—points that Chaucer's deft play with multiple traditions might induce us to overlook.

The *Troybook* pictures a slightly modified image of the *anadyomene*. Explicating it, Lydgate demonstrates that poets, like mythographers, enjoy considerable interpretive license. Here the doves signify the innocence and cleanness of honest love (not, as Fulgentius would have it, ardent avian coitus); the red roses picture the freshness and fervor (not the shame) of young love, which fades in wintry old age; and the sea indicates the calms and storms, the mutable adversities, of love (2.2521–48). The image authorizes ardent youthful sexual passion. Since this image introduces the judgment of Paris, Lydgate hedges his sanction: although youth is the age of Venus, the man who chooses "lust" forsakes knighthood (2.2830–35). The overall import of the image and the conjoined sanction and warning recall the tenor and double attitude of much late medieval mythography. Also as in mythography, the image itself cannot predict the distinct features of the writer's often ambivalent attitudes toward sexuality. Significantly, Lydgate appropriates for the poet the role of commentator by including the mythographic image and the gloss in the text of the poem. Glosses often interrupt medieval poems, appearing as a block in the column of verse; Lydgate turns the gloss into part of the verse. He consolidates verse and gloss, presenting the author as sole authority over poetic meaning.

Lydgate is not wedded to a particular image, explanation, or strategy. His *Reason and Sensuality* portrays the deities according to stock courtly conventions—not surprisingly, since this poem renders into English the French "Love's Chess Game" (*Les Echecs amoureux*). Here Venus displays above all a noble social status:

> Queynte of array, who lyst take hede,
> A cote y-lacyd al of Rede,
> Rycher than outher silke or golde . . .
> But wel I wot, men myghte se
> Hir shappe throgh-out, so was hit maked,
> Lych as she had in soth be naked;

> A lace of golde, ful ryche at al,
> Gyrt about hir medil smal,
> On her fyngres everychon
> Rynges with many ryche ston.
> (1555–57, 1562–68)

As the description proceeds, she gains a chaplet of roses (but, the narrator notes, no kerchief over her hair), a fiery brand, a golden apple, and flocks of doves. Although this image and the *anadyomene* develop out of similar classical models and overlap to some extent, we can easily discern separate emphases in the medieval representational conventions. One expresses a seemingly natural sexuality, and the other emphasizes the artificiality of cultured sexual love. Where the mythographers aim to strip poetic fictions away from the deities, romance writers strive, as here, after fictional embellishment. Mythography turns the deities into figures of sensual love; romances make them patrons of the literary love conventions belonging to the gentle classes. Courtly traditions often suggest that the deities' wealthy dress and noble accoutrements correspond to the dictum that only the noble can love. In their fictional trappings of wealth and nobility, the king and queen of love picture less the moral end of sensuality than its social setting.

Lydgate does not leave this iconology to the mercies of our unaided understanding. The goddess Diana explicates it, and she proves an unsympathetic mythographer determined to advance a rigorous sexual code. Diana's etymology derives *venus* from *venym* (3386–88). This analysis of contemporary French conventions in terms of a conceptual model developed for ancient literature demonstrates one way of combining courtly imagery with mythographic commentary. Even given Diana's extensive commentary within the poem, one scribe finds interpretation inadequately directed, and consequently supplements Diana's exposition with marginal Latin mythographic formulas. Where Diana reads Venus as *venym*, the scribe informs us that this is "Venus, goddess of pleasure" ("venus dea voluptatis," gloss to 3383). Similarly, the scribe glosses Venus's first appearance with this condensed version of mythography: "Venus, that is concupiscence of the flesh or a planet that inclines to concupiscence, and signifies the life of pleasure due to the flesh."[79] Mythographic hermeneutics can, as here, become mechanical displays of shallow learning. This scribal explication, even more than Diana's analysis, implies that we should read Venus according to some stable moral system, yet the very doubling of authoritative systems finally calls them into question. Although neither Diana nor the scribe actually constrains the more ambiguous and interesting implications of the poem itself, the text with its scribal additions exposes attempts to grant priority to authoritative (mythographic) systems of interpretation.

Lydgate at times permits images of the deities to enter more fully into the play of poetic meaning. For instance, the *Temple of Glass* initially refers to Venus, quite sketchily, as the *anadyomene*: "she sate fleting in the se" (53). The lovers in the poem describe her as a planet, a star of comforting light. The narrator eventually depicts Venus as a unified carnal and spiritual force, a planetary goddess holding tightly to the fiery chain of eternal love. None of these descriptions gains a mythographic commentary, and each complicates the deity's import. The Venuses of *Troybook*, *Reason and Sensuality*, and *Temple of Glass* exemplify once again the range of refigurations and reinterpretations possible even for one writer. Lydgate at one point develops an iconographic commentary for a mythographic image, at another point applies etymology to a courtly image, and at still another point offers an astrologized *anadyomene* without a mythographic gloss. Even more obviously than Chaucer, Lydgate continually describes and deciphers the deities anew, combining and revising traditions to suit his immediate purposes. And scribes may in turn always supplement any of these artistic decisions with "correct" interpretations.

The Lydgatean *Assembly of Gods* begins with descriptions of the Olympian deities, not in their mythographic nudity but apparelled as medieval nobility. These portraits eventually gain an authoritative explication, but only after a delay that introduces a functional occasion of interpretive uncertainty. In accordance with courtly conventions, Cupid embodies nothing so much as an aristocratic display of wealth:

> Then was there set the god Cupido,
> All fresshe & galaunt & costlew in aray.
> With ouches & rynges he was beset so
> The paleys therof shone as though hit had be day.
> A kerchyef of plesaunce stood over hys helme ay.
> The goddesse Ceres he lookyd in the face
> And with oon arme he hyr dyd enbrace.
>
> (295–301)

Likewise, Venus imitates a romance heroine:

> Dame Venus with colour crystallyne,
> Whoos long here shone as wyre of goold bryght.
> Cryspe was her skyn, her eyen columbyne,
> Ravysshyd myn hert her chere was so lyght.
> Patronesse of plesaunce, be namyd well se myght.
> A smokke was her wede, garnysshyd curyously.
> But above all other she had a wanton ey.
>
> On her hede she weryd a rede copyr crowne.
> A nosegay she had made full pleasauntly.
>
> (372–80)

Venus and Cupid seem, most of all, living humans. In them the poet animates the life of "plesaunce," a life dependent on the wealth and leisure detailed here. They are not allegorical abstractions; Lechery and Sensuality enter under separate cover. Throughout the middle section of the poem (an allegorical battle of the vices and virtues), we are left to our own understanding of the initial poetic images. Then Doctrine, like any mythographer, strips away the false poetic fables to reveal the Christian truth. This turns out to be the mythographers' historical explanation: ancient poets recounted fables, but rural folk misunderstood them and worshipped the humans divinized in the tales. Paganism arises from literalist misreadings of figurative language. The opening images of the deities anticipate this explication: the gods and goddesses seem human because they were originally human. Thus the poet ultimately advances a commonplace mythographic explanation of the pagan deities, though this commentary does not actually constrain the narrative description. Venus's copper crown, for instance, refers not to historicizing but to astrological explanations. A single hermeneutic proves inadequate to address the narrative unity of diverse conventions.

Throughout the middle section of the poem, before Doctrine's intervention, the portraits of the deities illustrate the inescapable ambiguity of poetry as well as the dangers of misreading. The initial poetic images invite the audience to duplicate the pagan misreading—to understand these figures literally, as deities. Doctrine's deferred correction comes as a shock, enforcing the message that literature remains always "derke as a myste, or a feynyd fable" (1988). The poem finally argues that each and every poetic figure requires the mediation of Doctrine, of an authoritative system of reading: an impossible recipe for poetry, but a superb witness to anxieties about poetic fables. The *Assembly of Gods* does not follow its own recipe, but, like some of Lydgate's poetry, it does quite aptly illustrate how mythographic hermeneutics may be manipulated in attempts to stabilize poetic figures. Lydgate and this poet together indicate that mythographic modes of thought are entirely commonplace in late medieval culture, always available for new appropriations.

Contested Interpretations

While mythographers can be poets, ignoring conventional hermeneutics and inventing their own symbolic systems (I think especially of Bernard Silvestris, Boccaccio, and Christine de Pizan), poets and scribes can follow standard mythographic hermeneutics slavishly. Particularly in the later Middle Ages, a vast terrain exists on which poetic and mythographic discourses intermingle, and on which the relative values of ambiguity and clarity, of symbolic suggestiveness and moral specificity, are contested. Chaucer and Lydgate fully establish that poets respond diversely to the mythographers' interpretive models. If Chaucer grants free interpretive authority to his audiences, Lydgate and the author of the *Assembly of Gods* both to some extent, in some places, limit audience authority. All of them, however, set poets in the authoritative place of commentators; all contest the ascendancy of separate Latin interpretive systems. We would do well to read such contests simply as contests, seeking to understand what issues of interpretive authority or representation are at stake, seeking to appreciate where authority or meaning is rendered questionable and how. Obviously, mythography does not constitute an invariably privileged and invulnerable way of reading in this milieu. Even for Lydgate, it offers no more than convenient suggestions about interpretive models.

Mythographies and poems alike draw our attention to the deities' potential for refiguration and multivalence. The great beauty of the *anadyomene* and blind Cupid is in fact their essential ambiguity, their capacity to absorb meaning from their contexts. Mythography and ancient literature may influence the imagery, but each poetic context creates meaning anew—as each mythographic context does. Traditions do not, after all, determine the nuances and implications of any literary moment; rather, unique literary contexts always create traditions anew. Mythography and poetry alike therefore advise us to listen for the "uniqueness of a literary phenomenon," and not to heed the sirens singing of an "atemporal continuity of tradition."[80]

As poets combine and recombine diverse traditions, they illuminate the familiar in unfamiliar ways, teaching us to see the everyday from novel perspectives. Each literary context to some extent denaturalizes conventions. Through Lydgate's verse, we stumble on not always brilliant juxtapositions of courtly and mythographic conventions, appeals to what seem at times merely diverse explanatory and representational models. Lydgate also reveals a very circumspect integration of commentary and poetic conventions, a cautious poetic arrogation of the right to gloss references to the deities. Through Chaucer's poems, we discover suggestive affinities among seemingly disparate ideals of sexual love, sensuality, class ideologies, and poetry. He introduces mythographic, courtly, and cosmological conventions to each other, and all are enlarged by their meeting. As significantly, with the *House of Fame* (and then again and variously with *Parliament of Fowls*, *Troilus and Criseyde*, the *Prologue* to the *Legend of Good Women*), Chaucer becomes the poet of Venus and Cupid. Later English treatments of the deities often respond not only to his essentially humanist and classicizing poetic project but also to his self-definition as the Ovid of English poetry. At the center of that project, Chaucer and consequently his successors place Venus and Cupid, figures much enriched by their long passage through the byways of mythography, the invocations of poets, and the celebration of courtly rites.

Chapter 5

Myths of a Venereal Nature

> I, being born a woman and distressed
> By all the needs and notions of my kind,
> Am urged by your propinquity to find
> Your person fair, and feel a certain zest
> To bear your body's weight upon my breast:
> So subtly is the fume of life designed,
> To clarify the pulse and cloud the mind,
> And leave me once again undone, possessed.
>   Edna St. Vincent Millay

> Biologically man takes the initiative. Woman receives and is feminine.
>   Dr. Graham Leonard, bishop of London (1985), quoted by
>   Joan Smith, *Misogynies: Reflections on Myths and Malice*

Modern critics sometimes distinguish between mythographic (moralized) and astrological Venuses, with the former generally "bad" and the latter vaguely "good." The antithesis, of course, oversimplifies both hermeneutics. Many later medieval mythographies include astrological commentary, confounding any strict difference between the discourses; and moralizing no more consistently produces a wholly "bad" Venus than, to anticipate the argument of this chapter, astrology develops an utterly "good" one. In practice, moral and astrological hermeneutics are anything but mutually exclusive. As we have discovered already, both mythographic and poetic appeals to natural orders serve to rationalize and justify moral orders. By appealing to a natural order—whether in astrology, physiology, medicine, theology, canon or civil law, mythography, or poetry—writers present sexuality as part of an unalterable and inherent universal order.[1] Ideological systems and values are nonetheless always embedded in ideas of nature, for nature is a cultural invention, in the Middle Ages as now.[2] Part of the hermeneutic value of nature is simply that it presents these ideological systems as objective and immutable facts. This is not to deny the technical side of astrology, which continues to receive valuable study in relation to literature, but to remind us that technical details are not the whole of any science.[3] As the category of nature provides a seemingly unalterable basis for many contingent sexual and moral codes, the particular human orders appear divinely and eternally authorized. When Venus's meaning lies in the book of nature, therefore, medieval readers discern a singularly authorized sexuality—though that does not prevent their discerning many different sexualities.

Medieval natural hermeneutics for Venus exhibit an inherent double character from their basis in both ancient Roman nature religion and eastern astrology.[4] In keeping with the ancient traditions, mythographers generally explain the deities either as anthropomorphized natural forces (as when Jupiter represents thunder; Venus, sensual passion; and Saturn, time) or as planets that exercise particular influences over material nature. Although the Greek Eros was once a revered and powerful cosmogonic generative force, Cupid never gained a similar Roman prominence.[5] Natural interpretation typically has nothing to say about him. With Venus, the syncretic character of the Roman heritage often renders the precise nature of nature ambiguous. That is, ideas about innate sexual impulses and about astral influences over sexuality overlap, and we cannot always specify which one is relevant to any particular representation. We encounter this confusion with Boccaccio's attempt to separate "astral" and "moralized" Venuses, which leaves both Venuses symbolizing equivocally interrelated forces of nature. Obviously, it is not always possible to distinguish between a specifically astral Venus and a less clearly defined natural force. Venus may refer us at once to astrology and a "law of kynde," to external influences over material bodies and to an internal force of sexual desire. In her the origins of sexual desire look equivocal, at once within and without. Throughout the Middle Ages, this central ambiguity in the natural Venus testifies to her complex ancient origins in nature religion and astrology (and, as we will find, to diverse ideas about the origins of sexual desire).

The fact that many natural interpretations indirectly implicate astrology furthers the potential for ambiguity.[6] In scientific-natural explanations of Venus and sexuality, for instance, we discover that medicine and humor physiology alike are linked to astrology: medicine depends on a theory of humors bound up in a cosmology that includes astral influences.[7] (Thus Chaucer's Physician studies astronomy.) Any discussion of sexual and reproductive physiology explicitly or implicitly, wittingly or not, involves astrology. Hence astrology to some extent provides the scientific basis of medieval natural interpretations whether or not Venus appears specifically as a planet. This is true even for medieval writers who oppose astrology as an element of pagan superstition, since astrology cannot be entirely eliminated from the natural sciences. For example, although Isidore of Seville objects to some aspects of astrology, he accepts the connection between astral influences and the body, and he includes medicine and astrology in the quadrivium.[8] Likewise, the immensely and enduringly popular *Secretum secretorum* directs us to astrology for the maintenance of good health.[9] Although astrology provokes much controversy in the Middle Ages, a pragmatic acceptance of some astral influence over human life was unquestionably commonplace.

Medieval astrology is not particularly scientific before the time of the Crusades, when Europe rediscovered key Greek texts in Arabic translations.[10] Two major authorities, Ptolemy (second century C.E.) and Abu Ma'shar (787–886, known as Albumasar in the Latin west), were translated in the twelfth century and quickly achieved preeminence.[11] These and other translations provoked in mythography as in many other discourses a sudden interest in the stars, and from the twelfth through the fifteenth century astrology fostered a particular kind of mythographic classicism: scientific explanations of the pagan deities. In time, interest in science gave way in some quarters to suspicion of Arabic learning, linked in some minds with the supposedly fatalistic paganism of the medieval Latin west. Mythographic and poetic negotiations of astrology, as of any other ancient hermeneutic, thus reveal the shifting contexts and politics of classicism. Despite their historical fluctuations, however, astrological or simply natural interpretations of the deities repeatedly serve to delineate a seemingly fixed and manifest cosmic reality, an authoritative and indisputable truth.

Little of the science ever entered mythography, which even in the later Middle Ages typically displays an attraction to the hermeneutic potential of the stars rather than detailed information about astrology. Alberic may serve to exemplify this tendency. Writing when translation provoked renewed interest in astrology, he offers an astrological interpretation of a scene in Virgil's *Aeneid* that reveals a very generalized notion of planetary influences: Venus, a beneficent planet, mediates the harmful influences of Mars and Saturn (harmful in the sense of injurious to erotic desire).[12] What we meet with most often in mythography as in poetry is either this sort of popularized science or a philosophized astrology. For metaphysical readings of the stars, mythographers and poets were indebted not to astrologers but to natural philosophers such as Boethius (ca. 480–524) and Nicole Oresme (d. 1382), who defined the limits of astral influences, their subordination to providence, and their relation to human free will.[13] This is the intellectual basis for the astrology we discover in ecclesiastical iconology throughout the later Middle Ages, implying the all-encompassing order of the Christian universe.[14] In sum, medieval astrology presents us on the one hand with a science having usually hidden ideological implications, and on the other with overtly ideological deployments of that science.

Representations of the planetary deities necessarily negotiate a complex set of relations between Christianity and paganism, between human free will and destinal influences, and among philosophy, theology, and science. In natural interpretations of Venus, whether specifically astrological or not, what is most clearly at stake—and often most clear—is ideologies of sex. Mythography and poetry alike depend on the seemingly fixed authority of nature to articulate in the planetary deity the ever-changing historical and personal constructions of sexual desire. As we have already found, many medieval writers represent Venus and Cupid so as to legitimate a naturally irresistible youthful sexual appetite; many depict the deities so that sexuality appears a natural, innate compulsion, regardless of age.[15] The deities may likewise serve to authorize as natural procreation, sexual pleasure, heterosexual intercourse in the "missionary" position, homosexuality, physical pollution, incest, adultery, or the madness of sexual passion. The labels "natural" and "unnatural" depend on context. They define ideological agendas, not absolutes in human behavior or social values.[16] When these distinct moralities are defined as natural, though, they seem to express a universal and unchanging morality. Of course, the concept of nature is no more unified than that of morality and, as we have already discovered, ideas of natural sexuality vary considerably. Natural interpretations, like others, are always interested, bound to particular contexts, and political. Writers may invoke nature to rationalize sexuality, to legitimate certain sexualities, to universalize specific moral codes or social mores, or to dictate the relations between the individual and society. Nature is not a stable objective order but a human construct—in mythography, not surprisingly, a series of constructs—revealing ideological biases.

With this principle established, we may take up the question of how ideologies inhere in particular representations. As we will find, the basic mythographic hermeneutics disclose interested negotiations of natural sexualities; in particular, astral physiology in both mythography and poetry manifests class and gender biases embedded in ideas of nature. The planetary influence of Venus need not, democratically, affect all alike and equally. Familiarity with the natural traditions will therefore allow us to appreciate anew how science may legitimate or undermine or simply complicate social mores.

Natural Sexualities

Natural hermeneutics manifest a persuasive power and flexibility in their mythographic contexts, and several examples may help to clarify and make more specific the ways in which these hermeneutics may be used to encode ideological imperatives. Besides offering astrological readings of epic literature, Alberic develops a number of more general natural interpretations. With the story of Venus and Adonis, Alberic focuses on the image of Venus weeping for her slain lover:

Remigius says that Venus mourns with flowing tears for Adonis slain by the boar, because the beauty of earth (signified by Venus) mourns for the sun (designated by Adonis) when it descends to its southern zone. The sun was slain by the filth and cold of winter, as if by a boar's tusks. Then the earth brings forth its tears of rain showers and streams.[17]

We might note in passing that this explanation differs from one Alberic offers elsewhere: Remigius's picture of two Venuses, one chaste and the other given to pleasure. The present account forcefully revises Venus's cosmological generative vitality, replacing springtime and exuberant youthful passion with the deprivations of winter. With Venus a symbol of sexual deprivation rather than plenitude, we view the pleasures of spring in retrospect, from the mournful perspective of winter, knowing youthful beauty and pleasure only through their absence. This perspective yields a touching evocation of pleasures realized vividly in their loss. Venus here signifies a precisely articulated natural sexuality: she illustrates an approved passionate feminine sexual desire for the masculine (reading heterosexuality into the book of nature), an endorsed feminine passivity (extending a cultural norm to the cosmos), and an authorized grief for sexual deprivation in a figurative winter of old age (sanctioning youthful sexual pleasure). With this myth of naturalized heterosexuality and feminine passivity, and through the poignant recollection of ephemeral youthful sexuality, Alberic illustrates how natural interpretations naturalize ideology.

Such an encyclopedic text does not, however, produce a strictly unified concept of nature. Venus also represents a beneficent planetary force that may moderate the influence of malevolent planets, in effect fostering sexual desire without consideration for the season of life. She elsewhere symbolizes the physiology and evanescence of *libido* (desire, passion, lust; 155), a universal feature of the postlapsarian human condition.[18] In each case, the appeal to nature makes moral good and social order look indisputable and always everywhere identical, but these various passages collectively witness to contradictions among ideas about natural sexuality. If youthful desire is recalled fondly at one point, at another all desire produces only the "sting of regret" ("poenitudinis stimulus," 155). Repeatedly affirming the immutability of natural orders conceals the mutability of human attitudes toward sexuality. Nature does not provide a fixed moral category; it offers only the illusion of one. Encyclopedism heightens the effect of such contradictions: whereas a moralizing hermeneutic generates a jaded detachment from sexual satiation, a natural hermeneutic invites a desirous memory of the excitement preceding that satiation. The alternation between bliss and woe might best be read as expressing ambivalence. Or, in Shakespeare's far more eloquent words, sexual desire appears "A bliss in proof, and, prov'd, a very woe, / Before, a joy propos'd, behind, a dream."[19] Point of view significantly affects judgment.

Giovanni del Virgilio, with *Ovidian Allegories* (*Allegorie Ovidiane*, ca. 1330–50), may help to trace out how natural interpretations naturalize sexual ideologies. Here the tale of Mars and Venus reveals that people, however virtuous, sometimes fall into *luxuria* (licentiousness, luxury, extravagance), since "victory is rare in this contest."[20] Similarly, in the story of Vulcan and Pallas, Vulcan is a wise man but fights a losing battle against the far-reaching implications of luxuriousness (48). Both tales sympathetically present even the wise and virtuous as naturally susceptible to the whole panoply of vices labeled *luxuria*. Thus Virgilio depicts sexual sin as both inevitable and eminently excusable: nature authorizes a measure of sexual license. At the same time, Virgilio repeatedly pictures sexual desire as the ocean from which Venus was born; immersed in this ocean, men drown in *libido* (for instance, Aesacus, 95; and Diomedes, 101). The recurrent metaphor portrays men as physically helpless and inadequate, diminutive in relation to their vast seas of desire, experiencing a recurrent terror of being consumed, smothered, or drowned. At times the imagery suggests castration anxiety, a masculine fear of the all-swallowing vulva.[21] According to this theme, heterosexual desire is at once unavoidable and terribly fearful: *libido* naturally overwhelms us. (Men are especially, but not exclusively, affected.) A fear of sexual desire accompanies the limited sexual license. Whatever explicit ethical lessons Virgilio advances, his text manifests deep ambivalences about natural sexuality—and a vivid sense that sexual desire is naturally ungovernable.

The undeclared ideologies informing natural interpretations consistently reward investigation, and not only to recover such tacit equivocations and ambivalences. Let us consider evidence of more obviously dominant ideological biases: Virgilio variously explicates a story in which Venus rides a fish across the Euphrates River (*Ovidian Allegories*, 63). The thousand eggs of one fish signify her procreative capacity, or the tale indicates that she was born in the sea, or that she is a salty humor, or that she is like the foam of blood (presumably semen, a combination of blood and hot air according to some theories).[22] A unified concept emerges from these readings, for the procreative capacity is based on the salty humor of blood and on the foamy semen derived from it. (We will return shortly to this physiology; for the moment I want to focus on the ideology advanced under cover of these natural interpretations.) The natural Venus most commonly represents this association of procreation, blood, and semen. This almost invariably serves to justify an idea of naturally procreative sexuality: in other words, the unity of blood, semen, and procreation depicts a sexuality in accord with the most basic orthodox ecclesiastical ideologies—the reproductive teleology of sex. Sexual desire, sexual capacity, and procreation are apparently inextricable. Desire equates with procreation.

This representation of Venus, like many others we have examined, implicitly supports orthodox Catholic ideals of natural sexuality. Various and numerous aspects of sexuality contested in ecclesiastical milieus—

such as theologians' debates over the role of pleasure in a Christian life or canonists' interrogations of the legal niceties of sexual positions and motives for intercourse[23]—simply disappear in such popular representations. What we encounter here is not sophisticated and nuanced theology or canon law but simply the Church's bottom line: procreative sex is natural. As Boccaccio bluntly expresses it in a gloss on the *Teseida*, "all natural couplings [aim] at procreation."[24] The feature of Catholic teaching on sexuality that disseminates most widely is just this division between "natural" (procreative) and "unnatural" (nonprocreative) sexuality.[25] Indeed, preaching and pastoral instruction are typically limited to communicating just this model. Some ecclesiastics worried that more detailed education would teach the ways of deviance. The flip side of this inculcated ignorance is that the laity sometimes believed there was no sin in marital sex.[26] Although the laity generally understood that sexual relations must be natural, a sexually active layperson did not necessarily comprehend just what "nature" dictated in terms of everyday practice. Witness the instruction provided by Chaucer's *Parson's Tale*:

Eek whan man destourbeth concepcioun of a child, and maketh a womman outher bareyne by drynkynge venenouse herbes thurgh which she may nat conceyve, or sleeth a child by drynkes wilfully, or elles putteth certeine material thynges in hire secree places to slee the child, or elles dooth unkyndely synne, by which man or womman shedeth hire nature in manere or in place ther as a child may nat be conceived, or elles if a woman have conceyved, and hurt hirself and sleeth the child, yet is it homycide. (575–76)

The Parson's indefinite terms ("drynkes," "material thynges," "unkyndely synne") do not tell anyone how to commit these sins against nature, though the whole clearly prescribes a normative model of procreative intercourse. Youthful sexual desire and activity are perhaps widely celebrated or excused precisely because they do not necessarily transgress against this, the most essential rule (though adolescent sexual activity was not necessarily believed always to coincide with reproductive capacity).[27]

The distance is great between the widespread and popular idea of a vaguely natural procreative sexuality and the theological calculations of the hierarchical degrees of sinfulness pertaining to sexual positions, motives for seeking sexual intercourse, and various kinds of physical pleasure. While the Church obviously shaped the most widely acknowledged ideology of natural sex, it purposefully exercised a limited role in influencing lay understandings of sexuality. Representations of Venus (and many other portrayals of sexuality) typically offer up far simpler notions of natural sexuality than those developed by theologians and canonists. Consequently, with Venus and Cupid we discover how the rule of procreation could be united with commonplace social mores—such as the irresistibility of youthful desire, the enjoyment of physical pleasure, and the expression of love. Hence the deities of love help to disclose how medieval constructions of sexuality mediate among lay practices and discourses and the various ecclesiastical discourses (theological, pastoral, homiletic) that invent "natural" sexuality.

Alberic, Giovanni del Virgilio, and Chaucer's Parson all demonstrate the power of humans to find in the cosmos itself support for their truths. In defining natural sexualities, each presents particular norms—youthful sexual pleasures, the overwhelming force of sexual desire, a union of desire and procreation—in the guise of universal facts, as if derived from a rational investigation of nature. With each case, the final authority of nature precludes challenges to the moral and social orders promoted. Ideas of nature, like other hermeneutic categories, nonetheless manifest the proposed joys, remembered surfeits, psychic anxieties, equivocations, and ambivalences inherent in any discussion of human sexuality.

Ideology and Physiology

Natural hermeneutics may vary widely, but many depend on standard concepts of astrology and physiology. The sexual physiology associated with Venus is fairly straightforward and constitutes perhaps the most widely known of the medieval natural explanations: the planet reigns over sexuality because it governs heat and moisture. According to most medieval medical theories, sexual desire results from superfluous physical moisture, especially from an excess of blood, the bodily fluid (and the humor) identified with heat and moisture.[28] Thus iconology pictures Luxury displaying an excess of blood.[29] Since innate heat and moisture govern the accumulation of this superfluity, Venus's sway over those qualities typically defines her power over sexual desire. In fact, correspondences of humors, elements, and planets are anything but consistent throughout the period, yet the mythographic planetary Venus characteristically governs the excess warmth and moisture that produce sexual appetite.[30] As a more general natural force, she signifies the end effect but not the causal chain. This set of associations requires no remarkable faith in astrology and was widely reported in the early Middle Ages as well as later. The basic link between Venus, warmth, and moisture emerges in natural interpretations in the works of Fulgentius, Isidore, and Alberic.[31] Accordingly, Venus's marriage to Vulcan indicates that venereal works require heat, figured by the smith's fire.[32] The union of Venus, warmth, and moisture often becomes explicitly astrological in later texts. Though neither Pierre Bersuire nor Thomas Walsingham shows particular interest in astrology, for instance, both mention that Venus is literally a planet and associated with warmth (Vulcan's fire) and moisture (the sea), elements that together arouse concupiscence.[33] This connection also produces a vegetable Venus: Naevius notes that "eating 'Venus that has felt Vulcan's power,'" is an allegory about consuming "boiled vegetables."[34]

This basic sexual physiology readily supports a mandate of procreative intercourse, for sexual desire and procreation depend on an identical balance of humors and heat. The conditions that allow for procreation—temperate heat, temperate moisture—also sustain sexual vigor. In the natural order, then, sexual appetite, pleasure, and procreation appear to constitute a unity. According to this scientific model, there is no procreation without sensual delight. On the other hand, a deficiency in heat or moisture produces both a lack of desire and sterility. This was theoretically supposed to happen in old age, when a loss in bodily heat and blood were thought to predict and explain sexual incapacity.[35] According to this physiology, the process of aging eventually brings about sexual restraint (which permits wisdom and religiosity to flourish). Natural order makes youth the proper time for sexual activity, but also perhaps the only time. "Gather ye rosebuds while ye may"—"when youth and blood are warmer"[36]—takes on a certain urgency in this scheme of things, for warmth, like time, is always fleeting. Medieval explanations of natural sexuality prepare the ground for a Renaissance flowering of *carpe diem* verse.

As mythographers develop the sexual physiology that constitutes this normative mythographic outline of Venus's natural-astral import, they often explicitly recognize its implications for the rational "care of the self," to borrow a phrase from Foucault. Fulgentius witnesses to the most common mythographic formulation. He explicates the fable of Venus's birth as a story about physiological processes:

> a piece of poetic folly meaning nothing less than that Saturn is called Chronos in Greek, for in Greek *chronos* is the word for time. The powers of the seasons, that is, crops, are totally cut off by the scythe and, cast into the liquids of the belly, as it were into the sea, needs must produce lust. For abundance of satiety creates lust, as Terence says: "Venus grows cold without Ceres and Bacchus." (*Fulgentius the Mythographer*, 66)[37]

The effects of food and wine follow inexorably from the standard physiology: food and especially wine produce moisture and heat, and consequently sexual desire. Fulgentius identifies a lucid causal chain behind the universal quality of *libido*, the inherent flaw that mars all postlapsarian men and women.[38] The food and wine that sustain life also foster sensuality. At the same time, the apparent universality is undercut by the association between Venus and a specific kind of plenitude—an abundance of food and drink—possible only for the wealthy: she connotes *luxuria* in the economic sense of the word, as well as in its sexual sense. It seems that the wealthy alone can afford the sexual desire of which all are guilty.

Fulgentius cites Terence as his authority for this yoking of Venus, Ceres, and Bacchus. Much earlier in the history of mythography, Cicero also cited Terence, and the line reappears over and over in medieval (and later) texts: Isidore, the Second Vatican Mythographer, William of Conches, Bernard Silvestris, Alberic, and Walsingham (to name a few) all repeat it.[39] Similarly, the mythic trio guarantees love in the *Eve of St. Venus* (*Pervigilium Veneris*).[40] They suggest much the same in Chaucer's *Parliament of Fowls* (275–76). The idea of food and wine creating sexual desire is also widely recounted without the mythological representatives. Alan of Lille in the *Plaint of Nature* argues that food boils up into lust.[41] Chaucer's Pardoner contends that "the fyr of lecherye ... / is annexed unto glotonye" (*Pardoner's Tale*, 481–82)—this after the pilgrims have stopped for food and drink.[42] Gower in *Confessio Amantis* attributes sexual desire to Cupid's brand heating the stomach (5.1485–88). Because wine especially stimulates sexual appetite, it may serve as a remedy for lovesickness, which is to say that sexual intercourse may cure lovesickness. Interestingly, roses and myrtle are also remedies for lovesickness and imply the same cure.[43] The direct cause-and-effect relationship between food and sex persists into the seventeenth century with Ben Jonson's epigram "On Gut":

> Thus in his belly can he change a sin:
> Lust it comes out, that gluttony went in.[44]

With some transmutations the reputed intimacy of food and sex retains its vitality through the nineteenth century, when Mr. Graham's crackers and Mr. Kellogg's cereal flakes were supposed to curb sexual desire and youthful masturbation.[45] The idea may now be in its decadence.

This astral-physiological explanation of sexual desire establishes the grounds and limits of self-control. The most likely method of sexual control suggested by this physiology is diet: a diet of cold and dry elements was often (not always) thought to suppress sexual desire. The well-known link between food, wine, and sexual desire therefore encourages religious fasting and temperance. Just as eating and drinking create sexual desire, fasting diminishes it.[46] Mythographers may explicitly or implicitly develop this idea. For example, Boccaccio notes that fasting people, weakened in their natural powers, rarely desire intercourse, and he several times draws attention to the connection between food and sexual desire.[47] He unites an explanation of causes with the means of self-governance. (If one aspires to sainthood, or to monastic sanctity, this is only the starting line in the lifelong marathon to arrive at perfect chastity.) We might compare the very different use of food in cures for lovesickness, treatments that according to the mythographers' physiology would stimulate sexual desire.[48] The treatment again likely implies coitus as the cure for lovesickness. Plainly, diet may serve many purposes in the pursuit of sexual control, for it promises (through lengthy discipline—this is no quick fix) a means of manipulating the fluid balances that foster or inhibit physical desire. In brief, then, the natural Venus may refer us to the astral-physiological origins of sexual desire, and to the impact of feast or famine on desire. She introduces us as well to problematic methods of controlling sensuality.

Children of the Planet

As a planetary force, Venus particularly affects the physical and psychic orientation of those born under her sway, the "children of the planet." The idea of children of the planets comes into prominence in the late fourteenth century, and raises in a slightly different way the questions of self-governance implicit in Venus's primary natural influence.[49] Chaucer offers in the *Squire's Tale* a verbal image of the planet's children that may serve to outline the basic pictorial tradition. The "Tartre kyng," Cambyuskan, enters his Presence Chamber,

> Ther as they sownen diverse instrumentz
> That it is lyk an hevene for to heere.
> Now dauncen lusty Venus children deere,
> For in the Fyssh hir lady sat ful hye,
> And looketh on hem with a freendly ye.
>
> (270–74)

In the sky above her children sits Venus with her astrological signs or zodiacal houses—here, Pisces, a sign in which she is especially powerful. On earth, children of the planet manifest their sanguinity: dancing, making music, showing their "lusty" character. Chaucer's image is perhaps most intriguing for its immediate ambiguities, its lack of clues to an explanatory discourse. Does it refer to philosophical discussions about free will? To medical accounts of the age and physical conditions requisite for amorous activities? To ecclesiastical disapproval of astrology and (Arabic) astral determinism? To all or none of these? The phrase "lyk an hevene" holds us in suspense among the possibilities of censure or sanction.[50] Once again, Chaucer simply presents an image, relying on the context to associate it with other marvels of an eastern aristocracy—brass horses that function as magic carpets, mirrors that reveal the truth, and rings that decode the speech of birds. The sensuality of the scene dramatically portrays Venus's children as aristocratic youth: young people dancing, wining and dining, filled with "lustiheed" and "jolitee." The idea of "children of the planet" here seems a consummate eastern and aristocratic fiction, a fable about oriental sensuality and magic and nobility. Astrology permits Chaucer to characterize the east as both mysterious other and familiar hierarchical home.

Although Christine de Pizan does not elaborate an astrological explanation of Venus—indeed, she continually calls attention to the fact that she passes over such interpretations—the *Epistle of Othea* clearly if briefly indicates the star's influence over its children.[51] This may help further to fill in the pictorial tradition. The illustrative program for the *Epistle* includes miniatures of each of the planetary deities and their children; according to Millard Meiss, this constitutes the first known instance of the visual motif.[52] In these illustrations, Venus is pictured fashionably dressed, gathering in her lap the hearts of her children, while on earth comparably stylish men and women hold their hearts up to her. At least one manuscript offers a caption: pagans worshipped Venus as goddess of love because the planet influences amorousness.[53] We might remark that Venus here reigns not over the sexual organs, as we might expect from scientifically oriented discussions of her astral influence, but over the heart. This forms an apparently standard association in zodiacal illustrations.[54] Accordingly, Christine's Venus influences sensual and aristocratic heterosexual love rather than exercising her more typically limited mythographic force over sexual desire. In other words, Christine conflates desire and love: sexual desire and sexual acts express love. That the couples and Venus are pictured in courtly guise restricts sensual love to a social class, and Venus presides once again over a specifically courtly sensuality. Nobles appear by native right children of the planet, an ideological imperative having nothing to do with the science of the stars. While commenting on Venus, Christine passes over the opportunity to moralize about sexuality in order to warn her audience, the young *chevalier*, against indulging in idleness and vanity. She perceives little if any danger in sensual love itself—love improves the noble man (she is here silent about its consequences for women)—but she recognizes a considerable threat in the leisure and vanity that invite young men to love and may lead them into more perilous adventures. Thus Christine adapts astrology to the norms of a romanticism constrained by social standing and discretion.

Boccaccio goes further than most mythographers in detailing Venus's astral influence over those born under her sway, the children of the planet.[55] Parading his astrological erudition, he follows Albumasar in associating the planetary Venus *magna* with the cold, moist, phlegmatic humor—not with the moisture and heat usual in mythography. She nonetheless influences sexual desire.[56] Boccaccio identifies another, nonplanetary natural Venus (Venus *secunda*) with heat, moisture, blood, and—once again—sexual desire (*Genealogy*, 1: 143, 149–50). With this double sexual physiology, desire seems somewhat ludicrously immanent and, in medical terms, untreatable. The effect is inadvertent, for Boccaccio's design of separating Venuses brings out confusions implicit in the discrepancies among medical theories of sexuality.[57] Overlooking this difficulty, he goes on to recount the astral Venus's influence over writing and poetry, song, dance, sculpture, physical beauty, procreation, humility among friends, voluptuousness, cheerfulness, deceitfulness, credulousness, generosity, eating and drinking. The list goes on to detail what I can only describe as a life of pleasure (1: 143). As a specifically sexual force, Venus *magna* has a feminine and phlegmatic complexion, encourages humans to procreate, and provokes "all sorts of illicit sexual activity and wantonnesses, and a multitude of couplings."[58] That in this she acts as one of the "beneficent" planets advertises the disjunction between Boccaccio's (and others') notions of astrological beneficence and moral good.

In strictly scientific terms, the beneficent planets' influences are not entirely propitious, whatever morality (or poetry) they sponsor. Astrologers such as Ptolemy attribute mixed influences—harmful as well as salutary—to all the planets.[59] Hence Alberic carefully distinguishes damaging (retrograde) from fortunate planetary influences (for example, *Gods and Allegories*, 155, 231). Other mitigating factors include astrological sign and proximity to other planets. Astrology presents us with planets that merely tend toward beneficent or malevolent influences. In Boccaccio's portrait of Venus's influence, this translates into such social advantages as benignity and liberality (and poetic ability), and such disadvantages as a weak spirit and excessive lasciviousness. Popularizations of the science undertaken by other writers simplify the tendency of planetary beneficence. In such representations we often end with Venus having a wholly salutary effect, especially on sexual desire and capacity. Showing a slightly more complex understanding of the science than this, Boccaccio offers us a fairly well-rounded portrait of the children of Venus. Notably, he does not with this Venus moralize the voluptuousness he recounts in such appreciative detail, though in commenting on his other two Venuses he at points denounces precisely these acts and inclinations. When Boccaccio develops natural interpretations, he may reserve or modify moral judgments. Science and nature at once legitimate sexuality and remove it from the realm of overt moral commentary. Such a splicing together of natural and moral interpretation, of approval and condemnation, is of course unexceptional in medieval commentary on sexuality.

Astrological influences can become very much more detailed and extensive than even Boccaccio would suggest.[60] Astrologers and medical writers give Venus specific biological responsibilities in generation. The planet may control the embryo's formation of ears, fingers, nose, and sexual organs (the correlation of nose and genitalia anticipates comedy); and Venus establishes the innate capacity for sexual desire. She may affect behaviors as well as bodies. Albubather (such names speak of the Arabic presence in medieval astrology) indicates that Venus's positions relative to Mars and Mercury in a horoscope predict whether the child conceived will be a fornicator and have illegitimate offspring, while Albohali credits Venus with causing marital infidelity (Giovanni Pontano restricts this to an influence over women). Some speculations are voyeuristic and indicate peculiar social uses for astrology. Abenragel (eleventh century) tells us how to use astrology to determine when a neighbor will indulge in sexual intercourse (given the lack of privacy in the period, spending time on such calculations hardly seems worthwhile).[61] Abraham ibn Ezra reveals that a natal horoscope with Venus in the twelfth or seventh house predicts that an individual will have intercourse daily. And Guido Bonatti (mid-thirteenth century) asserts that one configuration of Venus portends a man who prefers a woman to take the superior position in intercourse, a lascivious preference according to some standards of the time.[62] While many philosophers would dispute the effect of the planet on sexual positions and inclinations, such detailed inquiries into the possible physical and behavioral effects of the planet serve to demonstrate the innocuousness of the basic mythographic formulation and its distance from the fatalism attributed to Arabic astrology.

Women and Venus

While both men and women would appear susceptible to Venus's astral influences, women were often deemed more vulnerable than men to venerean influences. Women, thought to be colder than men, accumulated great excesses of moisture that were purged through menstruation; men's inherently warmer bodies were not similarly overburdened.[63] Ptolemy and many after him consequently label Venus a feminine planet because associated with moisture, the quality most characteristic of women.[64] Venus, with her power over heat and moisture, "naturally" controls women through the interlinking of menses, sexual desire, and procreative capacity. Like young people and aristocrats, women are, especially, children of Venus. With each group this idea takes on slightly different implications. While science authorizes the refinement of the nobility and justifies youthful irresponsibility, it creates a view of women as distressed by superfluities of moisture (not by sex and gender systems). Women are naturally venereal. Rationalizing this gender inequity, Boccaccio submits that women are "very fervently aroused in venereal heat" because they have cold and moist complexions.[65] The distinction between such ideologically weighted uses of astrology and astrology *per se* is clear if we compare the gender distinctions in Ptolemy's *Tetrabiblos*, which outlines equivalent male and female "imperfections" (for instance, 4.5). Because women are moister than men, however, they are commonly imagined to be more prone to despondency, envy, lovesickness, and sexual stimulation.[66] For much the same reasons, women are often thought to be more vulnerable than men to the stimulating effects of food and wine. As part of his advice to women, Robert of Blois recommends avoiding gluttony in order to hinder a "bold excess below the waist" (presumably he is not referring to weight gain).[67] Medieval science justifies the idea of women as sexually overdetermined, and authorizes cultural myths about feminine sexual insatiability and constant feminine sexual availability. As science reifies this set of misogynistic cultural values, inscribing them on the body, ideology appears masked as physiology—as innocent natural fact. Physiology becomes destiny.

The repeated "natural" connection between women and Venus does not necessarily require any particular scientific prop. Augustine, for example, identifies Venus (as Libera) with the emission of feminine seed, Liber with male seed.[68] The link between women and Venus (by which I mean also *venus*, sexual intercourse) is at bottom ideological rather than scientific. Such a gender bias is not at all inevitable. The planet (or goddess, or natural force) could as logically affect primarily men. The production of semen was supposed, like menstrual fluids, to be dependent on warmth and moisture, and, in fact, sperm was sometimes thought to be generated from blood.[69] If the planet governs warmth, moisture, and blood, the production of semen as well as menstruation is necessarily implicated. Indeed, male and female humors and fluid balances could be seen as substantially the same.[70] The planet or natural law can theoretically constrain both sexes equitably: Chaucer's Wife of Bath and Troilus are equally plausible children of Venus.

In much medieval literature, Venus nevertheless governs women in particular, and science certainly corroborates this pattern. Jean de Meun's conclusion to the *Romance of the Rose* famously writes women as inherently subject to the fiery arrows of a natural Venus. A similar gender bias is evident in much late medieval English literature, and accounts for numerous men praying that Venus influence their beloved ladies. Several examples should suffice to sketch out this pattern and some of its implications. Lydgate in the *Complaint of a Lover's Life* identifies Venus with a law of "kynde" that would release true lovers from their pains by eliminating feminine "daunger": if cultural constraints were removed, natural feminine sexual desire and "pitee" would provide the remedy for love. That is, feminine assent to masculine importunings is natural (women are liable to "pitee," to sexual availability, and thus to Venus), and feminine resistance violates nature. This is a common paradigm in both English and French literature, and turns men's desire into women's responsibility. (A similar logic permits women's resistance to sex—*woman's* action or lack thereof—to define rape.)[71] Like Lydgate, James I in the *Kingis Quair* also imagines an astral Venus facilitating the (natural) remedy for love: feminine compliance. This gender model enforces and rationalizes heterosexuality, takes for granted a masculine right to the sexual pleasures of youth, and authorizes misogynistic views of women as at once full of pity and sexually insatiable. Women are, by this model, essentially children of Venus.

Lydgate's and James's poems also and perhaps as significantly emphasize the importance of a woman's consent to sexual union, in this using the natural tradition to reinforce ecclesiastical ideology. Although women are naturally sexually desirous, men must still wait upon their consent. This implicit message in turn supports a central Catholic precept: consent creates a marriage.[72] The doctrine values individual choice over such considerations as family ambition. This is actually a troublesome doctrine throughout the later Middle Ages, in part because it mandates the validity of clandestine marriages (that is, informal unions based on private consent and consummation, not presided over by the clergy).[73] The privacy of these unions means that neither party can later prove consent was given. Subsequent renunciation of the vows, a divorce as informal as the marriage, and bigamy become possible. Clandestine marriage presents "sely" upper-class women in particular with a socially dangerous situation—potential renunciation of the vows, abandonment, and irremediable loss of reputation.

For all the social problems tied up with the doctrine of consent, problems conspicuous in later medieval England, Lydgate among others shows a strong allegiance to the ideal. Indeed, Lydgate's *Temple of Glass* ends with a scene delineating a clandestine union.[74] Venus binds the lovers in a golden chain of eternal love, locks their hearts with a golden key, and dictates their vows of truth to each other, emphasizing that they must not "chaunge for no nwe" (1128) according to the fashion of the day.[75] Replicating marriage ritual, the couple finally kneels and takes vows before Venus. They agree to an eternal bond, though their physical union apparently awaits the removal of the woman's obscure impediment to marriage.[76] Venus's chain binding these lovers together contrasts with another chain binding the woman, an image of her present unavailability. The two chains picture an opposition between natural desire and legal duty, between natural and human law. Venus takes the side of natural desire, and nature here accords with eternal love. As Venus's golden chain unites the couple in eternal love, then, the natural and sacramental become one.[77] Venus's particular insistence on the man's truth and fidelity serves to protect the woman from the potential dangers of this clandestine bond, as does the deferred consummation.

Astrology functions in this poem to support a very precise, and precisely specified, ecclesiastical ideology: true and passionate love within a clandestine marriage. That Venus sponsors constant truth in loving, that the sacramental bond is natural, identifies these values with a divinely ordered cosmos. In that cosmos, women are again children of Venus. The woman initiates things by praying to Venus for her chosen love; the man, straightaway wounded by love, prays that Venus create a "remedie" by warming the woman (715–28). In the *Temple of Glass* women and other children of Venus participate in an order that naturalizes the compulsion of ardent and youthful sexual love, but that also insists on the necessity of individual consent, on truth to vows of love, and on a tenuous ecclesiastical regulation of sexuality (through the validity of clandestine marriage). Lydgate thus enlists nature to defend youthful rights to love, to sexual pleasure, and to a personal choice of partner.

James I and Lydgate indicate the flexibility of astrological concepts, the simplicity of appealing to the heavens in order to justify and naturalize particular social orders. For both, as for Jean de Meun, Boccaccio, and numerous other medieval writers, a venerean nature implicates women especially. Yet such is the utility of the astral Venus that misogynistic constructions of feminine sexuality hide within what seems a scientifically verifiable and merely natural order.

Flesh and Spirit

Astrology and natural interpretations invite questions about the relation between flesh and spirit. For instance, if diet may to some extent regulate desire, desire also arises in the mind and is controlled (or not) by reason. Internal and external forces are ambiguously interconnected in the creation of desire: sexual urges arise from both matter (according to medicine and astrology) and mind (according to love literature and, again, medicine). We might recall Andreas Capellanus asserting that the imagination generates sexual love, a conventional idea of desire ultimately based on medicine.[78] In seeking the origins of sexual desire, we discover ambiguous relations among internal and external, physical and subjective forces, planets and the individual imagination. We might most sensibly conclude that medieval discourses locate sexual desire in both mind and body.[79]

This is a feature of medieval sexuality that takes shape in the patristic period and changes little with the passing of centuries. As Peter Brown remarks, this conceptualization of sexuality separates pagan from Christian care of the self:

The body is no longer treated as a self-contained system, whose smooth functioning (due to an austere regime) enabled the wise man to put his body "in brackets," as it were, in order to concentrate, undisturbed, on the long labor of self-reformation through the mind. For good or ill . . . body and mind had become compacted. . . . it was precisely the intimacy of sexuality, and its apparent position on the shadowy borderline of body and mind, that enabled men such as John Cassian to look to it for the first, unmistakable signs of the mighty works of deliverance wrought by God in the recesses of the soul.[80]

The ancient regulation of the self through diet and long discipline—through measured efforts of the supreme individual will—grows implausible, at least for the average Christian. To the extent that medieval theologians and others follow Augustine, they discover a sharp disjunction between human will and sexual feelings, a discord between will and body that speaks always of the concupiscence resulting from original sin. For Augustine, the original Edenic hierarchy of reason over appetite toppled with the original fault. As theologians after Augustine scrutinize human sexual desire, they too trace out the effects of concupiscence in the ungovernable perversity of the human will. Theology can thus regard with great pessimism the possibility of a rational control of sexuality: the very instrument of control is itself disordered.[81]

According to theological and scientific views of the body, medical discourses, and arts of love alike, we can discern no simple division between flesh and spirit, and no clear-cut means for governing the flesh. Yet a lucid hierarchy of reason over appetite serves as the basis of medieval philosophizing about astrology: according to the stock formula, the heavens influence the body but leave the will free. Plainly, theology and medicine and philosophy promote conspicuously different perspectives and conclusions. The philosophical binary of will and flesh serves to affirm the ideology of free will. Like all binaries, of course, it suppresses untidy details—in this case, the ambiguous origins of sexual desire, the irremediable entanglement of body and mind. Theology, on the other hand, explores precisely that entanglement. The persistent reiteration of the philosophical binary throughout the medieval period indicates that the questions it attempts to answer keep recurring, even though apparently resolved many times over.[82] In other words, the often-reiterated proofs of free will testify to the abiding presence of doubts, and to the problems raised by the doctrine of original sin. Reflecting on the natural Venus, we can appreciate why such doubts would arise, why the hierarchized opposition of flesh and spirit would seem at best tenuous. The possibility of an astral influence over sexuality profoundly deepens the shadows cast by concupiscence and original sin. Though numerous medieval writers affirm the freedom of the will, equally numerous popular representations of astrology along with many theological debates disclose less philosophical surety. If natural philosophy sometimes seems utterly confident about the power of the free will, other discourses do not always agree.

Numerous works would provide evidence of this, but let us consider just one, the "Pageant of Knowledge," a popular work by Lydgate that discloses an attitude toward astrology not quite in keeping with the standard philosophical formula. (This is typical of his works.)[83] A didactic public pageant, this text explains the seven estates, the seven parts of prudence, the foundation of the seven liberal arts, and the disposition of the planets, zodiacal signs, elements, complexions, and seasons. Here "Venus, full of new fangylnes, / Makyn men unstable here in her lyvyng."[84] Just as Venus makes people "unstable," Saturn disposes them to melancholy, Mars to war, and so on. While each planet inclines people toward particular temperaments and actions, the zodiacal signs also rule parts of the body. Enmeshed in this cosmic web, humans manifest the mutability of the world. All things function, as Venus does, to make humans "unstable." As the pageant forcefully details the limits of human action, Lydgate raises a question at the end of each succeeding stanza (except the last): "How shuld a man than be stedfast of lyvyng?" (145).

Lydgate does not resolve this question by proffering the philosophical commonplace that we should identify with supernatural constancy and thereby transcend the flesh; nor does he recommend that reason should dominate the physical members, control the will, select a more appropriate diet, or find a marital partner. He answers instead that the influences of planets, zodiacal signs, elements, humors, and seasons all teach that in fact we "cannat be stedfast in lyvyng" (152). Consequently, in the spring when heat and moisture abound (the time and conditions of Venus's precedence), "gret lust he doth recover" and "meynt with dred ys mannys governance" (243, 245). The possibility of self-governance in any season or age grows increasingly dubious as each stanza multiplies the constraints on human action and reiterates the inevitability of human unsteadfastness. The pageant ends not by advising alterations in diet or increased fasting, but simply by recommending prayers for grace, contrition, and shrift. Failures of self-control constitute the expected norm: the pageant teaches the necessity of confession and penance by detailing pervasive human weaknesses.[85] Reason and science account for submissions to sensual desire; supernatural intervention is restricted to supplying the grace of contrition for the inevitable acquiescence to sensuality. And this deployment of astrology comes in popular instruction offered by a monk of indisputable orthodoxy. If we recall the *Temple of Glass*, we may perceive the mutability of such natural orders. The astral Venus may as easily legitimate human instability as constant human truth, and problems of self-governance as readily as the necessity of freely willed consent.[86] Yet in each representation nature seems a final, immovable, and unchanging authority.

Lydgate's focus on the limits of free choice and self-control provides a ready-made rationalization for lapses in human governance, and he is certainly not alone in articulating and justifying a pragmatic acceptance of human limitations. In response to such popular science, philosophers and preachers may assert the freedom of the human will. The idea that self-governance is unfeasible (especially but not at all exclusively in youth) nevertheless has an understandable and enduring popular appeal, more than adequate rational legitimation in medieval science, and ample recognition within ecclesiastical discourses.[87] The theme of human limitations here as elsewhere implies the survival of "a muted but tenacious tendency" in early Christianity "to treat sexuality as a privileged ideogram of all that was most irreducible in the human will."[88]

We should note the diverse attitudes about sexual desire and self-governance developed within various discourses. This diversity perhaps most clearly reveals itself in the central differences between philosophical-theological and astrological-medical discussions of sexuality: whereas theologians may forbid sexual intercourse as a sin (except under elaborate constraints),[89] physicians may prescribe it as essential for health.[90] Similarly, medical writers regularly convey information about contraception, forbidden by the Church.[91] The theological model holds that reason should attempt to rule the sensual passions, though lapses are expected. This model would imply that "eschewing is the only remedy," and a heroic one at that.[92] The scientific model, on the other hand, develops a system of material cause and effect: heat and moisture produce desire, which accordingly intensifies in youth, in the spring, after food and drink. This model proposes a regulation of the self through physical means such as diet, coitus, or masturbation. If one system assumes the shaky precedence of the mind, other modes of thought rely on the sure paths of the flesh. Which cure should the sufferer take, if any? Would any cure be effective?

Since the hierarchy of mind over body, so dear to some theologians and philosophers, is obviously neither universal nor unchallenged in medieval culture, the answer to such questions is not foreordained. Further, as we have seen, representations of nature often suggest that no cure would be effective, that sexual desire is inevitable and inevitably leads to coitus (and, occasionally, to procreation). Clearly, concentrating on any single discourse (whether Boethian philosophy or Salernitan medicine or Arabic astrology) can offer insight into only a small part of medieval culture. If we would digest a larger bite of the culture, we need to take in more than one discourse; we need also to appreciate how such discourses may differ from each other in their perspectives and conclusions—and to reflect on what they collectively render ambiguous.[93] In the case of Venus and sexuality, what appears most ambiguous is simply the nature of the relations between the individual and the cosmos, reason and desire, the will and the flesh.

Venereal Orders and Disorders

Ideas about natural sexuality vary considerably. We may recall that Alan of Lille defines natural sexual intercourse as heterosexual, unpleasurable, and procreative—toilsome work to be undertaken with due regard for its utilitarian end. Alberic repeats a commonplace idealization of youth as the natural season of sexual vigor and joy, yet also includes a retrospective rejection of those fleeting pleasures. Giovanni del Virgilio presents natural sexuality as inevitable and, it seems, inevitably procreative. Chaucer's Parson is less concerned about the sensual pleasure of procreative acts than about the imperative that nothing thwart generation. Lydgate in the "Pageant of Knowledge" pictures natural sexual desire as an innate drive bound not for procreation but simply for sensual gratification; in the *Temple of Glass* he obliges lovers to take vows of constancy, with marriage now the natural fulfillment of sexual desire. Finally, many writers associate women in particular with venerean influences, and this myth depicts women as naturally acceding to male desires—as caught between the mandates of culture and those of nature. The seemingly fixed category of nature everywhere disguises the fact of significant medieval variations in just what is imagined to constitute natural sexuality. Nature is a convenient ideological category, not an unchanging constant.

If natural interpretations often embody in Venus various and sundry sexual ideologies—sex must be and naturally is procreative, and its proper time is youth and spring—in mythography they as frequently publish disparities among medieval discourses on sexuality. The mythographers' natural-astrological Venus may illuminate nothing quite so well as the differences among the discourses that articulate medieval sexualities. In mythography cultural heterogeneity appears particularly marked, because the diverse hermeneutics derived from medicine, astrology, and theology are closely juxtaposed and manifestly unreconciled with each other. The mythographic compiler generally indicates no preference among the conflicting models, authorizing no single explanation but rather contradictory and heterogeneous systems of interpretation. As mythography and poetry alike indicate, the discursive multivalence and the disparities among conceptual models necessarily provoke questions about the relation between body and mind, about the grounds and limits of self-governance. Mythographers typically leave such questions open, as, of course, may poets (or medical doctors or theologians).

Because mythographic natural interpretations are often accompanied by disjunctive moralizations, discursive contradictions may stand out in sharp relief: sexuality both must and may not be controlled. This contradiction forms one of the most routine of medieval perspectives on sexuality, so often repeated as to become unremarkable—and to seem natural. As a consequence, discourses about sexuality, whether addressed to laity or clergy, tend to establish the inevitability of sin, and hence the necessity of confession. Most simply, many (not all) medieval discourses work together to invent a sexuality shadowed by guilt; in doing so, they implicitly legitimate the primacy of confession in the Church's discursive control of sexuality.[94] This tendency does not preclude parodic comedy or a wide range of other responses. Jean de Meun ends the *Romance of the Rose* with much laughter over the natural procreative rule, as he depicts a lover whose procreative achievement cannot establish his moral innocence. Chaucer mockingly portrays the procreative motive in the elderly January's analysis of marriage and in his labored attempts at consummation. The humor of such parodies depends on their foil, on the prevalent seriousness of the official rule.[95]

Notably, Venus's genial astral influence over warmth, moisture, blood, spring, youth, desire, and conception does not challenge any crucial theological imperatives. Questions about the limits of self-governance, which originate in early Christianity and persist without possibility of definitive resolution, do not contest the most basic Catholic teaching on sexuality: the rule of natural sex for procreation. Representations of the natural Venus almost always implicitly support this rule, for warmth, moisture, coitus, pleasure, and procreation form an apparently indivisible unity. Hence, although modern critics often propose that we interpret Venus according to a binary opposition of lust and chastity (with these terms usually corresponding to extramarital and marital sex), this is obviously too rigorous a distinction, particularly for the later Middle Ages.[96] Orthodox natural sexuality, as popularly understood, does not disallow passion or sensual pleasure in marriage. Indeed, the prevalence of legal prostitution in medieval Europe indicates nothing if not a widespread cultural acceptance of masculine sexual license, and a concern that desire be directed into "natural," heterosexual relations—even outside marriage.[97] Venus's astral or (more broadly understood) natural influence violates no essential theological dicta, no commonplace social norm.

In the end, Venus may embody a natural, orthodox sexuality both in spite of and because of her associations with sensual pleasure and sin. She represents the force of concupiscence (or, more positively, of love) that overwhelms reason but that also fulfills reason in assuring the generative continuity of life. She calls attention both to the link between human and cosmos and to the division within the human soul—both to created order and to the flaw chiseled deeply into that order at the time of the Fall.

Chapter 6

Unnatural Acts

> Sunt mihi naturae iura novanda meae.
> (I must devise new laws for my nature.)
> Ovid, *Art of Love*

> Every act of becoming conscious
> (it says here in this book)
> is an unnatural act
> Adrienne Rich,
> "The Phenomenology of Anger"

The last chapter concentrated on delineating the ways in which ideology is naturalized—whether in representations of procreative sexuality, in astral physiology, under the guise of "children of the planet" Venus, or through a poetic image of a natural-sacramental bond uniting two lovers. Mythography and poetry alike showed how mutable and contingent cultural values may be depicted as eternal and unchanging—as divinely authorized. It is certainly not the office of poetry merely to legitimate cultural systems, however. In the Middle Ages, as now, poetry often unveils the unnaturalness of what we commonly allow to be natural, and the ideologies that hide in supposedly nonideological terrain. The present chapter accordingly seeks the unnatural acts of poetry—the acts that make us conscious of both nature and social orders as human fabrications. I will begin this investigation with the ways venerean astrological conventions enter into Chaucer's *Wife of Bath's Prologue*, and then proceed to his adaptation of natural traditions in the *Parliament of Fowls*.

On Consulting a Learned Astronomer

Astrology discloses ideology provocatively in the *Wife of Bath's Prologue*, for the Wife includes astrology among the authoritative discourses by which she defines herself.[1] In the course of her exposition, she refers to a preeminent scientific authority, Ptolemy in the *Almagest* (324–25). The improbability of a Wife of Bath knowing this text firsthand, let alone citing it, calls attention to her use of supremely learned and Latin traditions: astrology joins exegesis, commentary, sermons, and compilation in her intellectual arsenal. The passing casual reference to Ptolemy identifies her as a (most unlikely) scientific authority in an ancient, learned, elite, and above all masculine discourse, a discourse she may be appropriating from Jankyn. As we have seen, this discourse represents women as quite essentially what the Wife claims to be: a child of Venus, sexually defined by men. The translation of that scientific discourse into the Wife's *Prologue*, however, incisively denaturalizes it, proclaims it to be about men writing women rather than about an immutable natural order.[2]

The Wife recapitulates the primary features of the astrological-medical discourse we traced in the last chapter. She explains the planet's influence over her horoscope: "Venus me yaf my lust, my likerousnesse" (611)—in other words, the inclination to enjoy sexual pleasure.[3] She equivocates over the link between this native inclination and her actions:

> I folwed ay myn inclinacioun
> By vertu of my constellacioun;
> That made me I koude noght withdrawe
> My chambre of Venus from a good felawe.
> (615–18)

"I folwed" asserts self-control over a native predisposition, which passes insensibly into the seeming constraint of "I koude noght withdrawe." The lines turn on the tension between her innate "inclinacioun" and her active pursuit of it, between matter and mind.[4] At the same time, the fancy rhyme *inclinacioun/constellacioun* suggests a distinctly stylized control of the self. Astral physiology thus enters into her self-definition not as a universal natural truth, but as equivocation that may be turned into excuses and verbal exhibitions. The translation from general scientific principle to individual application—and from masculine institutions of Latin learning to a woman's speech in English poetry—deprives the authoritative discourse of its authority. The Wife tells us about the familiar venereal effects of wine on women, and produces a similar effect:

> And after wyn on Venus moste I thynke,
> For al so siker as cold engendreth hayl,
> A likerous mouth moste han a likerous tayl.

> In wommen vinolent is no defence—
> This knowen lecchours by experience.
> (464–68)

In scientific discourses the erotic effect of wine on women constitutes a simple, universal natural phenomenon, as certain as hail when the temperature drops. Here the rhyme *hayl/tayl* aptly connects the natural phenomenon and its specific application. In the Wife's overtly interested use of the scientific discourse, the universal explanation all too obviously serves the purposes of self-justification. Interestingly, the last line quoted suspends the experience between men and women, making a feminine experience of defenselessness indistinguishable from a masculine (and feminine) experience of sexual desire. A supposedly nonideological natural truth rationalizes the experience of sexuality as eroticized powerlessness. In short, the Wife crafts a defense out of her feminine defenselessness, or at least out of a pose of defenselessness.

The Wife completes her scientific self-representation by positing a contest between clerks, who are children of the planet Mercury, and women, children of Venus. While clerks naturally love "wysdam and science," women pursue "ryot and dispence" (699–700), and this explains their acrimonious relations:

> Therfore no womman of no clerk is preysed.
> The clerk, whan he is oold, and may noght do
> Of Venus werkes worth his olde sho,
> Thanne sit he doun, and writ in his dotage
> That wommen kan nat kepe hir mariage!
> (706–10)

The link between old age, "wysdam and science," and masculine impotence is trenchantly pictured in the "olde sho." Drier than old leather, the aged male is utterly devoid of the moisture, blood, and heat needed for coitus. The clerk "in his dotage" has no choice but to relinquish sexuality and turn to wisdom; he merits no applause for his conversion to learning. The Wife's shoes, "ful moyste and newe" (*Gen. Pro.* 457), correspond to her perpetually youthful sexuality, the sexuality of women as inscribed by those clerks.[5] According to the scientific model, women are sexually overdetermined—as are aristocrats and youths (we might recall Jankyn with his "feet so clene and faire," 598).

As the Wife outlines her paradigm of venerean women, Chaucer denaturalizes the misogyny of the scientific model by showing its affinity with more immediately recognizable misogynistic discourses: exegesis, Jerome's *Adversus Jovinianum*, the book of wicked wives from which Jankyn reads. The Wife's use of these misogynistic discourses forcefully points up the fact that there are no other official discourses. Men write women, and men write women as the venereal other. Sexuality appears always "a problem raised for the self by the other," as Peter Brown astutely comments: "Seen by the aged, the intensity of sexual feeling was dismissed as a problem for the hot-blooded young. Seen by men, sexual desire was feared as a source of disruption, only too frequently brought upon them by the wiles of women."[6] Astrological medicine constructs sexuality from what Brown describes as the "privileged viewing-point of the old and the male," so that youths and women are particularly "other" and therefore the "problem." By making the Wife of Bath an astrologer, Chaucer rejects the "privileged viewing-point" that conceives women and youths as sexually insatiable; he invalidates the scientific illusion of a universal human perspective yielding nonideological truths. He reveals that scientific traditions are constructed from particular, limited, and interested human perspectives.[7] And he demonstrates that science may be appropriated for many purposes, all of them having personal and political implications. Far from expressing sacral truth or immutable nature, science articulates particular human ideologies. (Ptolemy is well chosen for this end: one can find in his work, as in the Bible or an encyclopedic mythography, support for almost any position.)

The Wife's practice of exegesis evidences a similar effect, and Ralph Hanna's argument on this point may help us to understand the Wife's astrological hermeneutics as part of a larger pattern: "The Wife calls attention to aspects of Jerome's voice which place it, which show it to be, not God's voice, but simply that of another human being. At that level, it has become desacralized, has lost any position beyond appeal which it might have occupied, and has become analyzable."[8] Likewise, with the Wife's uses of astrology the "universal truths" of science show themselves to be specifically masculine inventions, contingent and human notions rather than unchanging features of a divine order. The obvious misogynies of exegesis and the more invisible misogynies of astral physiology prove mutually supportive and mutually revealing. Both discourses lose their privileged status; both exhibit inadequacies in their treatment of women.

Clearly, the project of translating Latin traditions into the vernacular may call institutional systems and the ideologies sustaining them into question. The traditions are opened to multiple interpretations when translated into English, and they forsake their ideological stability when read by the "untrained" and the "unfit." In the act of translating authoritative texts, the Wife dramatizes the potentially dangerous reading skills of the "untrained." It is therefore not surprising that the *Wife of Bath's Prologue* is one of the *Canterbury Tales* most subject to marginal scribal annotations. These annotations attempt to reinstate what the Wife so blatantly overturns: the ideologically "neutral," authoritative reputation of learned Latin traditions.[9] Within Chaucer's poem those traditions are literally marginalized, as the Wife appropriates for her own purposes masculinist myths about women, including scientific myths about feminine, youthful, or aristocratic children of Venus. If the denaturalization of each imported misogynistic discourse is readily grasped, however, the *Prologue* as a whole seems above all equivocal (and that effect is only enhanced by the tale). For even as the Wife exposes institutionalized misogynies, she also authorizes misogynistic fears of woman's sexual insatiability, of woman's garrulousness, and of woman's lies.[10] Modern critics can discern in her both protofeminism and antifeminism, and that is perhaps the point. Misogynists and the Wife are finally locked into a perpetual waltz, each defined by and defining the moves of the other. Her *Prologue* takes her audience through the steps of her life's dance, making them desire a change both in the obligatory tune and in the compulsory moves. The discourse she opposes dictates the terms of her argument, and she cannot invent a wholly new science on her own. Appropriating the masculinist discourse, she adopts as well its narrow view of women.

The Textual Production of Desire

With the *Parliament of Fowls*, Chaucer presents natural sexuality as a cultural artifact, a product of books. This implication emerges in the poem's first stanzas and becomes emphatic with the retelling of Cicero's *Dream of Scipio* (*Somnium Scipionis*), the dream-vision of an ornately artificial natural Venus, and the vision of Nature purportedly derived from Alan of Lille. As each image of natural sexuality arrives under the authority of particular books or literary conventions, Chaucer emphasizes the multiplicitous (and inadequate) human inventions of natural orders.[11] Ideas of natural sexuality evidently differ as much as do any other human traditions. Separately, each textually inspired sequence in the *Parliament of Fowls* discloses a construction of seemingly natural sexuality; yet together these conflicting perspectives unsettle the idea of nature and dispute the possibility of a single natural sexual code.[12] That Chaucer ends the poem with a return to still "othere bokes" (695) promises an endless parade of ideas, among which he may (or may not) find "som thyng for to fare / The bet" (698–99). Throughout this quasi-encyclopedic vision of natural order, the burden of reconciling sometimes disparate traditions falls wholly on the reader.

The poem opens with Chaucer's narrator learning about the god of love by the simple expedient of reading about him "ful ofte in bokes":

> The lyf so short, the craft so long to lerne,
> Th'assay so hard, so sharp the conquerynge,
> The dredful joye alwey that slit so yerne:
> Al this mene I by Love, that my felynge
> Astonyeth with his wonderful werkynge
> So sore, iwis, that whan I on hym thynke
> Nat wot I wel wher that I flete or synke.
>
> For al be that I knowe nat Love in dede,
> Ne wot how that he quiteth folk here hyre,
> Yit happeth me ful ofte in bokes reede
> Of his myrakles and his crewel yre.
> There rede I wel he wol be lord and syre;
> I dar nat seyn, his strokes been so sore,
> But "God save swich a lord!"—I can na moore.
>
> (1–14)

These opening stanzas emphasize this Cupid's literary conventionality by reproducing stock Ovidian formulas: the antitheses of Alan of Lille's and Jean de Meun's famous definitions of sexual love—its "dredful joye";[13] the subjection of all men to the "wonderful werkynge" of this god; the feudal service of the lover to love; and the irresistibility and pain of love. Two stanzas suffice to depict sexual love in terms of the lordship of love and the subjection of the lover, an Ovidian pattern of domination and eager submission (although recognizably Ovidian, the medieval conventions have of course flowed quite far from the fountain of Ovid's texts).

A brief comparison with *Troilus and Criseyde* may help to clarify these conventions and their import here. Troilus falls in love when the great and angry god of love shoots his arrow, a mythic scenario that raises passionate love to a high literary register. Troilus soon experiences the contraries of love ("O quike deth, O swete harm," 1.411), is straightaway subject to the god of love (1.206–31), and is rapidly improved in all virtues (1.1072–85). Chaucer draws on the familiar Ovidian conventions in order to depict Troilus's love as naturally noble and ennobling—temporarily. Even here Chaucer does not simply affirm the conventions. If Troilus seems at first sight the "typical lover of the French lyric," Chaucer gradually undermines precisely the values of that mode.[14] The *Parliament of Fowls*, however, introduces the same conventions as a quaint custom reported by books, not as epitomizing an inevitable, natural, noble (masculine) experience of love. The conventions are thoroughly denaturalized, and the narrator announces his distance from them. From the perspective of the nonparticipant narrator, the stock conventions appear as overblown literary artifices rather than as the questionably natural consequences of noble love. Although Chaucer manipulates the literary conventions differently in these two poems, both poems denaturalize French conventions and values for poetry, and both associate those conventions with the figure of Cupid. The great god of love myth typically defines noble sexual behavior as an important convention that establishes the natural differences among social classes, but Chaucer again and again reveals its contingency. With the *Parliament of Fowls* Chaucer turns Cupid into a sign of a domineering literary tradition that this poet, at least, will not endorse.

As the narrator continues, Cupid's brand of amatory poetry takes its place in a larger library, becomes just one of many books containing the "sondry usages" of love:

> Of usage—what for lust and what for lore—
> On bokes red I ofte. (15–16)

Books hold the varied human customs of pleasure and learning, and the narrator is interested in the diversity of the "usages" preserved within them. He views past literary representations of human customs as the fertile earth from which writers continually bring forth new crops (22–25). This brief reflection on the manifold uses of books accomplishes a transition from one "usage" of love—the god of love in his Ovidian guise—to another, Cicero's *Dream of Scipio*. The abrupt turn from Cupid to Scipio exemplifies the typically paratactic structure of the poem, its progress from one book to another and another and another without the author explicitly relating each to some organic whole. The poem mirrors not nature but successive literary instances of human customs (Ovidian, Ciceronian, Chartrian) that represent nature in accordance with particular exigencies. Cicero and his commentator Macrobius are concerned with the relations not of social classes, as Cupid is, but of body and soul, earth and heaven. The two passages require us to view love from the disparate perspectives bound into courtly and philosophical discourses. Chaucer does not imply an equal competition between these perspectives: Cupid receives mocking, doubtful treatment, whereas Cicero earns diffident approval. The comparison favors Cicero without giving him an exclusive or uncontested right to define human sexual relations. His reported teaching takes precedence only over the grossly inadequate conventions associated with Cupid. Interestingly, Cicero's text provides the narrator with great pleasure, and this evidently establishes its superiority: "To rede forth hit gan me so delite / That al that day me thoughte but a lyte" (27–28). Cupid's poetics fail because they astonish without pleasing.

Passing on to Cicero's *Dream of Scipio*, the narrator elaborates this second "usage" of love. According to this account of things, those who seek "commune profit" arrive in the place "that ful of blysse is and of soules cleere" (76) sooner than do the lecherous, who after death must reel painfully about the earth before gaining their reward. Scipio's dream contrasts one who seeks common profit with "likerous folk." Since the lecherous are classed with "brekers of the lawe" (78), sensuality seems to parallel civil disobedience. If we expect a binary opposition between the pursuit of sensuality and the love of common profit, we might infer that common profit involves a legal exercise of sexuality. Critics sometimes import a legalistic principle—the rule of procreative sex—to satisfy this expectation. Whether or not the poem as a whole supports such a standard, this passage does not articulate it. The dream of Scipio develops a contrast more enigmatic than clear between common profit and lechery, and the distinction between licit and illicit sexualities is no more than a faint suggestion.

We might attempt to appreciate this obscurity rather than removing it. The dream of Scipio nebulously aligns civil legality with religious virtue, hence civil with divine systems of justice, and the very ambiguity of this alignment is historically provocative. For in the late fourteenth century the state is increasingly entering into the regulation of sexuality—

creating just this apparent correspondence between civil and divine legal systems.¹⁵ As the state takes on the hitherto predominantly ecclesiastical role of defining licit and illicit sexual acts, however, it does not merely duplicate ecclesiastical law. The multiplication of civil and ecclesiastical authorities and legal systems renders potentially ambiguous precisely what Chaucer's poetry does. How are human and divine laws related? Which sexual acts are licit, which illicit? With its elusive intimations of licit and illicit sexualities, the dream of Scipio provokes these questions. The poem does not have to answer the questions it raises; indeed, a simple answer would deny the potent implications of the questions.¹⁶ By means of ambiguity, Chaucer lends aesthetic form to the possibility of anxious irresolutions in sexual norms and values. Deftly bringing uncertainties to consciousness, he accomplishes a poetic unnatural act. Ambiguity (like multiplicity) is the point rather than something to be argued away.

Chaucer does not reconcile these initial, conflicting perspectives with each other, but augments the poem's diversity by stringing together further near-oppositions. As he begins his dream, he invokes Venus, introducing yet another literary "usage" of love. This invocation creates an apparent opposition between the verse of Cupid's "makers," who (purportedly) develop the courtly clichés laughingly passed over in the opening stanzas, and the venerean poetics of Chaucer. That is, first he explicitly takes his poetics out of the narrow arena occupied by the French makers, shunning the pose of Cupid's lover-poet and refusing a prescriptive view of love and chivalry; then he assigns his poetry to the patronage of Venus. The petition to Venus associates her with "enditing," with a poetry that goes beyond that of the makers to encompass a broader ethical purposiveness and to provide a point of view suitable for an audience beyond the merely courtly (very much as in the invocation to Book 2 of the *House of Fame*):¹⁷

> Cytherea, thow blysful lady swete,
> That with thy fyrbrond dauntest whom the lest
> And madest me this sweven for to mete,
> Be thow myn helpe in this, for thow mayst best!
> As wisly as I sey the north-north-west,
> Whan I began my sweven for to write,
> So yif me myght to ryme, and endyte!
> (*Parliament of Fowls*, 113–19)

Venus carries her firebrand, as in the *Romance of the Rose*, indicating her power over sensual desire. The enjambment and parallel verbs—"with thy fyrbrond *dauntest* whom the lest / And *madest* me this sweven for to mete"—fuse the pleasures of sex with those of the dream. To invoke Venus's aid in this way is to call frankly upon sensuality, to stress the pleasures of narrative verse, especially, perhaps, the music of rhyme royal. Venus's power over sensuous pleasures (over rhyme in particular) aligns her with the ideal of musicality in the French lyric mode, but Chaucer names his venerean poetics "enditing" and "ryming," not "making." (Later, Scipio promises that if the narrator has "connyng for t'endite," he will find matter in the garden; 167.) The invocation thus unifies poetic delights and the values of "enditing," which is very close to the union the narrator discovers in Cicero's account of Scipio's dream. The vaguely cosmological turn of the allusive reference to the "north-north-west" generalizes Venus's power, as is appropriate to the classicizing style and purposes of the "enditing" she sponsors.[18] As the references to "fyrbrond" and "north-north-west" combine in one figure the goddess of sensual pleasure and the cosmological deity who presides over poetry, Chaucer implies a synthesis of the maker's priority of sensuously pleasing poetry and the enditer's ambition that pleasure not be the sole end of the text.[19]

As in the *House of Fame*, Chaucer integrates fleshly desire and intellectual (classicizing) effort, sensual appetite and poetry. He rejects only the subjects and stereotypical personae of Cupid's makers; he does not repudiate one of their vital goals—to give sensuous pleasure through musical verse. Adopting this aesthetic, he identifies it with Venus, in many ways a more plausibly sensuous figure than Cupid would be. French conventions, reductively represented in the opening stanzas, seem distinct from and inferior to this classicizing venerean poetics. The apparent opposition between Cupid's lover-poets and Venus's dreamer disguises the debt to the French tradition and aligns Chaucer instead with classical and classicizing writers—chiefly with Cicero, Macrobius, and Ovid, poet of Venus. (This gesture only deepens the disguise, for French poets as well as the Italians pioneered the literary use of mythology.)[20] The emphasis on pleasure furthers the resonance between the narrator's dream and the dream of Scipio.

These depictions of Cupid and Venus as alternative poetic patrons give way to portraits that complicate those first views. The narrator dreams he walks through a garden containing a temple in which Venus occupies a small corner.[21] The temple passage returns love to the register of myth in order to depict a traditionally aristocratic natural sexuality, and in order once again to denaturalize that class-coded understanding of sensual love.[22] The narrator first passes through a *locus amoenus* into a scene that closely recalls the *Romance of the Rose* with its walled garden and teeming personifications (though here the French poem is mediated through Boccaccio, for Chaucer adapts this scene from the temple of Venus in the *Teseida*). In Chaucer's garden, "oure lord" Cupid stands beside a well, sharpening arrows for Wille to temper (212). This allegorical image limits Cupid's power to the sharpening of desire's arrows, and subordinates even that power to human will, which determines whether they slee or wound.[23] The mythic god of love becomes, once again, an emblem of sensual desire. This image comments retrospectively on the opening stanzas, and on the conventions of French poetry (such as the *Romance of the Rose*) alluded to therein. If Gallic Ovidian protocol views desire as an overpowering and lordly force, a tyrant over the will, another "usage" treats desire as subject to the will. The much-celebrated, overwhelming force of aristocratic love in the Gallic fashion appears here as neither an innate noble endowment nor a necessarily commendable social norm. The poetic fiction of a lover's submission to the almighty god of love becomes just one literary model, one contingent "usage" of love. At the same time, Cupid's arrows do not constitute just a simple moral allegory. Their power to slay anticipates the lovers whose deaths are later depicted on the temple wall, for in this mutable world the arrows of death always shadow love. Consistent with his iconological ambiguities, Cupid holds weapons poised between death and desire, implying their union in the cyclical order of generation.

The allegorical Cupid heads up a parade of courtly personifications (218–29) that return us to the aristocratic prerequisites for love. The list of personifications stresses exclusionary class ideals, for wealth (Aray) and aristocratic social mores (Curteysie, Gentilesse, Flaterye, Messagerye) necessarily accompany pleasure (amplified into Plesaunce, Lust, Delyt, and Desyr). Beute and Youthe encompass the reputedly natural qualities of noble lovers. Foolhardynesse and Meede intrude into this conventionally genteel company, along with a much disfigured Craft, who "can and hath the myght / To don by force a wyght to don folye" (221). With these figures, Chaucer hints at ignoble "usages" that persistently, and in his works visibly, attend the idealizing fictions of noble love.

The garden with its Cupid, well, and courtly personifications creates the expectation that Jean de Meun's *Romance of the Rose* Venus will soon arrive on the scene as the "natural" sexual appetite, the goddess of torches, arrows, and roses. Following Boccaccio's *Teseida*, however, Chaucer revises that vision of "natural" sexuality. Chaucer removes Boccaccio's Venus from an outdoor setting on Mount Citherea and places her in an elaborately detailed temple that transforms familiar natural conventions into excrescences.[24] This treatment denaturalizes Jean de Meun's depiction of "natural" sexuality. Here the planetary metal, brass, forms into a solid temple, upon which perches a positive superfluity of doves—"many an hundred peyre" (238). Dancers, traditionally children of the planet, circle the temple in disheveled array, "yer by yeere" in their unrelenting office of gaiety (236). Inside, venereal heat and moisture concretize into "sykes hoote as fyr" (246), continually generated by desire, continually circling and fueling altars. The roses traditionally adorning Venus transmute into floral garlands for Priapus.[25] In the image of Priapus, Chaucer links the natural imagery of heat, moisture, and the *spiritus* of sighs with perdurable male erection. This god stands "with hys sceptre in honde" (256), wielding his permanently arrested erection, and thereby illustrating one physical consequence of all this heat and moisture (a desire uncomfortably "forever warm and still to be enjoyed").[26] His presence makes this literally a phallocentric temple. Further on in the temple tour, Ceres and Bacchus stand next to Venus, recalling the dictum that Venus grows cold without food and wine. One final characteristic of the natural Venus is her particular sway over women. The broken bows of "many a mayde" hang on her wall (287). At the end of the poem, the formel eagle anticipates joining them, and vows only that "I wol nat serve Venus ne Cupide, / Forsothe as yet" (652–53).[27] She apparently expects to serve them—to participate in the compulsory privilege of the nobility. But narrative delay is the principle of Venus's temple and of sexuality among the elite: it establishes social difference.

The venerean "natural" conventions of planetary metal, doves, roses, heat and moisture, food and wine, and feminine sexual inclinations all appear in the *Parliament of Fowls*, and perhaps constitute the promised "newe science" that comes out of "olde bokes" (24–25). By representing these natural conventions in the too numerous mythic agents of sexual desire and love, Chaucer denies their naturalness and foregrounds their participation in a class-specific myth of sexuality. The mythological temple cohort expresses the fictive artificiality of this sexuality, with its preternatural frustration and its endless (windy, poetic) reproduction of desire. As the temple description repeats and repeats again, in image after image, the sexual physiology associated with Venus, that repetition renders all too visible the well-known natural effects of the astral Venus on her children. The preeminent features of natural sexual physiology are estranged from the realm of the unquestioned, from the sphere of the natural. In sum, the overwrought mythological description turns the reputedly natural features of noble desire into the recognizable products of high culture. This serves to reinforce the treatment of Cupid and, by implication, of French poetry in the poem's opening and in the temple precincts.

Chaucer's description of Venus details her wealth and rank, but does not merely repeat her usual courtly attributes. Venus disports with Richesse, "ful noble and hautayn of hyre port" (262). Her hair bound with "golden thred" (267), Venus lies on a "bed of gold" (265), a marvelously extravagant display of excess wealth. "A thousand savours sote" (274) evoke luxury in its modern as well as medieval senses. This conjunction of riches and sensual pleasure add up to a Venus of the entitled. Chaucer's imagery details a specifically "noble" sexuality, dependent on a wealth and leisure that exclude commoners. While Venus's portrait encodes an aristocratic sexuality, though, it also reifies ambivalence. Her "gilte heres" are both bound "with a golden thred" (267) and "untressed as she lay" (268), picturing at once restraint and license. Similarly, with her upper body naked, "men myghte hire sen" (270), but

> The remenaunt was wel kevered to my pay,
> Ryght with a subtyl coverchef of Valence—
> Ther was no thikkere cloth of no defense.
>   (271–73)

The covering does not stop sight but entices it. This image of the thin veil eroticizes what happens when Venus is painted in the sea, the water simultaneously revealing and concealing her. Water or veil forms a passable barrier expressive of both desire and its interdiction.[28] The way the "subtyl coverchef" invites and interferes with sight is paralleled by the confusing linguistic opacity of "no thikkere cloth of no defense," which tantalizes and thwarts comprehension. This veil over the body of the goddess suggests the conventional veil of fiction over hidden mythographic truths, even while the expression denies that the veil hides anything. The veil teasingly asserts that the image of the goddess signifies a transparent meaning, which nevertheless remains "wel kevered to my pay." Chaucer once again re-creates poetic ambiguities in response to mythographic hermeneutics and theories of the fictive "veil."

This image appreciably complicates the initial treatment of Venus, raising questions about the earlier easy equation between sensual and poetic delights. Thus far, in fact, the pleasures associated with texts surpass sexual desire or experience. Still, reading also generates unsatisfied desires. Finishing the dream of Scipio leaves the narrator

> Fulfyld of thought and busy hevynesse;
> For bothe I hadde thyng which that I nolde,
> And ek I ne hadde that thyng that I wolde.
> (89–91)

The temple of Venus similarly creates a need for "solace" (297). Reading about Cupid astonishes and confuses the narrator, just as the inscription over the gate to the garden perplexes him, places him tensely "betwixen adamauntes two" (148). Whether privileged or not, whether approved or not, texts produce distinct effects consistently described in terms of unsatisfied desires. In the temple as well as in the invocation, Venus sponsors the perpetual production of just such unsatisfied desires; she presides over something more forceful than an aesthetic dependent chiefly on the musicality of verse, more unsettling than the celebration of courtly values. Together, the invocation to Venus and the temple description insist on an affective and sensual poetics that generates desire without satisfying it.

It has long been a habit of Chaucerians to view the portrait of Nature (and/or the dream of Scipio) as delineating a love in opposition to that represented by Venus—whether those two loves are considered divine and earthly, selfish and selfless, natural and courtly, procreative and barren, or some combination of these and other loves.[29] These readings are sometimes supported by reference to the accepted meanings of Venus and Nature in Chaucer's avowed source for the last section of the poem, Alan of Lille's *Plaint of Nature*. Such dichotomies certainly impose a comprehensible order and lucidity on Chaucer's depiction of sexuality. Chaucer's poem, however, presents something less determinate and more ambiguous than Alan's prosimetrum has been understood to offer.[30] Here Nature's precepts concern the birds' mutual pleasure rather more than any procreative rule.[31] She speaks to facilitate the birds' "ese, in fortheryng of youre nede" (384). The conjunction of "ese" and "nede" perhaps anticipates the Wife of Bath's dictum that organs of generation were created "for office and for ese / Of engendrure" (*Pro.* 127–28). But Nature is not explicit about the "engendrure" side of things. She requires only that the birds choose mates "as I prike yow with plesaunce" (389), according to a hierarchical social order and feminine consent.

A standard of procreative sexuality does not clearly separate Nature from Venus. The heat and moisture of Venus's temple, the presence of Priapus, Venus, Ceres, and Bacchus, all indicate in a mythic register the physiology of pleasure, but also that necessary to generation. Nature more clearly presides over the pleasures than over any utilitarian end of sexual acts. That Chaucer does not in this poem allude to the conventional theological justification for sexual pleasure is suggestive, for his silence on this point distances us from the idealizing moral certainty inherent in the theologians' neat opposition of procreative/nonprocreative sex. In short, throughout the poem he obscures conventional moral categories, rendering ambiguous the standards by which sexual desire and love (and ultimately literature) are to be judged. Instead of unfolding binary oppositions between Cupid and Venus, Scipio and Venus, Venus and Nature, natural and courtly, reproductive and barren, moral and immoral, celestial and earthly, conjugal and extramarital sexualities, Chaucer presents ambiguously defined, conflicting, and overlapping perspectives throughout his poem. And he closes without resolving the issues raised in the course of surveying these many "usages" of love. His poem, like his dream, generates the unsatisfied desire it repeatedly defines as the affective virtue of texts.

Although much is ambiguous here, particular social mores are clear-cut. Nature establishes courtly standards for mating: "God sende hym hire that sorest for hym syketh!" (404). This explicit standard turns out to be functionally inappropriate (for the royal tercel as well as the goose), but Nature offers no other. She is primarily concerned with the preservation of social hierarchy, *gentillesse*, and feminine consent. Within her order, the lesser birds discover immediate "blisse and joye" (669), while the elite tercelets achieve their cultural difference in love service and a prolongation of suffering. The poem returns in the end to its initial portrayal of the "natural" order of exclusionary noble difference, of pain in love. Whereas Chaucer introduces this convention as an amatory custom found only in certain disturbing books, he proceeds to place it in increasingly "natural" venues, ever more subtly questioning ideas of nature implicit in Gallic and Ovidian amatory conventions. In the course of the poem, concepts of natural sexuality increasingly manifest their debt to human designs and to human exigencies. Natural sexualities appear what they are, the "products of historical human activity" to be comprehended "within the domain of the temporal and of specific societies," however they might seem fixed in the immutable order of the cosmos.[32]

Cosmic Aesthetics

Chaucer's *Wife of Bath's Prologue* and *Parliament of Fowls* exhibit the unnaturalness of what often seems natural in late medieval discourses: the construction of women as venereal, the values and mores of aristocratic culture, the possibility of a simple distinction between licit and illicit sexualities, between procreative and nonprocreative sex. Both poems render nature a problematic category, one called upon to endorse such human constructions as misogyny and social hierarchies. Yet for all Chaucer's foregrounding of these problematics, both poems at least overtly allow for that most basic orthodox ideal of natural—that is, procreative—sexuality. The Wife of Bath overtly claims her reproductive rights, and nothing in Venus's temple or Nature's garden seriously challenges the ideal. Even while serving to reveal the contingency and human artifice implicit in some ideas about nature and natural sexuality, Venus preserves uncontested and invisible the most basic construction of the Church. However denaturalized, the natural (astrological, cosmological) Venus signifies the ambiguous relations between sexual acts and procreation, between human will and sensual desires, between the order of the cosmos and human orders. With the *Parliament of Fowls*, she also witnesses to uneasy relations between sensual desire and rational arts; she suggests the powerful effect of literature, regardless of its ethical or moral aims, to arouse desires that may not be satisfied. By invoking Venus, Chaucer binds the affective qualities of literature to the musical, harmonious order of the cosmos. If this order appears finally dubious, obscured by our various constructions of it, the aesthetic order of poetry makes the mystery and confusion at least bearable—and hopefully rather more than that.

Chapter 7

Remedia Amoris

> I cannot keep my subject still. It goes along befuddled and staggering, with a natural drunkenness. I take it in this condition, just as it is at the moment I give my attention to it. I do not portray being: I portray passing. . . . My history needs to be adapted to the moment. I may presently change, not only by chance, but also by intention. This is a record of various and changeable occurrences, and of irresolute and, when it so befalls, contradictory ideas: whether I am different myself, or whether I take hold of my subjects in different circumstances and aspects. So, all in all, I may indeed contradict myself now and then.
>
> Montaigne, "Of Repentance"

At the beginning of the *Confessio Amantis*, Gower portrays Amans as a highly conventional literary lover who goes into the woods one fair May day to complain of his unrequited love and to beseech the love deities for a remedy. Such conventionality leads us to expect that Venus will promise the fulfillment of his desire (sex), her usual remedy for love, or that Cupid will enter with his retinue and permit the lover to hand over the keys to his heart. Instead, Venus appears and requires that he transform his sickness into seemingly endless speech: "I woll thou telle it on and on, / Bothe all thi thoght and al thi werk" (1.194–95). To this end, she refers him to her priest Genius, who will act as his confessor. And so the lover's confession begins, and so it progresses by rule through the sins, "on and on," book after book. This catechistic design exploits a startling affinity between literary love conventions and ecclesiastical standards: both effectively transform desire into discourse, be it poetry or verbal confession.[1] Gower's conflation of these generative verbal models calls attention to their similarities as well as to the difficulties of bringing them into a coherent union. If a literary lover wholeheartedly seeks the embraces of the beloved, the penitent must with similar zeal pursue less mundane aspirations. Amatory and penitential discourses may momentarily converge, but sooner or later they will inevitably diverge. The explicit motivation for the whole—amatory guidance—and the confessional design refer to potentially conflicted discourses about sexuality. By incorporating amatory as well as pastoral discourses, Gower accentuates the heterogeneity apparent in late medieval discussions of sexuality. He does not present us with a single hegemonic (ecclesiastical) discourse but rather invites contemplation of the relationships among the sundry and sometimes contradictory discourses that formulate medieval sexualities. Hence he invites us to appreciate more fully the flexibility inherent in those discourses—mythography among them—and the implications of bringing them into an unstable union.

Introducing Amans, Gower emphasizes the fictionality of this literary character, who plainly recalls conventional French representations of the lover-poet.[2] Indeed, a Latin marginal note pedantically calls attention to the fictive device of the persona by declaring that Gower here feigns the lover (at 1.60). Like many such literary lovers, Amans deifies sexual love, projecting his desires onto the all-powerful figures of Venus and Cupid.[3] Amans exists as a literary convention, and his meeting with the imagined supernatural representations of his love fulfills the expectations of that convention. In accordance with convention, he also participates in the religion of love. He eventually confesses that he sits in church with his "devocion" and "contemplacion" "only set on hire ymage" (5.7125–28), somewhat comically exemplifying idolatry. Patrick J. Gallacher has collected numerous other examples of Amans's religion of love, and we need not survey the evidence again.[4] Significantly, this adherence to a religion of love functions to characterize the lover as idolatrous: Amans deifies his own desires and worships idols of his own making. The conventional lover has fallen into a pseudo-pagan error of divinizing natural forces and humans. In sum, Gower depicts the frivolously devout Ovidian lover so as to show that he has reproduced pagan misconceptions of the divine, ingeniously misreading amatory conventions in order to re-create them.[5]

As Gower sketches out the overfamiliar traditions of amatory literature, he also places them under the temperate light of reason. Since Amans has fallen into a pseudo-pagan error, Genius corrects him by means of familiar mythographic explanations that demystify sexuality and its supposedly divine representatives. This correction forms one thread within the larger design of Genius telling tales in order to draw particular morals from them.[6] His methodology owes much to the hermeneutics developed within commentary traditions. Like many fourteenth-century mythographers and other commentators, Genius unifies his exposition according to a coherent scheme—he guides Amans through a structured confession of a slightly modified seven deadly sins. Each sin forms the focus for a single book of the poem, dictating the necessary transcendent meaning for all the tales in that book. In Books 5 and 7, Genius varies this design to offer extended instruction on particular topics—at which point he refers directly to mythographic hermeneutics, elaborating historical and astrological explanations of Venus and Cupid.[7]

Two brief examples should clarify Genius's method and permit us to contextualize his uses of mythography. In a book focused on the sin of covetousness, Genius tells a tale of a young, chaste king who falls ill and is advised by his physicians that the cure for his ailment is sexual intercourse.[8] His steward procures a woman (the steward's wife) for one medicinal night, during which this woman "doth al that sche mai to plese, / So that his herte al hol sche hadde" (5.2768–69). When the king discovers the steward's game, the steward is exiled for valuing gain instead of love, and the king marries the woman. Genius concludes from this that the lover should avoid covetousness, which generates dis-ease in marriage. The extramarital sexual pleasure, the informal divorce and remarriage, and the medical use of coitus escape any moralizing commentary because these aspects of the fiction are extraneous to the moral about covetousness. Genius often devises similarly mechanical moralizations that overlook obvious ethical issues. We might compare the tale of Babio, which falls a bit later in the book on covetousness. After the ungenerous Babio competes unsuccessfully with the liberal Croceus for Viola's favors, Genius concludes that the lover should be like Croceus, for in the end

> This Croceus, the bowe bende,
> Which Venus tok him forto holde,
> And schotte als ofte as evere he wolde.
>   (5.4860–62)

Genius accordingly recommends largesse as the surest way to coitus, and Amans earnestly promises to examine his conscience and amend any lack in the future. Importing this unabashedly Ovidian law of love into the moralization obviously confuses distinctions between erotic narrative and moralizing commentary, and dramatically raises the question of their appropriate relation. Certainly, not all of Genius's analyses are quite as problematic as these, though these are not exceptional cases. Such interpretations scattered throughout the text discover the sorts of moral questions potentially raised by the incorporation of both amatory and penitential perspectives.[9] Far from being a reliable authority, Genius embodies several contradictions and incongruities.[10]

Genius's frequently inapposite commentary and his flexible moral standards have invited some modern critics to treat him as an inept mythographer, unable to discern the "proper" moral implications of his tales.[11] But Genius simply unfolds interpretations that suit his overall design and immediate catechismal purpose, and his blatant (sometimes flat-footed) appropriation of ancient narrative strongly recalls mythographic analysis and commentary traditions. Genius is no more inept than most mythographers. Mythography can also provide analogues for the occasional surprise in Genius's morality and for his often blithely reductive commentary. What mythography cannot anticipate is the effect of Gower's coupling of erotic fiction and moralizing commentary. By translating (chiefly Ovidian) poetry as well as mythographic hermeneutics into one text, Gower foregrounds the disjunctions between them. The combination of narrative and hermeneutic arts discloses one of the central problems with conventional moralizing hermeneutics: they studiously avoid empirical methods of reading. In seeking transcendent truths about sin, Genius almost necessarily fails to treat his narratives persuasively. So does any mythographer in pursuit of a foreordained signification, though we do not need to notice this in mythography because the fiction and commentary are never so delicately balanced as they are in Gower's poem. Here, as critics have long recognized, the fully realized narratives repeatedly deny Genius's inappropriate and reductive interpretations.[12]

No simple formula can explain the relations between all the tales and morals in the *Confessio Amantis*; the text involves too many interpretive strategies and occasions and perspectives for a single explanation to suffice. Some disjunctions between tales and morals suggest merely that Gower sometimes nods and chooses a poor tale for the lesson at hand. More interesting are the many disparities that appear purposeful, and that reveal, as Charles Runacres persuasively demonstrates, "the need for more complex moral responses to ethical questions."[13] As such moralizations expose Genius's interpretive inadequacies, we realize how moralizing hermeneutics can all too easily simplify the ethical issues raised by narratives (or life). Genius's sometimes ludicrous readings and inconsistent ethical principles thus initiate questions about interpretation and about conventional Latin authority systems. His explications form a vivid commentary on the tradition of moralizing commentaries, serving gradually to undermine conventional interpretive models. In short, Gower incorporates a conventionally authoritative scholarly system of reading only to exhibit its limitations.

While Genius explicates his tales, he and Amans converse, often enough with the lover questioning or challenging Genius's analysis. Most famously, Amans contests the value of virginity (which interferes with procreation) and of crusading (since killing pagans precludes their conversion). Amans's disputes over particular interpretations assert the competence of individual readers to discern other meanings than those discovered by Genius. These dialogues represent interpretation as a process of negotiation between individual readers (with their own self-interested priorities and agendas) and conventional hermeneutics. Alongside or interspersed with this dialogic explication, Gower (or, less likely, a scribe) supplies Latin annotations, which may either summarize or modify Genius's conclusions. As Derek Pearsall and Winthrop Wetherbee have convincingly proposed, this scholarly apparatus can manifest significant differences from the poetic text. In Pearsall's words, the Latin annotations "are not means to the understanding of the English poem but instructions on how to read it according to the conventions of a specific code of reading."[14] The Latin glosses (and the final colophon) introduce yet another player into the interpretive game, all the more emphatically portraying reading as an individual and contingent act. Another feature of the text, Latin verses interspersed with the English, further complicates interpretation of the work as a whole (in part because these verses are bafflingly difficult to translate). This multiplication of authorities and voices, with all their differences from one another, forcefully argues against the possibility of any single, unquestionably authoritative model of interpretation. Although the scholarly frame to and design of the poem repeatedly, even redundantly, direct our attention to conventionally authoritative models of reading and writing, Gower presents them as always contested and limited paradigms. Human authority itself grows increasingly equivocal.[15]

In the overall structure of this text as well as in its details, the authority of any particular interpretive model appears merely local, temporary, and limited, always awaiting displacement by later, different models. As the seemingly authoritative traditions multiply in Gower's text, moreover, we understand them as part of a conspicuously fictive view of the world—as human inventions, not immutable divine truths.[16] In other words, we perceive the intellectual traditions as distinctly human artifacts with something less than indubitable authority, as sharing space with narrative art rather than replacing it. Gower's poem sets conventional hermeneutics themselves into the play of poetic meaning. His design authorizes, even invites, individualistic readings, even as the very length, conceptual diversity, and complexity of the poem perplex (and perhaps thereby generate) interpretation.

Mythographic hermeneutics constitute one of the discourses to which Gower grants a limited authority, and these hermeneutics contribute to a crucial turn in the poem: they help to effect the transformation of Amans from a conventionally frustrated, pseudo-idolatrous literary lover to an aged poet at greater peace with himself. Although their authority is limited, the hermeneutics nonetheless permit an efficacious response to pagan errors. As we have seen, Amans mystifies his love, transforms it into a religion. With a few prods from Amans, Genius consents to demystify sexual love by elucidating the love deities' historical and natural origins.[17] This multiplies authoritative definitions and thereby challenges the illusion of their explanatory adequacy. Much as the mythographers do, Gower offers multiple, seemingly unreconciled ways of understanding the ancient myths, both identifying and deferring originary meanings. Unlike mythographers, he locates these hermeneutics in the aesthetic order of poetry, implying a self-conscious design for such multiplicity. As a consequence, the poem encourages meditation on the relations among the various significances brought into sometimes uneasy, sometimes perplexing juxtaposition. Whereas encyclopedic mythography presents us with unexamined relationships among diverse unreconciled meanings, this poem turns the diverse meanings into the utterances of particular speakers, offering interpretations under the unequally authoritative patronage of Genius, Amans, a Latin scholar, and an English poet. The relation between individual speaker and discursive point of view grows apparent, as does the interested nature of the conclusions drawn.

The *Confessio Amantis* therefore does not grant authoritative priority to mythography, but treats it as a source of strategies by which to demystify Amans's love deities. This demystification officially begins in Book 5, when Genius asserts that a blindly irrational deification of natural forces constitutes the central flaw of paganism. The Chaldeans, Egyptians, Greeks, and Romans elevated stars, natural forces, and humans into gods and goddesses. Genius repeatedly stresses that in this they refused to follow reason; they willfully pursued their imaginative fictions rather than the truth.[18] Amans's initial perception of Venus and Cupid is analogous to this original pagan failure of reason—resulting from a fascination with imaginative fictive devices. Genius's analysis of paganism agrees with those of other medieval commentators—Bishop Bradwardine, Vincent of Beauvais, William of Conches, and Nicholas Trevet—who contend that pagans could, by the exercise of reason alone, arrive at a monotheism foreshadowing Christianity.[19] Genius accordingly returns the deities to the contexts of rational (that is, Christian) understanding by disclosing first their historical and then their natural origins—in short, by removing their fictive (imaginative) veils. The historical explanation treats Venus as an amorous woman who founded prostitution and was subsequently revered as goddess "of worldes lust and of plesance" (5.1443). Cupid was her incestuous son (5.1382–1443).[20] The elaborated spectacle of their incestuous, indiscriminate, commercial sexuality robs them of credibility and seemliness as sponsors of literary love. Hence direct mythographic explanation separates the deities from an aestheticized discourse, from a culturally elevated mythic register.

In the end Gower will complete this separation by silently absenting Cupid and by returning the planetary Venus to the heavens, implying Amans's final Christian understanding of her place in the natural order:

> Enclosid in a sterred sky,
> Venus, which is the qweene of love,
> Was take in to hire place above.
>   (8.2942–44)

Before that resolution is possible, Genius must replace faulty understandings of Venus, as a literary fiction and as a degraded historical figure, with an explanation of her natural powers. In other words, Genius must progressively redefine the forces Amans has mistakenly divinized. To this end, Genius develops a natural-astrological explanation of Venus, which falls within a review of Alexander's education (occupying most of Book 7). Once again, context is integral to Venus's meaning and bears close examination. Ascribing the natural explanation to Aristotle, Alexander's master, underwrites the authority of the account, its basis in natural reason; in this way Gower reinforces the bond between scientific discourses and elite authoritative masculine institutions. Yet in the *Confessio Amantis* authoritative systems are always limited, and Aristotelian astrology proves no exception.

The account of natural science in Book 7 is preceded by the tale of Nectanabus and Alexander (6.1789–2366), in which scientific authority becomes more than a little suspect. Nectanabus is an astrologer and magician who uses his arts to lie with a married woman and beget a child (the woman believes him to be a god, as does her husband in the end). The tale vividly exhibits the gullibility that permits humans to pose as gods. (This point more famously emerges from the story of Paulina and Mundus, another divine impersonator, 1.761–1059, and the fictional development of this theme reinforces Gower's historical interpretation of the deities.)[21] The child Alexander is born and in due time Nectanabus attempts to teach him astrology. Skeptical about the validity of this science, Alexander asks to hear Nectanabus's fortune and learns that he will be killed by his own son. Ignorant about his true parentage, Alexander pushes Nectanabus over the wall to disprove the prophecy, thereby fulfilling it. Events tacitly affirm the particular astrological prediction even as the tale expressly aligns astrology and magic with masculine arts of amatory deceit: the tale simultaneously acknowledges and denounces the power of astrology and its potential for abuse.

This tale implies that manifold difficulties arise with any attempt to determine what role astrology should play, or does play, in human affairs, and Genius's framing of the tale only accentuates these difficulties. He introduces the narrative with a fideistic dictum:

> The hihe creatour of thinges,
> Which is the king of alle kinges,
> Ful many a wonder worldes chance
> Let slyden under his suffrance;
> Ther wot noman the cause why,
> Bot he the which is almyhty.
> (6.1789–94)

Since justice operates obscurely, humans cannot know the causes of things. The narrative contrarily demonstrates that astrologers can foretell particular events in the future. In summing up the tale, Genius does not resolve this apparent contradiction, but offers still another view of divine order: "for o mis an other mys / Was yolde, and so fulofte it is" (6.2359–60). Whereas the introduction declares the enigmatic wonders of the "worldes chance," the distance between human and divine, the conclusion eliminates that distance and represents divine justice in easily comprehensible terms. Even that comprehensibility is limited, of course, since Alexander's casual patricide apparently earns no reciprocal "mis." The simplistic conclusion denies the questions raised by the narrative, foreclosing rather than coherently resolving its philosophical and ethical issues.

This story, with its veiled obscurities and with the questions it raises, leads (one very brief tale aside) to the education of Alexander, which includes astrology. In the midst of the description of heavenly bodies, Nectanabus reappears as Alexander's tutor. At this point Gower recounts the astronomer's identification of the fifteen stars (together with their stones and herbs) as objective scientific fact (7.1292–1438). The meaning of Nectanabus is obviously pliable: he can embody the evils of sorcery or stand for the felicitous matter of wisdom. Hence the second coming of Nectanabus exposes a lacuna between Gower's moralizing representation of astrological "sorcery" and his encyclopedic gathering of astrological lore. This lacuna perplexes the status of astrology in the poem, for Nectanabus's authoritative knowledge obviously does not produce the moral advantages that Genius supposes attend the acquisition of learning. What then is the point of repeating Alexander's studies? The status of astrology, the value of its insights, and its relation to divine and ethical orders all come into question even as Gower asserts its Aristotelian authority. This authority system, like all others, manifests its own limitations. Knowledge of astrology (or any other art) plainly gives one authority only over specifically limited matters, such as the classification of stars, or the traditional understanding of astral influences. This science can reliably disclose the character of Venus's planetary power but cannot answer the questions it provokes.

The limitations of authority systems become still more apparent with the specific introduction to astrology. Gower opens the topic by carefully defining the limits of planetary influences: "a wise man will rule the stars with the help of God."[22] This commonplace formula invokes a hierarchical relationship between mind and body, and asserts the free exercise of individual will. Instead of resting on or developing this philosophical tag, however, Gower uses it to introduce disagreements between astrologers and divines. The assertion becomes just one in a series of conflicting perspectives (7.633–69). As Genius points out, astrologers posit that earthly matters are governed by the stars, while divines claim that humans should not fear the stars as long as they are "goode and wise." Genius himself advocates a third position: original natural law emphatically must work in all creatures unless a "miracle" occurs "thurgh preiere of som holy man" (7.662–63). The initial Latin portrait of a "wise man" grandly dominating the stars with the help of God fades into that of a "holy man" working miracles. Wisdom in the face of natural forces presents a distinct exception to the norm, and divine assistance seems a mysterious anomaly. As he proceeds, therefore, Gower heightens rather than resolves the discursive differences among philosophers, divines, and astrologers. He questions the relationship between mind and body only to introduce multiple authorities and defer answers. After offering his skeptical view of the limits of human governance, Genius moves on to describe the planets and their influences. With this, our encyclopedic march forward treads over the conflicting implications of the discourses gathered together, and wisdom becomes a matter of merely acquiring information (7.710–20).[23] Genius's descriptions of the arts, elements, humors, temperaments, planets, and zodiacal signs unfold as objective, uncontroversial accounts of the nature of things. The presentation detaches science from philosophical dilemmas, and Gower leaves it to the reader to integrate these disparate perspectives—and to determine the value of the information presented. The reader can always decide to decline the challenge.

The astrological account of Venus shows her exercising her familiar powers over her children:

>   this Planete
> The moste part is softe and swete;
> For who that therof takth his berthe,
> He schal desire joie and merthe,
> Gentil, courteis and debonaire,
> To speke his wordes softe and faire,
> Such schal he be be weie of kinde,
> And overal wher he may finde
> Plesance of love, his herte boweth

> With al his myht and there he woweth.
> He is so ferforth Amourous,
> He not what thing is vicious
> Touchende love, for that lawe
> Ther mai no maner man withdrawe,
> The which venerien is bore
> Be weie of kinde, and therefore
> Venus of love the goddesse
> Is cleped. (7.781–98)

The planet presides over sexual desire, sexual capacity, and pleasure. Venus's class-specific influence is once again apparent: lovers are "gentil, courteis and debonaire," skilled in the verbal arts of love. Because Genius identifies these class-bound standards closely with natural order, the genteel appear naturally lovers, naturally courteous. These social norms seem, as they so often do, innate qualities; an inescapable natural law ensures cultural norms and the signs of privileged class status. A bit later in the passage, this natural law not only marks a social class but also distinguishes the inhabitants of Lombardy, where Venus's influence particularly fosters "lecherie" (7.799). Such social (and nationalist) constraints on astrology demonstrate its ideological usefulness. Although science here as elsewhere authorizes this cultural appropriation of the natural order, such conspicuously ideological accounts of the planet take us far from the science of astrology. We may as a consequence find Gower's astrology, as George G. Fox does, a "puerile ... performance"; or we may, with Hamilton M. Smyser, discern in it "an ineptitude remarkable even in the annals of pedagogy."[24]

Such scornful responses perhaps too hastily dismiss the poetry along with the science, for the sophistication of a science is hardly the key to its poetic worth. By defining this cultural order of sexuality as natural and authoritative, Gower affirms its legitimacy, granting to socially contingent values the ephemeral illusion of an immutable natural order understood through the seemingly nonideological exercise of reason. By thus defining the astral influence, Gower identifies a particular construction of natural sexuality with the (albeit contested) authority of medieval science. The irresistible power of sexual desire, the pleasures and "joie" of sexual activity, and the gentility of love constitute the preeminent features of a rationally verified natural sexuality. Significantly, Gower's representation of natural sexuality is here constrained predominantly by social mores rather than by theological or canonistic rule (we might recall Christine de Pizan's similarly configured astrology). Like many others in the later Middle Ages, Gower detaches the "plesance" of sexual love from the procreative rule, the *sine qua non* of orthodox constructions of natural sexuality.[25] Even the sexual physiology associated with Venus, which elsewhere may implicitly support the procreative rule, does not enter into the portrait of her children. Instead, sexual "joie" and "plesance" appear the entire "lawe" and "weie of kinde," at least for the gentle classes and residents of Lombardy.

Natural sexuality does not, as it so often does, equate with morality; and Gower does not exclusively adhere to the ecclesiastical definition of natural sexuality. At the same time, the limited authority supporting the astrological scheme means that it may be rejected. This is not nature but only one possible construction of nature, and we have already been reminded that the divines would say otherwise. Gower's representation of astrology and natural law frankly depicts them as products of historical human activity. This denaturalization of conventional ideas of natural sexuality neatly parallels Chaucer's treatment of astrology in the *Wife of Bath's Prologue* and of nature in the *Parliament of Fowls*. Each poet makes visible the culturally invisible ideological bent of science and nature.

Elsewhere in Book 7 Gower elaborates a natural sexual physiology along lines familiar from our investigation of the mythographers' Venus, and the further details fill in this picture of natural sexuality without altering its basic lines. In reviewing the four temperaments of humoral theory, for example, Genius stresses that the sanguine temperament (hot and moist) enables sexual capacity and pleasure (7.421–28). The description emphasizes the sensual delights of love: the sanguine man "hath bothe will and myht / To plese and paie love his riht" (7.425–26). Although Gower does not link the temperament with Venus, the traditional connection explains the planet resting in the hot and moist sign of Virgo (7.1111–14). As always, the season for love is "lusti" May, when

> love of his pointure stingeth
> After the lawes of nature
> The youthe of every creature.
> (7.1048–50)

The commonplace seasonal privilege of youth becomes an inviolable natural law. The familiar portrait of a lover gradually fills in: a child of

Venus, an aristocratic youth with a sanguine temperament, sensitive to the stimulating influences of spring. Throughout this description, sexual activity equates with love, as it does for many late medieval mythographers and poets. In Gower's poem this portrait of the lover goes under the authority of Aristotle: a rational though disputable investigation of natural order confirms that a venerean life of pleasure seems irresistible. Reason demonstrates the naturalness of sexual compulsions that are both innate and expressed in accordance with culturally bound social mores.

How Gower treats natural law throughout the poem reinforces the implications of the astral Venus and the natural sexuality over which she presides. Indeed, the tales do not always make clear whether Venus is a literary-amatory convention, a historical woman, a planet, an anthropomorphized force of sexual desire, or fortune's twin and associated with the evanescence of things. She is not one but all of these. Venus is most generally a manifestation of Gower's ambiguous law of nature.[26] According to this law, sexual desire is naturally, normally irresistible. While conventional wisdom posits that the wise rule the stars, therefore, throughout the poem, over and over again, we read that few are wise and that even the wise are conquered by love. This theme evidently conforms to the teaching of Aquinas,[27] and it suggests in Gower's poem an acceptance of the limits of reason and hence of self-governance. For instance, the Prologue takes love's domination over many wise men as the theme for the whole work:

> Whan the prologe is so despended,
> This bok schal afterward ben ended
> Of love, which doth many a wonder
> And many a wys man hath put under.
> (73–76)

Continuing this theme, the first book opens with Latin verses proclaiming the universal rule of love ("Naturatus amor nature legibus orbem / Subdit"), a message fortified by the English verse,

> ther is noman
> In al this world so wys, that can
> Of love tempre the mesure,
> Bot as it falth in aventure.
> (1.21–24)

A gloss somewhat superfluously reiterates the point. The universal and amoral rule of "natural" love is also re-asserted at regular intervals.[28] In some versions of the poem, Genius goes so far as to declare that chastity is achieved not by reason but by grace alone (5.*6400–6404), with the gloss contending that "to live in the flesh yet beyond the flesh is a life more angelic than human."[29] Amans echoes this theme, confessing that "ther is in me non holinesse" when he glimpses his beloved (5.7162). In fact, Genius discusses chastity as a near impossibility:

> bot it be grace
> Above alle othre in special
> Is non that chaste mai ben all.
>   (7.4242–44)

Wise humans who rule the flesh and the stars are the elect few who receive a special divine grace. That Gower ends the lover's confession with tales of incest pointedly declares the immanence of sexual desire, from which almost no human relationship is immune, no private space exempt. A notoriously incestuous couple, Venus and Cupid help to weave this theme through the text. The poem thus continually portrays humans as naturally subject to the irresistible power of love, particularly though not exclusively in youth and in the spring and according to social class. With the astral Venus and physiology of Book 7, Gower gathers these threads together under the authority of Aristotelian science. Poetic themes, scientific discourse, and confessional instruction apparently all teach a coherent rule: sexual desire is normally inexorable and overpowering, the source of a sensual pleasure nearly impossible to forgo. The congruence and coherence of this message through the various Latin glosses and verses, the tales, Genius's moral expositions, and the education of Alexander reveal a common ground on which many discourses meet, affirming a point of agreement among the heterogeneous perspectives of amatory poet, confessor and penitent, astrologer, and learned scribe. In short, the law of nature predicts a nearly compulsory sexual desire and demonstrates the limits of human governance (obviously a common late medieval theme). As Venus sums up this pattern,

> Nature is under the Mone
> Maistresse of every lives kinde,
> Bot if so be that sche mai finde
> Som holy man that wol withdrawe

> His kindly lust ayein hir lawe;
> Bot sielde whanne it falleth so,
> For fewe men ther ben of tho.
> (8.2330–36)

Early and late, natural sexuality subdues almost all creatures.

Alongside this motif, Gower develops a theme of hierarchical order, in which reason governs the flesh as the king rules over the state (an analogy that invites reflections on both kingship and reason). This would neatly resolve the poem's many ambiguities if the relation between reason and passion (or the flesh) were more clearly and consistently defined, if the poem ended in such a way as to illustrate the hierarchy, or, for that matter, if the king seemed likely to be exempt from the rule of nature. In fact, though, the rule of reason over sexuality is ambiguous, unavoidably so since the Fall; the relations of soul and body, reason and concupiscence, are at best seen through a glass darkly.[30] Gower certainly advocates a rational moderation of sexual impulses, but that rational mean is determined by the always shifting contexts and tightly constrained purposes of the individual tales. Reason (like nature) serves as a flexible explanatory principle rather than as a fixed rule. Genius candidly equivocates over the supposed priority of reason in relation to the natural law of sexual love:

> love is of so gret a miht,
> His lawe mai noman refuse,
> So miht thou thee the betre excuse.
> And natheles thou schalt be lerned
> That will scholde evere be governed
> Of reson more than of kinde.
> (3.1194–99)

Although the rule of love is universal, humans should know the way of rational governance. The relation of reason to natural law is simply unclear.[31] Any idealized hierarchical order, moreover, always anticipates individual failure, for the Prologue ends by detailing the consequences of original sin, the corruption that permanently overturned the microcosm.[32] This microcosmic disorder evidences itself as the rule of blind love in the tales. As Hugh White puts it, "the world is an environment normally fatal to our pursuit of moral perfection."[33]

The predetermined failure of self-governance leads inexorably in Genius's confessional discourse to a predictable theological conclusion: eschewing is the only remedy. At this point, Gower brings Venus and Cupid on the scene to participate in the lover's cure. Gower describes Venus as blind, drawing on a metaphor that has gathered extensive implications in the course of the poem, all of which reverberate here. Most obviously, blindness links Venus to Cupid, whose blindness earlier signifies irrationality:

> love is of a wonder kinde,
> And hath hise wittes ofte blinde,
> That thei fro mannes reson falle.
> (3.1323–25)

At another point, blindness figures Cupid's specifically incestuous desire: he and Venus were "bothe al one" since he "yhen hadde none / To se reson" (5.1411–13). The figure of Cupid's blindness identifies a condition of psychological sightlessness, an inability to see with the eyes of reason. Cupid actually has "yhen wrothe" (1.140) and apparently not sightless in his first appearance, so these descriptions of his blindness evidence an unstable iconology (much the same occurs with Venus).

Gower does not restrict blindness to Cupid. Blindness also signifies pagan idolatry, the ancient divinization of natural forces (for instance, in the Latin verses before 5.747). Further extending the figurative implications of blindness, Fortune and Venus both turn blind wheels. At various points, Amans and other lovers, covetousness, and avarice are all labeled blind. Gower places the conventional detail of Cupid's blindness into a complex figurative concatenation of sexual desire, love, irrationality, incest, idolatry, paganism, assorted sins, and fortune. Through these figurative associations, sexual desire appears in ever-changing relation to the social orders of family and community, to religious dogma, and to the cosmic order of fortune. Sexual desire comes to seem always and unremittingly immanent—implicit in the mutable order of fortune's wheel as well as in the closest familial circle. Even as blindness delineates this interdependence of human and cosmic orders, though, the figure suggests more than it delimits. Rather than referring Cupid's blindness to a specific moral code, Gower sets the figure into a continual play of poetic meaning on the nature and limitations of rational insight. He develops a poetry of figurative ambiguities rather than an argument. The absence of a detailed and fixed iconography for Venus and Cupid calls attention to Gower's refusal to pin them down within a single tradition, and to his aesthetic decision that they represent a wide range of the ambiguous social and ideological implications of sexuality.

Her blindness thus finally associates Venus iconologically with Cupid, irrational desire, pagan error, and, more significantly, with fortune (8.2385). As the twin of fortune, Venus is, at the end of the poem as elsewhere, linked to cyclical mutability, and this import underlies her closing counsel to Amans, which describes the place of old age on the wheel of fortune. In keeping with her close ties to fortune and nature, Venus directs Amans not to her routine natural cure for love—sex—but to another, also natural, cure: the impotence of old age. Gower begins the poem with the lover's appeal to the god and goddess of love, a stock formula of amatory poetry, but gradually displaces that convention in favor of natural traditions and figurative ambiguities.

The Venus of court poetry is replaced by the Venus of natural hermeneutics, and the original goddess of love comes to symbolize the mutability of human fortunes and desires. The point of Venus's kinship with fortune becomes apparent as she details Amans's age and physical incapacity through a sequence of dazzling metaphoric changes that vividly evoke the mutability of all living things: he is "noght sufficant / To holde love his covenant"; though his will is good "more behoveth to the plowh"; his "fieble astat" would keep him from winning the race; a man cannot bargain when he "lacketh forto paie"; and his green grass is turned to hay (8.2419–37). This transformative metaphoric sequence affirms the value of sexual as well as linguistic play, keeping before the audience the attractions of vigorous sexuality even (or perhaps especially) at the point of its individual decline.[34] As the wheel turns down for one, it raises another, and new life takes its turn in the race. In their rapid transformations, these fleeting metaphors evoke the ephemeral quality of life and youth, the always transitory character of human desire. Venus's blindness, recalling blind fortune, ultimately depicts the mutability as well as the irrationality of sexual desire.

Amans then forsakes what has already faded, a sexual capacity as evanescent as life. Venus's metaphoric vision of mortality effects in Amans the sensation of quasi death that intriguingly replicates the symptoms of lovesickness; he feels a sudden chill, turns pale, and faints. He has a vision in which lovers dispute his case, some saying that the old should not love, some that love's flame has no regard for age (8.2750–82). Within this vision, Venus and Cupid cure him of love by releasing him from his desire. That is, the remedy of love is the cessation of desire, which comes only with the gross infirmity of age. Amans is not cured by an exertion of willed reason over passion, or by prayer, but by the physiological effects of old age.[35] He now recognizes an analogy between his life and the year's seasons, in which the delight of growing things precedes their overthrow. Venus's metaphorical demonstration of transience here swells into a single extended metaphor capturing Amans's retrospective account of his life's seasons:

> I made a liknesse of miselve
> Unto the sondri Monthes twelve,
> Wherof the yeer in his astat
> Is mad. (8.2837–40)

From his present experience of wintry decay, Amans the more wistfully recalls the delights of summer and the passionate evanescence of youthful sexuality. The rueful tone suitable to this perspective, and the metaphoric intensity of expression, would surely excuse the audience determining "To love that well, which thou must leave ere long."[36] This farewell to love keenly evokes the transitoriness of life, the appeal of passionate youth as well as the inevitability of death. The blind Venus testifies to the unity of sexual desire and transience in the cyclical order of nature.

Amans becomes rational in his winter of old age. This conclusion follows logically from the recurrent scientific view of human action as conditioned largely by biology—by the heat and moisture of blood, by the irresistible power of youthful and vernal sexual desire, by the effects of cold and dry humors in old age. Gower clinically details Amans's faded color, cloudy eyes, sunken cheeks, wrinkled face, white hair (8.2820–31), cataloging the physiological aspects of aging. As Hugh White notes, however, nature is hardly consistent in this remedy, for even in Amans's final vision the assembly of love includes old men.[37] The natural effects of age permit Amans's "beau retret" from love, but nature's operations remain as ambiguous and uneven as they are throughout the poem. Gower does not paint an utterly comprehensible nature but one that withholds its mysteries, and he leaves nebulous the always perplexing relation between reason and passion. Since Gower places this complex portrayal of human limitations into the context of confession, the remedy for the inevitable human limits and failures is always immediately apparent. If sin is as inevitable as desire, it has a remedy: institutionalized speech about motives and actions, the transformation of desire into discourse. The confessional structure answers the thematic content, and the structure quite exquisitely complements the theme. Gower places structure and theme in a dialectical relationship rather than a hierarchical one.

In the *Confessio Amantis*, mythographic hermeneutics allow Gower to rationalize the deities' existence, and hence to reverse Amans's recapitulation of pagan error. Through this literary lover, the issues implicit in medieval negotiations of the classical and contemporary poetic heritage assume a new immediacy and urgency. Thus the poem offers a stunning new perspective on conventional and French literary fictions of love—a perspective that descries in literary convention the enduring vitality of ancient pagan error. The mythographic challenge to read the ancient past according to Christian revelation becomes the poetic problem of reading the present. As Gower appropriates mythographic strategies in order to comment on contemporary Ovidian and French literature—breaking a French butterfly on a wheel made for an ancient Roman variety—he indicates the continued need for mythography to address faulty understandings of the divine. His fiction reinvigorates the conceptual justification for mythography. In brief, mythography does not help Gower to allegories or ideas about two loves; instead, it shows him how to strip away the imaginative fictive veils over historical and natural truths, and how to correct pagan and pseudo-pagan errors.

Gower's incorporation of disparate discourses is surely not the product of an unwitting encyclopedism. Certainly, he emphasizes heterogeneity through his numerous discursive perspectives: the Latin scholar with his glosses, the Latin poet with his verses, Genius and Amans in their dialogues, the shifting narrative and didactic points of view, and the academic reviews of the nature of things. With Venus and Cupid, Gower exploits the multiplicity of traditions—literary amatory conventions, historicizing and astrologizing hermeneutics, natural law—so as to remake their meanings. The initial literary conventions of the love deities are assimilated to explanatory traditions, and then rewritten as natural forces. Within the poem, all the diverse traditions form an integrated whole, within which each convention, each discourse, each perspective enters into endlessly fascinating interplay with the others. The poem does not offer a single meaning but, rather, engaging invitations to reflect on the perspectives that create meaning and on the discourses that construct sexualities. We can of course resist the poem and select a single discourse (penitential, for instance) through which to read it. To the extent that humans tend to be uncomfortable with unresolved ambiguities, the text certainly invites this readerly activity.

We might nevertheless choose simply to respect Gower's design, which calls into question the relationships between human wisdom and cosmic orders, between mind and body, between theological and scientific perspectives, without advancing the sure answers of a hegemonic discourse. Indeed, the presentation of each authority as limited prevents any one (including the catechistic) from asserting absolute primacy. While medieval disciplinary discourses present the relation between mind and body variously and even indeterminately, Gower foregrounds the resultant ambiguities of this relationship. He thereby allows the audience to "break through the automatism of everyday perception."[38] Like Chaucer, Gower denaturalizes received wisdom, desacralizes supposedly divine authority. And like Chaucer, by bringing these diverse conceptual traditions into a satisfying aesthetic order, Gower puzzles thought precisely because he reveals ambiguities rather than advancing a singular, simplistic ideational clarity. Such ambiguities surely fulfill one of the more vital offices of poetry: rather than resolving us of all our ambiguities, Gower, like Chaucer, makes us able to contemplate them.

Chapter 8

Venus, Cupid, and English Poetry

> A conversation begins
> with a lie. And each
>
> speaker of the so-called common language feels
> the ice-floe split, the drift apart
>
> as if powerless, as if up against
> a force of nature
>   Adrienne Rich, "Cartographies of Silence"
>
> Words are to lie with
> believe me
> believe me
>   Ursula K. LeGuin, "More Useful Truths"

In the *House of Fame* and *Parliament of Fowls*, Chaucer shapes Venus and Cupid into unequal patrons of poetic and other amatory arts. For Chaucer as for Lucretius, Ovid, and many other writers, Venus embodies a poetic union of intangible ideas and tangible realities; she symbolizes the inextricable intimacy between mind and body, poetic effects and sensuality. She also suggestively binds poetry to the allusive order of the cosmos, to "natural" generative forces. When, in the *House of Fame* and *Parliament of Fowls*, Chaucer links the traditional *genetrix* with the *anadyomene*, he emphasizes the importance of sensuousness to his aesthetic. These early poems reveal that Venus presides over both "making"—with its emphasis on musical, sensually pleasing verse—and "enditing," which enlarges upon the makers' subjects and audiences, and refers us to a classicizing aesthetic. According to the originary myth memorialized in the house of Fame, Chaucer's sensual and classicizing aesthetic discovers in Ovid its fictive *auctor*. This concept of Venus is obviously mediated by Roman,

French, and Italian poetry far more significantly than by mythography, but Chaucer draws on the standard mythographic image in order to capture her ambiguities and sensuous appeal. Contrasting with her, Cupid implicates an artificial and outmoded poetic convention, governing genteel lover-poets who sigh out their painful desires. Cupid refers us to the makers, and to Chaucer's scrutiny of their sometimes limited courtly values and subjects. We find these mythic representations of Chaucer's poetics further elaborated in *Troilus and Criseyde* and the *Prologue* to the *Legend of Good Women*; we might pause briefly to speculate about this intriguing pattern of self-fashioning, and about how it and other traditions were received by later medieval writers. As we will find, Chaucer's paradigms add to the always multiplying traditions of the deities' fame.

Chaucer most fully develops his classicizing vision of Venus in *Troilus and Criseyde*, Book 3, which invokes her as the "blisful light" that "adorneth" the third planetary sphere (3.1–2). The description recalls that Venus is also known as Phosphoros, the light-bearer, which leads to her association with mental illumination. In addition, she epitomizes the "plesance of love" (3.4). Responsible for both light and pleasure, she alludes to the cosmological force we encountered in Lucretius's *On the Nature of Things*, Ovid's *Fasti*, the *Eve of St. Venus*, and Boccaccio's astrologized Venus *magna*.[1] Chaucer's hymn to this Venus fully integrates sexuality, cosmic order, and poetry. Once again, she hints at the conjoined sensuous and intellectual appeal of Chaucer's vernacular poetics. She also symbolizes a civilizing and uniting power, as she teaches Mars to be "corteys" and to eschew vice for the sake of her "joies" (3.25–28). She brings sexual joy and accord between friends. If we compare this depiction of Venus closely with what Chaucer found in Boccaccio's *Filostrato* (his primary source) and with the traditions of cosmological love, we must conclude, with Peter Dronke, that Chaucer's Venus embodies "all her aspects, from sexuality to providential love."[2] Beseeching her aid, Chaucer shapes a lyrical classicizing hymn that beautifully proves the sensuous, musical pleasures possible in English verse:

> In hevene and helle, in erthe and salte see
> Is felt thi myght, if that I wel descerne,
> As man, brid, best, fissh, herbe, and grene tree
> Thee fele in tymes with vapour eterne.

> God loveth, and to love wol nought werne,
> And in this world no lyves creature
> Withouten love is worth, or may endure.
>
> (3.8–14)

The alternation of masculine and feminine rhyme, the light echoes achieved by occasional alliteration, the open vowel sounds concentrated in the last lines of the stanza, the easy stress shifts, all exemplify a well-crafted musicality. The finely wrought stanzas throughout *Troilus and Criseyde* in fact testify to a new refinement in poetry, which Chaucer explicitly associates with a sensuous force of love that unites poetic and cosmic orders.

The narrator finally seeks Venus's help for his poetic art:

> Ye folk a lawe han set in universe,
> And this knowe I by hem that lovers be,
> That whoso stryveth with yow hath the werse.
> Now, lady bryght, for thi benignite,
> At reverence of hem that serven the,
> Whos clerc I am, so techeth me devyse
> Som joye of that is felt in thi servyse.
>
> (36–42)

This "lady bryght" may provide insight and teach poetic arts just as she may foster sexual joys. The "joye" of sexual love becomes analogous to the pleasures of the text, and the stanza's final rhyme, *devyse/servyse*, and the enjambment enforce this correlation. Chaucer declares himself the "clerc" of Venus—not her poet, but her clerk, an avowedly didactic office in keeping with the aims of "enditing."[3] This hymn to Venus superbly fulfills ideals perhaps more evident in French poetry than in the often rough English verse of Chaucer's time: the principle that poetry should compare with the more obvious sensual pleasures. In other words, Chaucer once again adopts the goal of the makers to impart pleasure, and gives this ambition an air of classicizing sophistication by locating it in the register of myth. While the makers limit themselves to the codified arts of Cupid, Chaucer ventures into Venus's third heaven, and thereby slyly claims an even greater poetic sensuousness as well as a wider subject matter. As the coup de grâce, he names himself Venus's clerk: one who helps and teaches the servants of love. Finally, here as elsewhere, Chaucer associates Venus *genetrix*, the nourishing mother, with his own mother tongue—with the language learned in childhood, "where language has its deepest psychic roots," as Walter Ong posits.[4] Indeed, Venus fully represents Chaucer's early ambitions for his poetics and his mother tongue.

Chaucer's myth of poetry repeatedly disavows the makers' patron, Cupid, as insufficiently alive to their goal of giving pleasure, and replaces the god with Venus, who signifies a poetics at once classicizing and native, at once clerkly and sensuous. *Troilus and Criseyde* complicates this pattern, for Cupid's meaning here shifts between pagan and Christian ("O love, O Charite!" 3.1254), as he transforms from dubious patron of amatory arts to ambiguous god of love and back again. Yet Chaucer's early poems generally treat Cupid more simply, and he often appears as the figurehead of comically limited love poetry. The *House of Fame*, *Parliament of Fowls*, and *Knight's Tale* all develop this paradigm. In the *Prologue* to the *Legend of Good Women*, Chaucer sharpens his running commentary on Cupid by pointedly describing the god's literary tyranny. Cupid now appears as the great god of love, in the guise most closely associated with the French literary legacy:

> Yclothed was this myghty god of Love
> Of silk, ybrouded ful of grene greves,
> A garlond on his hed of rose-leves
> Stiked al with lylye floures newe.
> But of his face I can not seyn the hewe,
> For sikerly his face shon so bryghte
> That with the glem astoned was the syghte;
> A furlong-wey I myhte hym not beholde.
> But at the laste in hande I saw hym holde
> Two firy dartes as the gleedes rede,
> And aungellych hys winges gan he sprede.
> And al be that men seyn that blynd is he,
> Algate me thoughte he myghte wel yse
>
> (G 158–70)

Chaucer's narrators are chronically "astoned" by Cupid. The god chills and confuses them. He is a hard taskmaster, rigidly insisting on a narrow treatment of love, on fidelity to clichés about "sely," "trewe" women and "fals," deceitful men. His angel-like presence here forcefully alludes to his appearance in the *Romance of the Rose*, a central text in this literary tradition. As the *Prologue* to the *Legend of Good Women* binds the poet to precisely limited themes and subjects, Chaucer traces them back to this suggestively Gallic Cupid, patron of the literary traditions Chaucer rewrites. As Anne Middleton astutely demonstrates, "The God of Love, it seems, keeps his devoted servants on a rather short tether: placating him requires the writer to renounce epic subjects and their complex narrative sweep, and the broadly human rather than cultic ethical questions that attend them."[5] Throughout his poetry, Chaucer burdens the figure of Cupid with his critique of the makers' poetics. His Cupid signifies their limitations in theme, matter, human interest, and social milieu. The *Prologue* to the *Legend of Good Women* sums up Chaucer's long critique, even while depicting the poet as uncomfortably still subject to this Cupid's tyranny.

Chaucer's replacement of Venus for the makers' Cupid adopts their goal of pleasure but roots it firmly in the classical past. Like Boccaccio and Dante, Chaucer develops Venus as the symbol of his poetics: she represents his interest in love but also in its cosmic setting, and perhaps most of all she embodies his desire to create in the sometimes clumsy and unpracticed vernacular a poetry that will yield sensuous pleasures at once vivid and refined. She symbolizes his aspiration to a poetic union of sensuality and art, flesh and intellect. The outlines of the classical Venus *genetrix* remain recognizable in this Chaucerian myth, but she has been reinterpreted through French and Italian poetry. In the course of her medieval passage, she has been invested with high vernacular and poetic ideals. She represents in Chaucer's several invocations a classicizing dream of vernacular sensuousness and eloquence, while Cupid points to a model of French making that Chaucer both follows and modifies.

Chaucer thus repeatedly turns Venus and Cupid into symbols of poetic influences. Cupid calls attention to a dominant masculine (French) influence over poetry and amatory codes; Venus suggests a (classicizing) poetics submissive to a feminine generative influence, and to the mother tongue. By referring his poetry variously to these deities' patronage, Chaucer articulates a poetic self-definition: his opposition to the French makers, subjects of Cupid, and his alliance with Ovid, poet of Venus (and, at times, of Cupid). Actually, of course, this model both disguises and reveals the influences over Chaucer's poetry. The mocking rejection of Cupid's arts suppresses Chaucer's very real debt to the French makers' poetic theory and practice, especially the makers' experiments with classicizing allusions and their ideals about the sensuous effects of verse. His treatments of Cupid imply rather the anxieties than the absence of influence. Similarly, Venus refers us to a long line of poets—including Ovid, Dante, and Boccaccio—who exert a profound influence over Chaucer's art, and to whom he alludes by invoking her aid. Although the embodiment of feminine generative forces, she refers us to exclusively masculine poetic reproduction. Just as in the story of her birth, then, she illustrates a patriarchal masculine creation, in the absence of women. The denial of one poetic father in Cupid leads only to the affirmation of another in Ovid. Venus and Cupid thus disclose complex and equivocal poetic myths of self-fashioning: Chaucer's own representation of his simultaneous dependence on and independence from other poets.[6]

Chaucer's self-fashioning as the poet of Venus and his rejection of Cupid were sometimes recognized, sometimes imitated, and variously commented upon by his contemporaries and successors. Eustache Deschamps acknowledges the self-mythologizing and praises the "grant translateur" in terms Chaucer would have appreciated: "great Ovid in your poetry" ("Ovides grans en ta poëterie"). Deschamps also names Chaucer England's god of love, not Love's servant.[7] Just as Chaucer both imitates and departs from Ovid and others, however, later poets also revise Chaucer's myths; and there are always models besides those Chaucer provides. Several examples should suffice to outline some prominent features of contemporary and later developments.

Gower likely takes a hint from Chaucer about the Gallic literary conventions, though Gower invents his own mythographic strategies in order to challenge them. Still, at the end of the *Confessio Amantis*, Gower imagines himself *in propria persona* as a maker, a poet of Venus. He straightaway takes his leave of "making" (8.3152–57) and turns outside the poem (and away from poetry) to a love that cannot fail, to a love that transcends the limitations of the temporal, mutable, evanescent (venereal) order of things below the moon. By portraying himself as a maker, a poet of Venus, Gower defines "making" in terms of its primary subject, love, and in terms vitally limited by the makers' conventions for love and poetry. That is, Gower replaces the makers' Cupid with Venus, but venerean poetry now appears identical to that of the makers. This restriction of Venus to specific and narrow amatory conventions could testify to the absence of the Italian influence, which most likely guided Chaucer to the cosmological deity, though Gower could certainly have discovered her in Latin literature. In the end, Gower's Venus "enclosid in the sterred sky" (8.2942) could suggest the cosmological deity, delineating as if through a veil her ancient union of sensuality and intellect. But Gower stops short of Chaucer's classicizing invocations to the ancient patroness of sensuous poetry. Significantly, in one redaction of the poem Gower has Venus recommend that Chaucer, another of her poets, forsake making "ditees" and "songs" (*8.2945) and "make" instead "his testament of love" (*8.2955). However we might interpret this problematic passage, it suggests an accord with Chaucer on one crucial point: making is best united with broad affective goals and ethical purposiveness.[8] When Gower defines himself as a poet of Venus, he both compliments Chaucer (for imitation is indeed a compliment) and questions his myth of venerean enditing.

Gower does not merely echo Chaucer in a new key, and the *Confessio* also achieves a memorable independent revision of Ovid's Venuses and Cupids. We might recall that Ovid has Venus preside over the schooling of wild love in the *Art of Loving*, where she sponsors poetic and amatory civilizing arts. When Gower puts Venus in charge of training love, he turns that civilizing code into the confessional. His revision makes for a superb tongue-in-cheek commentary on the Ovidian arts of love (which in Ovid's time delivered a wonderfully barbed commentary against his poetic forebears). And, like Chaucer, Gower notably rewrites the Cupid of French tradition, subordinating the great god of love to Venus. On this point—on the necessity of finally setting their vernacular eloquence off from that of the French makers—they agree.

Elsewhere, treatments of Cupid suggest that he epitomizes aristocratic masculine amatory behavior as well as the French literary conventions that aestheticize it. Ever since Jean de Meun depicted Amor inviting the help of False Seeming for the conquest of the Rose, presenting deceit and hypocrisy as arguably vital to such amatory adventures, Cupid could and often did appear a champion of masculine amorous duplicity. Throughout the later Middle Ages, in French as well as English literature, he exemplifies the artifices of a disreputable amatory code that false lovers employ to deceive women, and he provokes a recurring concern about the ethics of masculine amatory arts. During the Quarrel of the Rose, Cupid not surprisingly gathers much of the hostility directed against his code of courteous cunning. He becomes a sign not only of English reactions to French influences but also of French debates about the nature and value of that influence.

As one of the participants in the Quarrel of the Rose, Christine de Pizan many times called for a repudiation of this stylized masculine treachery, which she viewed as evidence of Jean de Meun's misogyny. One of the more intriguing texts she produced to this end is *Epistle of the God of Love* (*Epistre au Dieu d'Amours*, 1399), which comments forcefully on the social and literary problems attending Jean's (and Ovid's) treatments of women. This epistle purports to be from Cupid to his true servants, calling upon them to join in the defense of women against the misguided men who slander them, and repudiating all men who speak falsely of or to women. There are two preeminent culprits: Ovid, with his *Art of Loving*, which would better be called "*The Art of Great Deceit, / Of False Appearances*"; and Jean de Meun, with his mighty engines aimed at nothing more than seduction "through frauds and schemes."[9] Both poets stand indicted for their advocation of deceits, false appearances, frauds. The judge is their own god of love ("dieu d'Amours") turned against them. Cupid emerges from this *Epistle* as one of Christine's wittiest rewritings of the *Romance of the Rose* and Ovidian conventions in general. Through the mouthpiece of this much-revised Amor, Christine deflates any masculine conceit about the prestigious arts of deceit: "A great assault for such a feeble place? / How can one leap so far so near the mark?"[10]

When Thomas Hoccleve translates this poem into English as the *Letter of Cupid* (1402), he too emphasizes the masculine Ovidian arts that dupe innocent women (which suggests, of course, that women must be protected from dangerous linguistic arts).[11] The significance of "fals apparence" (42) in Jean de Meun's poem justifies a critique of the masculine fraud and slander seemingly bound into conventional amatory arts. Hoccleve argues, furthermore, that this masculine gender role is taken in with school lessons from Ovid's text:

> And that book scolers lerne in hir childhede
> For they of wommen be waar sholde in age
> And for to love hem, evere been in drede,
> Syn to deceyve is set al hir corage.
>   (211–24, punctuation added)

Men learn misogyny and Latin grammar together. Modern theory can confirm Hoccleve on this point. Walter Ong provocatively describes Latin as "sex-linked, a language written and spoken only by males, learned outside the home in a tribal setting which was in effect a male puberty rite setting."[12] This masculine language presents misogyny as an apparently objective truth, and embracing it becomes a "male puberty rite." Hoccleve, like Christine and others, denaturalizes that masculine truth, displaying the particular voices that utter it and the socially contingent forces that shore it up. Cupid, the fabled originator of male deceits, now contests the rite of this male bonding by means of misogyny and Latin learning. During the Quarrel of the Rose, Cupid becomes a powerful sign of challenged literary influences and amatory conventions, in England as well as in France. He also develops into a vehicle for a prolonged social critique of specific class behaviors and values identified with him. The noble god of love seems, in the end, to lead a pack of devious slanderers.

These texts may serve to hint at a combined concern for women and critique of upper-class men, which often surfaces in the later Middle Ages. We can find this concern overtly expressed in the works of Chaucer, for instance in the *Legend of Good Women*, and it emerges as well in many lesser-known texts. As we discern this repeated social commentary, we come to view "gentil" women as if they stood in a social jungle, perpetually assailed by the dangers of masculine deception, flattery, and force; above all, women appear in need of (bourgeois?) protection. At the same time, men seem mere puppets of their own sexual desires, debased shadows of the sometime noble servants of love. In this, both sexes manifest the slow waning of the Middle Ages, the wearing out of the old myths about love, the development of new social and literary expectations. Yet those old myths, long-lived as myths are, endure well into the Renaissance—playing, for example, into the comedy of Shakespeare's *Much Ado About Nothing*, which depends for part of its humor on the longstanding serious concern about male arts:

> Men were deceivers ever,
> One foot in sea, and one on shore,
> To one thing constant never.
> (II.iii.63–65)

From the women troubadours to Benedick, men are marked out as creatures constant only to change, and for that are applauded, condoned, mocked, catechized, adored, and scorned in turn. The wild boy who must be schooled in amatory arts, the boy who eventually grows into a young prince with tyrannical inclinations, Cupid leads the procession through the ages. Mythographers are perhaps merely astute when they explain that his wings signify his mutability.

Writers negotiate the available traditions in diverse ways, but we might finally content ourselves with glancing briefly at how two Chaucerian poets, James I and Robert Henryson, enter into the discussion. We find revisions of specifically Chaucerian Venuses and Cupids in the *Kingis Quair*, usually attributed to James I of Scotland. Here Cupid is predictably linked to devious masculine arts of love, while Venus becomes a distinctly medievalized cosmological force. Imitating Chaucer, the narrator early in the poem queries the fable of love's tyranny, strategically aligned with lovers' "feynit chere" (251, comparable with Jean de Meun's False Seeming):

> O Lord, quhat may this be,
> That Lufe is of so noble myght and kynde,
> Lufing his folk? and suich prosperitee,
> Is it of him, as we in bukis fynd?
> May he oure hertes setten and unbynd?
> Or all this is bot feynyt fantasye?
>
> (253–59)

The prestigious convention of the God of Love clearly suffers a decline in some later Middle English poetry, and it becomes conventional to doubt this "fantasye" of love. As this narrator asks, "Quahat makis folk to iangill of him in veyne?" (266) Within the ensuing dream-vision that takes the narrator into the sphere of Venus, the poet depicts her and Cupid according to familiar models, but their context once again shapes their nuances. Cupid is both the great god of love and angelic, thus resembling his ancestors in the *Romance of the Rose* and Chaucer's *Prologue* to the *Legend of Good Women*:

> in a chiere of estate besyde
> With wingis bright, all plumyt bot his face,
> There sawe I sitt the blynde god Cupide,
> With bow in hand that bent full redy was.
>
> (652–55)

Venus learns modesty:

> Fond I Venus upon hir bed that had
> A mantill cast over hir schuldris quhite,—
> Thus clothit was the goddesse of delyte.
>
> (670–72)

One is not entirely startled when this goddess takes the unprecedented course of referring the lover to Minerva, subjecting sexual love to wisdom. The imagery prepares for an integration of sensual love and reason, eroticism and spirituality. The poet does not disappoint this expectation, for he proceeds to revise both amatory conventions and Boethian philosophy.

The dominant deity in her own planetary sphere, Venus details her authoritative code of love in a complaint reminiscent of but far different from that delivered by Alan of Lille's Nature. Venus charges men with breaking yet another seemingly natural (and very Lydgatean) law of love: steadfast truth to one lover. Notably, failure to lead a "lusty lyf" also earns her disapproval (799–861). In her turn, Minerva too speaks against the false men who deceive "sely" women (932–45). The *Kingis Quair* proposes that truth in love is both a natural law of Venus and the standard of Minerva: constant love satisfies both desire and reason. This is certainly a rewriting of Chaucer's and others' Venuses and Cupids. While one tradition makes Cupid into the leader of false lovers, this poet, like Christine de Pizan and Hoccleve, insists he reform his ways. Although the cosmological Venus displaces the god of love, suggesting the planet's greater influence over lovers, she also subjects herself and lovers to wisdom. The wise seem at last capable of ruling the stars.

With the *Testament of Cresseid*, Henryson more radically rewrites Chaucer's myths of Venus and Cupid, starting with the ideal of a venerean poetics. The *Testament* opens with the narrator suffering from the cold of a northern spring as he stands in his oratory and watches Venus rise. Henryson pointedly refuses to invoke her aid for this poem that answers Chaucer's *Troilus and Criseyde*:

> I traistit that Venus, luifis quene,
> To quhome sum tyme I hecht obedience,
> My faidit hart of lufe scho wald mak grene,
> And therupon with humbill reverence
> I thocht to pray hir hie magnificence;
> Bot for greit cald as than I lattit was
> And in my chalmer to the fyre can pas.
>
> Thocht lufe be hait, yit in ane man of age
> It kendillis nocht sa sone as in youtheid,
> Of quhome the blude is flowing in ane rage;
> And in the auld the curage doif and deid

> Of quhilk the fyre outward is best remeid:
> To help be phisike quhair that nature faillit
> I am expert, for baith I have assaillit.
>
> (22–35)

He proceeds to mend the fire and pour a drink, remedying the cold of age. Henryson evidently appreciates that Venus signifies a union of sexuality and poetic pleasures in Chaucer's poem—and pretends to reject that for his own. Henryson eventually embodies in Venus the mutability of the sublunar realm, the evanescence of youth, warmth, and love. She aligns with the cosmological power of fortune, not, as Chaucer has it in *Troilus and Criseyde*, with the love that binds all things together in mutual concord. These are related cosmic forces, to be sure, but they are not identical. By emphatically not invoking Venus, Henryson defines his poetics in opposition to Chaucer's. At the same time, Henryson's stanzas clearly imitate Chaucer's rhyme royal grace, albeit with a Scottish burr.

Henryson further departs from Chaucer's models by picturing the courtly goddess as an emblem of inconstancy. Venus descends into Cresseid's vision

> cled in ane nyce array,
> The ane half grene, the uther half sabill blak,
> With hair as gold kemmit and sched abak;
> Bot in hir face semit greit variance,
> Quhyles perfyte treuth and quhyles inconstance.
>
> (220–24)

This description unites courtliness with the ephemerality of fortune, symbolizing their unity in the narrative. Love and beauty are, as both Cresseid and the narrator learn, brittle as glass, evanescent as the warm blood of youth. Venus's appearance sums up this theme, concretizing a lesson about the mutability of life and love. Cupid appears only briefly in the *Testament of Cresseid*, as a revengeful judge determined to exact justice against Cresseid. He manifests in this role a dynamic confusion between pagan and Christian systems, for he presides over a tribunal that falls somewhere between a court of love and a conjunction of astrological influences. Like Venus, he invites questions about the relationship between sexual love and natural orders, between human and supernatural orders. These questions perhaps imply the extent of Henryson's engagement with Chaucer's poem.

Such cursory gestures toward these complex and fascinating poems do not, of course, suffice as anything more than an outline of some patterns taking shape in later Middle English literature. Yet even a passing glance affirms that Venus and Cupid continue to signify contested literary and other values, that with Chaucer they become and thereafter remain important signs of how English poets negotiate competing literary traditions. Chaucer treats both deities as representatives of aesthetic and amatory codes, and they locate important priorities in his vernacular poetics. His contemporaries and successors rewrite his myths of love as well as his myths of poetry, but sometimes they keep Venus and Cupid as signposts marking the new ways. In these developments, the Quarrel of the Rose, changing relations between French and English literatures, and altering moral and aesthetic standards all come into play.

Perhaps we might conclude that Chaucerian poets define themselves both by imitating and by revising Chaucer's and others' myths. Harold Bloom contends that "Poetic Influence—when it involves two strong, authentic poets—always proceeds by a misreading of the prior poet, an act of creative correction that is actually and necessarily a misinterpretation."[13] There are, perhaps, a larger number of "strong, authentic" poets than Bloom was willing to admit. More likely, influence is never so simple as a "misreading" or "misinterpretation." As Chaucer, Gower, Christine de Pizan, Thomas Hoccleve, James I, and Henryson confirm, poets both learn from each other and create anew what they learn; they manifest both debt and originality. And they often employ Venus and Cupid to signify those rival tendencies within their art.

Afterword

> these things are important not because a
> high-sounding interpretation can be put upon them but because they are useful.
>
> Marianne Moore, "Poetry"

For all the potential interest of mythographic and encyclopedic traditions, the texts that delineate those traditions are very often treated in medieval studies only as positivist sources of accurate historical meaning. Simplified ideas of mythographic "two Venuses" or "moralized" Venuses form just a few links in the seemingly endless chain forged by this pervasive critical practice. Over the past few decades, medievalists have fashioned this chain into a bridge across an absolute divide: between canonical, belletristic texts that need interpretation and sensitive attention to nuances, and other texts that offer up transparent, immediately accessible meanings. This is a problematic divide and difficult to justify. Mythographies, like commentary and exegetical traditions, do not yield fixed historical meanings but rather continual renegotiations of meanings; iconography similarly discloses that the extrapoetic is no less ambiguous than the poetic.

Mythographies, like a great deal of other medieval noncanonical and Latin literature, occupy a curious space in medieval studies, a space almost wholly exempt from close critical analysis and from literary theory, which one evidently needs only when reading canonical literature (and especially poetry). Within the most sophisticated theoretical approaches to, for example, Chaucer's works, we run across wholly untheorized, positivist, and naïvely historicist uses of mythography. While there are many untheorized readings, however, there are no untheoretical ones; and this is as true with medieval Latin literature, including encyclopedias, as with a modern novel. The dominant untheorized practice discloses a lack of thoughtfulness that attends naturalized biases against noncanonical other literature. Rather than continuing to handle mythography with a peculiar combination of disdain for its "unliterary" texture and deference to its authority, we should treat its verbal texture as amenable to critical analysis, and its authority as an always unstable formation, exposed to challenges. Mythographies contain fascinating material, open intriguing questions, and definitely merit further study both for their own sake and in relation to poetry and other genres. That mythography cannot tell us what poetry means does not argue that medievalists should ignore it, commentaries, exegesis, and the like. Instead, we should reexamine these traditions, attending thoughtfully to what they consist of, what they can tell us about medieval habits of reading, what appeal they might hold forth, if not for us personally, then perhaps for someone somewhere in another episteme. If mythographies and commentaries cannot finally tell us the meaning of poetic allusions to mythic figures, birds, beasts, or gems, we may nonetheless gain provocative insights into numerous topics of current interest, such as constructions of sexuality, gender, or hermeneutics. The interest and appeal of any text lies in the critic's imagination; the centrality and value of any tradition is what we make of it.

Much as we have made mythography peripheral to the critical enterprise, so have we made ecclesiastical discourses central to the study of medieval sexualities. But no single discourse can possibly elucidate everything about medieval sexuality, no matter how vital or dominant that discourse may have been. Ecclesiastical writing did indeed have profound impact on conceptualizations of sex and sexuality, as on most aspects of medieval culture. Yet if we study ecclesiastical writing in isolation, we are unable fully to detect even the nature of that impact. Sexuality is inscribed in many discourses, and, now that we have studies of some of them, it is perhaps time for us to turn our attention more fully to their interactions, to how they conflict with and complement one another. As we do so, we should remember that each discourse suggests particular and limited points of view, and that each implies its own privileged system of judgment. These discursively bound perspectives often remain segregated from one another, and that is telling; they may also at times be brought into dialogic relations, and that is surely at least as intriguing.

If this book has suggested new ways of engaging and theorizing this kind of interdisciplinary study, new ways of thinking about the relationships between mythography and poetry, about the tensions and ambiguities implicit in medieval sexualities, about the potentially complex quality of poetic allusions to myth, it has fulfilled its most important purposes. In the end, though, the merit of this as of any study is what it permits others to discover, how it encourages others to take the conclusions in directions unimagined by the author. Modern critical discourse shares this at least with medieval mythographies and commentaries: each discourse depends on the continual appropriation of interpretive paradigms for new purposes. Writers from Augustine of Hippo and Remigius of Auxerre to Chaucer and Henryson would appreciate the vigorous continuity of the interpretive project.

Reference Matter

Notes

~~~

INTRODUCTION

1. Because I do not later develop this identification in any detail, it seems only fair to refer the reader to those who do: Woolf, *English Religious Lyric*, 165–67; and Robert Taylor, "Figure of Amor," 310–11.

2. Seznec, *Survival of the Pagan Gods*; Tuve, *Allegorical Imagery*; Allen, *Friar as Critic*. One could also consult any reliable classical dictionary to gain a sense of just how complex and confused the ancient figures are: e.g., *Lempriere's Classical Dictionary*.

3. Cadden, *Meanings of Sex Difference*, argues similarly about related discourses.

4. The contention of Foucault, *History of Sexuality*, 33. Payer, *Sex and the Penitentials*, esp. 54, would support the idea of local and temporary homogeneities in medieval discourses about sexuality.

5. Amply demonstrated, both individually and collectively, by Kelly, *Love and Marriage*; Boswell, *Christianity, Social Tolerance, and Homosexuality*; Flandrin, "Sex in Married Life," 114–29; Otis, *Prostitution in Medieval Society*; Noonan, *Contraception*; Brundage, *Law, Sex, and Christian Society*; Brown, *Body and Society*; Rossiaud, *Medieval Prostitution*; Greenberg, *Construction of Homosexuality*, 242–98; Wack, *Lovesickness*; Richards, *Sex, Dissidence and Damnation*; Baldwin, "Five Discourses on Desire"; Cadden, *Meanings of Sex Difference*; Payer, *Bridling of Desire*.

CHAPTER 1

1. E.g.: Dronke, "L'amor che move il sole"; Wetherbee, "The Literal and the Allegorical," 273–74, and *Platonism and Poetry*, 196–97; Boitani, "Chaucer's Temples of Venus"; Ferrante, *Woman as Image*, 43–61, see also 154–55; Quilligan,

"Words and Sex," 202, and "Allegory, Allegoresis, and the Deallegorization of Language," 172–73; Robert Taylor, "Figure of Amor."

2. The most extensive survey of Cupid takes courtly love as its guiding light: Ruhe, *Le Dieu D'Amours*.

3. My admittedly whimsical denomination for a "courtly love" originating in the monastery of Fontevrault: Bloch, *Medieval Misogyny*, esp. 178–83.

4. Academics can at present use the term only by disregarding reams of argument: see esp. Moore's wittily acerbic "Courtly Love." Boase, *Origin and Meaning of Courtly Love*, offers a good survey of scholarship, but even he fails to settle on a definition for the term he studies. It is worth noting that in the seminal work of Gaston Paris, the meanings given "amour courtois" vary: see Kelly, "Gaston Paris's Courteous and Horsely Love," and "Varieties of Love." I do not find "fine amour" or "fyn lovynge" adequate replacements for "courtly love" because each term has its own complex range of specific meanings: see Reiss, "Chaucer's *fyn lovynge*"; and Burnley, "*Fine Amor.*"

5. Carroll, *Through the Looking Glass*, in *Alice in Wonderland*, 163.

6. Lewis, *Allegory of Love*, remains an excellent study of the differences between French and English literary loves. German revisions of French conventions are cogently discussed by Jackson, "Faith Unfaithful."

7. See, e.g., Macey on dualism, *Patriarchs of Time*; and Friedrich on *The Meaning of Aphrodite*.

8. E.g., Augustine, *City of God*, 14.7: "a rightly directed will is love in a good sense and a perverted will is love in a bad sense," trans. Bettenson, 557.

9. I do not use the term "bipolar opposition" from any penchant for jargon but simply as the most precise identification of a theoretical position. The term derives from the work of Saussure, though he refers to "reciprocal opposition": see *Course in General Linguistics*, esp. 101–39; Hawkes provides a brief introduction to the concept within structuralism, *Structuralism and Semiotics*, 24–25. My use of the term draws upon post-structuralist thought; a review of this usage is given by Scott, "Deconstructing Equality-Versus-Difference," 36–38. For the moment, we may take "bipolar opposition" to designate two elements (for example, male and female) defined by their opposition to each other, an opposition that generally appears hierarchical.

10. Panofsky, *Studies in Iconology*, 95–169, with a discussion of these images on 148–53. Dronke, "L'amor che move il sole," provides a valuable further analysis of the relevant Platonic traditions.

11. Robertson, "The Subject of the *De amore*," revised and included in *A Preface to Chaucer*, 24–31, 124–27, et passim.

12. Robertson, *Preface to Chaucer*, 205, 297–98, 316–17, 357–59, 365–73, etc.

13. Ibid., 198–202, 391–503.

14. Patterson usefully reviews some of the issues in *Negotiating the Past*, 3–74.

15. Economou, "Two Venuses," 20.

16. E.g., in *Goddess Natura*, 85, Economou includes Fulgentius in a list of mythographers who repeat an idea of two Venuses; n. 54 documenting this cites not Fulgentius's *Mythologies* (which at any rate does not double Venus) but John Ridewall's *Fulgentius Metaphored*, a fourteenth-century rewrite of Fulgentius's text. Economou repeats the error in "Two Venuses," 21.

17. Hollander, *Boccaccio's Two Venuses*.

18. See Peck, "Problematics of Irony," for a complementary critique of this basic methodology.

19. Ruhe, *Le Dieu d'Amours*, 46–58, similarly surveys two mythographic loves: *schlecht* and *gut*, analogous to *impurus* and *purus* in courtly love. Mulryan, "Venus, Cupid, and the Italian Mythographers," also focuses on dualisms.

20. Panofsky, *Studies in Iconology*, 144–45. These writers' concept of the universe actually makes three figures a more logical choice: see 132–45.

21. Robertson, *Preface to Chaucer*, 126, citing John Scotus Eriugena, *Annotationes in Marcianum*, ed. Lutz, 13.

22. John Scotus Eriugena, *Annotationes in Marcianum*, ed. Lutz, 13. Dronke, "L'amor che move il sole," 408–10, posits that John contributes significantly to ideas about cosmic love by uniting two traditions: love as moving the universe and love as the goal toward which all moves. Attention to any one of John's descriptions of Venus merely hides such innovations.

23. John Scotus Eriugena, *Annotationes in Marcianum*, 67.

24. Ibid., 191–92: "omnis libido delectatione carnalium sensuum nascitur."

25. Robertson briefly notes that mythographies advance multiple interpretations (*Preface to Chaucer*, 250, 298–99), yet he has had a greater influence in his more developed and forceful assertion that mythographers and poets understood the deities *in bonum* and *in malum* (297–98, 391–503). Similarly, Heinrichs in *Myths of Love* recognizes multiplicity in theory (23) but rejects it as a possibility in literature (59, 118).

26. Green, "Alan's *Planctus*," 660–72. Green later explicitly endorses the "historicist" value of mythography to the understanding of poetry: "Classical Fable and English Poetry."

27. Foucault, *History of Sexuality*, 83. For Foucault, this is the *modus operandi* of power; whatever his surface resemblance to Robertson, of course, Foucault evidences a self-consciousness about how binaries function that witnesses to the more central difference between the two scholars. Foucault in later volumes of the *History* revises his initial concepts, but they remain influential.

28. "Veneres ergo duas legimus esse, legitimam scilicet et petulantie deam. Le-

gitimam Venerem legimus esse mundanam musicam, id est equalem mundanorum proportionem, quam alii Astream, naturalem justiciam, vocant. Hec enim est in elementibus, in sideribus, in temporibus, in animantibus. Impudicam vero Venerem et petulantie deam dicimus esse carnis concupiscentiam que omnium fornicationum mater est." Bernard Silvestris, *Commentary on the First Six Books of the "Aeneid,"* ed. Jones and Jones, 9 (Book 1, ll. 10–15); trans. Schreiber and Maresca, *Commentary on the First Six Books of Virgil's "Aeneid,"* 10–11. (I alter this translation slightly.)

29. Dronke, "L'amor che move il sole," 413, with an insightful discussion of Bernard following.

30. In agreement with Wetherbee, *Platonism and Poetry*, 120.

31. Dronke, *Fabula*, 100–106.

32. The Venuses have different origins: Venus *caelestis* is the daughter of Uranus, and Venus *vulgaris* the daughter of Zeus and Dione. For Renaissance Neoplatonic ideas of Venus, see Panofsky, *Studies in Iconology*, 143–45, and *Renaissance and Renascences*, 185–87, 198–200.

33. "Duae sunt Veneres, una casta et pudica quae praeest honestis amoribus, quae etiam fertur uxor Vulcani, altera voluptuaria libidinum dea, cuius filius est Ermafroditus. Sic etiam sunt duo amores, alter bonus et pudicus quo virtutes et sapientia amantur; alter impudicus et malus, quem ad distinctionem boni amoris pluraliter amores dicimus." Remigius, *Remigii Autissiodorensis Commentum in Martianum Capellam*, ed. Lutz, 180; see also 135–36.

34. Copeland, *Rhetoric, Hermeneutics, and Translation*, 75, proposes an analogous conclusion about the relation of these texts.

35. Courcelle, *La Consolation*, 244–48.

36. *Mythographus secundus*, in *Scriptores rerum mythicarum*, ed. Bode, 74, 84–86, 106–7, 116, 123, 150.

37. *Gods and Allegories*, in *Scriptores rerum mythicarum*, ed. Bode, 239. It is worth noting that Ridewall in turn rewrites this idea: see *Fulgentius Metaphored*, ed. Liebeschütz, 78. For the earlier development of this concept, see Ruhe, *Le Dieu d'Amours*, 46–53.

38. See Alton, "Mediaeval Commentators on Ovid's *Fasti*," 136, marginalia for 4.1.

39. Howard, *Chaucer*, 310.

40. Yeager, *Gower's Poetic*, 180–87.

41. Twycross, *Medieval Anadyomene*; Mulryan, "Venus, Cupid, and the Italian Mythographers"; Ruhe, *Le Dieu d'Amours*, esp. 46–58; Schreiber, "Venus in the Medieval Mythographic Tradition"; Steinberg, "The Comedy of Love" (this article unfortunately distorts medieval traditions). A more recent survey, Heinrichs's *Myths of Love*, esp. 1–52, explicitly regards poets and mythogra-

phers as developing identical moral commonplaces. Nonmythographic methodologies inform the dated but still informative studies of Venus and Cupid by Neilson, *Origins and Sources of the Court of Love*, and Spencer, "Literary Lineage of Cupid."

42. Patterson, *Chaucer and the Subject of History*, 225.

43. E.g., ibid., 64–65 and n. 60, 134–35 and n. 125.

44. This has been quite persuasively demonstrated by Allen, *Friar as Critic*.

45. For Boccaccio's three Venuses, see *Genealogy* 3. 22, 3. 23, 11. 4; and see also Boitani, *Chaucer and Boccaccio*, 93; Mulryan, "Venus, Cupid, and the Italian Mythographers," 35–36, 39. Scholars are so preconditioned to discover two loves that Schreiber finds only two of Boccaccio's three: "Venus in the Medieval Mythographic Tradition," esp. 522. For the other references, see Fulgentius, *Fulgentius the Mythographer*, trans. Whitbread, 66, 72–73, 88–90, 125–26; Richard of Fournival, *Consaus D'Amours*, in Shapiro, *Comedy of Eros*, 100–102.

46. Fleming, *Classical Imitation*, 143–46, contributes a good concise exposition of Augustine's attitudes toward paganism.

47. Augustine, *City of God*, 4.10 (trans. Bettenson, 148).

48. E.g., Knowlton, "Goddess Nature," 245; Green, "Alan's *Planctus*," 649–74; Economou, *Goddess Natura*, 85–86, and "Two Venuses," 24–29; Friedman, "L'Iconographie de Venus," 63; Yeager, *Gower's Poetic*, 181.

49. E.g., Fleming, *Study in Allegory and Iconography*, 192.

50. "In lacrimas risus, in luctus gaudia verto, / In planctum plausus, in lacrimosa jocos, / Cum sua Nature video decreta silere, / Cum Veneris monstro naufraga turba perit; / Cum Venus in Venerem pugnans illos facit illas / Cumque sui magica deviret arte viros." Alan of Lille, *Plaint of Nature*, Metrum 1.1–6.

51. Economou's contention: *Goddess Natura*, 85–87, and "Two Venuses," 24–25, though here he seems to be thinking of Cupid and Jocus rather than of two Venuses *per se*.

52. E.g., Stehling, trans., *Medieval Latin Poems*, poem 65, ll. 29–40; poem 36; see also Boswell, *Christianity, Social Tolerance, and Homosexuality*, 186–87, 262–64.

53. Lewis and Short, *A New Latin Dictionary*, note that "Venus" is sometimes a euphemism for sexual intercourse or venery. My reading here concurs with that of Nitzsche, *Genius*, 99–101. Critics have regarded Venus as a figure for procreation or desire, which may be euphemistic versions of my argument: Bethurum Loomis, "Venus," 187–89; and Wetherbee, *Platonism and Poetry*, 195. Payer overlooks this Latin usage (and many others) when he discovers in the Middle Ages no word for sex closer than *venereus* and *venerea*, concluding from this that "the absence of Latin terms for sex and sexuality points to the absence of cor-

responding concepts" (*Bridling of Desire*, 14). I find this an overstatement; although many texts avoid dealing with abstractions, they nonetheless clearly treat of sex and sexuality (e.g., Constantine the African's *De Coitu*).

54. "Terrestrium animantium materiande propagini Venerem destinavi, ut varias materias in rebus materiandis excudendo substerneret.... Et ut instrumentorum fidelitas prave operationis fermentum excluderet, ei duos legitimos malleos assignavi quibus et Parcharum inaniret insidias resque multimodas essentie presentaret.

"Incudum etiam nobiles officinas eiusdem artificio deputavi precipiens, ut eisdem eosdem malleos adaptando rerum effigiationi fideliter indulgeret, ne ab incudibus malleos aliqua exorbitatione peregrinare permitteret." (Alan of Lille, *Plaint of Nature*, Prose 5.21–30)

55. This is Aristotle's model. For the medicine, see Bullough, "Medieval Medical and Scientific Views of Women," 487; Jacquart and Thomasset, *Sexuality and Medicine*, e.g., 37; and Laqueur, *Making Sex*, 41–42, 55–57, etc. We might note that this model compensates for male anxiety about paternity.

56. See Tuve, *Allegorical Imagery*, fig. 107, 108.

57. Quoted by Foucault, "Battle for Chastity," 19–20.

58. We might also compare the idea of the artisan in Alan's time: see Le Goff, *Intellectuals*, 57, 62.

59. Noonan, *Contraception*, 171–99.

60. Alan of Lille, *Plaint of Nature*, Prose 5.66–72. Alford, "Grammatical Metaphor," 751–52, and Ziolkowski, *Grammar of Sex*, 13–49, quite ably elucidate Alan's grammatical metaphors. See also Thomas of Erfurt, one of the Modistae, who sets forth an interestingly parallel gender system. Thomas reads the gender of nouns as masculine if the "mode of signifying" is a "property of acting," feminine if the property is "of being acted upon," and neuter if the property is "indeterminate," *Grammatica speculativa*, 178–79, cf. 216–17 on verbs.

61. Ziolkowski, *Grammar of Sex*, 35.

62. Barkan, *Gods Made Flesh*, 132, commenting on the medieval and especially Chartrian confusion of Venus and Nature (119–36). See also Green, "Alan's *Planctus*," 666–70.

63. Dronke, "L'amor che move il sole," studies this thoroughly.

64. Alan of Lille, *Plaint of Nature*, Prose 1, Prose 2.18–63, Metrum 4, Prose 9.41–56; and *Anticlaudianus*, 1.187–206, though compare 2.242–60, which grants the role to Concord.

65. Robertson, *Preface to Chaucer*, 105–10, 127, 370–77; Hoffman, "Canterbury Tales," 60–70, amplifies the interpretation, equating the sensual Venus with all women; McCall also modifies Robertson's reading, *Chaucer Among the Gods*, 64–86. More recently, Blanch and Wasserman further enlarge on the central idea: "White and Red in the *Knight's Tale*."

66. E.g., Wood, *Chaucer and the Country of the Stars*, 72.
67. This is the gloss on which Hollander depends, *Boccaccio's Two Venuses*, 53–65; more recently, Wallace, *Chaucer and the Early Writings of Boccaccio*, 66, accepts Hollander's reading.
68. "Perciò che per la sua influenzia tutti i congiugnimenti naturali a procreare alcuna cosa," *Teseida*, 466; trans. Boitani, *Chaucer and Boccaccio*, 204.
69. Boitani contends as I do for disjunctions: *Chaucer and Boccaccio*, 14–19, 31–32. Anderson, *Before the "Knight's Tale,"* 186 n. 44, concisely reviews the scholarship on this question and offers a persuasive analysis.
70. For a skeptical assessment of Chaucer's access to Boccaccio's glosses, see Pratt, "Conjectures." On the other hand, Boitani detects Chaucer using the glosses for verbal details: *Chaucer and Boccaccio*, 113–16. I find the evidence inconclusive.
71. Dronke analyzes Boethius along these lines, "L'amor che move il sole," 402–4.
72. I argue this point slightly more fully in "Saturn of the Several Faces," 302; see also Anderson, *Before the "Knight's Tale,"* 192–224.
73. For extended comparisons of the two poets leading to similar conclusions, see Pratt, "Conjectures," and "Chaucer's Use of the *Teseida*," 613–20; Boitani, "Chaucer's Temples of Venus," and *Chaucer and Boccaccio*; Wallace, "Chaucer and Boccaccio's Early Writings," and *Chaucer and the Early Writings of Boccaccio*, 141–43; Anderson, *Before the "Knight's Tale."* I do not speak of Hubertis M. Cumming's *The Indebtedness of Chaucer's Works to the Italian Works of Boccaccio*.
74. The astrological-philosophical aspect of the tale is concisely discussed by Wood, *Chaucer and the Country of the Stars*, 45–47; and Minnis, *Chaucer and Pagan Antiquity*, 40–47.
75. Spearing also emphasizes the tale's repression of the feminine: *Medieval Poet as Voyeur*, 155–56. Crane, "Medieval Romance and Feminine Difference," proposes that Emelye and Diana disrupt the tale's order. See also Hansen, *Chaucer and the Fictions of Gender*, 209–23, for a reading that emphasizes the threat women (especially Amazons) pose to men. I am sorry to discern less potential for feminine disruption or threat in the tale than Crane and Hansen do.
76. I think of the brilliant analyses by Patterson, *Chaucer and the Subject of History*, 165–230; and Wallace, "Chaucer and the Absent City."
77. Respectively, Robertson, *Preface to Chaucer*, 51, and Bakhtin, *Rabelais and His World*, 1–58.
78. For the concupiscent Venus, see note 67 to this chapter. Compare also Whitlark, "Chaucer and the Pagan Gods," 69, linking excessive love (concupiscence) and idolatry. Minnis, *Chaucer and Pagan Antiquity*, 113–16, identifies the Venus of concupiscence with Boccaccio's gloss and the mythographers,

and then refers Chaucer's Venus to the astrologers, who, Minnis contends, depict a Venus sponsoring married, mystical, holy love and other blessings. I find this an unpersuasive summation of astrology; see Chap. 5 below for astrology.

79. This constitutes one perennial division in criticism of the tale; the following exemplify in my view the landmark studies: Muscatine, "Form, Texture, and Meaning in Chaucer's *Knight's Tale*"; Anderson, *Before the "Knight's Tale,"* 192–224; and Patterson, *Chaucer and the Subject of History*, 165–230. Various misapprehensions were introduced into the ongoing discussion by Tatlock, *Development and Chronology*, 231–33; Fairchild, "Active Arcite, Contemplative Palamon"; Marckwardt, *Characterization*; Curry, *Chaucer and the Medieval Sciences*, 119–63; and Brooks and Fowler, "Meaning of Chaucer's *Knight's Tale*." Curry, Brooks, and Fowler present very faulty but widely accepted evidence: my "Saturn of the Several Faces," 305–6, analyzes some of the problems; and see also Gaylord, "Role of Saturn," 190 n. 47, with whom I agree that "Curry's study, so full of lore, is finally quite useless": Saturn does not side with Venus, as Curry has him do; Curry's sources for Saturnian physiognomy are too long after Chaucer's time to be applicable (Brooks and Fowler do not remedy this problem); and the physiognomy is inconclusive.

80. E.g., Wood, *Elements of Chaucer's Troilus*, 39–40, 113, 166; Fleming, *Classical Imitation*, 65–70 et passim; Heinrichs, *Myths of Love*, 102–3, 114, 259.

81. See the Introduction, note 5.

82. Cf. Tuve, *Allegorical Imagery*, e.g., 70, and Copeland, *Rhetoric, Hermeneutics, and Translation*.

83. *European Literature*, 122.

84. Robertson makes this goal explicit, *Preface to Chaucer*, 52–137, 286–390; Heinrichs adopts it in *Myths of Love*, 23–50.

85. *Toward an Aesthetic of Reception*, 9.

86. See Allen, *Friar as Critic*, 117–51; Tuve, *Allegorical Imagery*, 142, lamenting the "willingness to read a poet as saying anything that would preserve the source relationship"; and similarly Copeland, *Rhetoric, Hermeneutics, and Translation*, 4, regretting "the way that mythography has traditionally been read, as a set of learned footnotes to what are then designated as 'primary' texts."

87. MacCormack, "Nature, Culture and Gender: A Critique," 5. We could also refer the phenomenon to psychoanalytic models, such as Freud's idea of split affect (affection/sensuality), as discussed by Delany, "Slaying Python." Unfortunately, I lack the sophistication in psychoanalysis needed to develop this reasoning.

88. The classic account of nature/culture gendering is Ortner's brilliantly provocative "Is Female to Male as Nature Is to Culture?" For other developments of the idea, see Rosaldo's "Woman, Culture, and Society"; Barnes, "Gen-

etrix:Genitor :: Nature:Culture"; and Ortner and Whitehead, Introduction to *Sexual Meanings*.

89. Lewis, *Allegory of Love*, 121; see also Fansler, *Chaucer and the "Roman de la Rose,"* 59.

90. Within post-structuralist feminist writing, e.g., language and gender can constitute parallel bipolar oppositions. Dallery, "Politics of Writing," 53, argues that "the logical ordering of reality into hierarchies, dualisms, and binary systems presupposes a prior gender dichotomy of man/woman." See also Homans, "Feminist Criticism and Theory," 171.

91. I am indebted throughout this study to analyses of gender and difference from a variety of disciplinary perspectives. If I do not elsewhere refer specifically to these works, that simply means the debt is pervasive, always already operative. See Chodorow, "Family Structure and Feminine Personality"; Rubin, "Traffic in Women"; Rogers, "Woman's Place"; MacCormack, "Nature, Culture and Gender: A Critique"; Shapiro, "Anthropology and the Study of Gender"; Leacock and Nash, "Ideologies of Sex"; Gilbert and Gubar, "Sexual Linguistics"; Scott, *Gender and the Politics of History*; Bordo, "Feminism, Postmodernism, and Gender-Scepticism"; Butler, *Gender Trouble*; Rhode, *Theoretical Perspectives on Sexual Difference*. Recently, several medieval scholars have developed similar approaches: Cadden, *Meanings of Sex Difference*; Clover, "Regardless of Sex"; Frantzen, "When Women Aren't Enough."

92. My debt to Derrida, particularly to his reading of Saussure, will be obvious here and throughout this study: *Of Grammatology*, 27–65. I have also found very valuable Scott, "Deconstructing Equality-Versus-Difference"; Dallery, "The Politics of Writing"; and Butler, *Gender Trouble*.

93. See Curtius, *European Literature*, 116 n. 26; Boswell, *Christianity, Social Tolerance, and Homosexuality*, 243–66.

94. See Paglia's contrafeminist deployment of gender binaries in *Sexual Personae*.

95. See Pearsall, "Interpretative Models for the Peasants' Revolt"; and see the quite different but complementary discussion offered by Rider, "Other Voices."

96. The centrality of Augustine of Hippo to modern readings of the Middle Ages ensures the thematic predominance of such a model in many studies that touch on medieval sexuality, as recently evidenced, e.g., in Laqueur's reading of the Middle Ages, *Making Sex*, 59–61. That Foucault assumes Augustine's influence and a medieval ethos of licit/illicit sexuality furthers the scholarly popularity of such a model (*History of Sexuality*).

97. See the Introduction, note 5.

98. Bennett, "Medievalism and Feminism," submits an excellent history of this feminist position.

99. This is not the place for extended discussion of medieval sign theory, so I would refer the reader to a fine introductory analysis by Coletti, *Naming the Rose*.

100. "Jupiter apud poetas accipitur multis modis," gloss at 1029.

101. Altieri, "Hermeneutics of Literary Indeterminacy," persuasively exposes this false dichotomy.

102. Bakhtin, *Dialogic Imagination*, 259–422.

103. In this aim, I am particularly indebted to Rhode's reflections on the state of scholarship on gender and sexuality: *Theoretical Perspectives on Sexual Difference*, esp. 6.

104. The most illuminating recent studies of sexual renunciation draw subtle conclusions about just what renunciation could mean in its cultural context: Bynum, *Holy Feast and Holy Fast*; and Brown, *Body and Society*.

105. The groups ably surveyed by Richards, *Sex, Dissidence and Damnation*.

CHAPTER 2

1. E.g., Allen, "Commentary as Criticism"; and Hyde, "Boccaccio: The Genealogies of Myth."

2. See also surveys of the traditions by Seznec, *Survival of the Pagan Gods*, 11–147; Allen, *Friar as Critic*, 29–53; Schreiber, "Venus in the Mythographic Tradition"; Barkan, *Gods Made Flesh*, 103–17; and Chance, "Medieval Apology for Poetry." I am of course indebted to all of these studies, as well as to Copeland's analysis of related traditions (*Rhetoric, Hermeneutics, and Translation*), and to Minnis's very useful study of biblical exegesis: *Medieval Theory of Authorship*. For a very good bibliography of mythographic literature, see Kaske, *Medieval Christian Literary Imagery*, 104–29.

3. Noonan, *Contraception*, 171–99.

4. See Noonan, *Contraception*, 292–95; Rossiaud, *Medieval Prostitution*, 72–85, 104–28; Payer, *Bridling of Desire*, 61–72, 79–83, 110, 118–31.

5. The most notable omission is the *Ovide moralisé*, though since Bersuire and Christine de Pizan consulted it, it enters indirectly. For good analyses of the *Ovide moralisé*, see Schreiber, "Venus in the Mythographic Tradition"; and Copeland, *Rhetoric, Hermeneutics, and Translation*, 107–26.

6. Minnis, *Medieval Theory of Authorship*, 42, and Copeland, *Rhetoric, Hermeneutics, and Translation*, 63–86, survey other texts that demonstrate this phenomenon.

7. Cf. the complementary discussion by Allen, "Eleven Unpublished Commentaries."

8. See Wilkins, *University of Chicago Manuscript*, 4–6.

9. As an example of the resulting confusion, we might note how several

scholars have attempted without obvious success to determine whether Chaucer used Bersuire's text, and if so, what edition: see Wilkins, "Descriptions of Pagan Divinities"; Steadman, "Venus' *Citole*"; Quinn, "Venus, Chaucer, and Peter Bersuire"; Panofsky, *Renaissance and Renascences*, 78 n. 2; Engels, on Bersuire 1966, p. xvi; and Twycross, *Medieval Anadyomene*, 5–14.

10. Reynolds, "Sources, Nature, and Influence," 95.

11. Elliott and Elder, "Critical Edition."

12. E.g., Raschke compiles the Third Vatican Mythographer's sources, "De Alberico mythologo"; Coulter, "Genealogy of the Gods," 327–34, reviews Boccaccio's sources; Campbell, *L'Epître d'Othéa: Etude sur les Sources de Christine de Pisan*, 142–54, concentrating on the *Ovide moralisé*; Laistner, "Fulgentius," delineates Fulgentius's influence on later writers; Allen, "An Anonymous Twelfth-Century 'De Natura Deorum,'" 357–64, traces its sources and influences; Whitbread, "Fulgentius and Dangerous Doctrine," intelligently treats Fulgentius's uses of his sources; Ruhe, *Le Dieu d'Amours*, 46–58, identifies parallels in several mythographies; MacFarlane analyzes "Isidore of Seville on the Pagan Gods"; and Reynolds studies the "Sources, Nature, and Influence of the *Ovidius Moralizatus* of Bersuire." Introductions to critical editions and translations add further details.

13. Quoting Alberic: "Mars igitur complexu Veneris *pollutus*, id est, virtus libidinis illecebris *corrupta*," *Gods and Allegories*, in *Scriptores rerum mythicarum*, ed. Bode, 231; see also Fulgentius, *Mythologies*, in *Opera*, ed. Helm, 2.7.

14. See Payer, *Sex and the Penitentials*, 21, 45, 47, 49–50, 118. The language is originally Ovid's, but the medieval mythographic contexts alter his implications.

15. "Quid est enim voluptas Veneris nisi mera insania?" Lactantius Placidus, *Commentarios in Statii Thebaida*, ed. Jahnke, 262.

16. Brown, ed., "An Anonymous *Liber de natura deorum*," 25: "Ea propter turpitudinem suam maritum contemnens ... amans cum eodem [Marto] saepe adulteravit."

17. Reported by Tuve, *Allegorical Imagery*, 308.

18. Loukopoulos, ed., "Classical Mythology in the Work of Christine de Pisan," Ph.D. diss., Wayne State University, 1977, no. 56.

19. Shakespeare, *Macbeth* I.vii.1–2.

20. Tuve, *Allegorical Imagery*, 285–311, offers an insightful analysis of how and why some of Christine's allegories fail.

21. Walsingham, *Mysteries of the Gods*, ed. van Kluyve: "vir fortis in Venerem dissolvitur," 72; and "Iuxta eum [Vulcan] pingebatur dii irridentes eum, qui eum de celo propter suam turpitudinem expellere confinguntur," 39.

22. Guibert of Nogent, *Self and Society*, 150.

23. In *Lydgate: Poems*, ed. Norton-Smith, 390, 392.

24. Hill, "La Vieille's Digression," 114; see also Wood, *Chaucer and the*

Country of the Stars, 120–30, for an emphasis on consistency in mythographic moralizations of the myth.

25. For parallel changes in intellectual life, see Colish, *Mirror of Language*; and see also Le Goff, *Intellectuals*, esp. 9–20, 81–88, 104–5 on changes in the status of pagan texts.

26. Cicero, *De natura deorum*: "*Venus prima* Caelo et Die nata, cuius Eli delubrum vidimus, *altera* spuma procreata, ex qua et Mercurio Cupidinem secundum natum accepimus, *tertia* Iove nata et Diona, quae nupsit Volcano, sed ex ea et Marte natus Anteros dicitur, *quarta* Syria Cyproque concepta, quae Astarte vocatur, quam Adonidi nupsisse proditum est" (3.59; 2: 1124–28; cf. also Venus Coa at 1.75; 1: 390–92). And "*Cupido primus* Mercurio et Diana prima natus dicitur, *secundus* Mercurio et Venere secunda, *tertius* (qui idem est Anteros) Marte et Venere tertia" (3.60; 2: 1131–32; cf. also 3.58). Boccaccio, *Genealogy*, offers for Venus: "De Venere magna VIa Celi filia," essentially the planet (1: 142); "De secunda Venere Celi VIIa filia et matre Cupidinis," a moralized figure (1: 148); and "De Venere Iovis XIa filia, que peperit Amorem," the wife of Vulcan (2: 543). For Cupid and Amor we get: "De Amore primo Herebi filio" (1: 46); "De Mercurio secundo Liberi et Proserpine filio, qui genuit Cupidinem et Auctolium" (1: 81); "De Cupidine primo, secundi Mercurii filio" (1: 83); "De Cupido Veneris filio" (1: 152); "De Cupidine Io Martis filio, qui genuit Voluptatem" (2: 451), "De Amore XIIo Iovis filio" (2: 545), as well as various appearances in others' fables. It is not impossible that I missed a figure.

27. For a lucid account of some confusions, see MacMullen, *Paganism in the Roman Empire*.

28. Seznec, *Survival of the Pagan Gods*, 11–13, 37–42, 84–87, outlines the ancient traditions; Cooke, "Euhemerism," 396–400, also sketches out ancient historical traditions. The more detailed study by Cumont remains eminently readable and informative: *Astrology and Religion*.

29. This phenomenon has been persuasively and thoroughly established: see Seznec, *Survival of the Pagan Gods*; Tuve, *Allegorical Imagery*, who thinks of this as "new Christian wine" in "old classical bottles" (70); and Copeland, *Rhetoric, Hermeneutics, and Translation*, 42, 55, 106. Cf. also McCall, *Chaucer Among the Gods*, 2–14, who focuses on continuity.

30. Cogent overviews of euhemerism are given by Cumont, *Astrology and Religion*, who places the strategy in its ancient context; Cooke, "Euhemerism," 396–410; and Seznec, *Survival of the Pagan Gods*, 11–36. Dumézil, *Archaic Roman Religion*, 2: 492, analyzes Lactantius's influential historical account of Venus as a prostitute (see also Cooke, "Euhemerism," 400–401).

31. *Augustine*, 266. See also Barkan, *Gods Made Flesh*, 96–103, who offers an illuminating discussion of Augustine and paganism.

32. E.g., Augustine, *City of God*, 6.8, 7.27. Cooke, "Euhemerism," 396, points out two other common rationales for the continued worship of these fig-

ures: 1) audiences, imagining the poets' invented fables about divine power to be real, worshipped those powers; 2) the "divine" powers were astrological.

33. See Kelly, *Devil, Demonology and Witchcraft*, 31–34, 43–57.

34. For Augustine's appeal to his immediate audience, see Brown, *Augustine*, 299–312.

35. For insightful analyses of medieval etymologizing, see Curtius, *European Literature*, 495–500; Allen, *Friar as Critic*, 15–17 et passim; Bloch, *Etymologies and Genealogies*, 30–63; Colish, *The Mirror of Language*, 11–39, 113–20; and Amsler, *Etymology and Grammatical Discourse*.

36. Augustine, *City of God*, 6.9 (trans. Bettenson, 246).

37. *On Christian Doctrine*, trans. Robertson, 85–86 (*Patrologia Latina*, 34, col. 70). I must pass over the intricacies of Augustine's sign theory, but acknowledge a debt to Markus, "St. Augustine on Signs," and to Colish, *Mirror of Language*, 8–53.

38. Brown, *Augustine*, 259–69, offers an informative contextualization; see also Allen, *Friar as Critic*, 11–12; and Minnis, *Medieval Theory of Authorship*, 40–72.

39. Fulgentius, *Mythologies*, in *Opera*, ed. Helm; Fulgentius, *Fulgentius the Mythographer*, trans. Whitbread. I cite the original text by page number and refer to it generally or in translation by book and section (e.g., 1.2). For useful introductions to Fulgentius's works and influence, see Whitbread's introduction and Laistner, "Fulgentius in the Carolingian Age."

40. "Certos itaque nos rerum praestolamur effectus, quo sepulto mendacis Greciae fabuloso commento quid misticum in his sapere debeat cerebrum agnoscamus," Fulgentius, *Mythologies*, 11. Whitbread, "Fulgentius and Dangerous Doctrine," analyzes his treatment of the past.

41. "Calliope ludibundo palmulae tactu meum vaporans pectusculum poeticae proriginis dulcidinem sparsit," Fulgentius, *Mythologies*, 8; and "percussaque mollius cervice quam decuit" (10).

42. "In utroque sexu vapore aetatis extincto libido commoritur. . . . omne enim caloratae iuventutis igniculum torpidae veternositatis algescit in senio," Fulgentius, *Mythologies*, 63. We find many similar comments from late antiquity through the Middle Ages: see Brown, *Body and Society*, 79–80, 135, 378.

43. "Afrodis dicta est—afros enim Grece spuma dicitur—sive ergo quod sicut spuma libido momentaliter surgat et in nihilum veniat, sive quod concitatio ipsa seminis spumosa sit" (Fulgentius, *Mythologies*, 39).

44. Jacquart and Thomasset, *Sexuality and Medicine*, 59–60.

45. We can discern a similar combination of acceptance and condemnation in natural philosophy: see Cadden, *Meanings of Sex Difference*, 216.

46. Isidore of Seville, *Etymologies*, ed. Lindsay; all citations refer to vol. 1. Rabanus Maurus, *De universo*, *Patrologia Latina*, 111, col. 432, repeats Isidore's material on Venus and Cupid.

47. E.g., Fulgentius, *Mythologies*, 3.6; Isidore, *Etymologies*, 8.11.80.

48. See Ferrante, *Woman as Image*, 67, 71; and Panofsky, *Studies in Iconology*, 113, and fig. 84–85.

49. Holquist, "Politics of Representation," 164.

50. Alberic, *Gods and Allegories*, in *Scriptores rerum mythicarum*, ed. Bode. Rathbone introduces the attribution "Master Alberic of London"; see also Seznec, *Survival of the Pagan Gods*, 170–72. There seems to have been an earlier edition of this text, which in the best of all possible worlds would bear investigation: see Burnett, "A Note on the Origins of the Third Vatican Mythographer."

51. This is generally recognized as the quintessential mythography: see Tuve, *Allegorical Imagery*, 224–28; and Schreiber, "Venus in Mythographic Tradition," 519–20.

52. D'Alverny very usefully details translating activity, "Translations and Translators"; Tester, *A History of Western Astrology*, 98–201, provides an excellent overview. For the larger context of mythographic hermeneutics in this time, see also Häring, "Commentary and Hermeneutics"; and Le Goff, *Intellectuals*, 14–20.

53. I allude to Barthes's discussion of semiology, *Mythologies*, 109–59.

54. Cicero, *De natura deorum*, 2.69 (2: 733): "Quae autem dea ad res omnes veniret Venerem nostri nominaverunt, atque ex ea potius venustas quam Venus ex venustate." Dumézil, *Archaic Roman Religion*, 2: 421–22, proposes that the abstract neuter *venus* must originally have expressed the sense of a worshipper charming a god, thus the idea of *venustas* associated with Venus, who became feminine on the model of Aphrodite.

55. See Cadden, *Meanings of Sex Differences*, 100, 200.

56. Both in *Scriptores rerum mythicarum*, ed. Bode.

57. Brown, ed., "An Anonymous *Liber de natura deorum*"; fully described by Allen, "An Anonymous 'De Natura Deorum.'"

58. See Allen, "An Anonymous 'De Natura Deorum,'" 361–64.

59. Minnis, *Medieval Theory of Authorship*, 75–94.

60. *Fulgentius Metaphored*, ed. Liebeschütz. Liebeschütz unfortunately did not edit the final section of the work, on Venus and the voluptuous life, and I have not been able to examine the manuscript. Venus appears incidentally in an edited section on Saturn, and in a descriptive verse. Allen, "Commentary as Criticism," and Smalley, *English Friars and Antiquity*, 109–21, describe Ridewall's text in some detail; see also Allen, *Friar as Critic*, who extensively discusses Ridewall's and others' intellectual contexts.

61. Allen, "Commentary as Criticism," 32.

62. See Liebeschütz's introduction, 34.

63. Quoted by Le Goff, *Intellectuals*, 55.

64. Smalley, *English Friars and Antiquity*, provides a definitive study of the group, later supplemented by Allen, *Friar as Critic*.

65. There are several modern editions of Bersuire's text:

Reductorium morale, Liber XV, cap. i, De formis figurisque deorum, ed. Engels, Werkmateriaal 1 (1960). This is the 1st or A (Avignon) edition of 1340, first printed in 1509 in Paris, attributed to Thomas Walleys. It consists of explanations of images of the deities.

Reductorium morale, Liber XV, cap. ii–xv, "Ovidius moralizatus," ed. Engels, Werkmateriaal 2 (1962). This is the remainder of the 1st (Avignon) ed. of the text, a commentary on Ovid's *Metamorphoses*.

Reductorium morale, Liber XV: "Ovidius moralizatus," cap. i, De formis figurisque deorum, ed. Engels, Werkmateriaal 3 (1966). This is the 2d or P (Paris) edition, completed by 1362 (the year of Bersuire's death). This, the longer of the two versions, is likely the one Chaucer knew (if he did), and I refer to it throughout as *Appearances and Figures*.

"Petrus Berchorius, *Reductorium morale, Liber XV: "Ovidius moralizatus," cap. ii*," ed. Van der Bijl (1971). This was appended to the P ed. I cite this as "Ovidius moralizatus, cap. ii."

Reynolds has translated the text, and I have consulted but not cited his translation: *Ovidius Moralizatus*, Ph.D. diss., University of Illinois, 1971.

For fuller descriptions of Bersuire's text and method, as well as bibliographic essays, see Panofsky, *Renaissance and Renascences*, 78 n. 2; J. Engels, Introduction to Bersuire 1966, "L'Edition critique de l'*Ovidius moralizatus*," "Berchoriana I," and "Berchoriana I (suite)"; Allen, *Friar as Critic*; Twycross, *Medieval Anadyomene*, 3 n. 3; Reynolds, "Sources, Nature, and Influence."

66. "Simili modo fecerunt poete qui in principio fabulas finxerunt, quia scilicet per huius modi figmenta semper aliquam veritatem intelligere voluerunt" (Bersuire, *Appearances and Figures*, 1); "In the same way [as Scriptural poets] the poets did who in the beginning devised stories, indeed because through fictions of this sort they wished always to understand some truth." Copeland, *Rhetoric, Hermeneutics, and Translation*, 76–81, astutely analyzes this methodology.

67. Allen, *Friar as Critic*, provides a lucid and thorough analysis of the method. The *Ovide moralisé* employs the same strategy: see Copeland, *Rhetoric, Hermeneutics, and Translation*, 112.

68. Bersuire, *Appearances and Figures*, 23: "Venus enim in mari genita fingitur pro eo quod luxuria ab opulencia & deliciarum fluxibus generatur. Ideo cuidam meretrici videtur loqui Scriptura, Ysa. XXIII: Transi terram tuam quasi flumen, filia maris"; Isaias 23:10, Douay Rheims trans.

69. Twycross, *Medieval Anadyomene*, 27–45, traces out a logic in this leap.

70. Argued fully by Allen, *Friar as Critic*; Reynolds, "Sources, Nature, and Influence," 89–92.

71. Van Kluyve, "Introduction" to *Mysteries of the Gods*, xiv.

72. *Genealogie deorum gentilium libri*, ed. Romano, 2 vols. I cite this text by volume and page: e.g., 1: 150.

73. See note 26 to this chapter.

74. Schreiber, "Venus in Mythographic Tradition," 528–30, also points to some of the overlaps among the Venuses.

75. The tension between these plots is insightfully studied by Hyde, "Genealogies of Myth."

76. See Marino, "Prometheus."

77. Woodbridge, "Boccaccio's Defence of Poetry," summarizes Boccaccio's position.

78. *Boccaccio on Poetry*, trans. Osgood, 42; cf. 36–54, 123. Gullace offers a useful if not entirely persuasive recent analysis of Boccaccio's idea of the veil: "Medieval and Humanistic Perspectives in Boccaccio's Concept and Defense of Poetry."

79. Hyde, "Genealogies of Myth" offers this double reading of the structure.

80. See Wilkins, *University of Chicago Manuscript*, 17, and "Genealogy of the Genealogical Trees of the *Genealogia deorum*."

81. Lewis, *Allegory of Love*, and Seznec, *Survival of the Pagan Gods*, provide the classic statements about the death and revivification of the gods.

82. I refer to Loukopoulos's edition, from MS Harley 4431; trans. Chance, *Letter of Othea to Hector*. I cite the *Epistre* according to Christine's section numbers. Cf. also *The Epistle of Othea*, trans. Scrope, based on MS. H. 5 of St. John's College, Cambridge. Christine's *Epistre* has received excellent critical commentary, and I am particularly indebted here to the following studies: Tuve, *Allegorical Imagery*, 285–311; Ignatius, "Christine de Pizan's *Epistre Othéa*: An Experiment in Literary Form"; Willard, *Christine de Pizan*, 91–99; Hindman, *Painting and Politics*; Kellogg, "Christine de Pizan as Chivalric Mythographer."

83. Keen, *Chivalry*, confirms that this in fact constitutes the essential medieval definition of chivalry.

84. Hindman, *Painting and Politics*, details the political commentary.

85. Again, Keen, *Chivalry*, provides a confirming historical context.

86. For discussions of gender ideology in Christine's works, cf. Finkel, "Portrait of Woman"; Reno, "Feminist Aspects of Christine's *Epistre*"; and the essays collected by Bornstein, ed., *Ideals for Women*.

87. Delany insightfully compares Christine with radicals of her time, in a polemical correction of the critical tendency to idealize Christine: "Mothers to Think Back Through."

88. Giovanni del Virgilio, *Allegorie Ovidiane*, ed. Ghisalberti.

89. See Wimsatt, *Chaucer and His French Contemporaries*, 64–69, 192.

90. I am indebted to Brownlee's provocative reading of the *Livre du chemin de long estude*, which achieves a similar effect: "Literary Genealogy and the Problem of the Father."

91. Wetherbee, *Platonism and Poetry*, 36–48, and Dronke, *Fabula*, 13–78, present details about variations in the theory in the twelfth century; the twelfth-

century formulations do not preclude later reformulations, addressed by Allen, *Friar as Critic*, 3–28; and Minnis, *Medieval Theory of Authorship*, 140–44. For fascinating discussions of the implications of the "veil," see also Barkan, *Gods Made Flesh*, 111–17; and Dinshaw, *Chaucer's Sexual Poetics*.

92. See Wetherbee, *Platonism and Poetry*, 40–45; Dronke, *Fabula*, 23–25, 32.

93. Such binaries are central to Robertson's ideas about how to read medieval texts (*Preface to Chaucer*, 52–137, 286–390); I find him overgeneralizing medieval ideas about the fictive veil.

CHAPTER 3

1. See, e.g., Mâle, *Gothic Image*, 1–22.

2. See Schapiro, "On the Aesthetic Attitude in Romanesque Art"; I am grateful to Kirk Ambrose for this reference and for stimulating discussions about iconography.

3. Tuve, *Allegorical Imagery*, 317–22, 331, perceptively analyzes limitations of concrete detail; see also Mitchell's discussion of the conventions and limits of visual images, *Iconology*, 5–52.

4. See Spencer, "Lineage of Cupid," 123–27, 129–44; and Grigson, *Goddess of Love*, 65–70 (a very well illustrated study). Histories of Roman religion do not generally treat of Cupid, though he was worshipped in Venus's temple. For instance, Dumézil in *Archaic Roman Religion* provides a thorough historical account of Venus: the rise to importance in the time of the Julians (1: 241; 2: 540–49), etymology (2: 421–22), the integration of Venus of Eryx into Trojan legend (2: 452–54, 457–89). Cupid does not appear.

5. I.e., "Venus" names a number of different local goddesses in the Roman empire: for good accounts of syncretism, see Palmer, *Roman Religion and Roman Empire*, 51–55, 122–23; and MacMullen, *Paganism in the Roman Empire*, 1–10.

6. For details, see Lawrence, "*Birth of Venus* in Roman Art," with excellent illustrations; Grigson, *Goddess of Love*; Heckscher, "Anadyomene in the Medieval Tradition"; Lloyd-Morgan, "Roman Venus." For a concise review of ancient traditions, see also Twycross, *Medieval Anadyomene*, 97–102.

7. See esp. Lawrence, "*Birth of Venus* in Roman Art."

8. Grigson identifies swans as Apollo's bird, and argues that associating Venus with swans gives her a role in the creation of poetry and song (*Goddess of Love*, 204–5).

9. See Lloyd-Morgan, "Roman Venus," 184.

10. See Buono, "From Goddess to Virgin"; and Heckscher, "Anadyomene in the Medieval Tradition."

11. Panofsky cites an intriguing twelfth-century report of viewing ancient ruins: *Renaissance and Renascences*, 72–73.

12. See Smith, "Mythological Figures and Scenes in Romano-British Mosaics," items 17–25, 103–7, 132.

13. For the mosaics, see Lawrence, "*Birth of Venus* in Roman Art," 11, 16, and figs. 2, 3; and Twycross, *Medieval Anadyomene*, 18–19.

14. "Hanc etiam nudam pingunt, sive quod nudos sibi adfectatores dimittat sive quod libidinis crimen numquam celatum sit sive quod numquam nisi nudis conveniat. Huic etiam rosas in tutelam adiciunt; rosae enim et rubent et pungunt, ut etiam libido rubet verecundiae opprobrio, pungit etiam peccati aculeo; et sicut rosa delectat quidem, sed celeri motu temporis tollitur, ita et libido libet momentaliter, fugit perenniter. In huius etiam tutelam columbas ponunt, illa videlicet causa, quod huius generis aves sint in coitu fervidae. . . . Hanc etiam in mari natantem pingunt, quod omnis libido rerum patiatur naufragia. . . . Conca etiam marina portari pingitur, quod huius generis animal toto corpore simul aperto in coitu misceatur." *Fulgentius the Mythographer*, 66–67; *Mythologies*, 40.

15. See also Twycross, *Medieval Anadyomene*, 18–23, for the type.

16. See Twycross, *Medieval Anadyomene*, 70–88; and Friedman, "L'Iconographie de Venus."

17. Fulgentius, *Mythologies*, 66–70; *Fulgentius the Mythographer*, 88–90.

18. Panofsky and Saxl demonstrate that such a separation of classical image from classical meaning is common in the Middle Ages; they view this as a regrettable falling away from classical standards, an art-historical deviation corrected in the Renaissance: "Classical Mythology in Mediaeval Art." Such a devaluation of medieval conventions seems to me unnecessary.

19. "Aut libidine mollitur aut homicidiis cruentatur aut rapina succenditur aut livoribus rancidatur," Fulgentius, *Mythologies*, 37; *Fulgentius the Mythographer*, 64.

20. See Brundage, *Law, Sex, and Christian Society*, 63–65, 70, 80–82, 90–92; and for parallels with the penitentials, Payer, *Sex and the Penitentials*, 4, 21, 45, 47, 49–50, 54, 118, 121. Cf. also Fuchs, *Sexual Desire and Love*, 35–41, for an intriguing discussion of the logic underlying the judgment.

21. Heckscher, "Anadyomene in the Medieval Tradition," 129–33; and Lawrence, "*Birth of Venus* in Roman Art," 13 and n. 30.

22. See Noonan, *Contraception*, 56–139; Brundage, *Law, Sex, and Christian Society*, 89–93.

23. Isidore, *Etymologies*, 8.11.76–80; cf. Macrobius, as discussed by Wetherbee, *Platonism and Poetry*, 119–20. I discuss the fable here as if it were the image because the description of Cupid invites, I believe, a parallel visualization of Venus. Sharpe's Introduction to "Isidore of Seville: The Medical Writings," 1–37, provides a good overview of Isidore's medical knowledge.

24. "[Cupid] alatus pingitur, quia nihil amantibus levius, nihil mutabilius invenitur. Puer pingitur, quia stultus est et inrationabilis amor. Sagittam et facem tenere fingitur. Sagittam, quia amor cor vulnerat; facem, quia inflammat." Isidore, *Etymologies*, 8.11.80.

25. Panofsky, *Studies in Iconology*, 104–5.

26. The visual analogue for this description would be a figure Panofsky labels *Amor carnalis*: *Renaissance and Renascences*, 94–95 and figs. 64–67.

27. On the Stoics, see Noonan, *Contraception*, 46–49, 76–81; Brundage, *Law, Sex, and Christian Society*, 18–21, and 138, on Isidore's stoicism in particular. Payer, *Bridling of Desire*, valuably studies the medieval theological relation between reason and appetite. The influence of Augustine, *Contra Faustum Manichaeum*, is apparent on Isidore: see MacFarlane, "Isidore of Seville on the Pagan Gods," 30.

28. Brundage, *Law, Sex, and Christian Society*, 134–38, discusses conflicts in Isidore's time between Church and laity. For evidence of resistance to the official sexual code, see also Payer, *Sex and the Penitentials*, 4, 120–21; and Boswell, *Christianity, Social Tolerance, and Homosexuality*, 137–66.

29. *Mythographus primus*, in *Scriptores rerum mythicarum*, ed. Bode, 33.

30. *Mythographus secundus*, in *Scriptores rerum mythicarum*, ed. Bode, 84–86.

31. "Venerem in mari natantem fingunt, quia omnis libido rerum patitur naufragia" (84); Porphyry is the cited source for this often-repeated idea.

32. Though the affair of Venus and Mars concludes with this moral: "Nam virtus [i.e., Mars], corrupta libidine [Venus], sole teste apparet, et turpiter catenata fervoris constrictione tenetur" (85).

33. This seems not to appear in ancient art: Lawrence, "*Birth of Venus* in Roman Art," 11. I name the father "Saturn" for convenience, but paternity varies: see my "Saturn of the Several Faces," 292. Venus can also be born from her conch shell, without an apparent *genitor*.

34. "Fingitur autem Venus nata per damnum, quia omnes vires usu venereo debilitantur, qui sine damno non geritur" (84). In his turn, Alberic adds that the sea indicates the sweat coitus always produces, *Gods and Allegories*, 155; and Walsingham, *Mysteries of the Gods*, 7, repeats Alberic's account.

35. See Bullough, "Medical and Scientific Views," 487–88; and Jacquart and Thomasset, *Sexuality and Medicine*, 48–70.

36. I have found several scholars helpful in examining the split between beliefs in paternity and scientific proof for it: Barnes, "Genetrix:Genitor :: Nature:Culture"; Montrose, "Shaping Fantasies," 36–42; and Laqueur, *Making Sex*, 56–59, who writes "believing in fathers is like, to use Freud's analogy, believing in the Hebrew God" (57).

37. "Quia venerea res sine amore exerceri non potest" (86).

38. Noonan, *Contraception*, does not include any theologians of this period with the Second Vatican Mythographer's attitude; see his 303–30, and Brundage, *Law, Sex, and Christian Society*, 67, 80, 82–84, 138–39.

39. "Mentem vulnerat amor" (86).

40. "Puer etiam fingitur, quia sicut pueris per imperitiam facundia, sic quoque nimium amantibus per voluptatem deficit" (86).

41. Wack, *Lovesickness*, 64.

42. See Chap. 1.

43. "Ut medicorum indicant libri, haec arbor plurimis mulierum necessitatibus apta est" (Alberic, *Gods and Allegories*, 229).

44. "Ex voluptatis desiderio amorem nasci certum sit" (ibid., 239).

45. Noonan, *Contraception*, 171–99, argues that the twelfth century witnesses a revival of rigorous Augustinianism, i.e., a rejection of pleasure. Walsingham repeats this interpretation (*Mysteries of the Gods*, 156), but in his time the idea is more commonplace.

46. Brundage, *Law, Sex, and Christian Society*, 234–39, 273–74.

47. "Quia turpitudinis est stulta cupiditas, et quia imperfectus est in amantibus, sicut in pueris, sermo" (Alberic, *Gods and Allegories*, 239).

48. Gower, *Confessio Amantis*, gloss at 3.155: "intolerabilis iuventutis concupiscencia."

49. See Rossiaud, *Medieval Prostitution*; Brundage, *Law, Sex, and Christian Society*, 91, 301, 303–5, 317; Richards, *Sex, Dissidence and Damnation*, 38–41; Cadden, *Meanings of Sex Difference*, 147–48; and Richard of Fournival, *Consaus D'Amours*, "Advice on Love," in *Comedy of Eros*, trans. Shapiro, 107.

50. See also Le Goff, *Intellectuals*, 25.

51. "Itidemque Amores duo; alter bonus et pudicus, quo sapientia et virtutes amantur; alter impudicus et malus, quo ad vitia inclinamur." Alberic, *Gods and Allegories*. Cf. the discussion of Remigius, Chap. 1. Walsingham, *Mysteries of the Gods*, 156–57, repeats the account but distinguishes between the chaste Pallas as wife of Vulcan, and the unchaste Venus as mother of Hermaphrodite.

52. Panofsky analyzes this feature in depth, *Studies in Iconology*, 104–12.

53. Panofsky, *Studies in Iconology*, 123–28.

54. "Ovidius moralizatus, cap. ii," ed. Van der Bijl, 32–33: "Vel dic de Cupidine, qui duplici telo erat armatus, quod iste est Deus amoris, Dei filius quia s., sicut dicitur I *Ioh*, 'Deus caritas est.' Sagitte ipsius sunt divina mandata, duplici s. penna impennata i. in duplici caritate fundata. Sed revera de istis telis unum erat acutum et aliud obtusum, in quo s. notatur quod aliqua sunt mandata affirmativa, alia negativa; prima sunt boni amoris inflammativa, secunda sunt mali amoris repressiva. . . .

"Vel dic quod Cupido est luxuriosus qui, licet sit Veneris filius et lascivus, sagittas tamen divinorum eloquiorum portat."

55. Bersuire, *Appearances and Figures*, 22–25. Twycross, *Medieval Anadyomene*, 21–45, accounts for why Venus now carries the shell that once carried her, and explores Bersuire's innovations in interpreting that shell.

56. Twycross, *Medieval Anadyomene*, 27–45, analyzes this iconography in depth.

57. I agree with Twycross, *Medieval Anadyomene*, 44–45, that Bersuire intends the full range of connotations for *luxuria*.

58. I take these details from Panofsky, *Renaissance and Renascences*, 86–87, and figs. 56–58.

59. The Paris version specifies which hand, but the earlier Avignon edition does not (*Reductorium morale, Liber XV, cap. i, "Appearances and Figures,"* ed. Engels, 1960, p. 15).

60. In Ridewall, *Fulgentius Metaphored*, ed. Liebeschütz, 118 and plate 18 (a facsimile of the folio on Venus). Seznec, *Survival of the Pagan Gods*, 170–79, and Twycross, *Medieval Anadyomene*, 4–14 analyze the sources of the *Notebook*.

61. "Pingebatur ergo Venus puela pulcerima, nuda et in mari natans et in manu sua dextera concham marinam continens atque gestans. Que Venus rosis candidis et rubeis sertum gerebat in capite ornatum et columbis circa se volantibus comitabatur. Vulcano, deo ignis rustico turpissimo, in coniugium erat assignata, qui stabat ad eius dexteram, et coram ipsa tres astabant iuvencule nude, que tres Gracie dicebantur. Ex quibus duarum facies versus nos adverse erant, tercia vero dorsum in contrarium vertebat. Huic et Cupido, filius suus alatus et cecus, assistebat, qui sagita et arcu, quos tenebat, Appolinem sagitaverat, propter quod deos contra se turbatos timens ad matris gremium fugiebat, cui et illa sinistram porrigebat." *Notebook*, 118.

62. In agreement with Twycross, *Medieval Anadyomene*, 16–17.

63. Bodleian Library, MS Fairfax 16, a facsimile of which has been ed. by Norton-Smith.

64. E.g., Boccaccio, *Genealogy* 1: 46–47. One Cupid's wings show the swift passage of youth (1: 83). Boccaccio does not develop iconography for Cupid, son of Venus *magna*, though this seems to be the conventional winged youth (1: 144, 146–47). Still another Cupid is supposed to be the son of Venus *secunda*, but he is excluded from her iconography, for which Boccaccio follows Fulgentius (1: 148–52).

65. See Wack, *Lovesickness*, 79.

66. Boccaccio cites Francesco de Barbarino as his source for these details: Panofsky, *Studies in Iconology*, 115–20, and figs. 88–91 studies the image.

67. See Neumann, *Great Mother*, plates 62, 63, 126 and discussion.

68. "Quod a cignis eius trahatur currus, duplex potest esse ratio, aut quia per albedinem significant lautitiam muliebrem, aut quia dulcissime canant, et maxime morti propinqui, ut demonstretur amantum animos cantu trahi, et quod cantu amantes fere desiderio nimio morientes passiones explicent suas." Boccaccio, *Genealogy*, 1: 147.

69. For further detail on planetary influences, see below, Chap. 5.

70. The seeming variance between naturalism and moralism in Boccaccio's career has provoked critical controversy. E.g., Scaglione, *Nature and Love*, finds Boccaccio retreating from naturalism after writing the *Decameron*; while Hollander, *Boccaccio's Two Venuses*, finds Boccaccio always a moralist. The controversy is based, I think, on a misapprehension of ecclesiastical standards and a failure to recognize how common this variance and double perspective are in medieval culture.

71. See Kelly, *Love and Marriage*, 245–85; Noonan, *Contraception*, 292–95; Brundage, *Law, Sex, and Christian Society*, 364–69; Payer, *Bridling of Desire*, 61–72, 79–83, 110, 118–31. Rossiaud, *Medieval Prostitution*, 72–85, 104–28, interestingly, explores some implications of this "victory for the flesh."

72. See Chap. 5 below.

73. Allen, *Friar as Critic*, discusses this method in the context of homiletic exegesis.

74. "Poete dupplicem dicunt deam Venerem. Unam, quam dicunt deam ordinate et caste delectacionis, aliam dicunt esse Venerem, quam ponunt deam lascivie et carnalis voluptatis." Ridewall, *Fulgentius Metaphored*, 78.

75. Walsingham in his turn also revises Remigius's two Venuses (*Mysteries of the Gods*, 156–57).

76. "Blandimenta feminea corporum," Ridewall, *Fulgentius Metaphored*, 77.

77. "Corpore nudata, equore delata, / virore plantata, cute dealbata, / floribus ornata, ungentis afflata, / graciis stipata et concha locata." Ibid., 116, with the illustration in plate 10. This text glosses "afflata" with "vel linita"; I quote the line without the gloss, which spoils the meter.

78. See Friedman, "John de Foxton's Continuation of the *Fulgentius metaphoralis*."

CHAPTER 4

1. "*Compilatio* and the Wife of Bath," 11.

2. This chapter is greatly indebted to recent discussions of the relations between Latin and vernacular: Hanna, "*Compilatio* and the Wife of Bath"; Wallace, *Chaucer and the Early Writings of Boccaccio*; Copeland, *Rhetoric, Herme-*

neutics, and Translation; Wetherbee, "Latin Structure and Vernacular Space"; Minnis, *Medieval Theory of Authorship*, 160–210, and "De Vulgari Auctoritate." I would also refer the reader to Michael J. Bennett, who provocatively argues that the royal court could have contributed to the flourishing of vernacular literature ("Court of Richard II"), and to Yeager, *Gower's Poetic*, 1–44, on what it means for Chaucer and his contemporaries to translate any tradition into English.

3. See Hexter, *Ovid and Medieval Schooling*.

4. Mack, *Ovid*, 58; see also 53–69.

5. For the complex tradition in which both poems participate, see Dronke, "L'amor che move il sole," 393–95, 406.

6. See Dronke, "L'amor che move il sole," 407, n. 64.

7. This is a recurrent metaphor in Ovid's amatory verse: see Copley, *Exclusus Amator*, 125–40. Although Copley is an unsympathetic reader of Ovid, he usefully traces out the traditional elements.

8. See Dronke, "L'amor che move il sole."

9. "Omnis generis fornicationes atque lascivias et coitus multitudinem," Boccaccio, *Genealogy*, 1: 143.

10. Her planetary children are described: "acute meditationis in compositionibus carminum," ibid., 1: 143. Ptolemy relates Venus to poetry only in combination with Mercury: *Tetrabiblos*, 4.4.

11. Hollander's argument in *Boccaccio's Two Venuses*, 112–16.

12. For a study of related visual traditions, see Van Marle, *Iconographie*, 2: 415–55.

13. See Panofsky, *Studies in Iconology*, 101–3, for the iconology; Dahlberg, trans., reproduces splendid samples: *Romance of the Rose*.

14. See also Robert Taylor, "Figure of Amor," for Cupid's backgrounds in Provençal literature.

15. For a good discussion of this, see Robert Taylor, "Figure of Amor."

16. Tuve, *Allegorical Imagery*, 278, fig. 100.

17. Hindman reproduces and discusses Christine's iconology: *Painting and Politics*, 77–99, 122–23, and figs. 11, 38, 74, 85. I deal with the iconology of Christine's planetary Venus in Chap. 5, and with her remaking of the courtly Cupid in Chap. 8.

18. See Wimsatt, *Chaucer and His French Contemporaries*, 4, 41, 61, 83–84.

19. Koonce, *Chaucer and the Tradition of Fame*, 89–136, argues that this is one of the "two Venuses" of Boccaccio's gloss on the *Teseida*. Koonce ignores iconography: Boccaccio's blind Cupid does not appear with Venus, either in the *Genealogy* or in the gloss; Bersuire's blind Cupid does attend Venus, but of course Bersuire does not include the "two Venuses." Ruggiers, "Unity of Chaucer's *House of Fame*," 263–64, proposes a conflation of Venus, Fame, and Fortune;

though in my view this fails adequately to differentiate traditions, it nonetheless insightfully emphasizes the close relation between Venus and Fame in the poem.

20. Twycross, *Medieval Anadyomene*, 70–88, proposes Idleness in *Romance of the Rose* as the source for the comb; see Chaucer's *Romaunt of the Rose* A, 565–79, 599. Friedman, "L'Iconographie de Venus" mentions other instances of the comb. For the scholarly debate surrounding the source of Chaucer's iconology, see above, Chap. 2 note 9.

21. Boitani also notes the significance of the temple setting, "Chaucer's Temples of Venus," 17–21. For its medievalization, see Sypherd, *Studies in Chaucer's "Hous of Fame,"* 80–86; Bennett, *Chaucer's Book of Fame*, 12–14; Braswell, "Architectural Portraiture." See also Kendrick, "Chaucer's House of Fame and the French Palais de Justice."

22. Minnis, *Chaucer and Pagan Antiquity*, 32–40, persuasively outlines medieval reasoning about pagan idolatry; Twycross, *Medieval Anadyomene*, 61–62, points out that Chaucer uses the mythographers' image only for the pagan idol. Kolve conveys examples of the visual tradition, which emphasizes pagan idols: *Chaucer and the Imagery of Narrative*, 113 (fig. 48), 151 (fig. 60). Whitlark, "Chaucer and the Pagan Gods," 70–71, places the narrator in the condemnable place of the pagans, which seems unlikely.

23. Wallace, *Chaucer and the Early Writings of Boccaccio*, 70–72.

24. In agreement with J. A. W. Bennett, *Chaucer's Book of Fame*, 16–24.

25. Cooper similarly argues that in *House of Fame* Chaucer rejects the tradition of a moralized Ovid, "Chaucer and Ovid," 74–75.

26. In agreement with several critics, who find that Chaucer emphasizes his difference from his often conflicting sources, his departures from traditional uses of conventions: see Clemen, *Chaucer's Early Poetry*, 67–121; J. A. W. Bennett, *Chaucer's Book of Fame*, 1–51; and Delany, *Chaucer's "House of Fame."*

27. See Olson, "Deschamps' *Art* and Chaucer's Literary Environment" and "Making and Poetry."

28. Copeland proposes that in the *Prologue* to the *Legend of Good Women* "Chaucer defines the terms of translation as an overt act of exegetical appropriation" (*Rhetoric, Hermeneutics, and Translation*, 186); evidently, he begins to work out this strategy as early as the *House of Fame*.

29. See Wallace, *Chaucer and the Early Writings of Boccaccio*, 5–22, on Chaucer's *House of Fame* and Dante's vernacular ideal; see also Karla Taylor, *Chaucer Reads*, 20–49, for an insightful discussion of how Chaucer uses Dante. Minnis, "De Vulgari Auctoritate," 41–51, proposes that Chaucer's refusal conventionally to authorize his poetry indicates a rejection of vernacular *auctoritas*, but this seems to me to overstate the uneasinesses of Chaucer's vernacular ideal. I agree with

Taylor that Chaucer actually manifests some ambivalence about authentication, *Chaucer Reads*, 38–49.

30. Critics sometimes posit that Venus's temple represents the world of (French) love literature: e.g., Shook, "*House of Fame*"; Boitani, "Chaucer's Temples of Venus," 20; McCall, *Chaucer Among the Gods*, 50, 57. This perception demonstrates how thoroughly Chaucer succeeds in changing Latin traditions, though it passes somewhat too hastily over the fact that they are Latin traditions, albeit mediated by French and Italian poetry.

31. *Aeneid*, 1.407–9: "Quid natum totiens, crudelis tu quoque, falsis / ludis imaginibus? cur dextrae iungere dextram / non datur ac veras audire et reddere voces?"

32. J. A. W. Bennett, *Chaucer's Book of Fame*, 28–46, cogently analyzes Chaucer's retailoring of Virgil's *pius* Aeneas; Delany, *Chaucer's "House of Fame,"* 48–57, traces the conflicts in Ovid's and Virgil's accounts of Aeneas, which contribute to this lowering.

33. See Fyler's assessment of how Ovid read Virgil, focusing on Ovid's deflation of Virgilian epic: *Chaucer and Ovid*, 1–22.

34. Fulgentius, *Mythologies*, 2.1, establishes the dominant mythographic understanding of Paris's decision; see also Alberic, *Gods and Allegories*, 241, recapitulated by Walsingham, *Mysteries of the Gods*, 170. Medieval commentators generally accept Aeneas as Virgil presents him, an exemplum of virtuous man: e.g., Bernard Silvestris in *Commentary on the "Aeneid,"* on which see Wetherbee, *Platonism and Poetry*, 105–11. Like Chaucer, Silvestris rewrites Virgil's Venus *genetrix*, but into *mundana musica* rather than into the *anadyomene*.

35. See Hall, "Chaucer and the Dido-and-Aeneas Story," 155–58; and Delany, *Chaucer's "House of Fame,"* 48–57.

36. I allude to Rubin, "Traffic in Women."

37. Critics tend to divide between finding Chaucer a partisan of Dido and discovering her utterly condemned. For recent instances of the former, see Spearing, *Readings in Medieval Poetry*, 86, 89; Mann, *Chaucer*, 7–16; and Minnis, "De Vulgari Auctoritate," 45–48. For the latter, see Koonce, *Chaucer and the Tradition of Fame*, 111–23. Such polarized readings suppress either Chaucer's direct commentary or his tone: J. A. W. Bennett recognizes both, *Chaucer's Book of Fame*, 30–39. Hansen, *Chaucer and the Fictions of Gender*, 87–107, reads Dido as a stereotype of "everywoman"—"weak," victimized, subjugated—an argument that requires us to overlook the effects of class on gender norms.

38. Benson, "Courtly Love and Chivalry," 244–51, usefully sketches out the social consequences of conventional love talk such as Aeneas's.

39. Vance, "Chaucer's Poetics of Inflation" sets these stylistic variations against a fascinating economic context.

40. Critics have frequently remarked that this poem is about poetry or tex-

tuality or language. For representative examples of this position, see Shook, "House of Fame," 341–54; Fyler, *Chaucer and Ovid*, 23–64; Vance, "Chaucer's Poetics of Inflation," 17–37; Gellrich, *Idea of the Book*, 167–201; Spearing, *Readings in Medieval Poetry*, 92–93; Kiser, *Truth and Textuality*, 25–41; and Kruger, "Imagination and Complex Movement." Karla Taylor, *Chaucer Reads*, 219 n. 2, supplies a recent full bibliography of similar critical positions.

41. See Wallace, *Chaucer and the Early Writings of Boccaccio*; and Yeager, *Gower's Poetic*, 11–13.

42. *Chaucer Reads*, 37; I am much indebted to this sophisticated analysis of influence; and to Copeland's *Rhetoric, Hermeneutics, and Translation*, which thoroughly establishes this potential of translation.

43. See Wimsatt, *Chaucer and His French Contemporaries*, 43–76, 190–209.

44. *Riverside Chaucer* compiles the sources: Chaucer borrows from Boccaccio's *Teseida*, 1. 1–3, 11. 63, for Venus and the Muses of Elicon and Parnassus; and from Dante's *Divine Comedy, Inferno*, 2.7–9, for the Muses and memory (I read Dante's "mente" and Chaucer's "thought" as both referring to memory); cf. *Paradiso* 1.10–12 for the treasury of memory.

45. Cf. Joyner, "Parallel Journeys," 18, who finds Venus here representative of "all worldly attractions that can lure the mind," in contrast to the Apollo invoked for Book 3; and McCall, *Chaucer Among the Gods*, 57, who similarly reads the invocation as recalling "the discredited art world of Venus's temple." They assume, as I do not, strict representational unity.

46. See Martianus Capella, *De nuptiis Philologiae et Mercurii*, ed. Dick, 1.28, for the correlation of Muses and planets; trans. Stahl and Johnson, *Martianus Capella and the Seven Liberal Arts*, 2: 16 (numbered 1.27); Dante's *Convivio* also provides a key medieval statement on parallels between the planets and liberal arts: see Mazzotta, "Light of Venus." Seznec, *Survival of the Pagan Gods*, 73–76, 133–35, 137–43, and Wood, *Chaucer and the Country of the Stars*, 55–57, present evidence for the prevalence of the correspondences.

47. Olson, "Deschamps' *Art* and Chaucer's Literary Environment," 718; see also Olson, "Making and Poetry"; and Wimsatt, *Chaucer and His French Contemporaries*.

48. Middleton, "Chaucer's 'New Men,' " 25.

49. Chaucer could have derived his treatment also from the *Pervigilium Veneris*: see Donaldson, "Venus and the Mother of Romulus."

50. See Wimsatt, *Chaucer and His French Contemporaries*.

51. Wimsatt, ibid., provides an admirable study of Chaucer's relation to these writers. See also Sypherd, *Studies in the "House of Fame,"* 129–32; Fansler, *Chaucer and the "Roman de la Rose,"* 56–72; Fisher, "Chaucer and the French Influence." Overbeck, "Man of Gret Auctorite," 157–61, recognizes Chaucer's debt to French traditions in portraying Cupid and concludes that Cupid is

the poem's expected "man of gret auctorite," a conclusion that overshoots the evidence and that deals unconvincingly with the traditions.

52. See Wimsatt, *Chaucer and His French Contemporaries*, 77–107.

53. Vance argues similarly about erotic texts, "Love's Concordance," 48–50.

54. For other aspects of Chaucer's poetics, see Everett, "Reflections on Chaucer's 'Art Poetical' "; Payne, *Key of Remembrance*; Kean, *Chaucer and the Making of English Poetry*, 1: 1–66; Lenaghan, "Clerk of Venus."

55. Bethurum Loomis and Leyerle similarly remark that the poem demonstrates Chaucer's "encyclopedic taste" or the "encyclopedic . . . tendency of [his] poetic imagination": respectively, "Center of the *Parlement of Foules*," 49; and "Chaucer's Windy Eagle." Kean, *Chaucer and the Making of English Poetry*, 1: 86–111, also emphasizes the multiplicity of literary traditions; as do Karla Taylor, *Chaucer Reads*, 20–49, and Ruffolo, "Literary Authority and the Lists of Chaucer's *House of Fame*."

56. See Wimsatt, *Chaucer and His French Contemporaries*.

57. I agree with those who find the parts of this poem disparate—see Muscatine, *Chaucer and the French Tradition*, 107–15; Payne, *Key of Remembrance*, 129–39—though I think the parts are also more than merely disparate.

58. Derrida, *Of Grammatology*, 10–26, very provocatively explicates such mythologizing.

59. I am indebted to Muscatine's analysis of the tale's symmetries and orders, particularly its use of aesthetic and chivalric order as a bulwark against ever-impending chaos (*Chaucer and the French Tradition*, 175–90); Jordan, *Chaucer and the Shape of Creation*, 154–84, usefully extends Muscatine's analysis, emphasizing the construction of order.

60. McCall, *Chaucer Among the Gods*, 63–72; and Kolve, *Chaucer and the Imagery of Narrative*, 105–32, cogently analyze the amphitheater along these lines.

61. Knight's provocative analysis of the tale's treatment of chivalric ideology, especially his sense of the conflicts between the ideals of chivalric romance and the practices of medieval cavalry, underlies my reading: *Chaucer*, 83–90. I am further indebted to Huizinga, *Waning of the Middle Ages*, 1–114, which remains a valuable essay on the tensions between chivalric ideals and practices; and to Keen, *Chivalry*. Patterson, *Chaucer and the Subject of History*, 165–230, provides a challenging reading of the tale as representing a "crisis of chivalric identity"; and Leicester, *Disenchanted Self*, 221–382, suggestively treats of a "disenchantment" with the institution of chivalry.

62. See Ciavolella, "Mediaeval Medicine and Arcite's Love Sickness."

63. The most extreme, and the most thought-provoking, analysis of this cultural pattern is by MacKinnon, *Toward a Feminist Theory of the State*, 126–54; interestingly, Keen, *Chivalry*, also points out the eroticism of chivalric combat. Howard has usefully illuminated the connection between sexuality and ag-

gression in other of Chaucer's works as well as in this tale: "Thwarted Sexuality in Chaucer's Works," 243–49.

64. See, e.g., attempts to resolve the issue in favor of a venerean Palamon or martial Arcite: Tatlock, *Development and Chronology of Chaucer's Works*, 231–33; Fairchild, "Active Arcite, Contemplative Palamon"; Marckwardt, *Characterization in Chaucer's "Knight's Tale,"* 1–23; French, "Lovers in the *Knight's Tale*"; Frost, "An Interpretation of Chaucer's *Knight's Tale*"; Curry, *Chaucer and the Medieval Sciences*, 119–63; Schmidt, "Tragedy of Arcite"; Brooks and Fowler, "The Meaning of Chaucer's *Knight's Tale*"; McCall, *Chaucer Among the Gods*, 63–84; Minnis, *Chaucer and Pagan Antiquity*, 109–21; and Perryman, "False Arcite."

65. Cf. Leicester, *Disenchanted Subject*, 267–73, who reads the temple as the embodiment of the Knight's perception of "the structure of jealousy and rivalry that . . . is the truth of chivalric eros" (270), with Venus representing a masculine suspicion of feminine sexuality. I think this misses the tone and overdetermines some of the detail.

66. Chaucer takes the details of Venus's temple essentially from Boccaccio and the *Romance of the Rose*; for source study, see Boitani, "Chaucer's Temples of Venus," 27–31, and *Chaucer and Boccaccio*, 89–95; Kolve, *Chaucer and the Imagery of Narrative*, 85–157, insightfully compares the texts. Kean, *Chaucer and the Making of English Poetry*, 2: 3–5, 21–28, asserts that Chaucer bases his temple descriptions on Children of the Planets (*Planetenkinder*) traditions. Twycross, *Medieval Anadyomene*, 51–54, and Kolve, *Chaucer and the Imagery of Narrative*, 115–30, provide more closely reasoned arguments on this point. (Minnis, *Chaucer and Pagan Antiquity*, 113–16, argues for a beneficent planetary Venus, but he is not concerned with iconology.) As Kolve indicates (118), the description of Venus does not strongly suggest children of the planet, though the temple of Mars does, with its depiction of the human activities sponsored by the planet. In fact, Venus is the least astrologized of the tale's deities. I discuss children of the planets in Chap. 5.

67. See Lowes, "Loveres Maladye"; and Wack, *Lovesickness*, 60–62, 89, 146–76.

68. Aers, *Community, Gender, and Individual Identity*, 117–52, argues perceptively about the masculine establishment of gender and class identity through love conventions.

69. Arcite endures lovesickness. Palamon falls in love with the conventional blanches and sighs; interestingly, he has Theban opium at the time of his prison escape (1472), a drug used to treat lovesickness: Emerson, "Chaucer's 'Opie of Thebes.'"

70. See Benson, "Courtly Love and Chivalry."

71. Moi astutely uncovers this ideology: "Desire in Language."

72. Benson, "Courtly Love and Chivalry," 245–50, outlines the social norms.

73. For possible sources of the citole, see Twycross, *Medieval Anadyomene*, 27–70; Steadman, "Venus' *Citole*," 623, infers it connotes "sophisticated pastimes."

74. See Patterson, *Chaucer and the Subject of History*, 179–98; and Saul, "Chaucer and Gentility."

75. Howard, *Idea of the Canterbury Tales*, 227–37, takes in both the humor and the pathos of the poem, and my sense of a laudatory critique is indebted to his sensitive response to the whole of Chaucer's complex tone.

76. *Christianity, Social Tolerance, and Homosexuality*, 253.

77. Bodleian MS Fairfax 16, ed. Sieper, 89.

78. See Schirmer, *Lydgate*, 277.

79. "Venus id est carnalis concupiscencia vel planeta que inclinat ad concupiscenciam et significat vitam voluptuosam que debetur carnalibus," glossing 1444.

80. Jauss, *Toward an Aesthetic of Reception*, 9.

CHAPTER 5

1. See Noonan, *Contraception*, and Payer, *Bridling of Desire*, on the theological production of "natural" sexuality; Helen Rodnite Lemay, "Lectures on Female Sexuality," and Bullough, "Medical Views of Women," on the naturalization of medical misogyny; Wack, *Lovesickness*, on medical rationales for a cultural pattern of desire; and for biology and physiology, see Laqueur, *Making Sex*; Thomasset, "Nature of Woman"; and Cadden, *Meanings of Sex Difference*. I find Boswell's comments on ideologies of nature also thought-provoking (*Christianity, Social Tolerance, and Homosexuality*, 303–32).

2. MacCormack, "Nature, Culture and Gender," offers a concise, cogent analysis. For discussions relevant to modern sciences, cf. also Sherif, "Bias in Psychology"; and Keller, "Gender/Science System."

3. For studies of astrology relevant to later Middle English literature, see Eade, *Forgotten Sky*; North, *Chaucer's Universe*; Smyser, "View of Chaucer's Astronomy"; and Wood, *Chaucer and the Country of the Stars*, who attempts to place astrology also in its philosophical contexts. Curry, *Chaucer and the Medieval Sciences*, though often cited by literary critics, is thoroughly unreliable, usually because his "scientific" evidence is inappropriate.

4. I am indebted to Cumont's lucid treatment of Roman traditions, *Astrology and Religion*. For a brief introduction to the subject, see Seznec, *Survival of the Pagan Gods*, 37–58.

5. For the Greek Eros, see Spencer, "Lineage of Cupid," 123–24.

6. In the following overview and throughout this chapter I am gratefully indebted to several admirable discussions of ancient and medieval astrology:

Laistner, "Western Church and Astrology"; Seznec, *Survival of the Pagan Gods*, 37–83; Helen Rodnite Lemay, "Stars and Human Sexuality"; Carey, "Astrology at the English Court"; Richard Lemay, "True Place of Astrology in Medieval Science and Philosophy"; North, "Medieval Concepts of Celestial Influence"; and Tester, *History of Western Astrology*, 98–201.

7. For fine introductions to astrological medicine, see Helen Rodnite Lemay, "Stars and Human Sexuality"; and Siraisi, *Medieval and Early Renaissance Medicine*.

8. See Laistner, "Western Church and Astrology," 74–75; and Wedel, *Mediaeval Attitude Toward Astrology*, 27–28.

9. See, e.g., the versions of the *Secretum secretorum* ed. by Manzalaoui.

10. See Laistner, "Western Church and Astrology," 82; Richard Lemay, "True Place of Astrology," 63–64; and d'Alverny, "Translations and Translators." Tester, *History of Western Astrology*, 152 n. 91, provides a convenient chart of translations.

11. For an excellent discussion of these writers, see Tester, *History of Western Astrology*, 63–88, 157–61.

12. "Veneris enim praesentes radii intervenientes aneroticos, id est noxios planetas temperant, Martem videlicet et Saturnum, qui si ortum geniturae radiis suppulsaverint, vitae rationem intercidere aestimantur." Alberic, *Gods and Allegories*, 230: cf. the less strained astrology on 234–35.

13. For Oresme, see Wood, *Chaucer and the Country of the Stars*, 8–12 (in addition, Wood quite usefully studies the philosophical issues); North, "Concepts of Celestial Influence," 14–16; Tester, *History of Western Astrology*, 197–99; and Le Goff, *Intellectuals*, 133.

14. See Wood, *Chaucer and the Country of the Stars*, 51–57; and Kamborian, "Children of the Planets."

15. The contingency of this idea is perhaps most apparent if we compare a radically different concept: Girard argues that sexual desire may be mimetic and mediated (borrowed from the Other), not inherent, individual, or necessarily arising from the Self: *Deceit, Desire, and the Novel*.

16. Noonan, *Contraception*, thoroughly analyzes the Church's naturalization of sexual mores; Payer, *Bridling of Desire*, offers a careful further study specific to theology of the later Middle Ages.

17. "Venus, inquit [Remigius of Auxerre], Adonem ab apro interfectum fusis lacrimis plangit, quia terrae pulchritudo, quae per Venerem significatur, plangit solem, qui per Adonem designatur, ad australes circulos descendentem, spurcitia et rigore hiemali quasi dentibus apri interfectum; tuncque lacrimas imbrium et fluentorum terra producit." Alberic, *Gods and Allegories*, 238–39.

18. For the theological import of *libido* in the later Middle Ages, see Payer, *Bridling of Desire*, 54.

19. Sonnet 129, ll. 11–12, *Riverside Shakespeare*.

20. "Per Martem et Venerem intellige homines virtuosos, qui tamen aliquando decipiuntur per luxuriam. Quia in hac pugna est victoria rara." Giovanni del Virgilio, *Ovidian Allegories*, 55. Whereas theologians distinguish between *luxuria* ("a vice that is freely acquired") and *libido* ("an integral part of the constitution of fallen human nature" (Payer, *Bridling of Desire*, 54), Virgilio suggestively confuses them.

21. E.g., "Circes igitur convertit inguina Sille in ora canina quia sicut canes sunt voraces in tantum quod numquam sibi saturi videantur imo revertuntur super illud quod vomunt, ita femina libidinosa dicitur vorare cuncta." Giovanni del Virgilio, *Ovidian Allegories*, 98–99. I am indebted to Griffin's perceptive study of images of castration anxiety, *Satires Against Man*, 79–129.

22. For the genesis of semen from blood, see MacFarlane, "Isidore on the Pagan Gods," 29; Jacquart and Thomasset, *Sexuality and Medicine*, 54–55; and Laqueur, *Making Sex*, 35.

23. Noonan, *Contraception*; Brundage, *Law, Sex, and Christian Society*; and Payer, *Bridling of Desire*, 61–131, detail these issues.

24. Gloss to 7.50, trans. Boitani, *Chaucer and Boccaccio*, 204.

25. My conclusion agrees with and is indebted to Noonan, *Contraception*, 258–74; see also Payer, *Bridling of Desire*, 18–41, 61–72; Cadden, *Meanings of Sex Difference*, 219. This naturalization of the procreative rule is still very much apparent, and still a vigorously debated issue in the Catholic Church: see, e.g., Steinfels, "Papal Birth-Control Letter Retains Its Grip."

26. Kelly, *Love and Marriage*, 272–73; see also Payer, *Bridling of Desire*, 128–29.

27. Cadden, *Meanings of Sex Difference*, 147–48.

28. I rely for sexual physiology in this section of my argument on Helen Rodnite Lemay, "Lectures on Female Sexuality"; Bullough, "Medical Views of Women"; Jacquart and Thomasset, *Sexuality and Medicine*; Laqueur, *Making Sex*; and Cadden, *Meanings of Sex Difference*.

29. Kosmer, "Lecherie," 6–8.

30. The planetary Venus is linked to moisture, heat, and blood—or to moisture, cold, and phlegm. There is no single, stable, authoritative correlation of planets, elements, and humors (or, more simply, no single theory of human physiology) for the Middle Ages or Renaissance. (I am indebted to William Ingram, who called this confusion to my attention.) Richard of Wallingforth in *Exafrenon pronosticacionum temporis* gives an intelligible system: Mars, the sun, and sometimes Mercury are linked to hot and dry qualities, thus fire; Jupiter and

Venus to hot and moist, thus air; the moon to cold and moist, thus water; and Saturn, sometimes Mercury, to cold and dry, thus earth (*Richard of Wallingforth*, 1: 200). Ptolemy, *Tetrabiblos*, 1.4, outlines a similar correspondence of qualities and planets. According to Klibansky, Panofsky, and Saxl, *Saturn and Melancholy*, 129 and n. 8, similar correspondences of planets and elements in *Liber Aristotelis de cclv indorum voluminibus* are as follows: Venus and the sanguine temperament (i.e., air); Mars and fire, choler; Saturn and earth, melancholy; the moon and water, phlegm. Venus is also associated with the sanguine temperament (thus with moisture and heat) in the title piece of Marten de Vos's 1581 series on planets: Phlegm is Diana, Choler Minerva, and Melancholy a Nun (*Saturn and Melancholy*, 388 n. 42). Marten van Heemskerck designed illustrations of the four temperaments, correlated with seasons, elements, planets: the moon governs the phlegmatic, Mars rules the choleric, Jupiter and Venus jointly preside over the sanguine, and Saturn over the melancholic (*Saturn and Melancholy*, 397). Venus is credited with enhancing sexual desire by her power over blood (sanguine temperament, moist and hot elements) in the eleventh-century Salernitan *Regimen sanitatis* (Bullough, "Medical Views of Women," 498–99). In all these texts, the correspondence between the planetary Venus and moisture, heat, blood, and the sanguine temperament explains her dominance over sexual desire.

But one of the most influential of Arab astrologers in the Middle Ages, Abu Ma'sar, wrote against the correlation of planets and humors. The scheme he rejects: Mars and the choleric, Jupiter and the sanguine, Saturn and the melancholic, Venus with the moon and the phlegmatic (*Saturn and Melancholy*, 127–28 and n. 5). Since Abu Ma'sar is the astrologer on whom mythographers most rely, they can gain from him this union of Venus with the cold, moist, phlegmatic humor. For western thought, the "decisive event" in correspondences is the same scheme in the translation of the eleventh-century Alcabitius's *Introductorium maius* (*Saturn and Melancholy*, 130–32). Richard of Wallingforth explicitly reconciles traditions, relating Venus in ascension to heat, moisture, and inclinations to lechery—and in her nadir to cold, moisture, and phlegm (*Exafrenon*, 215). But we should not place too much reliance on a single authority. Even the identifications of Saturn and the melancholic, Mars and the choleric are less than absolute: Alberic gives Saturn power over phlegm because the planet is cold (*Gods and Allegories*, 154). Burrow, *Ages of Man*, 5–54, lucidly details further possibilities for variation and confusion among correspondences of planets, ages, and humors; and see also Sears, *Ages of Man*, 25–31.

Variety being the astrological norm, natural mythographic correspondences are remarkably cohesive. When interpreted as *libido*, Venus is physically related to warmth, moisture, and blood, as the physiological causes of sexual desire. Whether or not this set of correspondences agrees with a strictly astrological concept of her influence will depend on which, if any, astrological scheme(s) the mythographer employs. I take the association of Venus with warmth, moisture, blood, and thus sexuality as a steady physical-natural tradition, whether astrological or not. This correspondence of blood, a sanguine temperament, and desire is in any event ubiquitous in the Middle Ages, for which see also Wack, *Lovesickness*, 100.

31. Fulgentius, *Mythologies*, 2.1; Isidore, *Etymologies*, 8.11.76–77 (both discussed above, Chap. 2); Alberic, *Gods and Allegories*, 154–55.

32. Isidore, *Etymologies*, 8.11.78; Digby Mythographer, "An Anonymous *Liber*," 25 (ed. Brown); Walsingham, *Mysteries of the Gods*, 20.

33. Bersuire, *Appearances and Figures*, 22–23; Walsingham, *Mysteries of the Gods*, 32.

34. *Oxford Classical Dictionary*, 2d ed.

35. E.g., Isidore, *Etymologies*, 8.11.78: "Frigidus in Venerem senior," from Virgil, *Georgics*, 3.97 (this source grants the idea a certain currency, though there are certainly innumerable other expressions of the idea in antiquity). Alberic's *Gods and Allegories* offers that "in senectute inquietationis libidinum obliviscuntur. Senectus enim quod frigida et humorosa sit" (240); "senex est a calore iuventutis destitutus et frigiditate laborat (minuitur enim in iis sanguis, unde et tremunt)" (154). Burrow, *Ages of Man*, 135–89, offers a complementary argument and provides further evidence; see also Sears, *Ages of Man*, 47–53; Brown, *Body and Society*, 79–80, 135, 378; and Demaitre, "Care and Extension of Old Age," 9, 16, 18.

36. Robert Herrick, "To the Virgins, to Make Much of Time," in *Ben Jonson and the Cavalier Poets*, ed. Hugh Maclean, 121, ll. 1, 10.

37. "Illud nihilominus ostendere volens poetica vanitas quod Saturnus Grece Cronos dicitur; chronos enim Grece tempus vocatur. Abscisae ergo vires temporis, id est fructus, falce quam maxime atque in humoribus viscerum velut in mari projectae libidinem gignant necesse est. Saturitatis enim abundantia libidinem creat, unde et Terentius ait: 'Sine Cerere et Libero friget Venus.'" Fulgentius, *Mythologies*, 2.1.

38. For the theology involved, see Brown, *Body and Society*, 387–427; and Payer, *Bridling of Desire*, 42–60.

39. Cicero, *De natura deorum*, 2.61 (2: 691–92); Isidore, *Etymologies*, 1.37.9; *Mythographus secundus*, 87; William of Conches, *Philosophia mundi*, quoted by Dronke, *Fabula*, 26, 102; Bernard Silvestris, *Commentary on the "Aeneid,"* ed. Jones and Jones, 10; Alberic, *Gods and Allegories*, 155; Walsingham, *Mysteries of the Gods*, 6. Further citations are given in *De natura deorum*, 2: 691–92 n. "illud Terenti."

40. In *Catullus, Tibullus, and Pervigilium Veneris*, ed. and trans. Mackail, st. 12.

41. Alan of Lille, *Plaint of Nature*, prose 5.128–30, 166–68, prose 6.7–11 (Sheridan trans. 163, 165, 169).

42. Chaucer also presents the idea in the *Physician's Tale*, 58–59, *Parson's Tale*, 836, *Wife of Bath's Prologue*, 464, and *Troilus and Criseyde*, 5.208.

43. See Wack, *Lovesickness*, 41, 45, 81, 104.

44. Epigram 118.5–6 in *Ben Jonson*, ed. Ian Donaldson; cf. Jonson's *Underwood* 47.13: "They have glutted in and lechered out that week."

45. Reported by Highwater, *Myth and Sexuality*, 163–64. Foucault, *History of Sexuality*, 121–22, aptly contextualizes this nineteenth-century concern for diet and children's sexuality.

46. See Foucault, "Battle for Chastity"; Bynum, *Holy Feast and Holy Fast*; Brundage, *Law, Sex, and Christian Society*, 103; and Brown, *Body and Society*, 78, 224–25, 419.

47. Boccaccio, *Genealogy*, 1: 150, and *Teseida*, gloss to 7.50.

48. See Wack, *Lovesickness*, 70, 104–5.

49. Friedman, "L'Iconographie de Venus," 63–67, surveys the visual tradition. For an introduction to the concept of children of the planets, see Seznec, *Survival of the Pagan Gods*, 69–76; Klibansky, Panofsky, and Saxl, *Saturn and Melancholy*, constitutes an admirably thorough study of one planetary tradition, while illuminating all the others. A very useful account of visual traditions may be found in Fuchs's *Die Ikonographie der 7 Planeten*.

50. Cf. Wood, *Chaucer and the Country of the Stars*, 99–101, who argues for a philosophical reading.

51. We might expect Christine to offer more astrology than she does: her father was court astrologer to Charles V, and that she was fairly learned in the science is demonstrated by Willard, "Christine de Pizan: Astrologer's Daughter"; and by Hindman, *Painting and Politics*, 77–89.

52. Meiss, *French Painting in the Time of Jean de Berry*, 1: 26, 2: plate 87. Hindman relates the illustrations of children of the planets to various influences on the *Epistle* and to Christine's purposes, *Painting and Politics*, 77–99, and plate 11; see also Tuve, *Allegorical Imagery*, 296–98.

53. Harley MS 4431, ed. Loukopoulos, 7.

54. See Seznec, *Survival of the Pagan Gods*, 66–68.

55. Cf. Klibansky, Saxl, and Panofsky, *Saturn and Melancholy*, 174–75, on Boccaccio's science; and Wood, *Chaucer and the Country of the Stars*, 40–42, on his philosophy.

56. The physiology here differs radically from that offered in the gloss on *Teseida*, 7.50, which argues that cold humors create sexual incapacities. For the problematic parallels between planets and humors, see note 30 to this chapter.

57. Diversities among ancient and medieval medical theories are beautifully laid out by Cadden, *Meanings of Sex Difference*, 13–104.

58. "Omnis generis fornicationes atque lascivias et coitus multitudinem," 1: 143.

59. Ptolemy, *Tetrabiblos*, 2.8, 3.4, 3.12–14, etc.; cf. the positive and negative influences attributed to Venus according to astrological sign in John de Foxton's *Liber cosmographiae*, reported by Friedman, "Remedies for Fortune," 322.

60. I draw the details in this paragraph from Helen Rodnite Lemay, "Stars and Human Sexuality," supplemented by Tester, *History of Western Astrology*. Ptolemy, *Tetrabiblos*, offers extensive further minutiae.

61. Brilliantly analyzed in the essays collected by Ariès and Duby, *History of Private Life*.

62. Woman in the superior position was a transgression of what canon law defined as an acceptable sexual position, and popular opinion seems at least sometimes to have concurred: see Noonan, *Contraception*, 163, 170, 225–26, 238–39; and Rossiaud, *Medieval Prostitution*, 110. For a cogent discussion of Bonatti, see Tester, *History of Western Astrology*, 189–90.

63. For this physiology, see Cadden, *Meanings of Sex Difference*, 23, 33, 97–98, 170–77, 184–85.

64. Ptolemy, *Tetrabiblos*, 1.6; Helen Rodnite Lemay, "Stars and Human Sexuality," 127–37, documents other astrologers. Friedman, "Remedies for Fortune," mentions a complementary gender distinction in the reckoning of horoscopes: one sign points to different male and female fortunes.

65. "Mulieres, quarum complexio ut plurimum frigida et humida est . . . in calorem et Venerem acrius excitantur." Boccaccio, *Genealogy*, 1: 145. The *Prose Salernitan Questions* similarly unite women, moisture, and (greater) sexual desire (Baldwin, "Five Discourses on Desire," 818); see Cadden, *Meanings of Sex Difference*, 97–98, for other authorities.

66. Wack, *Lovesickness*, 114–15.

67. *Le Chastoiement des Dames*, "Advice to Ladies," in *Comedy of Eros*, trans. Shapiro, 74.

68. Augustine, *City of God*, 6.9, 7.3.

69. Laqueur, *Making Sex*, 35; and Jacquart and Thomasset, *Sexuality and Medicine*, 52–60.

70. Laqueur, *Making Sex*, 35–43.

71. MacKinnon, *Toward a Feminist Theory of the State*, 134, analyzes this logic.

72. Brundage, *Law, Sex, and Christian Society*, 187–88, 235–38, 262–69, 288, 332–36, 361–64.

73. See Kelly, *Love and Marriage*, 163–76, though the entire study focuses on this topic; Brundage, *Law, Sex, and Christian Society*, 238–39, 276–77, 334–36, 354–55, 361–64, 414–15, 440–43, 487–88, 496–502.

74. Lydgate, *Poems*, ed. Norton-Smith, 1278–84. The reading of a clandestine marriage here is original with Kelly, *Love and Marriage*, 291–93.

75. Pearsall, *Lydgate*, 104–15, emphasizes this theme.

76. On the impediment, see Norton-Smith, in Lydgate's *Poems*, 178n, 184n, and his "Lydgate's Changes in the *Temple of Glas*"; and see also Ebin's analysis, *Lydgate*, 29–35. Schirmer's hypothesis—that the poem was commissioned for a wedding—seems unlikely, given the impediment and delay: *Lydgate*, 37–38.

77. Norton-Smith explicates the image similarly: "Lydgate's Metaphors."

78. Wack, "Imagination, Medicine, and Rhetoric."

79. This is one aspect of Brown's argument in *Body and Society*, and has recently been reasserted by Partner, "No Sex, No Gender," 423–33.

80. Brown, "Bodies and Minds," 491–92.

81. For excellent overviews of how this theology develops, see Brown, *Body and Society*, 387–447, and Payer, *Bridling of Desire*, 42–60.

82. For accounts of the major philosophical dilemmas and resolutions, see Wedel, *Mediaeval Attitude Toward Astrology*; Wood, *Chaucer and the Country of the Stars*; and Tester, *History of Western Astrology*. Wetherbee, "Latin Structure and Vernacular Space," brilliantly perceives how irresolution inheres in the dialogic structure of Boethius's work, one of the major influences over this formula.

83. Wedel, *Mediaeval Attitude Toward Astrology*, 155, considers Lydgate a "firm believer in celestial influence." I find the idea of astrological "belief" or "disbelief" a misdirection, especially in Wedel's antithesis of "popular" and "Church" beliefs. I mean not to repeat this antithesis but merely to discriminate between a technical science and its translation into more widely disseminated and popular texts.

84. In Lydgate, *Minor Poems*, 137–38, the version based on MS Trinity R. 3. 21; the version in MS Harley 2255 leads to about the same conclusions. The "Pageant" is briefly discussed by Schirmer, *Lydgate*, 104; and Pearsall, *Lydgate*, 183–84.

85. Burrow, *Ages of Man*, 30–31 argues similarly on the basis of other of Lydgate's works; see also 95–134 for a wider selection of evidence leading to the same conclusion.

86. Though elevating marriage in the *Temple of Glass*, Lydgate also composes antimatrimonial literature, indicating in another way the contingency of his thought: Richard Firth Green, "Three Fifteenth-Century Notes" discusses the antimatrimonial end of a mumming.

87. For ecclesiastical discourses, see Brundage, *Law, Sex, and Christian Society*, 91, 301, 301–3, 317; Brown, *Body and Society*; and Payer, *Bridling of Desire*, 9, 59.

88. Brown, "Bodies and Minds," 481.

89. Brundage illustrates this wittily and memorably: *Law, Sex, and Christian Society*, 162. See also Payer, *Bridling of Desire*, 89–110.

90. This difference emerges vividly in Noonan, *Contraception*; and Wack, *Lovesickness*.

91. Noonan, *Contraception*, 200–230.

92. This is a dominant hierarchical and masculinist model; we should recognize other possibilities, for women creatively exploited it and invented other models: see Bynum, *Holy Feast and Holy Fast* and *Jesus as Mother*; and Newman, *Sister of Wisdom*.

93. Sears, *Ages of Man*, 99–103, concisely exemplifies the possibility of discursive variations, and it emerges throughout Wack's study of *Lovesickness*, Baldwin's analysis of "Five Discourses on Desire," and Cadden's *Meanings of Sex Difference*.

94. Foucault, *History of Sexuality*, 19–21, 33, contends that auricular confession expresses a homogeneous medieval sexuality. I find him both wrong (confession is not the only medieval discourse on sexuality, and medieval sexuality is not homogeneous) and more right than he knew (many discourses lead to the confessional).

95. Bakhtin, *Rabelais and His World*, provocatively illuminates the interdependence of official systems and such laughter.

96. Kelly, *Love and Marriage*, 245–85, outlines a wide range of views from the late medieval debate over whether passion can be sinless in marriage.

97. See Rossiaud, *Medieval Prostitution*, and Otis, *Prostitution in Medieval Society*.

CHAPTER 6

1. My understanding of the Wife's treatment of discourses is informed by Aers, *Chaucer, Langland, and the Creative Imagination*, 147–51; Hanna, "*Compilatio* and the Wife"; Knapp, "Alisoun and the Reappropriation of Tradition"; Mann, *Chaucer*, 70–86; Patterson, *Chaucer and the Subject of History*, 280–321; and Galloway, "Marriage Sermons, Polemical Sermons, and the *Wife of Bath's Prologue*." See also Cox's "Holy Erotica and the Virgin Word," focused on the Wife's problematic appropriation of masculine discourse. Dinshaw, *Chaucer's Sexual Poetics*, 113–31, offers an intriguing analysis of the Wife's relation to misogynistic discourses. While rejecting D. W. Robertson's criticism (28–39), Dinshaw bases much of her discussion on his rigidly hierarchized binary oppositions (carnality/spirituality, text/gloss, fictive veil / exegetical truth), which I think need revision.

2. My argument that the *Prologue* displays the human production of astrology resembles Leicester's position in *Disenchanted Self*, 107–13. For a discussion of the (especially modern) gender politics of men writing women, see Hansen, *Chaucer and the Fictions of Gender*, 26–57.

3. The technical features of her horoscope are studied by Hamlin, "Astrology

and the Wife"; Wood, *Chaucer and the Country of the Stars*, 11, 172–80, with a focus on the "mental blindness" of her astral determinism; Massó, "Tensión astrológica y la Comadre de Bath"; and North, *Chaucer's Universe*, 289–303. These studies essentially confirm the Wife's analysis: Venus gave her an inclination to "lust" and "likerousnesse," and Mars bestowed "sturdy hardynesse" (611–12). Or, as Massó concisely summarizes it: "Su agresividad es amorosa, su amor, marciano" (114). Curry, *Chaucer and the Medieval Sciences*, 91–118, bases his study of the Wife on imperfect evidence; Wood, 177–79, and North, 300–301, develop sound critiques.

4. Leicester, *Disenchanted Self*, 108–9, reads these lines similarly.

5. Matthews persuasively discusses the stereotype of old age and her exemption from it, "Wife of Bath and All Her Sect." Burrow, *Ages of Man*, 158, finds her sexuality unseasonable, but misogynistic rhetoric paints women just so.

6. Brown, "Bodies and Minds," 484 (also for the following quote).

7. Karla Taylor perceptively demonstrates much the same effect in Chaucer's treatment of Dante, *Chaucer Reads*, 33–34, 37. This is apparently not specific to any one discursive tradition or poem.

8. Hanna, "*Compilatio* and the Wife," 8.

9. Ironically, Caie takes the glosses' "historical" authority as evidence of a "correct" reading of the poem: "Significance of the Early Chaucer Manuscript Glosses."

10. Recently, Mann has helpfully explored the "symbiotic relationship" between masculine oppression and feminine "bullying," *Chaucer*, 79 (see 70–86); and Galloway has similarly discussed how the Wife "has both refuted male authority and provided all the more reason for men to watch over her," "Marriage Sermons, Polemical Sermons, and the *Wife of Bath's Prologue*," 18.

11. My reading agrees with David Aers, "Authority, the Knower, and the Known," that the poem demonstrates the contingent human basis of seemingly transcendent authority systems; and with Knight, *Chaucer*, that "the notion of God's natural harmony is employed to mask conflict, the only instance of Nature having real power is an ideological device rather than a divine principle at work" (30). Furthermore, my argument begins in much the way that Leicester's does (though we soon part company), in "The Harmony of Chaucer's *Parlement*." Finally, I agree with and am indebted to a number of critics who have submitted that the *Parliament* presents (whether structurally, thematically, or stylistically) a variety of conflicting views of love: Bronson, "In Appreciation," 201–2; Bethurum Loomis, "Center of the *Parlement*"; McDonald, "An Interpretation"; Frank, "Structure and Meaning"; J. A. W. Bennett, "*Parlement*," 12–13; Muscatine, *Chaucer and the French Tradition*, 115–23; Clemen, *Chaucer's Early Poetry*, 122–69; Payne, *Key of Remembrance*, 139–44; Baker, "*Parliament*,"

363–65; Hutchinson, "Literary Entertainment"; Fyler, *Chaucer and Ovid*, 81–95; Quilligan, "Allegory, Allegoresis, and the Deallegorization of Language," 170, 175–82; Leonard, *Laughter in the Courts of Love*, 48–52; Strohm, "Politics and Poetics," 109–10.

12. For very different recent analyses of natural order and desire, cf. Olsson, "Poetic Invention and Chaucer's *Parlement*"; and Peck, "Love, Politics, and Plot."

13. J. A. W. Bennett, "*Parlement*," 26–31, elucidates this convention of "love's duality."

14. Wimsatt argues this in detail, *Chaucer and His French Contemporaries*, 149–61.

15. See Brundage, *Law, Sex, and Christian Society*, 487–550.

16. Clemen argues similarly about the poem, *Chaucer's Early Poetry*, 124, 166, as does McCall, *Chaucer Among the Gods*, 59–63.

17. I am here, as in my discussion of the *House of Fame* (Chap. 4), greatly indebted to several excellent studies of Chaucer's poetics: Payne, *Key of Remembrance*, emphasizing emotional effect (77–90); Olson, "Deschamp's *Art* and Chaucer's Literary Environment," and "Making and Poetry," enlarging on the ideals of the makers; Middleton, "Chaucer's 'New Men,'" analyzing the diction of "making" and "enditing" and the ideals associated with each; and Wimsatt, *Chaucer and His French Contemporaries*, on theories of "natural music." Cf. also Polzella, "Poet and Lover"; and Kiser, *Truth and Textuality*, 42–55.

18. The invocation to Venus "north-north-west" has occasioned much discussion, for it has been thought astronomically impossible to see Venus in that position from London. Kelly, *Chaucer and the Cult of Saint Valentine*, 117–19, postulates a sensible resolution of the astronomical difficulty, which would remove the interpretive problem. Bronson establishes the standard ironizing reading by offering that the narrator does not see Venus, and that the poem is not inspired by her: "In Appreciation," 204–8. Bronson later wittily posits that the astronomically impossible direction might be better read as geographical, with this passage an interpolation: "*Parlement* Revisited," 249–52. Many critics follow his ironizing lead: e.g., McDonald, "An Interpretation," 446; Clemen, *Chaucer's Early Poetry*, 139; and Selvin, "Shades of Love," 153. Smyser, "View of Chaucer's Astronomy," suggests that the inexactitude proves Chaucer is not yet concerned with astrology. Other critics propose that the narrator misunderstands Venus and petitions the wrong party: e.g., Huppé and Robertson, *Fruyt and Chaf*, 109; Pelen, "Form and Meaning of the Old French Love Vision," 299. For astronomical discussions, cf. also Lazarus, "Venus in the 'north-north-west'"; North, *Chaucer's Universe*, 326–41.

19. Bennett, "*Parlement*," 56–60, argues, much as I do, that the invocation unites the planet and goddess.

20. See Wimsatt, *Chaucer and His French Contemporaries*, 43–76, 190–209.

21. Helpful analyses of Chaucer's treatments of his sources and the meaning of his temple and its precincts are developed by Bronson, "In Appreciation," 209–11; McDonald, "An Interpretation," 448–51; Bennett, "*Parlement*," 62–132; Clemen, *Chaucer's Early Poetry*, 142–46; Boitani, "Chaucer's Temples of Venus," 21–27, and "Style, Iconography, and Narrative," 190–92; Walls, "Patience"; Donaldson, "Venus and the Mother of Romulus"; Wallace, *Chaucer and the Early Writings of Boccaccio*, 143–46.

22. The conventional class features of the description have been established by Emslie, "Codes of Love," 4–5; and by Frank, "Structure and Meaning," 533–36.

23. This reading derives from that of Huppé and Robertson, *Fruyt and Chaf*, 115–16.

24. My interpretation generally agrees with J. A. W. Bennett, "*Parlement*," 94–147 (Venus embodies the confusing ambivalence of love). For other readings, see Lumiansky, "Philosophical Interpretation," 85–87 (Venus symbolizes "worldly pleasures"); McDonald, "An Interpretation," 446–51 (Venus suggests a courtly, barren love); Bethurum Loomis, "Center of the *Parlement*," 39–50 (Venus is a subordinate aspect of Nature); Clemen, *Chaucer's Early Poetry*, 146–48 (Venus and Cupid are neither moralized nor contrasted with natural love); Muscatine, *Chaucer and the French Tradition*, 115–23 (an ironically and ambiguously depicted Venus); Huppé and Robertson, *Fruyt and Chaf*, 117–22 (Venus is a "prostitute goddess," 121, symbolizing the deceptive pleasures of lechery); Selvin, "Shades of Love," 151–53 (Venus is nonprocreative *cupiditas*); Baker, "Parliament," 359, 363–65 (Venus is a symbolic part of natural love); Robertson, "Courtly Love as an Impediment," 6–7 (Venus and Cupid signify "lecherous desire"); Economou, *Goddess Natura*, 127–38 (two Venuses: "celestial," 127, in the invocation, and of "excessive sensuality," 137, in the temple), and "Two Venuses," 31; Hutchinson, "Literary Entertainment," 146–47 (the depiction of Venus calls the "courtly-love ambience" into question); Pelen, "Form and Meaning of the Old French Love Vision," 297–305 (Venus equates with "venereal disorder," 301); McCall, *Chaucer Among the Gods*, 59–63 (the temple and invocations develop the "puzzling character of love," 63); Olsson, "Poetic Invention," 20, 25–26 (Chaucer's Venus—like Boccaccio's—is to be understood *in malum*, as "frustrated love," 25).

25. Emerson Brown offers a very fine analysis of Priapus as an emblem of frustrated desire: "Priapus and the *Parlement*."

26. John Keats, "Ode on a Grecian Urn," l. 26 (*Norton Anthology of Poetry*, 3d ed.).

27. For a recent thorough discussion of the formel's choice, see Hansen, *Chaucer and the Fictions of Gender*, 108–40.

28. I borrow this idea from Riffaterre's stunning analysis of Proust, "Mind's Eye," 38–39. Spearing, *Medieval Poet as Voyeur*, 216, concentrates on the narrator's "scopophilia" in this "red-light district," which seems to me a caricature of the passage, though I would agree that one finds here a "fetishization of what is concealed and forbidden."

29. See Goffin, "Heaven and Earth"; Lumiansky, "Philosophical Interpretation"; Emslie, "Codes of Love," who finds both "duality" and "overlapping" between Venus and Nature, 4–5; McDonald, "An Interpretation," 444–57; Huppé and Robertson, *Fruyt and Chaf*, 122; Selvin, "Shades of Love," 146–60; Economou, *Goddess Natura*, 125–50; Kelley, "Antithesis in the *Parlement*"; Pelen, "Form and Meaning of the Old French Love Vision," 297–305; Howard, *Chaucer*, 310–16.

30. Others have likewise proposed that Chaucer does not develop mutually exclusive models of love. I think J. A. W. Bennett, "*Parlement*," 98–147, quite persuasively establishes the essential similarities between Venus and Nature, and the centrality of ambiguity to the meaning of the poem. See also Clemen, *Chaucer's Early Poetry*, 146–51; Payne, *Key of Remembrance*, 139–44; Baker, "*Parliament*," 364–65; Leicester, "Harmony of Chaucer's *Parlement*," 26–29; Fyler, *Chaucer and Ovid*, 88–92; Heffernan, "Wells and Streams in Three Chaucerian Gardens," 339–45; Aers, "Authority, the Knower, and the Known," 8–11.

31. In general agreement with Emerson Brown, "Priapus and the *Parlement*," 266–74, who points out the difficulty of reconciling the birds' mating and a conservative ecclesiastical standard.

32. Respectively, Rubin, "Traffic in Women," 204; Stimpson, "Ad/d Feminam," 177.

CHAPTER 7

1. Lewis, *Allegory of Love*, 198–200, originates a quite different sense of the affinity here, the idea that social and ecclesiastical norms are identical. Compare also Minnis's assertion that sins are identical in amorous (or pagan) and Christian contexts, "Moral Gower," 58–61; and Yeager's argument that the exemplum form emphasizes the homiletic purposes of the amatory narratives, "Gower and the Exemplum Form."

2. Burrow deftly traces the conventions: "Portrayal of Amans," 5–11.

3. Critics have regularly interpreted Gower's Venus according to a model of two loves: see Economou, "Genius in Alan de Lille, Jean de Meun, and Gower," 114–16; Gallacher, *Love, the Word, and Mercury*, 138–43, 147–48; Hatton, "Role of Venus and Genius"; Yeager, *Gower's Poetic*, 180–87, 260. The poem's conclusion perhaps invites this reading in that the recommendation of *caritas* and transcendence of the flesh clearly opposes Amans's earlier love, yet

even so I find the model of two loves imposing a reductive clarity on Gower's determinedly ambiguous poetry, which develops a number of not easily synthesized loves.

4. Gallacher, *Love, the Word, and Mercury*, 44–76; Gallacher argues that the religion of love potentially confuses "amorous persuasion" with prayer, and that Gower condemns this confusion. This is a graver reading than mine and discovers greater moral clarity.

5. Yeager's very perceptive discussion of Gower's "radical revision of amorous discourse" informs my analysis, *Gower's Poetic*, 66–113 (quote on 109). Compare Calin, who contends that since French poets also undermine amatory conventions, Gower should be regarded as following rather than critiquing those conventions: "Continuity in the Tradition of French *Fin'Amor*." His point about French poetry is well taken, though I find a significant distinction between Gower's strategies and those of the French poets Calin cites.

6. For excellent studies of Genius, see Nitzsche, *Genius in Antiquity and the Middle Ages*, 125–30; Denise Baker, "Priesthood of Genius"; and Simpson, "Genius's 'Enformacioun.'"

7. The most extensive published study of Gower and mythography takes for granted that he relies on allegorical readings of myth, and does not mention other hermeneutics: Gallacher, *Love, the Word, and Mercury*.

8. Wack, *Lovesickness*, explores the relevant medical tradition.

9. Peck, "Problematics of Irony," argues similarly about Genius's shifting positions.

10. Simpson, "Genius's 'Enformacioun,'" 163–79.

11. Hatton, "Role of Venus and Genius," and "Gower's Use of Ovid"; Hiscoe, "Ovidian Comic Strategy," and "Heavenly Sign and Comic Design." Peck, "Problematics of Irony," offers a thoughtful and compelling analysis of the weaknesses in this line of argument. Both Hatton and Hiscoe base their conclusions on the assumption that mythographers are especially dour in their treatment of sexual mores, though we have found that mythographers of the later fourteenth century tend to demonstrate a range of liberal views attuned to social mores (we might compare Christine de Pizan, Bersuire, Ridewall, and Boccaccio). Gower's debts to several mythographies (among them Bersuire's text and the *Ovide moralisé*) would further argue against Hatton's and Hiscoe's presuppositions regarding single correct readings of myth. For Gower's mythographic sources, see Dilts, "Gower and the *De genealogia deorum*"; and Mainzer, "Gower's Use of the 'Mediaeval Ovid.'"

12. For excellent appreciations of Gower's narrative art, see Lewis, *Allegory of Love*, 198–222; and Pearsall, "Gower's Narrative Art." My understanding of the relations of tales to morals is much indebted to Runacres, "Art and Ethics,"

126–30; and to Wetherbee, "Genius and Interpretation." For other useful studies of this relationship, see Burrow's comments, *Ricardian Poetry*, 83–85; Farnham, "Art of High Prosaic Seriousness"; and Bunt, "Exemplum and Tale."

13. Runacres, "Art and Ethics," 125.

14. Pearsall, "Gower's Latin," 24; Wetherbee, "Genius and Interpretation," and "Latin Structure and Vernacular Space." My analysis is also similar to those of Minnis, *Medieval Theory of Authorship*, 177–90, on the limited authority claimed by the glosses; Simpson, "Ironic Incongruence," on conflicts and irresolutions among literary and philosophical conventions; and Echard and Fanger, *Latin Verses*, with a preface by Rigg, xlvii–liv, on the interplay between Latin and English. For more positive recent valuations of the Latin apparatus than I offer, see Yeager, "'Our englisshe' and Everyone's Latin," and *Gower's Poetic*, 37; and Minnis, "Moral Gower and Medieval Literary Theory," and "De Vulgari Auctoritate," 51–63.

15. Farnham, "Statement and Search," arrives at similar conclusions.

16. Copeland perceptively investigates this fictional disguise of exegesis, *Rhetoric, Hermeneutics, and Translation*, 202–20.

17. See Yeager's thoughtful analysis of these strategies, *Gower's Poetic*, 172–79, 207–16.

18. E.g., 5.836, 1097, 1131–32, 1270–76. Peck, *Kingship and Common Profit*, 127–37, comments aptly on the relation between fantasy and reason elsewhere in the text.

19. For these commentators, see Minnis, *Chaucer and Pagan Antiquity*, 31–60.

20. The problem of how Venus's priest can ultimately reject her, especially in this euhemeristic account, has been laid to rest by Denise Baker, "Priesthood of Genius"; and Wetherbee, "Genius and Interpretation."

21. Gallacher, *Love, the Word, and Mercury*, 26–43, usefully details Gower's parodic allusions to the Annunciation in these tales.

22. "Vir mediante deo sapiens dominabitur astris" (after 7.632). Gower's "astrological determinism" has provoked mild controversy: for other analyses, see Tatlock, *Scene of the "Franklin's Tale"*; Wedel, *Mediaeval Attitude Toward Astrology*, 132–42; Fox, *Mediaeval Sciences*, 50–94 (my argument resembles his 92–94); Wood, *Chaucer and the Country of the Stars*, 38–39.

23. Yeager, *Gower's Poetic*, 277–78, offers a useful context for this problem: the principle of encyclopedic plenitude implies a value for knowledge for its own sake.

24. Respectively, *Mediaeval Sciences in the Works of Gower*, 83, and "View of Chaucer's Astronomy," 361. Wedel, *Mediaeval Attitude Toward Astrology*, 132–42, offers a more sympathetic analysis. Gower's sources for astrology are primarily

"unscientific" texts: see Hamilton, "Some Sources"; for an excellent recent evaluation of how Gower manipulates his sources, see Yeager, *Gower's Poetic*, 207–16.

25. Kelly, *Love and Marriage*, 274–80, presents further evidence of Gower's acceptance of passion and pleasure in marital sexuality, and demonstrates the incidental quality of procreation in the text. By contrast, J. A. W. Bennett, "Gower's 'Honeste Love,'" sets the currently dominant emphasis of Gower criticism, which insists on the procreative end of "honeste" love. The poem does not seem to me conducive to such a simple rule: for every evidence of one ethical code, we may marshal other evidence that refutes it. Gower's poem, like Ptolemy's *Tetrabiblos* and Alberic's *Gods and Allegories*, can support nearly any argument and counterargument; such encyclopedic texts are, I think, best not reduced to selectively simplistic coherence.

26. Several critics establish Venus's and nature's moral ambiguities: Baker, "Priesthood of Genius," 290–91; Cherniss, "Allegorical Figures." My understanding of natural law is also indebted to the analyses of Fisher, *Gower*, 160–70; White, "Nature and the Good"; Olsson, "Natural Law"; and Simpson, "Genius's 'Enformacioun.'" Cf. Collins, "Love, Nature and Law," for conclusions very different from those I reach; I find her ignoring the effects of original sin in conceptions of nature and law.

27. See Wedel, *Mediaeval Attitude Toward Astrology*, 67–69; and Tester, *History of Western Astrology*, 181.

28. E.g., 1.669–781, with love's blindness the point of the Mundus and Paulina tale; and 1.2620–28, with love's ungovernable character accounting for Albinus's end.

29. "In carne preter carnem vivere pocius vita angelica quam humana est."

30. My reading is supported by the detailed analyses of Simpson, "Ironic Incongruence," 628–30; and of White, "Division and Failure." The role of reason is of course debatable, and others emphasize its primacy as ideal: cf. Coffman, "Gower in His Most Significant Role"; Fisher, *Gower*, 156–203; Peck, *Kingship and Common Profit*; Minnis, "Moral Gower," 71–78; Chandler, "Memory and Unity"; Simpson, "Genius's 'Enformacioun.'"

31. Olsson, "Natural Law," 186, explicates this passage similarly, although he focuses on demonstrating the priority of reason in the conclusion of the poem. I would find this a more persuasive argument if the analysis dealt more closely with the actual cure of Amans, which does not depend on his becoming one of a few holy, wise men through moral conversion alone but is facilitated by the effects of age.

32. Wetherbee, "Latin Structure and Vernacular Space," 20–22, comments perceptively on the interpretive problems this passage initiates by not unfolding the moral implications of the divided human state. He concludes by em-

phasizing "the irresolution of the Prologue as a whole, its seeming failure to provide a single coherent view of the place of man in the natural economy" (22). The Prologue initiates ambiguities rather than a solution.

33. White, "Nature and Good," 2; see also Burrow, *Ricardian Poetry*, 104–11, on a common "image of man" in Ricardian poetry, focused on the "unsuspected weakness and perversity of human nature. *Nemo sine crimine vivit*" (111).

34. I am indebted to Minnis's sensitive reading of the poem's conclusion in "De Vulgari Auctoritate," 60–63.

35. Several scholars similarly contextualize the conclusion of the poem in terms of natural-scientific traditions: Burrow, *Ages of Man*, 160–61, 186–88, and "Portrayal of Amans," 14–20; Nitecki, "Figures of Old Age." Schueler, "Age of the Lover," proposes that old age is a constant feature of the portrayal, but this idea has been persuasively refuted by Burrow, "Portrayal of Amans," 12–15. Cf. also Cowling, "Gower's Ironic Self-Portrait," 70, who reads the conclusion as sacred parody, which I find an unconvincing response to the tone.

36. Shakespeare, Sonnet 73, l. 14, *Riverside Shakespeare*.

37. White, "Naturalness of Amans' Love."

38. So Jauss succinctly describes the effect of revising poetic forms, *Toward an Aesthetic of Reception*, 41.

CHAPTER 8

1. Ferris, "Venus and the Virgin," suggests that the Virgin provides the model for this Venus, but the reverse is more likely: Venus often served as a prototype for the Virgin, the Christian *alma mater*.

2. Dronke, "L'amor che move il sole," 422.

3. Lenaghan, "Clerk of Venus," also comments on this self-fashioning.

4. Ong, *Orality and Literacy*, 113.

5. Middleton, "Chaucer's 'New Men,'" 28.

6. I take this idea about influence from Karla Taylor's *Chaucer Reads*, a very persuasive analysis of Dante's influence which should provide a model for such investigations.

7. Quoted and trans. by Wimsatt, *Chaucer and His French Contemporaries*, 249–50.

8. See also Yeager, *Gower's Poetic*, 66–113.

9. "*Livre d'Art de grant decevance, / . . . et de faulce apparence*," 377–78; "par fraude et par cautelle," 396; trans. Fenster and Erler.

10. "A foible lieu fault il dont grant assault? / Comment peut on de pres faire grant sault?" 397–98.

11. There has been some discussion about the purposes and effects of Hoccleve's translation: see Jerome Mitchell, *Hoccleve*, 21–22; Fleming, "Hoccleve's 'Letter'"; Bornstein, "Anti–Feminism"; William Quinn, "Hoccleve's *Epistle*."
12. Ong, *Orality and Literacy*, 113.
13. Bloom, *Anxiety of Influence*, 30.

Bibliography

The following abbreviations are used in the Works Cited.

ChauR	*Chaucer Review*
EETS	Early English Text Society
EIC	*Essays in Criticism*
ELN	*English Language Notes*
ES	*English Studies*
JEGP	*Journal of English and Germanic Philology*
JMRS	*Journal of Medieval and Renaissance Studies*
MLR	*Modern Language Review*
MP	*Modern Philology*
MS	*Mediaeval Studies*
NLH	*New Literary History*
PL	*Patrologia Latina*, ed. J.-P. Migne (Paris, 1844–64)
PLL	*Papers on Language and Literature*
PMLA	*Publications of the Modern Language Association of America*
PQ	*Philological Quarterly*
RES	*Review of English Studies*
SAC	*Studies in the Age of Chaucer*
SP	*Studies in Philology*
TSLL	*Texas Studies in Literature and Language*

PRIMARY TEXTS

Alan of Lille. *Anticlaudianus*. Ed. R. Bossuat. Paris: Librairie Philosophique, 1955.
———. "Alan of Lille, 'De Planctu naturae.'" Ed. Nikolaus M. Häring. *Studi medievali* 3.19 (1978): 797–879.
———. *The Plaint of Nature*. Trans. James J. Sheridan. Toronto: Pontifical Institute of Mediaeval Studies, 1980.

Alberic. [*On the Gentile Gods and Their Allegories*] *De diis gentium et illorum allegoriis*. In G. H. Bode, ed., *Scriptores rerum mythicarum*.
The Assembly of Gods, or the Accord of Reason and Sensuality in the Fear of Death. Ed. Oscar Lovell Triggs. EETS es 69. London: Kegan Paul, 1896.
Augustine. *City of God* [*De civitate dei*]. Trans. Henry Bettenson. 1972; rpt. New York: Penguin, 1984.
———. *De doctrina Christiana*. PL 34.
———. *On Christian Doctrine*. Trans. D. W. Robertson, Jr. New York: Bobbs-Merrill, 1958.
Bernard Silvestris. *The Commentary on the First Six Books of the "Aeneid" of Vergil Commonly Attributed to Bernardus Silvestris*. Ed. Julian Ward Jones and Elizabeth Frances Jones. Lincoln: University of Nebraska Press, 1977.
———. *Commentary on the First Six Books of Virgil's "Aeneid."* Trans. Earl G. Schreiber and Thomas E. Maresca. Lincoln: University of Nebraska Press, 1979.
Bersuire, Pierre. *Reductorium morale, Liber XV, cap. i, "De formis figurisque deorum."* Ed. J. Engels. Utrecht: Instituut voor Laat Latijn, 1960.
———. *Reductorium morale, Liber XV, cap. ii-xv, "Ovidius moralizatus."* Ed. J. Engels. Utrecht: Instituut voor Laat Latijn, 1962.
———. [*On the Gods' Appearances and Figures*] *Reductorium morale, Liber XV, cap. i, "De formis figurisque deorum."* Ed. J. Engels. Utrecht: Instituut voor Laat Latijn, 1966.
———. "Petrus Berchorius, *Reductorium morale, Liber XV: "Ovidius moralizatus,"* cap. ii. Ed. Maria S. Van der Bijl. *Vivarium* 9 (1971): 25–48.
———. *The Ovidius Moralizatus of Petrus Berchorius: An Introduction and Translation*. Trans. William D. Reynolds. Ph.D. diss., University of Illinois, 1971.
Boccaccio, Giovanni. *Boccaccio on Poetry*. Trans. Charles G. Osgood. Princeton, N.J.: Princeton University Press, 1930.
———. [*Genealogy of the Gentile Gods*] *Genealogie deorum gentilium libri*. Ed. Vincenzo Romano. Bari: G. Laterza, 1951. 2 vols.
———. *Teseida*. In *Tutte le opere*, vol. 2. Ed. Alberto Limentani. Maggio: Mondadori, 1964.
Bode, Georgius Henricus, ed. *Scriptores rerum mythicarum Latini tres Romae nuper reperti*. 1834; rpt. Hildesheim: Georg Olms, 1968.
Brown, V., ed. [*Book on the Nature of the Gods*] "An Edition of an Anonymous Twelfth-Century *Liber de natura deorum*." *Mediaeval Studies* 34 (1972): 1–70.
Carroll, Lewis. *Alice in Wonderland*. Ed. Donald J. Gray. New York: Norton, 1971.
Chaucer, Geoffrey. *The Riverside Chaucer*. Ed. Larry D. Benson. 3d ed. Boston: Houghton Mifflin, 1987.

Christine de Pizan. [*Epistle of the God of Love*] *Epistre au dieu d'Amours*. In Thelma S. Fenster and Mary Carpenter Erler, eds. and trans., *Poems of Cupid, God of Love*. Leiden: E. J. Brill, 1990.

———. [*Epistle of Othea*] *L'Epistre Othéa*. Ed. Halina Didycky Loukopoulos. "Classical Mythology in the Work of Christine de Pisan, With an Edition of *L'Epistre Othéa* from the Manuscript Harley 4431." Ph.D. diss., Wayne State University, 1977.

———. *The Epistle of Othea*. Trans. Stephen Scrope. Ed. Curt F. Bühler. EETS 264. London: Oxford University Press, 1970.

———. *Letter of Othea to Hector*. Trans. Jane Chance. Newburyport, Mass.: Focus Information Group, 1990.

Cicero. [*On the Nature of the Gods*] *De natura deorum*. Ed. Arthur Stanley Pease. Cambridge, Mass.: Harvard University Press, 1955 (vol. 1), 1958 (vol. 2).

De deorum imaginibus libellus. [*Notebook on the Images of the Gods*] Ed. Hans Liebeschütz. In Ridewall, *Fulgentius metaforalis*. Leipzig: B. G. Teubner, 1926. Pp. 117–28, plates 16–32.

Digby Mythographer, *see* Brown, V., ed., "Anonymous Twelfth-Century *Liber*."

Eriugena, John Scotus. *Iohannis Scotti Annotationes in Marcianum*. Ed. Cora E. Lutz. Cambridge, Eng.: Mediaeval Academy, 1939.

First Vatican Mythographer, *see* Bode, G. H., ed., *Scriptores rerum mythicarum*.

Fulgentius, Fabius Planciades. [*Mythologies*] *Mitologiae*. In *Fabii Planciadis Fulgentii V. C. opera* . . . Ed. Rudolph Helm. Bibliotheca Teubneriana. Leipzig 1898; rpt. Stuttgart, 1970.

———. *Fulgentius the Mythographer*. Trans. Leslie George Whitbread. Columbus: Ohio State University Press, 1971.

Giovanni del Virgilio. [*Ovidian Allegories*] *Allegorie Ovidiane*. In "Giovanni del Virgilio, espositore delle «Metamorfosi»." Ed. Fausto Ghisalberti. *Il Giornale Dantesco* 34 (1933): 1–110.

Gower, John. *The English Works of John Gower*. Ed. G. C. Macaulay. EETS es 81, 82. London: Oxford University Press, 1900.

———. *The Latin Verses in the "Confessio Amantis": An Annotated Translation*. Trans. Siân Echard and Claire Fanger. With a preface by A. G. Rigg. East Lansing: Colleagues Press, 1991.

Guibert of Nogent. *Self and Society in Medieval France*. Trans. C. C. Swinton Bland (Harper, 1970). Ed. and rev. John F. Benton. Toronto: University of Toronto Press, 1984.

Guillaume de Lorris and Jean de Meun. *Romance of the Rose*. Trans. Charles Dahlberg. Hanover, N.H.: University Press of New England, 1971.

Henryson, Robert. *Testament of Cresseid*. In Denton Fox, ed., *Robert Henryson: The Poems*. Oxford: Clarendon, 1987.

Hoccleve, Thomas. *The Letter of Cupid*. In Thelma Fenster and Mary Carpenter Erler, eds. and trans., *Poems of Cupid, God of Love*. Leiden: E. J. Brill, 1990.
Hyginus. *The Myths of Hyginus*. Trans. and ed. Mary Grant. Lawrence: University of Kansas Press, 1960.
Isidore of Seville. [*Etymologies*] *Isidori Hispalensis episcopi Etymologiarum sive originum*. Ed. W. M. Lindsay. Vol. 1. Oxford: Clarendon, 1987.
———. "Isidore of Seville: The Medical Writings." Trans. William D. Sharpe. Transactions of the American Philosophical Society, n.s. 54.2. Philadelphia, 1964.
———. "Isidore of Seville on the Pagan Gods." Ed. Katherine Nell MacFarlane. Transactions of the American Philosophical Society, 70.3 (1980): 1–40.
James I. *James I of Scotland: "The Kingis Quair."* Ed. John Norton-Smith. Oxford: Clarendon, 1971.
Jean de Meun, *see* Guillaume de Lorris.
Lactantius Placidus. *Lactantii Placidi qui dicitur Commentarios in Statii Thebaida et Commentarium in Achilleida*. Ed. Richard Jahnke. Leipzig: Teubner, 1898.
Lucretius Carus, Titus. [*On the Nature of Things*] *De rerum natura*. Ed. and trans. Cyril Bailey. 3 vols. Oxford: Clarendon, 1947.
Lydgate, John. *John Lydgate: Poems*. Ed. John Norton-Smith. Oxford: Clarendon, 1966.
———. *The Minor Poems of John Lydgate*. Ed. Henry Noble MacCracken. EETS os 192. 1934; rpt. London: Oxford University Press, 1961.
———. *Reson and Sensuallyte*. Ed. Ernst Sieper. 2 vols. EETS es 84, 89. London: Oxford University Press, 1901, 1903.
———. *Troybook*. Ed. Henry Bergen. EETS es 97. London: Kegan Paul, 1906.
Martianus Capella. [*On the Marriage of Mercury and Philology*] *De nuptiis Philologiae et Mercurii*. Ed. Adolfus Dick. 2 vols. Stuttgart: B. G. Teubner, 1969.
———. *Martianus Capella and the Seven Liberal Arts*. Trans. William Harris Stahl and Richard Johnson, with E. L. Burge. 2 vols. New York: Columbia University Press, 1971.
Mythographus secundus, *see* Bode, G. H., ed., *Scriptores rerum mythicarum*.
Norton-Smith, John, ed. *Bodleian Library, MS Fairfax 16*. London: Scolar Press, 1979.
Ovid. [*Loves, Art of Loving*] *Amores, Medicamina faciei femineae, Ars amatoria, Remedia amoris*. Ed. E. J. Kenney. Oxford: Clarendon, 1961.
———. *Fasti*. 2d ed. revised by G. P. Goold. Trans. Sir James George Frazer. Loeb, 1951.
Pervigilium Veneris [*The Eve of St. Venus*]. In *Catullus, Tibullus, and Pervigilium Veneris*. Ed. and trans. J. W. Mackail. Loeb, 1913.
Ptolemy. *Tetrabiblos*. Ed. and trans. F. E. Robbins. Loeb, 1940.
Rabanus Maurus. *De universo*. PL 111.

Remigius of Auxerre. *Remigii Autissiodorensis Commentum in Martianum Capellam*. Ed. Cora E. Lutz. Leiden: E. J. Brill, 1962.
Richard of Wallingforth. *Richard of Wallingforth: An Edition of His Writings with Introductions, English Translations and Commentary*. Ed. J. D. North. 3 vols. Oxford: Clarendon, 1976.
Ridewall, John. [*Fulgentius Metaphored*] *Fulgentius metaforalis*. Ed. Hans Liebeschütz. Leipzig: Teubner, 1926.
Second Vatican Mythographer, *see* Bode, G. H., ed., *Scriptores rerum mythicarum*.
Secretum secretorum: Nine English Versions. Ed. M. A. Manzalaoui. EETS 276. London: Oxford University Press, 1977.
Shakespeare, William. *The Riverside Shakespeare*. Boston: Houghton Mifflin, 1974.
Shapiro, Norman R., trans. *The Comedy of Eros: Medieval French Guides to the Art of Love*. Urbana: University of Illinois Press, 1971.
Stehling, Thomas, ed. and trans. *Medieval Latin Poems of Male Love and Friendship*. New York: Garland, 1984.
Thomas of Erfurt. *Grammatica Speculativa of Thomas of Erfurt. An Edition with Translation and Commentary*. Trans. and ed. G. L. Bursill-Hall. London: Longman, 1972.
Virgil. *Aeneid*. Ed. R. D. Williams. 2 vols. London: St. Martin's Press, 1973.
Walsingham, Thomas. [*On the Mysteries of the Gods*] *De archana deorum*. Ed. Robert A. van Kluyve. Durham, N.C.: Duke University Press, 1968.

SECONDARY TEXTS

Aers, David. *Chaucer, Langland, and the Creative Imagination*. London: Routledge and Kegan Paul, 1980.
———. *Community, Gender, and Individual Identity: English Writing 1360–1430*. New York: Routledge, 1988.
———. "The *Parliament of Fowls*: Authority, the Knower, and the Known." *ChauR* 16 (1981–82): 1–17.
Alford, John A. "The Grammatical Metaphor: A Survey of Its Use in the Middle Ages." *Speculum* 57 (1982): 728–60.
Allen, Judson Boyce. "An Anonymous Twelfth-Century 'De Natura Deorum' in the Bodleian Library." *Traditio* 26 (1970): 352–64.
———. "Commentary as Criticism: The Text, Influence, and Literary Theory of the Fulgentius Metaphored of John Ridewall." In *Acta Conventus Neo-Latini Amstelodamensis*. Proceedings of the 2d International Congress of Neo-Latin Studies. Ed. P. Tuynman, G. C. Kuiper, and E. Kessler. Munich: Wilhelm Fink, 1979. Pp. 25–47.
———. "Eleven Unpublished Commentaries on Ovid's *Metamorphoses* and

Two Other Texts of Mythographic Interest: Some Comments on a Bibliography." In Chance, ed., *The Mythographic Art.* Pp. 281–89.

———. *The Friar as Critic: Literary Attitudes in the Later Middle Ages.* Nashville: Vanderbilt University Press, 1971.

Altieri, Charles. "The Hermeneutics of Literary Indeterminacy: A Dissent from the New Orthodoxy." *New Literary History* 10 (1978): 71–99.

Alton, E. H. "The Mediaeval Commentators on Ovid's *Fasti.*" *Hermathena* 44 (1926): 119–51.

Amsler, Mark. *Etymology and Grammatical Discourse in Late Antiquity and the Early Middle Ages.* Amsterdam: John Benjamins, 1989.

Anderson, David. *Before the "Knight's Tale": Imitation of Classical Epic in Boccaccio's "Teseida."* Philadelphia: University of Pennsylvania Press, 1988.

Ariès, Philippe, and Georges Duby, eds. *A History of Private Life: II. Revelations of the Medieval World.* Trans. Arthur Goldhammer. Cambridge, Mass.: Belknap Press of Harvard University Press, 1988.

Baker, Denise N. "The Priesthood of Genius: A Study of the Medieval Tradition." *Speculum* 51 (1976): 277–91.

Baker, Donald C. "The *Parliament of Fowls.*" In Beryl Rowland, ed., *Companion to Chaucer Studies.* London: Oxford University Press, 1968. Pp. 355–69.

Bakhtin, Mikhail. *The Dialogic Imagination: Four Essays.* Ed. Michael Holquist. Trans. Caryl Emerson and Holquist. Austin: University of Texas Press, 1981.

———. *Rabelais and His World.* Trans. Helene Iswolsky. Bloomington: Indiana University Press, 1984.

Baldwin, John W. "Five Discourses on Desire: Sexuality and Gender in Northern France around 1200." *Speculum* 66 (1991): 797–819.

Barkan, Leonard. *The Gods Made Flesh: Metamorphosis and the Pursuit of Paganism.* New Haven: Yale University Press, 1986.

Barnes, J. A. "Genetrix:Genitor :: Nature:Culture." In Jack Goody, ed., *The Character of Kinship.* Cambridge, Eng.: Cambridge University Press, 1973. Pp. 61–73.

Barthes, Roland. *Mythologies.* Trans. Annette Lavers. New York: Hill and Wang, 1972.

Bennett, J. A. W. *Chaucer's Book of Fame, An Exposition of "The House of Fame."* Oxford: Clarendon, 1968.

———. "Gower's 'Honeste Love.'" In John Lawlor, ed., *Patterns of Love and Courtesy: Essays in Memory of C. S. Lewis* (1966). Rpt. in Peter Nicholson, ed., *Gower's "Confessio Amantis": A Critical Anthology.* Cambridge, Eng.: D. S. Brewer, 1991. Pp. 49–61.

———. *The "Parlement of Foules": An Interpretation.* Oxford: Clarendon, 1957.

Bennett, Judith M. "Medievalism and Feminism." *Speculum* 68 (1993): 309–31.

Bennett, Michael J. "The Court of Richard II and the Promotion of Literature." In Hanawalt, ed., *Chaucer's England*. Pp. 3–20.
Benson, Larry D. "Courtly Love and Chivalry in the Later Middle Ages." In Robert F. Yeager, ed., *Fifteenth-Century Studies: Recent Essays*. Hamden, Conn.: Archon, 1984. Pp. 237–57.
Blanch, Robert J., and Julian N. Wasserman. "White and Red in the *Knight's Tale*: Chaucer's Manipulation of a Convention." In Wasserman and Blanch, eds., *Chaucer in the Eighties*. Syracuse, N.Y.: Syracuse University Press, 1986. Pp. 175–91.
Bloch, R. Howard. *Etymologies and Genealogies: A Literary Anthropology of the French Middle Ages*. Chicago: University of Chicago Press, 1983.
———. *Medieval Misogyny and the Invention of Western Romantic Love*. Chicago: University of Chicago Press, 1991.
Bloom, Harold. *The Anxiety of Influence: A Theory of Poetry*. New York: Oxford University Press, 1973.
Boase, Roger. *The Origin and Meaning of Courtly Love: A Critical Study of European Scholarship*. Manchester University Press; Totowa, N.J.: Rowman and Littlefield, 1977.
Boitani, Piero. *Chaucer and Boccaccio*. Medium Aevum monographs, ns 8. Oxford: Society for the Study of Mediaeval Languages and Literature, 1976.
———. "Chaucer's Temples of Venus." *Studi Inglesi* 2 (1975): 9–31.
———. "Style, Iconography, and Narrative: The Lesson of the *Teseida*." In Boitani, ed., *Chaucer and the Italian Trecento*. Cambridge, Eng.: Cambridge University Press, 1983. Pp. 185–99.
Bordo, Susan. "Feminism, Postmodernism, and Gender-Scepticism." In L. J. Nicholson, ed., *Feminism/Postmodernism*. New York: Routledge, 1990. Pp. 133–56.
Bornstein, Diane. "Anti-Feminism in Thomas Hoccleve's Translation of Christine de Pizan's *Epistre au dieu d'Amours*." *ELN* 19 (1981): 7–14.
———, ed. *Ideals for Women in the Works of Christine de Pizan*. n.p.: Michigan Consortium for Medieval and Early Modern Studies, 1981.
Boswell, John. *Christianity, Social Tolerance, and Homosexuality: Gay People in Western Europe from the Beginning of the Christian Era to the Fourteenth Century*. Chicago: University of Chicago Press, 1980.
Braswell, Mary Flowers. "Architectural Portraiture in Chaucer's House of Fame." *JMRS* 11 (1981): 101–12.
Bronson, Bertrand H. "In Appreciation of Chaucer's *Parlement of Foules*." *University of California Publications in English* 3 (1935): 193–224.
———. "The *Parlement of Foules* Revisited." *ELH* 15 (1948): 247–60.
Brooks, Douglas, and Alastair Fowler. "The Meaning of Chaucer's *Knight's Tale*." *Medium Aevum* 39 (1970): 123–46.

Brown, Emerson, Jr. "Priapus and the *Parlement of Foulys*." *SP* 72 (1975): 258–74.
Brown, Peter. *Augustine of Hippo*. Berkeley: University of California Press, 1967.
———. "Bodies and Minds: Sexuality and Renunciation in Early Christianity." In *Before Sexuality: The Construction of Erotic Experience in the Ancient Greek World*. Princeton, N.J.: Princeton University Press, 1990. Pp. 479–93.
———. *The Body and Society: Men, Women, and Sexual Renunciation in Early Christianity*. New York: Columbia University Press, 1988.
Brownlee, Kevin. "Literary Genealogy and the Problem of the Father: Christine de Pizan and Dante." *JMRS* 23 (1993): 365–87.
Brundage, James A. *Law, Sex, and Christian Society in Medieval Europe*. Chicago: University of Chicago Press, 1987.
Bullough, Vern L. "Medieval Medical and Scientific Views of Women." *Viator* 4 (1973): 485–501.
Bunt, G. H. V. "Exemplum and Tale in John Gower's *Confessio Amantis*." In W. J. Aerts and M. Gosman, eds., *Exemplum et Similitudo: Alexander the Great and Other Heroes as Points of Reference in Medieval Literature*. Mediaevalia Groningana Fasc. 8. Groningen: Egbert Forsten, 1988. Pp. 145–57.
Buono, Elisa. "From Goddess to Virgin: Transformations in the Eastern Empire." In *Survival of the Gods: Classical Mythology in Medieval Art*. Exhibition Catalogue, Brown University, Feb. 28–Mar. 29, 1987. Brown University: Dept. of Art, 1987. Pp. 85–95.
Burnett, Charles S. F. "A Note on the Origins of the Third Vatican Mythographer." *Journal of the Warburg and Courtauld Institutes* 44 (1981): 160–66.
Burnley, J. D. "*Fine Amor*: Its Meaning and Context." *RES* 31 (1980): 129–48.
Burrow, J. A. *The Ages of Man: A Study in Medieval Writing and Thought*. Oxford: Clarendon, 1986.
———. "The Portrayal of Amans in *Confessio Amantis*." In A. J. Minnis, ed., *Gower's "Confessio Amantis": Responses and Reassessments*. Cambridge, Eng.: D. S. Brewer, 1983. Pp. 5–24.
———. *Ricardian Poetry: Chaucer, Gower, Langland, and the "Gawain" Poet*. New Haven: Yale University Press, 1971.
Butler, Judith. *Gender Trouble: Feminism and the Subversion of Identity*. New York: Routledge, 1990.
Bynum, Caroline Walker. *Holy Feast and Holy Fast: The Religious Significance of Food to Medieval Women*. Berkeley: University of California Press, 1987.
———. *Jesus as Mother: Studies in the Spirituality of the High Middle Ages*. Berkeley: University of California Press, 1982.
Cadden, Joan. *Meanings of Sex Difference in the Middle Ages: Medicine, Science, and Culture*. Cambridge, Eng.: Cambridge University Press, 1993.

Caie, Graham D. "The Significance of the Early Chaucer Manuscript Glosses (With Special Reference to the *Wife of Bath's Prologue*)." *ChauR* 10 (1975–76): 350–60.
Calin, William. "John Gower's Continuity in the Tradition of French *Fin'Amor*." *Mediaevalia* 16 (1993, for 1990): 91–111.
Campbell, P. G. C. *L'Epître d'Othéa: Etude sur les Sources de Christine de Pisan*. Paris: Librairie Ancienne Honoré Champion, 1924.
Carey, Hilary M. "Astrology at the English Court in the Later Middle Ages." In Patrick Curry, ed. *Astrology, Science, and Society: Historical Essays*. Suffolk: Boydell Press, 1987. Pp. 41–56.
Chance, Jane. "The Medieval 'Apology for Poetry': Fabulous Narrative and Stories of the Gods." In Chance, ed., *The Mythographic Art*. Pp. 3–44.
———, ed. *The Mythographic Art: Classical Fable and the Rise of the Vernacular in Early France and England*. Gainesville: University of Florida Press, 1990.
Chandler, Katherine R. "Memory and Unity in Gower's *Confessio Amantis*." *PQ* 71 (1992): 15-30.
Cherniss, Michael D. "The Allegorical Figures in Gower's *Confessio Amantis*." *Res Publica Litterarum: Studies in the Classical Tradition* 1 (1978): 7–20.
Chodorow, Nancy. "Family Structure and Feminine Personality." In Michelle Zimbalist Rosaldo and Louise Lamphere, eds., *Woman, Culture, and Society*. Stanford, Calif.: Stanford University Press, 1974. Pp. 43–66.
Ciavolella, M. "Mediaeval Medicine and Arcite's Love Sickness." *Florilegium* 1 (1979): 222–41.
Clemen, Wolfgang. *Chaucer's Early Poetry*. Trans. C. A. M. Sym. London: Methuen, 1963.
Clover, Carol J. "Regardless of Sex: Men, Women, and Power in Early Modern Europe." *Speculum* 68 (1993): 363–87.
Coffman, George R. "John Gower in His Most Significant Role." In *Elizabethan Studies in Honor of George F. Reynolds* (1945). Rpt. in Peter Nicholson, ed., *Gower's "Confessio Amantis": A Critical Anthology*. Cambridge, Eng.: D. S. Brewer, 1991. Pp. 40–48.
Coghill, N. K. "Love and 'Foul Delight': Some Contrasted Attitudes." In John Lawlor, ed., *Patterns of Love and Courtesy: Essays in Memory of C. S. Lewis*. Evanston, Ill.: Northwestern University Press, 1966. Pp. 141–56.
Coletti, Theresa. *Naming the Rose: Eco, Medieval Signs, and Modern Theory*. Ithaca, N.Y.: Cornell University Press, 1988.
Colish, Marcia L. *The Mirror of Language: A Study in the Medieval Theory of Knowledge*. Rev. ed. Lincoln: University of Nebraska Press, 1983.
Collins, Marie. "Love, Nature and Law in the Poetry of Gower and Chaucer." In Glyn S. Burgess, ed., *Court and Poet: Selected Proceedings of the Third*

Congress of the International Courtly Literature Society. Liverpool: Francis Cairns, 1981. Pp. 113–28.
Cooke, John Daniel. "Euhemerism: A Mediaeval Interpretation of Classical Paganism." *Speculum* 2 (1927): 396–410.
Cooper, Helen. "Chaucer and Ovid: A Question of Authority." In Charles Martindale, ed., *Ovid Renewed: Ovidian Influence on Literature and Art from the Middle Ages to the Twentieth Century*. Cambridge, Eng.: Cambridge University Press, 1988. Pp. 71–81.
Copeland, Rita. *Rhetoric, Hermeneutics, and Translation in the Middle Ages: Academic Traditions and Vernacular Texts*. Cambridge, Eng.: Cambridge University Press, 1991.
Copley, Frank O. *Exclusus Amator: A Study in Latin Love Poetry*. Philological Monographs, American Philological Assn., no. 17. 1956.
Coulter, Cornelia C. "The Genealogy of the Gods." In Christabel Forsythe Fiske, ed., *Vassar Mediaeval Studies*. New Haven: Yale University Press, 1923. Pp. 317–41.
Courcelle, Pierre. *La Consolation de Philosophie dans la tradition littéraire: Antécédents et postérité de Boèce*. Paris: n.p., 1967.
Cowling, Samuel T. "Gower's Ironic Self-Portrait in the *Confessio Amantis*." *Annuale Mediaevale* 16 (1975): 63–70.
Cox, Catherine S. "Holy Erotica and the Virgin Word: Promiscuous Glossing in the *Wife of Bath's Prologue*." *Exemplaria* 5 (1993): 207–37.
Crane, Susan. "Medieval Romance and Feminine Difference in the *Knight's Tale*." *SAC* 12 (1990): 47–63.
Cumont, Franz. *Astrology and Religion among the Greeks and Romans*. New York: G. P. Putnam, 1912.
Curry, Walter C. *Chaucer and the Medieval Sciences*. 2d ed. New York: Barnes and Noble, 1960.
Curtius, Ernst Robert. *European Literature and the Latin Middle Ages*. Trans. Willard R. Trask. Princeton, N.J.: Princeton University Press, 1953.
Dallery, Arleen B. "The Politics of Writing (the) Body: Ecriture Féminine." In A. M. Jaggar and S. R. Bordo, eds., *Gender/Body/Knowledge: Feminist Reconstructions of Being and Knowing*. New Brunswick: Rutgers University Press, 1989. Pp. 52–67.
d'Alverny, Marie-Thérèse. "Translations and Translators." In Robert L. Benson and Giles Constable, with Carol D. Lanham, eds., *Renaissance and Renewal in the Twelfth Century*. 1982; rpt. Toronto: University of Toronto Press, 1991. Pp. 421–62.
Delany, Sheila. *Chaucer's "House of Fame": The Poetics of Skeptical Fideism*. Chicago: University of Chicago Press, 1972.
———. "'Mothers to Think Back Through': Who Are They? The Ambiguous

Example of Christine de Pizan." In Laurie A. Finke and Martin B. Shichtman, eds., *Medieval Texts and Contemporary Readers*. Ithaca, N.Y.: Cornell University Press, 1987. Pp. 177–97.

———. "Slaying Python: Marriage and Misogyny in a Chaucerian Text." In *Writing Woman*. New York: Schocken, 1983. Pp. 47–75.

Demaitre, Luke. "The Care and Extension of Old Age in Medieval Medicine." In Michael M. Sheehan, CSB, ed., *Aging and the Aged in Medieval Europe*. Toronto: Pontifical Institute of Mediaeval Studies, 1990. Pp. 3–22.

Derrida, Jacques. *Of Grammatology*. Trans. Gayatri Chakravorty Spivak. Baltimore: Johns Hopkins University Press, 1976.

Dickerson, A. Inskip. "Chaucer's *House of Fame*: A Skeptical Epistemology of Love." *TSLL* 18 (1976): 171–83.

Dilts, Dorothy A. "John Gower and the *De genealogia deorum*." *MLN* 57 (1942): 23–25.

Dinshaw, Carolyn. *Chaucer's Sexual Poetics*. Madison: University of Wisconsin Press, 1989.

Donaldson, E. Talbot. "Venus and the Mother of Romulus: The *Parliament of Fouls* and the *Pervigilium Veneris*." *ChauR* 14 (1980): 313–18.

Dronke, Peter. "L'amor che move il sole e l'altre stelle." *Studi medievali* ser. 3.6 (1965): 389–422.

———. *Fabula: Explorations into the Uses of Myth in Medieval Platonism*. Leiden: E. J. Brill, 1974.

Dumézil, Georges. *Archaic Roman Religion*. Trans. Philip Krapp. Chicago: University of Chicago Press, 1970. 2 vols.

Eade, J. C. *The Forgotten Sky: A Guide to Astrology in English Literature*. Oxford: Clarendon, 1984.

Ebin, Lois A. *John Lydgate*. Boston: Twayne, 1985.

Economou, George D. "The Character Genius in Alan de Lille, Jean de Meun, and John Gower." *ChauR* 4 (1970). Rpt. in Peter Nicholson, ed., *Gower's "Confessio Amantis": A Critical Anthology*. Cambridge, Eng.: D. S. Brewer, 1991. Pp. 109–16.

———. *The Goddess Natura in Medieval Literature*. Cambridge, Mass.: Harvard University Press, 1972.

———. "The Two Venuses and Courtly Love." In Joan M. Ferrante and Economou, with Frederick Goldin, Esther C. Quinn, Renata Karlin, and Saul N. Brody, eds., *In Pursuit of Perfection: Courtly Love in Medieval Literature*. Port Washington, N.Y., London: Kennikat, 1975. Pp. 17–50.

Elliott, Kathleen O., and J. P. Elder. "A Critical Edition of the Vatican Mythographers." Transactions of the American Philological Assn. 78 (1947): 189–207.

Emerson, Oliver Farrar. "Chaucer's 'Opie of Thebes Fyn.'" *MP* 17 (1919): 287–91.

Emslie, MacDonald. "Codes of Love and Class Distinctions." *EIC* 5 (1955): 1–17.

Engels, Joseph. "Berchoriana I: Notice Bibliographique sur Pierre Bersuire, Supplément au Repertorium Biblicum Medii Aevi." *Vivarium* 2.1–2 (1964): 62–112, 113–24.

———. "L'Edition critique de l'*Ovidius moralizatus* de Bersuire." *Vivarium* 9 (1971): 19–24.

Everett, Dorothy. "Some Reflections on Chaucer's 'Art Poetical.'" 1950; rpt. in Patricia Kean, ed., *Essays on Middle English Literature*. Oxford: Clarendon, 1955. Pp. 149–74.

Fairchild, Hoxie Neale. "Active Arcite, Contemplative Palamon." *JEGP* 26 (1927): 285–93.

Fansler, Dean Spruill. *Chaucer and the "Roman de la Rose."* Gloucester, Mass.: Peter Smith, 1965.

Farnham, Anthony E. "The Art of High Prosaic Seriousness: John Gower as Didactic Raconteur." In Larry D. Benson, ed., *The Learned and the Lewed: Studies in Chaucer and Medieval Literature*. Cambridge, Mass.: Harvard University Press, 1974. Pp. 161–73.

———. "Statement and Search in the *Confessio Amantis*." *Mediaevalia* 16 (1993, for 1990): 141–57.

Ferrante, Joan M. *Woman as Image in Medieval Literature: From the Twelfth Century to Dante*. New York: Columbia University Press, 1975.

Ferris, Sumner. "Venus and the Virgin: The Proem to Book III of Chaucer's *Troilus and Criseyde* as a Model for the Prologue to the *Prioress's Tale*." *ChauR* 27 (1993): 252–59.

Finkel, Helen R. "The Portrait of Woman in the Works of Christine de Pizan." *Les Bonne Feuilles* 3 (1974): 138–51.

Fisher, John H. "Chaucer and the French Influence." In Donald M. Rose, ed., *New Perspectives in Chaucer Criticism*. Norman, Okla.: Pilgrim Books, 1981. Pp. 177–91.

———. *John Gower, Moral Philosopher and Friend of Chaucer*. New York University Press, 1964.

Flandrin, Jean-Louis. "Sex in Married Life in the Early Middle Ages: The Church's Teaching and Behavioural Reality." In Philippe Ariès and André Béjin, eds., *Western Sexuality: Practice and Precept in Past and Present Times*. Trans. Anthony Forster. Oxford: Basil Blackwell, 1985. Pp. 114–29.

Fleming, John V. *Classical Imitation and Interpretation in Chaucer's Troilus*. Lincoln: University of Nebraska Press, 1990.

———. "Hoccleve's 'Letter of Cupid' and the 'Quarrel' Over the *Roman de la Rose*." *Medium Aevum* 40 (1971): 21–40.

———. *The "Roman de la Rose": A Study in Allegory and Iconography.* Princeton, N.J.: Princeton University Press, 1969.
Foucault, Michel. "The Battle for Chastity." In Philippe Ariès and André Béjin, eds., *Western Sexuality: Practice and Precept in Past and Present Times.* Trans. Anthony Forster. Oxford: Basil Blackwell, 1985. Pp. 14–25.
———. *The History of Sexuality.* Vol. 1. Trans. Robert Hurley. New York: Pantheon, 1978.
Fox, George G. *The Mediaeval Sciences in the Works of John Gower.* New York: Haskell, 1966.
Frank, Robert Worth, Jr. "Structure and Meaning in the *Parlement of Foules.*" *PMLA* 71 (1956): 530–39.
Frantzen, Allen J. "When Women Aren't Enough." *Speculum* 68 (1993): 445–71.
French, Walter Hoyt. "The Lovers in the *Knight's Tale.*" *JEGP* 48 (1949): 320–28.
Friedman, John B. "'Dies boni et mali, obitus, et contra hec remedium': Remedies for Fortune in Some Late Medieval English Manuscripts." *JEGP* 90 (1991): 311–26.
———. "L'Iconographie de Venus et de son miroir a la fin du moyen age." In Bruno Roy, ed., *L'Erotisme au Moyen Age.* Montreal, 1977. Pp. 53–82.
———. "John de Foxton's Continuation of the *Fulgentius metaforalis* of John Ridewall." *Studies in Iconography* 7–8 (1981–82): 65–79.
Friedrich, Paul. *The Meaning of Aphrodite.* Chicago: University of Chicago Press, 1978.
Frost, William. "An Interpretation of Chaucer's *Knight's Tale.*" *RES* 25 (1949): 289–304.
Fuchs, Bruno Archibald. *Die Ikonographie der 7 Planeten in der Kunst Italiens bis zum Ausgang des Mittelalters.* Inaugural dissertation, Munich, 1909.
Fuchs, Eric. *Sexual Desire and Love: Origins and History of the Christian Ethic of Sexuality and Marriage.* Trans. Marsha Daigle. Cambridge, Eng.: James Clarke; New York: Seabury Press, 1983.
Fyler, John M. *Chaucer and Ovid.* New Haven: Yale University Press, 1979.
Gallacher, Patrick J. *Love, the Word, and Mercury: A Reading of John Gower's "Confessio Amantis."* Albuquerque: University of New Mexico Press, 1975.
Galloway, Andrew. "Marriage Sermons, Polemical Sermons, and the *Wife of Bath's Prologue*: A Generic Excursus." *SAC* 14 (1992): 3–30.
Gaylord, Alan T. "The Role of Saturn in the *Knight's Tale.*" *ChauR* 8 (1974): 171–90.
Gellrich, Jesse M. *The Idea of the Book in the Middle Ages: Language Theory, Mythology, and Fiction.* Ithaca, N.Y.: Cornell University Press, 1985.
Gilbert, Sandra M., and Susan Gubar. "Sexual Linguistics: Gender, Language, Sexuality." *NLH* 16 (1985): 515–33.

Girard, René. *Deceit, Desire, and the Novel: Self and Other in Literary Structure.* Trans. Yvonne Freccero. Baltimore: Johns Hopkins University Press, 1965.

Goffin, R. C. "Heaven and Earth in the 'Parlement of Foules.'" *MLR* 31 (1936): 493–99.

Green, Richard Firth. "Three Fifteenth-Century Notes." *ELN* 14 (1976): 14–17.

Green, Richard Hamilton. "Alan of Lille's *De planctu Naturae.*" *Speculum* 31 (1956): 649–74.

———. "Classical Fable and English Poetry in the Fourteenth Century." In Dorothy Bethurum, ed., *Critical Approaches to Medieval Literature.* New York: Columbia University Press, 1960. Pp. 110–33.

Greenberg, David F. *The Construction of Homosexuality.* Chicago: University of Chicago Press, 1988.

Griffin, Dustin H. *Satires Against Man: The Poems of Rochester.* Berkeley: University of California Press, 1973.

Grigson, Geoffrey. *The Goddess of Love.* London: Constable, 1976.

Gullace, Giovanni. "Medieval and Humanistic Perspectives in Boccaccio's Concept and Defense of Poetry." *Mediaevalia* 12 (1989, for 1986): 225–48.

Hall, Louis Brewer. "Chaucer and the Dido-and-Aeneas Story." *MS* 25 (1963): 148-59.

Hamilton, George L. "Some Sources of the Seventh Book of Gower's *Confessio Amantis.*" *MP* 9 (1911–12): 323–46.

Hamlin, B. F. "Astrology and the Wife of Bath: A Reinterpretation." *ChauR* 9 (1974–75): 153–65.

Hanawalt, Barbara A., ed. *Chaucer's England: Literature in Historical Context.* Minneapolis: University of Minnesota Press, 1992.

Hanna, Ralph, III. "*Compilatio* and the Wife of Bath: Latin Backgrounds, Ricardian Texts." In A. J. Minnis, ed., *Latin and Vernacular: Studies in Late-Medieval Texts and Manuscripts.* Cambridge, Eng.: D. S. Brewer, 1989. Pp. 1–11.

Hansen, Elaine Tuttle. *Chaucer and the Fictions of Gender.* Berkeley: University of California Press, 1992.

Häring, Nikolaus. "Commentary and Hermeneutics." In Robert L. Benson and Giles Constable with Carol D. Lanham, eds., *Renaissance and Renewal in the Twelfth Century.* 1982; rpt. Toronto: University of Toronto Press, 1991. Pp. 173–200.

Hatton, Thomas J. "John Gower's Use of Ovid in Book III of the *Confessio Amantis.*" *Mediaevalia* 13 (1987): 257–74.

———. "The Role of Venus and Genius in John Gower's *Confessio Amantis*: A Reconsideration." *Greyfriar* 16 (1975): 29–40.

Hawkes, Terence. *Structuralism and Semiotics.* Berkeley: University of California Press, 1977.

Heckscher, William S. "The Anadyomene in the Medieval Tradition." Rpt. in Egon Verheyen, ed., *Art and Literature: Studies in the Relationship*. Durham, N.C.: Duke University Press, 1985. Pp. 127–64.

Heffernan, Carol Falvo. "Wells and Streams in Three Chaucerian Gardens." *PLL* 15 (1979): 339–56.

Heinrichs, Katherine. *Myths of Love: Classical Lovers in Medieval Literature*. University Park: Pennsylvania State University Press, 1990.

Hexter, Ralph. *Ovid and Medieval Schooling*. Munich: Arbeo-Gesellschaft, 1986.

Highwater, Jamake. *Myth and Sexuality*. New York: New American Library, 1990.

Hill, Thomas D. "La Vieille's Digression on Free Love: A Note on Rhetorical Structure in the *Romance of the Rose*." *Romance Notes* 8 (1966): 113–15.

Hindman, Sandra L. *Christine de Pizan's "Epistre Othéa": Painting and Politics at the Court of Charles VI*. Toronto: Pontifical Institute for Mediaeval Studies, 1986.

Hiscoe, David W. "Heavenly Sign and Comic Design in Gower's *Confessio Amantis*." In Julian Wasserman and Lois Roney, eds., *Sign, Sentence, Discourse: Language in Medieval Thought and Literature*. Syracuse, N.Y.: Syracuse University Press, 1989. Pp. 228–44.

———. "The Ovidian Comic Strategy of Gower's *Confessio Amantis*." *PQ* 64 (1985): 367–85.

Hoffman, Richard L. "The Canterbury Tales." In R. M. Lumiansky and Herschel Baker, eds., *Critical Approaches to Six Major English Works: "Beowulf" through "Paradise Lost."* Philadelphia: University of Pennsylvania Press, 1968. Pp. 41–80.

Hollander, Robert. *Boccaccio's Two Venuses*. New York: Columbia University Press, 1977.

Holquist, Michael. "The Politics of Representation." In Stephen J. Greenblatt, ed., *Allegory and Representation*. English Institute Papers ns 5. Baltimore: Johns Hopkins University Press, 1981. Pp. 163–83.

Homans, Margaret. "Feminist Criticism and Theory. The Ghost of Creusa." *Yale Journal of Criticism* 1.1 (1987): 153–82.

Howard, Donald R. *Chaucer: His Life, His Works, His World*. New York: Dutton, 1987.

———. *The Idea of the Canterbury Tales*. Berkeley: University of California Press, 1976.

———. "Thwarted Sexuality in Chaucer's Works." *Florilegium* 3 (1981): 243–49.

Huizinga, J. *The Waning of the Middle Ages: A Study of the Forms of Life, Thought, and Art in France and the Netherlands in the XIVth and XVth Centuries*. New York: St. Martin's Press, 1924.

Huppé, Bernard F., and D. W. Robertson, Jr. *Fruyt and Chaf: Studies in Chaucer's Allegories*. Princeton, N.J.: Princeton University Press, 1963.
Hutchinson, Judith. "*The Parliament of Fowls*: A Literary Entertainment?" *Neophilologus* 61 (1977): 143–51.
Hyde, Thomas. "Boccaccio: The Genealogies of Myth." *PMLA* 100 (1985): 737–45.
Ignatius, Mary A. "Christine de Pizan's *Epistre Othéa*: An Experiment in Literary Form." *Medievalia et humanistica* ns 9 (1979): 127–42.
Jackson, W. T. H. "Faith Unfaithful—The German Reaction to Courtly Love." In Newman, ed., *The Meaning of Courtly Love*. Pp. 55–76.
Jacquart, Danielle, and Claude Thomasset. *Sexuality and Medicine in the Middle Ages*. Trans. Matthew Adamson. Princeton, N.J.: Princeton University Press, 1988.
Jauss, Hans Robert. *Toward an Aesthetic of Reception*. Trans. Timothy Bahti. Minneapolis: University of Minnesota Press, 1982.
Jonson, Ben. *Ben Jonson*. Ed. Ian Donaldson. Oxford University Press, 1985.
Jordan, Robert M. *Chaucer and the Shape of Creation: The Aesthetic Possibilities of Inorganic Structure*. Cambridge, Mass.: Harvard University Press, 1967.
Joyner, William. "Parallel Journeys in Chaucer's *House of Fame*." *PLL* 12 (1976): 3–19.
Kamborian, Kelly. "Children of the Planets: Medieval Astronomical Imagery." In *Survival of the Gods: Classical Mythology in Medieval Art*. Exhibition catalogue, Dept. of Art, Brown University, 1987. Pp. 125–32.
Kaske, R. E., in collaboration with Arthur Groos and Michael W. Twomey. *Medieval Christian Literary Imagery: A Guide to Interpretation*. Toronto: University of Toronto Press, 1988.
Kean, P. M. *Chaucer and the Making of English Poetry*. 2 vols. London: Routledge, 1972.
Keen, Maurice. *Chivalry*. New Haven: Yale University Press, 1984.
Keller, Evelyn Fox. "The Gender/Science System: Or, Is Sex to Gender as Nature Is to Science?" *Hypatia* 2 (1987): 33–44.
Kelley, Michael R. "Antithesis as the Principle of Design in the *Parlement of Foules*." *ChauR* 14 (1979–80): 61–73.
Kellogg, Judith L. "Christine de Pizan as Chivalric Mythographer: *L'Epistre Othéa*." In Chance, ed., *Mythographic Art*. Pp. 100–124.
Kelly, Henry Ansgar. *Chaucer and the Cult of Saint Valentine*. Leiden: E. J. Brill, 1986.
———. *The Devil, Demonology and Witchcraft: The Development of Christian Beliefs in Evil Spirits*. Garden City, N.Y.: Doubleday, 1968.
———. "Gaston Paris's Courteous and Horsely Love." In Glyn S. Burgess and Robert A. Taylor, eds., *The Spirit of the Court: Selected Proceedings of*

the Fourth Congress of the International Courtly Literature Society. Cambridge, Eng.: D. S. Brewer, 1985. Pp. 217–23.
———. *Love and Marriage in the Age of Chaucer*. Ithaca, N.Y.: Cornell University Press, 1975.
———. "The Varieties of Love in Medieval Literature According to Gaston Paris." *Romance Philology* 40 (1986–87): 301–27.
Kendrick, Laura. "Chaucer's House of Fame and the French Palais de Justice." *SAC* 6 (1984): 121–33.
Kiser, Lisa J. *Truth and Textuality in Chaucer's Poetry*. Hanover, N.H.: University Press of New England, 1991.
Klibansky, Raymond, Erwin Panofsky, and Fritz Saxl. *Saturn and Melancholy: Studies in the History of Natural Philosophy, Religion, and Art*. London: Nelson, 1964.
Knapp, Peggy A. "Alisoun of Bathe and the Reappropriation of Tradition." *ChauR* 24 (1989–90): 45–52.
Knight, Stephen. *Geoffrey Chaucer*. Oxford: Blackwell, 1986.
Knowlton, Edgar C. "The Goddess Nature in Early Periods." *JEGP* 19 (1920): 224–53.
Kolve, V. A. *Chaucer and the Imagery of Narrative: The First Five Canterbury Tales*. Stanford, Calif.: Stanford University Press, 1984.
Koonce, B. G. *Chaucer and the Tradition of Fame: Symbolism in "The House of Fame."* Princeton, N.J.: Princeton University Press, 1966.
Kosmer, Ellen. "The 'noyous humoure of lecherie.'" *Art Bulletin* 57 (1975): 1–8.
Kruger, Steven F. "Imagination and the Complex Movement of Chaucer's *House of Fame*." *ChauR* 28 (1993): 117–34.
Laistner, M. L. W. "Fulgentius in the Carolingian Age." In Chester A. Starr, ed., *The Intellectual Heritage of the Early Middle Ages*. Ithaca, N.Y.: Cornell University Press, 1957. Pp. 202–15.
———. "The Western Church and Astrology during the Early Middle Ages." In *The Intellectual Heritage of the Early Middle Ages*. Pp. 57–82.
Laqueur, Thomas. *Making Sex: Body and Gender From the Greeks to Freud*. Cambridge, Mass.: Harvard University Press, 1990.
Lawrence, Marion. "The *Birth of Venus* in Roman Art." In Douglas Fraser, Howard Hibbard, and Milton J. Lewine, eds., *Essays in the History of Art Presented to Rudolf Wittkower*. London: Phaidon, 1967. Pp. 10–16.
Lazarus, Alan J. "Venus in the 'north-north-west'? (Chaucer's *Parliament of Fowls*, 117)." In Larry D. Benson and Siegfried Wenzel, eds., *The Wisdom of Poetry: Essays in English Literature in Honor of Morton W. Bloomfield*. Kalamazoo, Mich.: Medieval Institute Publications, 1982. Pp. 145–49.
Leacock, Eleanor, and June Nash. "Ideologies of Sex: Archetypes and Stereo-

types." In Leonore Loeb Adler, ed., *Cross-Cultural Research at Issue*. New York: Academic Press, 1982. Pp. 193–207.

Le Goff, Jacques. *Intellectuals in the Middle Ages*. Trans. Teresa Lavender Fagan. Cambridge, Mass.: Blackwell, 1993.

Leicester, H. Marshall, Jr. *The Disenchanted Self: Representing the Subject in the "Canterbury Tales."* Berkeley: University of California Press, 1990.

———, (Henry M., Jr.). "The Harmony of Chaucer's *Parlement*: A Dissonant Voice." *ChauR* 9 (1974–75): 15–34.

Lemay, Helen Rodnite. "Some Thirteenth and Fourteenth Century Lectures on Female Sexuality." *International Journal of Women's Studies* 1 (1978): 391–400.

———. "The Stars and Human Sexuality: Some Medieval Scientific Views." *Isis* 71 (1980): 127–37.

Lemay, Richard. "The True Place of Astrology in Medieval Science and Philosophy: Towards a Definition." In Patrick Curry, ed., *Astrology, Science, and Society: Historical Essays*. Suffolk: Boydell, 1987. Pp. 57–73.

Lenaghan, R. T. "The Clerk of Venus: Chaucer and Medieval Romance." In Larry D. Benson, ed., *The Learned and the Lewed: Studies in Chaucer and Medieval Literature*. Cambridge, Mass.: Harvard University Press, 1974. Pp. 31–43.

Leonard, Frances McNeely. *Laughter in the Courts of Love: Comedy in Allegory, from Chaucer to Spenser*. Norman, Okla.: Pilgrim Books, 1981.

Lewis, C. S. *The Allegory of Love: A Study in Medieval Tradition*. London: Oxford University Press, 1936; rpt. 1990.

Leyerle, John. "Chaucer's Windy Eagle." *UTQ* 40 (1971): 247–65.

Lloyd-Morgan, G. "Roman Venus: Public Worship and Private Rites." In Martin Henig and Anthony King, eds., *Pagan Gods and Shrines of the Roman Empire*. Oxford: Oxford University Press, 1986. Pp. 179–88.

[Loomis], Dorothy Bethurum. "The Center of the *Parlement of Foules*." In *Essays in Honor of Walter Clyde Curry*. Nashville, Tenn.: Vanderbilt University Press, 1954. Pp. 39–50.

Loomis, Dorothy Bethurum. "The Venus of Alanus de Insulis and the Venus of Chaucer." In James L. Rosier, ed., *Philological Essays: Studies in Old and Middle English Literature in Honour of Herbert Dean Meritt*. The Hague, Paris: Mouton, 1970. Pp. 182–95.

Lowes, John Livingston. "The Loveres Maladye of Hereos." *MP* 11 (1914): 491–546.

Lumiansky, R. M. "Chaucer's *Parlement of Foules*: A Philosophical Interpretation." *RES* 24 (1948): 81–89.

McCall, John P. *Chaucer Among the Gods: The Poetics of Classical Myth*. University Park: Pennsylvania State University Press, 1979.

MacCormack, Carol P. "Nature, Culture and Gender: A Critique." In Mac-

Cormack and Marilyn Strathern, eds., *Nature, Culture, and Gender*. Cambridge, Eng.: Cambridge University Press, 1980. Pp. 1–24.
Macey, Samuel L. *Patriarchs of Time: Dualism in Saturn-Chronos, Father Time, the Watchmaker God, and Father Christmas*. Athens: University of Georgia Press, 1987.
McDonald, Charles O. "An Interpretation of Chaucer's *Parlement of Foules*." *Speculum* 30 (1955): 444–57.
Mack, Sara. *Ovid*. New Haven: Yale University Press, 1988.
MacKinnon, Catharine A. *Toward a Feminist Theory of the State*. Cambridge, Mass.: Harvard University Press, 1989.
MacMullen, Ramsay. *Paganism in the Roman Empire*. New Haven: Yale University Press, 1981.
Mainzer, Conrad. "John Gower's Use of the 'Mediaeval Ovid' in the *Confessio Amantis*." *Medium Aevum* 41 (1972): 215–29.
Mâle, Emile. *The Gothic Image: Religious Art in France in the Thirteenth Century*. 1913; rpt. New York: Harper, 1958.
Mann, Jill. *Geoffrey Chaucer*. Atlantic Highlands, N.J.: Humanities Press, 1991.
Marckwardt, A. H. *Characterization in Chaucer's "Knight's Tale."* Contributions in Modern Philology no. 5, 1947.
Marino, Lucia. "Prometheus, or the Mythographer's Self-Image in Boccaccio's «Genealogie»." *Studi sul Boccaccio* 12 (1980): 263–73.
Markus, R. A. "St. Augustine on Signs." *Phronesis* 2 (1957): 60–83.
Massó, Pedro Guardia. "Tensión astrológica y la Comadre de Bath." In J. F. Galván Reula, ed., *Estudios literarios ingleses: Edad Media*. Madrid: Catedra Critica y Estudios Literarios, 1985. Pp. 107–19.
Matthews, William. "The Wife of Bath and All Her Sect." *Viator* 5 (1974): 413–43.
Mazzotta, Giuseppe. "The Light of Venus and the Poetry of Dante." In Arthur Groos, et al., eds., *Magister Regis: Studies in Honor of Robert Earl Kaske*. New York: Fordham University Press, 1986. Pp. 147–69.
Meiss, Millard. *French Painting in the Time of Jean de Berry: The Limbourgs and Their Contemporaries*. 2 vols. New York: Braziller, 1974.
Middleton, Anne. "Chaucer's 'New Men' and the Good of Literature in the *Canterbury Tales*." In Edward Said, ed., *Literature and Society*. 1978 Selected Papers from the English Institute. Rpt. Baltimore: Johns Hopkins University Press, 1980. Pp. 15–56.
Minnis, A. J. *Chaucer and Pagan Antiquity*. Cambridge, Eng.: D. S. Brewer; Totowa, N.J.: Rowman and Littlefield, 1982.
———. "De Vulgari Auctoritate: Chaucer, Gower and Men of Great Authority." In Yeager, ed., *Chaucer and Gower*. Pp. 36–74.

———. *Medieval Theory of Authorship: Scholastic Literary Attitudes in the Later Middle Ages*. 2d ed. Philadelphia: University of Pennsylvania Press, 1988.

———. "'Moral Gower' and Medieval Literary Theory." In Minnis, ed., *Gower's "Confessio Amantis": Responses and Reassessments*. Cambridge, Eng.: D. S. Brewer, 1983. Pp. 50–78.

Mitchell, Jerome. *Thomas Hoccleve: A Study in Early Fifteenth-Century English Poetic*. Chicago: University of Illinois Press, 1968.

Mitchell, W. J. T. *Iconology: Image, Text, Ideology*. Chicago: University of Chicago Press, 1986.

Moi, Toril. "Desire in Language: Andreas Capellanus and the Controversy of Courtly Love." In David Aers, ed., *Medieval Literature: Criticism, Ideology, and History*. n.p.: Harvester Press, 1986. Pp. 11–33.

Montrose, Louis Adrian. "'Shaping Fantasies': Figurations of Gender and Power in Elizabethan Culture." In Stephen Greenblatt, ed., *Representing the English Renaissance*. Berkeley: University of California Press, 1988. Pp. 31–64.

Moore, John C. "'Courtly Love': A Problem of Terminology." *Journal of the History of Ideas* 40 (1979): 621–32.

Mulryan, John. "Venus, Cupid, and the Italian Mythographers." *Humanistica Lovaniensia* 23 (1974): 31–41.

Muscatine, Charles. *Chaucer and the French Tradition: A Study in Style and Meaning*. Berkeley: University of California Press, 1957.

———. "Form, Texture, and Meaning in Chaucer's *Knight's Tale*." In *Chaucer: Modern Essays in Criticism*. New York: Oxford University Press, 1959. Pp. 60–82.

Neilson, William Allan. *The Origins and Sources of the Court of Love*. Harvard Studies and Notes in Philology and Literature 6. Boston: Ginn and Co., 1899.

Neumann, Erich. *The Great Mother: An Analysis of the Archetype*. Trans. Ralph Manheim. Bollingen series 47. 2d ed. New York: Pantheon, 1963.

Newman, Barbara. *Sister of Wisdom: St. Hildegard's Theology of the Feminine*. Berkeley: University of California Press, 1987.

Newman, F. X., ed. *The Meaning of Courtly Love*. Albany: SUNY Press, 1968.

Nitecki, Alicia K. "Figures of Old Age in Fourteenth-Century English Literature." In Michael M. Sheehan, CSB, ed., *Aging and the Aged in Medieval Europe*. Toronto: Pontifical Institute of Mediaeval Studies, 1990. Pp. 107–16.

Nitzsche, Jane Chance. *The Genius Figure in Antiquity and the Middle Ages*. New York: Columbia University Press, 1975.

Noonan, John T., Jr. *Contraception: A History of Its Treatment by the Catholic Theologians and Canonists*. Enlarged ed. Cambridge, Mass.: Harvard University Press, 1986.

North, J. D. *Chaucer's Universe*. Oxford: Clarendon, 1988.

———. "Medieval Concepts of Celestial Influence: A Survey." In Patrick Curry, ed., *Astrology, Science, and Society: Historical Essays*. Suffolk: Boydell, 1987. Pp. 5–17.

Norton-Smith, John. "Lydgate's Changes in the *Temple of Glas*." *Medium Aevum* 27 (1958): 166–72.

———. "Lydgate's Metaphors." *ES* 42 (1961): 90–93.

Olson, Glending. "Deschamps' *Art de Dictier* and Chaucer's Literary Environment." *Speculum* 48 (1973): 714–23.

———. "Making and Poetry in the Age of Chaucer." *Comparative Literature* 31 (1979): 272–90.

Olsson, Kurt. "Natural Law and John Gower's *Confessio Amantis*." *Medievalia et Humanistica* 11 (1982). Rpt. in Peter Nicholson, ed., *Gower's "Confessio Amantis": A Critical Anthology*. Cambridge, Eng.: D. S. Brewer, 1991. Pp. 181–213.

———. "Poetic Invention and Chaucer's *Parlement of Foules*." *MP* 87 (1989): 13–35.

Ong, Walter J. *Orality and Literacy: The Technologizing of the Word*. London: Routledge, 1982.

Ortner, Sherry. "Is Female to Male as Nature Is to Culture?" In Michelle Rosaldo and Louise Lamphere, eds., *Woman, Culture, and Society*. Stanford, Calif.: Stanford University Press, 1974. Pp. 67–87.

———, and Harriet Whitehead. "Introduction: Accounting for Sexual Meanings." In Ortner and Whitehead, eds., *Sexual Meanings: The Cultural Construction of Gender and Sexuality*. Cambridge, Eng.: Cambridge University Press, 1981. Pp. 1–27.

Otis, Leah L. *Prostitution in Medieval Society: The History of an Urban Institution in Languedoc*. Chicago: University of Chicago Press, 1985.

Overbeck, Pat Trefzger. "The 'Man of Gret Auctorite' in Chaucer's *House of Fame*." *Modern Philology* 73 (1975): 157–61.

Paglia, Camille. *Sexual Personae: Art and Decadence from Nefertiti to Emily Dickinson*. New Haven: Yale University Press, 1990.

Palmer, Robert E. A. *Roman Religion and Roman Empire: Five Essays*. Philadelphia: University of Pennsylvania Press, 1974.

Panofsky, Erwin. *Renaissance and Renascences in Western Art*. Stockholm: Almquist and Wiksell, 1960.

———. *Studies in Iconology: Humanistic Themes in the Art of the Renaissance*. 1939; rpt. New York: Harper and Row, 1962.

———, and Fritz Saxl. "Classical Mythology in Mediaeval Art." *Metropolitan Museum Studies* 4.2 (1933): 228–80.

Partner, Nancy F. "No Sex, No Gender." *Speculum* 68 (1993): 419–43.
Patterson, Lee. *Chaucer and the Subject of History*. Madison: University of Wisconsin Press, 1991.
———. *Negotiating the Past: The Historical Understanding of Medieval Literature*. Madison: University of Wisconsin Press, 1987.
Payer, Pierre J. *The Bridling of Desire: Views of Sex in the Later Middle Ages*. Toronto: University of Toronto Press, 1993.
———. *Sex and the Penitentials: The Development of a Sexual Code 550–1150*. Toronto: University of Toronto Press, 1984.
Payne, Robert O. *The Key of Remembrance: A Study of Chaucer's Poetics*. New Haven: Yale University Press, 1963.
Pearsall, Derek. "Gower's Latin in the *Confessio Amantis*." In A. J. Minnis, ed., *Latin and Vernacular: Studies in Late-Medieval Texts and Manuscripts*. Cambridge, Eng.: D. S. Brewer, 1989. Pp. 13–25.
———. "Gower's Narrative Art." *PMLA* 81 (1966). Rpt. in Peter Nicholson, ed., *Gower's "Confessio Amantis": A Critical Anthology*. Cambridge, Eng.: D. S. Brewer, 1991. Pp. 62–80.
———. "Interpretative Models for the Peasants' Revolt." In Patrick J. Gallacher and Helen Damico, eds., *Hermeneutics and Medieval Culture*. Albany: SUNY Press, 1989. Pp. 63–70.
———. *John Lydgate*. London: Routledge and Kegan Paul, 1970.
Peck, Russell A. *Kingship and Common Profit in Gower's "Confessio Amantis."* Carbondale: Southern Illinois University Press, 1978.
———. "Love, Politics, and Plot in the *Parlement of Foules*." *ChauR* 24 (1989–90): 290–305.
———. "The Problematics of Irony in Gower's *Confessio Amantis*." *Mediaevalia* 15 (1993, for 1989): 207–29.
Pelen, Marc M. "Form and Meaning of the Old French Love Vision: The *Fableau dou Dieu d'Amors* and Chaucer's *Parliament of Fowls*." *JMRS* 9 (1979): 277–305.
Perryman, Judith C. "The 'False Arcite' of Chaucer's *Knight's Tale*." *Neophilologus* 68 (1984): 121–33.
Polzella, Marion L. "'The Craft So Long to Lerne': Poet and Lover in Chaucer's 'Envoy to Scogan' and *Parliament of Fowls*." *ChauR* 10 (1975–76): 279–86.
Pratt, Robert A. "Chaucer's Use of the *Teseida*." *PMLA* 62 (1947): 598–621.
———. "Conjectures Regarding Chaucer's Manuscript of the *Teseida*." *SP* 42 (1945): 745–63.
Quilligan, Maureen. "Allegory, Allegoresis, and the Deallegorization of Language: The *Roman de la Rose*, the *De planctu naturae*, and the *Parlement of Foules*." In Morton W. Bloomfield, ed., *Allegory, Myth, and Symbol*. Harvard En-

glish Studies 9. Cambridge, Mass.: Harvard University Press, 1981. Pp. 163–86.

———. "Words and Sex: The Language of Allegory in the *De planctu naturae*, the *Roman de la Rose*, and Book III of *The Faerie Queene*." *Allegorica* 2 (1977): 195–216.

Quinn, Betty Nye. "Venus, Chaucer, and Peter Bersuire." *Speculum* 38 (1963): 479–80.

Quinn, William A. "Hoccleve's *Epistle of Cupid*." *Explicator* 45 (1986): 7–10.

Raschke, Robert. "De Alberico mythologo." *Breslauer Philologische Abhandlungen* 45 (1913): 1–137.

Rathbone, Eleanor. "Master Alberic of London, 'Mythographus Tertius Vaticanus.'" *Mediaeval and Renaissance Studies* 1 (1941): 35–38.

Reiss, Edmund. "Chaucer's *fyn lovynge* and the Late Medieval Sense of *fin amor*." In Jess B. Bessinger and Robert R. Raymo, eds., *Medieval Studies in Honor of Lillian Herlands Hornstein*. New York: New York University Press, 1976.

Reno, Christine M. "Feminist Aspects of Christine de Pizan's *Epistre d'Othéa à Hector*." *Studi Francesi* 71 (1980): 271–76.

Reynolds, William D. "Sources, Nature, and Influence of the *Ovidius Moralizatus* of Pierre Bersuire." In Chance, ed., *Mythographic Art*. Pp. 83–99.

Rhode, Deborah L., ed. *Theoretical Perspectives on Sexual Difference*. New Haven: Yale University Press, 1990.

Richards, Jeffrey. *Sex, Dissidence and Damnation: Minority Groups in the Middle Ages*. London: Routledge, 1991.

Rider, Jeff. "Other Voices: Historicism and the Interpretation of Medieval Texts." *Exemplaria* 1 (1989): 293–312.

Riffaterre, Michael. "The Mind's Eye: Memory and Textuality." In Marina S. Brownlee, Kevin Brownlee, and Stephen G. Nichols, eds., *The New Medievalism*. Baltimore: Johns Hopkins University Press, 1991. Pp. 29–45.

Robertson, D. W., Jr. "The Concept of Courtly Love as an Impediment to the Understanding of Medieval Texts." In Newman, ed., *The Meaning of Courtly Love*. Pp. 1–18.

———. *A Preface to Chaucer: Studies in Medieval Perspectives*. Princeton, N.J.: Princeton University Press, 1962.

———. "The Subject of the *De amore* of Andreas Capellanus." *MP* 50 (1953): 145–61.

Rogers, Susan Carol. "Woman's Place: A Critical Review of Anthropological Theory." *Comparative Studies in Society and History* 20 (1978): 123–62.

Rosaldo, Michelle Zimbalist. "Woman, Culture, and Society: A Theoretical Overview." In Rosaldo and Louise Lamphere, eds., *Woman, Culture, and Society*. Stanford, Calif.: Stanford University Press, 1974. Pp. 17–42.

Rossiaud, Jacques. *Medieval Prostitution.* Trans. Lydia G. Cochrane. Oxford: Basil Blackwell, 1988.

Rubin, Gayle. "The Traffic in Women: Notes on the 'Political Economy' of Sex." In Rayna Reiter, ed., *Toward an Anthropology of Women.* New York: Monthly Review Press, 1975. Pp. 157–210.

Ruffolo, Lara. "Literary Authority and the Lists of Chaucer's *House of Fame*: Destruction and Definition through Proliferation." *ChauR* 27 (1993): 325–41.

Ruggiers, Paul G. "The Unity of Chaucer's *House of Fame.*" *SP* 50 (1953): 16–29. Rpt. in Richard J. Schoeck and Jerome Taylor, eds., *Chaucer Criticism.* Vol. 2: *Troilus and Criseyde and The Minor Poems.* Notre Dame, Ind., and London: Notre Dame University Press, 1961. Pp. 261–74.

Ruhe, Doris. *Le Dieu d'Amours avec son Paradis: Untersuchungen zur Mythenbildung um Amor in Spätantike und Mittelalter.* Munich: Wilhelm Fink, 1974.

Runacres, Charles. "Art and Ethics in the 'Exempla' of *Confessio Amantis.*" In A. J. Minnis, ed., *Gower's "Confessio Amantis": Responses and Reassessments.* Cambridge, Eng.: D. S. Brewer, 1983. Pp. 106–34.

Saul, Nigel. "Chaucer and Gentility." In Hanawalt, ed., *Chaucer's England.* Pp. 41–55.

Saussure, Ferdinand de. *Course in General Linguistics.* Ed. Charles Bally and Albert Sechehaye with Albert Riedlinger. Trans. Wade Baskin. 1959; rpt. New York: McGraw-Hill, 1966.

Scaglione, Aldo D. *Nature and Love in the Late Middle Ages.* Berkeley: University of California Press, 1963.

Schapiro, Meyer. "On the Aesthetic Attitude in Romanesque Art." 1947. Rpt. in *Romanesque Art: Selected Papers.* New York: George Braziller, 1977. Pp. 1–27.

Schirmer, Walter F. *John Lydgate: A Study in the Culture of the XVth Century.* Trans. Ann E. Keep. London: Methuen, 1961.

Schmidt, A. V. C. "The Tragedy of Arcite: A Reconsideration of the *Knight's Tale.*" *EIC* 19 (1969): 107–16.

Schreiber, Earl G. "Venus in the Medieval Mythographic Tradition." *JEGP* 74 (1975): 519–35.

Schueler, Donald. "The Age of the Lover in Gower's *Confessio Amantis.*" *Medium Aevum* 36 (1967): 152–58.

Scott, Joan Wallach. "Deconstructing Equality-Versus-Difference: Or, the Uses of Poststructuralist Theory for Feminism." *Feminist Studies* 14 (1988): 33–50.

———. *Gender and the Politics of History.* New York: Columbia University Press, 1988.

Sears, Elizabeth. *The Ages of Man: Medieval Interpretations of the Life Cycle.* Princeton, N.J.: Princeton University Press, 1986.

Selvin, Rhoda Hurwitt. "Shades of Love in the *Parlement of Foules*." *Studia Neophilologica* 37 (1965): 146–60.
Seznec, Jean. *The Survival of the Pagan Gods: The Mythological Tradition and its Place in Renaissance Humanism and Art*. Trans. Barbara F. Sessions. Bollingen Series 38. New York: Pantheon, 1953.
Shapiro, Judith. "Anthropology and the Study of Gender." *Soundings* 4 (1981): 446–65.
Sherif, Carolyn Wood. "Bias in Psychology." In S. Harding, ed., *Feminism and Methodology*. Bloomington: Indiana University Press, 1979. Pp. 37–56.
Shook, Laurence K. "*The House of Fame*." In Beryl Rowland, ed., *Companion to Chaucer Studies*. London: Oxford University Press, 1968. Pp. 341–54.
Simpson, James. "Genius's 'Enformacioun' in Book III of the *Confessio Amantis*." *Mediaevalia* 16 (1993, for 1990): 159–95.
———. "Ironic Incongruence in the Prologue and Book I of Gower's *Confessio Amantis*." *Neophilologus* 72 (1988): 617–32.
Siraisi, Nancy G. *Medieval and Early Renaissance Medicine: An Introduction to Knowledge and Practice*. Chicago: University of Chicago Press, 1990.
Smalley, Beryl. *English Friars and Antiquity in the Early Fourteenth Century*. Oxford: Basil Blackwell, 1960.
Smith, D. J. "Mythological Figures and Scenes in Romano-British Mosaics." In Julian Munby and Martin Henig, eds., *Roman Life and Art in Britain: A Celebration in Honour of the Eightieth Birthday of Jocelyn Toynbee*. Oxford: British Archaeological Reports, 1977. Pp. 105–93.
Smyser, Hamilton M. "A View of Chaucer's Astronomy." *Speculum* 45 (1970): 359–73.
Spearing, A. C. *The Medieval Poet as Voyeur: Looking and Listening in Medieval Love-Narratives*. Cambridge, Eng.: Cambridge University Press, 1993.
———. *Readings in Medieval Poetry*. Cambridge, Eng.: Cambridge University Press, 1987.
Spencer, Floyd A. "The Literary Lineage of Cupid." *The Classical Weekly* 25 (1932): 121–27, 129–34, 139–44.
Steadman, John M. "Venus' *Citole* in Chaucer's *Knight's Tale* and Berchorius." *Speculum* 34 (1959): 620–24.
Steinberg, Theodore L. "The Comedy of Love: The Medieval Venus and Adonis and Shakespeare's *Venus and Adonis*." In Chance, ed., *Mythographic Art*. Pp. 235–45.
Steinfels, Peter. "Papal Birth-Control Letter Retains Its Grip." *New York Times*, Aug. 1, 1993: 1, 13.
Stimpson, Catharine R. "Ad/d Feminam: Women, Literature, and Society." In Edward W. Said, ed., *Literature and Society*. Baltimore: Johns Hopkins University Press, 1980. Pp. 172–92.

Strohm, Paul. "Politics and Poetics: Usk and Chaucer in the 1380s." In Lee Patterson, ed., *Literary Practice and Social Change in Britain, 1380–1530*. Berkeley: University of California Press, 1990. Pp. 83–112.
Sypherd, Wilbur Owen. *Studies in Chaucer's "Hous of Fame."* 1907; rpt. New York: Haskell, 1965.
Tatlock, John S. P. *The Development and Chronology of Chaucer's Works*. 1907; rpt. Gloucester, Mass.: Peter Smith, 1963.
———. *The Scene of the Franklin's Tale Revisited*. Chaucer Society, Ser. 2, No. 51. London and Oxford, 1914. Pp. 17–37.
Taylor, Karla. *Chaucer Reads "The Divine Comedy."* Stanford, Calif.: Stanford University Press, 1989.
Taylor, Robert. "The Figure of Amor in the Old Provençal Narrative Allegories." In Glyn S. Burgess, ed., *Court and Poet: Selected Proceedings of the Third Congress of the International Courtly Literature Society*. Liverpool: Francis Cairns, 1981. Pp. 309–17.
Tester, S. J. *A History of Western Astrology*. Woodbridge, Suffolk: Boydell Press, 1987.
Thomasset, Claude. "The Nature of Woman." Trans. Arthur Goldhammer. In Christiane Klapisch-Zuber, ed., *A History of Women in the West*. Vol. 2: *Silences of the Middle Ages*. Cambridge, Mass.: Belknap Press of Harvard University Press, 1992. Pp. 43–69.
Tinkle, Theresa. "Saturn of the Several Faces: A Survey of the Medieval Mythographic Traditions." *Viator* 18 (1987): 289–307.
Tuve, Rosemond. *Allegorical Imagery: Some Mediaeval Books and Their Posterity*. Princeton, N.J.: Princeton University Press, 1966.
Twycross, Meg. *The Medieval Anadyomene: A Study in Chaucer's Mythography*. Oxford: Society for the Study of Mediaeval Languages and Literature, 1972.
Vance, Eugene. "Chaucer's *House of Fame* and the Poetics of Inflation." *Boundary 2* 7 (1979): 17–37.
———. "Love's Concordance: The Poetics of Desire and the Joy of the Text." *Diacritics* 5.1 (1975): 40–52.
Van Marle, Raimond. *Iconographie de l'art profane au moyen-âge et à la renaissance*. La Haye: Martinus Nijhoff, 1932. Vol. 2.
Wack, Mary F. "Imagination, Medicine, and Rhetoric in Andreas Capellanus' *De amore*." In Arthur Groos et al., eds., *Magister Regis: Studies in Honor of Robert Earl Kaske*. New York: Fordham University Press, 1986. Pp. 101–15.
———. *Lovesickness in the Middle Ages: The "Viaticum" and Its Commentaries*. Philadelphia: University of Pennsylvania Press, 1990.
Wallace, David. "Chaucer and the Absent City." In Hanawalt, ed., *Chaucer's England*. Pp. 59–90.

———. "Chaucer and Boccaccio's Early Writings." In Boitani, ed., *Chaucer and the Italian Trecento*. Pp. 141–62.
———. *Chaucer and the Early Writings of Boccaccio*. Woodbridge, Suffolk: D. S. Brewer, 1985.
Walls, Kathryn. "Patience and Her 'Hil of Sond' in the *Parliament of Fowls*." *American Notes and Queries* 16 (1977): 34.
Wedel, Theodore Otto. *The Mediaeval Attitude Toward Astrology, Particularly in England*. New Haven: Yale University Press, 1920.
Wetherbee, Winthrop. "The Function of Poetry in the *De planctu naturae* of Alain de Lille." *Traditio* 25 (1969): 87–125.
———. "Genius and Interpretation in the *Confessio Amantis*." In Arthur Groos et al., eds., *Magister Regis: Studies in Honor of Robert Earl Kaske*. New York: Fordham University Press, 1986. Pp. 241–60.
———. "Latin Structure and Vernacular Space: Gower, Chaucer and the Boethian Tradition." In *Chaucer and Gower: Difference, Mutuality, Exchange*. Victoria: University of Victoria, English Literary Studies, 1991. Pp. 7–35.
———. "The Literal and the Allegorical: Jean de Meun and the *De planctu naturae*." *Mediaeval Studies* 33 (1971): 264–91.
———. *Platonism and Poetry in the Twelfth Century: The Literary Influence of the School of Chartres*. Princeton, N.J.: Princeton University Press, 1972.
Whitbread, Leslie G. "Fulgentius and Dangerous Doctrine." *Latomus* 30 (1971): 1157–61.
White, Hugh. "Division and Failure in Gower's *Confessio Amantis*." *Neophilologus* 72 (1988): 600–616.
———. "The Naturalness of Amans' Love in *Confessio Amantis*." *Medium Aevum* 56 (1987): 316–22.
———. "Nature and the Good in Gower's *Confessio Amantis*." In R. F. Yeager, ed., *John Gower: Recent Readings*. Kalamazoo, Mich.: Medieval Institute Publications, 1989. Pp. 1–20.
Whitlark, James S. "Chaucer and the Pagan Gods." *Annuale Mediaevale* 18 (1977): 65–75.
Wilkins, Ernest H(atch). "Descriptions of Pagan Divinities from Petrarch to Chaucer." *Speculum* 32 (1957): 511–22.
———. "The Genealogy of the Genealogical Trees of the *Genealogia deorum*." *MP* 23 (1925): 61–65.
———. *The University of Chicago Manuscript of the "Genealogia deorum gentilium" of Boccaccio*. Chicago: University of Chicago Press, 1927.
Willard, Charity Cannon. "Christine de Pizan: The Astrologer's Daughter." In *Mélanges à la mémoire de Franco Simone: France et Italie dans la culture européene I. Moyen Age et Renaissance*. Geneva: Slatkine, 1980. Pp. 95–111.

———. *Christine de Pizan: Her Life and Works*. New York: Persea, 1984.
Wimsatt, James I. *Chaucer and His French Contemporaries: Natural Music in the Fourteenth Century*. Toronto: University of Toronto Press, 1991.
Wood, Chauncey. *Chaucer and the Country of the Stars: Poetic Uses of Astrological Imagery*. Princeton, N.J.: Princeton University Press, 1970.
———. *The Elements of Chaucer's Troilus*. Durham, N.C.: Duke University Press, 1984.
Woodbridge, Elizabeth. "Boccaccio's Defence of Poetry: As Contained in the Fourteenth Book of the *De Genealogia Deorum*." *PMLA* 13 (1898): 333–49.
Woolf, Rosemary. *The English Religious Lyric in the Middle Ages*. Oxford: Clarendon, 1968.
Yeager, R. F., ed. *Chaucer and Gower: Difference, Mutuality, Exchange*. Victoria: University of Victoria, English Literary Studies, 1991.
———. "John Gower and the Exemplum Form: Tale Models in the *Confessio Amantis*." *Mediaevalia* 8 (1982): 307–35.
———. *John Gower's Poetic: The Search for a New Arion*. Cambridge, Eng.: D. S. Brewer, 1990.
———. "'Our englisshe' and Everyone's Latin: The *Fasciculus Morum* and Gower's *Confessio Amantis*." *South Atlantic Review* 46.4 (1981): 41–53.
Ziolkowski, Jan. *Alan of Lille's Grammar of Sex: The Meaning of Grammar to a Twelfth-Century Intellectual*. Cambridge, Mass.: Medieval Academy of America, 1985.

Index

In this index "f" after a number indicates a separate reference on the next page, and "ff" indicates separate references on the next two pages. A continuous discussion over two or more pages is indicated by a span of numbers. *Passim* is used for a cluster of references in close but not consecutive sequence.

Abu Ma'shar, *see* Albumasar
Alan of Lille, 22–27, 29, 37, 39, 146, 159, 166–67, 175, 208
Alberic, 16–21 *passim*, 45–46, 60–62, 63, 67, 73, 86–89, 95, 138–46 *passim*, 150, 159
Albumasar, 138, 149, 248 n 30
Allegory, 53–56, 64–66, 68, 70–72, 76–77. *See also* Moralization
Allen, Judson Boyce, 5, 22, 64
Amor, *see* Cupid
Andreas Capellanus, 155
Aphrodite, *see* Venus
Aquinas, Thomas, 94, 190
Assembly of Gods, 103, 129–30, 132–34
Astrology, 47, 60–61, 66, 68, 71, 93–95, 108–9, 136–61, 162–66, 184–90, 196, 247 n30. *See also* Physiology; Venus: planetary
Augustine of Hippo, 11, 15, 21–22, 51–54, 57, 62, 152, 155–56

Bakhtin, Mikhail, 29, 40, 59
Bernard Silvestris, 16–29 *passim*, 76, 134, 146

Bersuire, Pierre, 38, 45–46, 65–67, 70, 72–73, 89–91, 145
Binary opposition, 11, 16–19, 32–41, 169, 176, 218 n9
Bipolar opposition, *see* Binary opposition
Bloom, Harold, 210
Boccaccio, Giovanni, 119, 134, 147, 202–3; *Filostrato*, 199; *Genealogy of the Gentile Gods* (*Genealogia deorum gentilium*), 21, 45, 50, 67–70, 73–74, 89, 92–95, 108–9, 112, 137, 149–50, 154, 199; *Teseida*, 13–14, 27–29, 94, 112, 126, 143, 172–73
Boethius, 64, 139
Boswell, John, 128
Brown, Peter, 52, 155, 165

Cassian, John, 24
Chaucer, Geoffrey, 134–35, 197, 203–4, 208, 210; *Canterbury Tales*, 31, 138, 164; *Complaint of Mars*, 92; *House of Fame*, 103, 112–23, 127, 170–71, 198, 201; *Knight's Tale*, 20, 22, 27–31, 103, 112–13, 124–29, 201; *Legend of Good*

Women, 199, 201–2, 206–7; *Merchant's Tale*, 160; *Pardoner's Tale*, 146; *Parliament of Fowls*, 11, 19–20, 146, 162, 166–77, 189, 198, 201; *Parson's Tale*, 143–44, 159; *Squire's Tale*, 148; *Troilus and Criseyde*, 114, 152, 167–68, 199–201, 208–9; *Wife of Bath's Prologue*, 152, 162–66, 176f, 189
Chrétien de Troyes, 87–88
Christine de Pizan, 38, 47, 70–73, 74f, 101, 111, 134, 148–49, 189, 205–10 *passim*
Cicero, 50, 60, 64, 109, 146, 166–71 *passim*
Classicism, 59, 65–66, 69–70, 72, 79, 112–14, 120–21, 128, 135, 171, 199–204 *passim*
Courtly love, 9–11, 13
Cupid, 23, 50, 58–60, 68–69, 71–72, 79–85, 87–93, 97–99, 137, 139, 144, 146, 176; and poetry, 2–4, 103–5, 107, 111–12, 119–22, 167–71, 174–75, 199–210; blind or blindfolded, 89–90, 92f, 113–14, 117–18, 121, 125, 127, 134, 193–94; courtly, 109–12, 121, 128–29, 132–33, 172–73, 201–2, 204–9. *See also* Courtly love; Two loves
Curtius, Ernst Robert, 31

Dante Alighieri, 38, 73, 115, 118, 119–20, 202–3
De deorum imaginibus libellus, 91–92
Deschamps, Eustache, 203
Digby Mythographer, 47, 62
Dronke, Peter, 199

Economou, George D., 12–13, 20, 22
Encyclopedism, 4–6, 25, 39, 58, 60–62, 64, 67, 89, 123, 141, 167, 183, 196, 211
Eriugena, John Scotus, 14–15, 18, 21
Eros, *see* Cupid
Etymology, 52–54, 56–58, 60–61, 68, 74, 109, 131
Euhemerism, 51–54, 57–58, 68–70, 71, 74, 133, 184f, 196

First Vatican Mythography, 45–46, 62, 83
Foucault, Michel, 16, 145
Fox, George G., 188
Fulgentius, Fabius Planciades, 21, 45f, 54–57, 62, 64, 73, 81–82, 94, 96, 130, 145–46

Gallacher, Patrick J., 179
Giovanni del Virgilio, 72–73, 141–42, 144, 159
Gower, John, 20, 47, 88, 146, 178–97, 203–4, 210
Green, Richard Hamilton, 15
Guibert of Nogent, 47
Guillaume de Lorris, *see Romance of the Rose*
Guillaume de Machaut, 111–12, 121

Hanna, Ralph, III, 102, 165
Henryson, Robert, 208–10
Hermeneutics, mythographic, 48–60, 73–77, 100–103, 111, 129–35, 180–83, 196. *See also* Allegory; Astrology; Etymology; Euhemerism; Iconography; Moralization; Natural interpretation
Historicism, 5, 19–20, 30, 35–37, 48, 211. *See also* Euhemerism
Hoccleve, Thomas, 205–6, 208, 210
Hollander, Robert, 12–14, 20, 22
Howard, Donald R., 19–20
Humpty Dumpty, 10

Iconography, 50, 60–61, 63–64, 78–99, 102, 110–16, 118–20, 125–29, 130–34, 147–49, 170–75, 193–94, 201, 207–8, 209, 211
Iconology, *see* Iconography
Isidore of Seville, 57–58, 62, 64, 73, 82–83, 84, 105, 138, 145f

James I of Scotland, 153–54, 207–8, 210
Jauss, Hans Robert, 32
Jean de la Mote, 112

Jean de Meun, *see Romance of the Rose*
John de Foxton, 96

Lactantius Placidus, 47
Lewis, C. S., 20, 33
Liber de natura deorum, see Digby Mythographer
Lovesickness, 85, 124, 125–26, 146–47, 152, 194–95
Lucretius Carus, Titus, 25–26, 105–7, 112, 198–99
Lydgate, John, 134–35; *Complaint of a Lover's Life*, 47–48, 153; "Pageant of Knowledge," 156–59; *Reason and Sensuality*, 38, 103, 129–32; *Temple of Glass*, 132, 154–59 *passim*; *Troybook*, 103, 129–30, 132

MacCormack, Carol P., 33
Mack, Sara, 104
Macrobius, 169, 171
Marie de France, 87–88
Mars, 46–48, 61, 93, 124–25, 139, 141, 199
Martianus Capella, 18. *See also* Remigius of Auxerre
Middleton, Anne, 120, 202
Moralization, 4, 12–15, 20, 27, 29–31, 35–36, 55–56, 59–60, 66, 74–76, 82–83, 86–87, 94–95, 98–99, 114–15, 117–18, 131–32, 136, 141, 150, 180–82, 186, 211. *See also* Allegory
Mulryan, John, 20

Natural interpretation, 86–87, 94–95, 98–99, 136–61. *See also* Astrology; Physiology
Neoplatonism, *see* Platonism
Nicole Oresme, 139

Olson, Glending, 120
Ong, Walter J., 201, 205–6
Ovid, 25–26, 66, 119, 121–22, 167–68, 171, 198, 202–4; *Art of Loving (Ars amatoria)*, 104–5, 111, 205–6; *Fasti*, 18, 109, 199; *Heroides*, 115, 117–18; *Loves (Amores)*, 104–5, 109–12
Ovide moralisé, 73

Paganism, 26, 28, 49–54, 65, 75, 114, 129, 133, 137–38, 149, 155, 179–80, 183–84, 193, 196
Panofsky, Erwin, 12, 14, 19f, 22
Paris (judgment of), 56, 64, 81, 116, 130
Patterson, Lee, 20
Pervigilium Veneris (The Eve of St. Venus), 107–8, 146, 199
Physiology, sexual, 27, 56–57, 58, 74–75, 82, 84, 94–96, 98–99, 137–38, 142, 144–55, 157–58, 160, 163–64, 173–74, 176, 189–90, 195, 247 n30. *See also* Astrology
Platonism, 12, 14, 17, 23
Pleasure: sexual, 15, 18, 24–26, 30–31, 81–83, 87–98 *passim*, 140–41, 145, 160–61, 163, 174–76, 180, 188–91, 200, 209; textual, 39, 105–9, 112, 119–22, 169, 171, 175, 200, 202, 209
Poetics, vernacular, 2–4, 7f, 101–4, 111–12, 114–15, 118–23, 135, 165–66, 175, 177, 198–210. *See also* Cupid; Venus
Polysemy, 5–6, 15, 20–22, 38–41, 61, 66–67, 74–76, 79, 90–91, 97–98, 102, 183, 190
Post-structuralism, 6, 34
Procreation, 23–24, 26, 82–84, 94–95, 98–99, 142–45, 151, 158–60, 169, 175–77, 189
Ptolemy, 138, 150ff, 163, 165

Remigius of Auxerre, 18–19, 21, 85, 88–89, 95, 140
Richard of Fournival, 21
Ridewall, John, 45, 62–65, 70, 73, 95–96
Robert of Blois, 152
Robertson, D. W., Jr., 12–16, 19–20, 22, 29–30
Romance of the Rose, 11, 22, 33, 39, 47f,

110–11, 113–14, 121, 126–27, 152–53, 154, 160, 167, 171–73, 201, 204–7
Ruhe, Doris, 20
Ruiz, Juan, 11

Saturn, 26, 55, 63, 83–84, 86, 94–96, 139
Schreiber, Earl G., 20
Second Vatican Mythography, 18, 45–46, 62, 83–85, 146
Secretum secretorum, 138
Sexuality: discourses on, 5–7, 30–31, 43–44, 158–60, 169–70, 178–79, 191, 196–97, 212–13; and age, 56, 88, 96, 123–25, 141–45 *passim*, 151–52, 164, 189–91, 194–95; and social class, 110–14, 117–19, 124–29, 148–49, 151–52, 168, 172–74, 176–77, 188–91, 205–6. *See also* Physiology; Pleasure: sexual; Procreation
Seznec, Jean, 5, 22
Smyser, Hamilton M., 188
Statius, 28
Steinberg, Theodore L., 20

Taylor, Karla, 118
Three Graces, 86, 90–91, 92, 94
Tuve, Rosemond, 5, 22, 70
Two loves, 9–10, 11–22, 27, 28–29, 31–37, 40, 88–89, 136, 140, 175, 196, 211

Twycross, Meg, 20

Vatican mythographies, *see* Alberic; First Vatican Mythography; Second Vatican Mythography
Venus: planetary, 28–29, 90, 93–95, 108–9, 122, 132, 137–40, 141, 144–61, 163–64, 173–74, 177, 184, 186–90, 199–200, 203–4, 208, 247 n30; ancient, 50–54, 137; birth of, 55, 64, 82–84, 94, 146; *anadyomene*, 80–99, 100, 109, 113–14, 116–20, 125–34, 198; *genetrix*, 80–81, 105–9, 112, 115–16, 119–22, 198, 200, 202; bearded, 87, 96; and poetry, 104–10, 112, 119–22, 150, 170–71, 175, 177, 198–210; courtly, 110, 130–33, 149, 194, 209; blind, 193–94. *See also* Poetics, vernacular; Sexuality
Virgil, 107, 115–18, 120, 138–39
Vulcan, 15, 18, 46–48, 90, 92f, 113, 141, 145

Wallace, David, 114
Walsingham, Thomas, 47, 67, 89, 145f
White, Hugh, 192, 195
William of Conches, 17, 146

Yeager, R. F., 20

Library of Congress Cataloging-in-Publication Data

Tinkle, Theresa Lynn.
  Medieval Venuses and Cupids : sexuality, hermeneutics, and English poetry / Theresa Lynn Tinkle.
    p.   cm. — (Figurae)
  Includes bibliographical references and index.
  ISBN 0-8047-2515-2
  1. English poetry—Middle English, 1100–1500—History and criticism. 2. Sex in literature. 3. Poetry, Medieval—Roman influences. 4. Venus (Roman deity) in literature. 5. Cupid (Roman deity) in literature. 6. English poetry—Roman influences. 7. Love in literature. 8. Myth in literature. 9. Hermeneutics. I. Title.
II. Series: Figurae (Stanford, Calif.)
PR317.S48T56 1996
821'.109352—dc20   95-21795
                                                                                            CIP

∞ This book is printed on acid-free, recycled paper.

Original printing 1996
Last figure below indicates year of this printing
05   04   03   02   01   00   99   98   97   96